Emergency Regimes for Global Health

ELGAR STUDIES IN HEALTH AND THE LAW

Series Editor: Professor Amandine Garde, *University of Liverpool, UK*

This new and exciting series will tackle and explore important issues around Health and the Law as they become increasingly entwined in today's world. Public interest issues sparked by the media and new spaces of information and communication engage society on a more hands-on level, which inevitably impacts many aspects of the Law and Policies that we live by.

As a field of study, Health and the Law will encompass the legal and political ramifications of various health issues within national and international law. The various and numerous aspects relating to these broad areas include healthcare law, non-communicable diseases, prevention strategies, health policies, reproductive justice, social and mental health law, bioethics, and medicinal law. Elgar Studies in Health and the Law will also be an excellent forum to discuss and debate the diverse and growing range of issues that remain unexplored.

The primary mission of the series is to stimulate the development of original thinking across Health and the Law and to foster the best theoretical and empirical scholarship in the field. With valuable insights, open-minded approaches, and high quality authored and edited collections; this series will be of interest to academics and practitioners alike.

For a full list of Edward Elgar published titles, including the titles in this series, visit our website at www.e-elgar.com.

Emergency Regimes for Global Health

Law, Policy, and Institutions

Edited by

Amrei Müller

Assistant Professor, Sutherland School of Law, University College Dublin, Ireland

Silvia Behrendt

Director, Global Health Responsibility Agency (GHRA), Salzburg, Austria and Formerly Legal Consultant, International Health Regulations Secretariat, World Health Organization, Switzerland

ELGAR STUDIES IN HEALTH AND THE LAW

EE Edward Elgar PUBLISHING

Cheltenham, UK • Northampton, MA, USA

Published by

Edward Elgar Publishing Limited
The Lypiatts
15 Lansdown Road
Cheltenham
Glos GL50 2JA
UK

Edward Elgar Publishing, Inc.
William Pratt House
9 Dewey Court
Northampton
Massachusetts 01060
USA

Authorised representative in the EU for GPSR queries only: Easy Access System Europe – Mustamäe tee 50, 10621 Tallinn, Estonia, gpsr.requests@easproject.com

A catalogue record for this book is available from the British Library

Library of Congress Control Number: 2025950470

This book is available electronically in the **Elgar**online
Law subject collection
https://doi.org/10.4337/9781035341702

MIX
Paper | Supporting responsible forestry
FSC® C014540

ISBN 978 1 0353 4169 6 (cased)
ISBN 978 1 0353 4170 2 (eBook)
ISBN 978 1 0353 9210 0 (ePub)

Printed and bound in the UK by Short Run Press Ltd, Exeter EX2 7LW

Contents

List of contributors

Kai Ambos is Professor of Criminal Law and Criminal Procedure, Comparative Law, International Criminal Law and Public International Law at the Faculty of Law of Georg-August University Göttingen, Germany and he also serves as a Judge at the Kosovo Specialist Chambers, The Hague.

Silvia Behrendt is Director of the Global Health Responsibility Agency (GHRA), Salzburg, Austria, and was formerly legal consultant to the International Health Regulations Secretariat at the World Health Organization.

David Bell is a public health physician and biotech consultant in global health, and a former medical officer and scientist at the World Health Organization (WHO), Programme Head for malaria and febrile diseases at the Foundation for Innovative New Diagnostics (FIND) in Geneva, Switzerland, and Director of Global Health Technologies at Intellectual Ventures Global Good Fund in Bellevue, WA, USA.

David Dürr is a practising lawyer and notary in Basel and Zürich since 1979, and Professor emeritus of law at the University of Zürich, Switzerland.

Michael Geistlinger is a retired Professor of International Law, Comparative Constitutional Law and Administrative Law and Eastern European Law at the University of Salzburg, Austria.

David McGrogan is Associate Professor at Northumbria Law School, Northumbria University, United Kingdom.

Amrei Müller is Assistant Professor (*Ad Astra* Fellow) at the University College Dublin, Sutherland School of Law, Ireland.

Sreenath Namboodiri is an independent Legal and Policy Researcher and an LL.M. Candidate in International Law, The Graduate Institute of International and Development Studies, Geneva, Switzerland.

Marie-Luce Paris is Associate Professor at the University College Dublin, Sutherland School of Law, Ireland.

Nithin Ramakrishnan is Senior Researcher at the *Third World Network.*

Günter Reiner is Professor of Business Law and Tax Law at Helmut Schmidt University (University of the Bundeswehr), Hamburg, Germany.

Acknowledgements

This volume would not have come into existence without the support of many people and institutions. First of all, the editors would like to warmly thank Richard Bunworth and Tommy MacDiarmada for their excellent editing assistance. Very special thanks go to Suzanne d'Arcy, Research and Innovation Manager at the Sutherland School of Law, University College Dublin, for her tremendous organisational and administrative support. Her patience and efficiency in dealing with special requests was truly unparalleled.

We are thankful to Stephanie Tytherleigh at Edward Elgar Publishing for her continuous support during the long and challenging process of bringing the various contributions together in one edited volume; and to Professor Amandine Garde for accepting the volume in the 'Elgar Studies in Health and the Law' series. We would also like to thank the three anonymous reviewers for their constructive comments on the book proposal which encouraged us to think further about the book project.

We would also like to thank the Sutherland School of Law, University College Dublin, for supporting the discussions among chapter authors, research, writing and editing processes and the final publication of this book. We are also grateful for the generous financial support provided under the *Ad Astra* Start Up Grant by the University College Dublin.

Special thanks are owed also to all contributors to this volume, as well as to individual reviewers who commented on many of the chapters. Your contributions and participation made this project a stimulating and valuable experience. We hope that your chapters will be the basis for further open debate about global health emergency preparedness, prevention, and response law, policies, and institutions.

List of abbreviations

Term	Definition
ABS	Access and benefit sharing
ACT-A	Access to Covid-19 Tools Accelerator
AMR	anti-microbial resistance
APA	Advance Purchase Agreement
BMG	(German) Federal Ministry of Health
BMGF	Bill and Melinda Gates Foundation (today Gates Foundation)
BVerfG	Federal Constitutional Court (Germany) *Bundesverfassungsgericht*
BVerwG	Federal Administrative Court (Germany) *Bundesverwaltungsgericht*
C-TAP	Covid-19 Technology Access Pool
CBRN	chemical, biological, radiological, and nuclear
CDC	(US) Centre for Disease Control
CEPI	Coalition for Epidemic Preparedness Innovations
CESCR	UN Committee on Economic, Social and Cultural Rights
CFM	Coordinating Financial Mechanism
CHAI	Clinton Health Access Initiative, Inc.
ChEU	Charter of Fundamental Rights of the European Union
CJEU	Court of Justice of the European Union
CNCDH	National Consultative Commission on Human Rights (France) *Commission Nationale Consultative des Droits de l'Homme*
COVAX	Covid-19 Vaccines Global Access
DALYs	Disability-Adjusted Life Years
DARIO	Draft Articles on the Responsibilities of International Organisations

Term	**Definition**
EB	WHO Executive Board
ECDC	European Centre for Disease Prevention and Control
ECHR	European Convention on Human Rights
ECtHR	European Court of Human Rights
EEAS	European External Action Service
EID	new, emerging and re-emerging diseases
EMA	European Medicines Agency
EPI-WIN	Information Network for Epidemics
EU	European Union
EUL	Emergency Use Listing
EURATOM	European Atomic Energy Community
EWRS	EU Early Warning and Response System
FDA	US Food and Drug Administration
FIMI	Foreign Information Manipulation and Interference
GACVS	Global Advisory Group on Vaccine Safety
Gavi	Global Alliance for Vaccines and Immunization (today Gavi Alliance)
GG	Basic Law (Germany) *Grundgesetz für die Bundesrepublik Deutschland*
GHC	Global Health Clusters
GHS	Global Health Security
GHSA	Global Health Security Agenda
GMP	good manufacturing practices
GOARN	Global Outbreak Alert and Response Network
GPMB	Global Preparedness Monitoring Board
GSD	genetic sequence data
H-TAP	Health Technologies Access Pool
HaDEA	European Health and Digital Executive Agency
HERA	Health Emergency Preparedness and Response
HRCttee	UN Human Rights Committee
HRH	human right to health
ICCPR	International Covenant on Civil and Political Rights

Term	Definition
ICESCR	International Covenant on Economic, Social and Cultural Rights
ICH	International Council for Harmonisation of Technical Requirements for Pharmaceuticals for Human Use
ICJ	International Court of Justice
IFR	Infection Fatality Rate
IfSG	Infection Protection Act (Germany) *Infektionsschutzgesetz*
IHR	International Health Regulations
IHREC	Irish Human Rights and Equality Commission
IHRL	international human rights law
INB	Intergovernmental Negotiating Body
IPCR	EU Integrated Political Crisis Response
mRNA	messenger ribonucleic acid
NATO	North Atlantic Treaty Organization
NFP	National Focal Point
NGO	non-governmental organisations
NPHET	National Public Health Emergency Team (Ireland)
OECD	Organisation for Economic Co-operation and Development
PABS system	Pathogen Access and Benefit Sharing system
PCR test	polymerase chain reaction test
PEG-V	Product Evaluation Group-Vaccines
PHEIC	public health emergency of international concern
PIP Framework	Pandemic Influenza Preparedness Framework for the Sharing of Influenza Viruses and Access to Vaccines and other Benefits
PPP	public-private partnership
QALYs	Quality-Adjusted Life Years
RKI	Robert Koch Institute (Germany)
RNA	ribonucleic acid
RPQ	Regulation and Prequalification
SAGE	Strategic Advisory Group of Experts on Immunizations
SPAR-tool	Self-assessment State Party Annual Reporting Tool

Term	**Definition**
TAG-EUL-V	Technical Advisory Group-Vaccines
TFEU	Treaty on the Functioning of the European Union
TWN	Third World Network
UDHR	Universal Declaration of Human Rights
UN	United Nations
UNDP	United Nations Development Programme
UNESCO	United Nations Educational, Scientific and Cultural Organization
UNGA	United Nations General Assembly
UNIASC	United Nations Inter-Agency Standing Committee
UNICEF	United Nations Children's Fund
UNTS	United Nations Treaty Series
US	United States
VOC	variants of concern
WEF	World Economic Forum
WELLBYS	years of well-being
WGIHR	Working Group on the Amendments of the International Health Regulations
WGPR	Working Group on Strengthening WHO Preparedness and Response to Health Emergencies
WHA	World Health Assembly
WHASS	Special Session of the World Health Assembly
WHE	World Health Emergency Programme
WHO	World Health Organization
WHOC	Constitution of the World Health Organization
WMA	World Medical Association

Introduction: emergency regimes for global health law

Amrei Müller and Silvia Behrendt

1. THE BACKGROUND TO THE VOLUME

Under the 2005 International Health Regulations (IHR (2005)),[1] the Director-General of the World Health Organization (WHO) – with the advice of an expert Emergency Committee that he sets up – can declare a Public Health Emergency of International Concern (PHEIC),[2] something akin to a 'global health emergency'. The world experienced this on 30 January 2020 with the classification of the appearance of the SARS-CoV-2 virus as a PHEIC by the WHO Director-General and the Covid-19 Emergency Committee that he set up under the IHR (2005).[3] This global health emergency lasted for more than three years, until 5 May 2023.[4]

---

[1] International Health Regulations (2005) (adopted 23 May 2005, entered into force 15 June 2007) 2509 UNTS 79 (IHR (2005)).

[2] IHR (2005), article 12(4). A 'PHEIC' is defined in article 1 as an 'extraordinary event which is determined … (i) to constitute a public health risk through the international spread of disease and (ii) to potentially require a coordinated international response'. Additional qualitative criteria for the declaration of a PHEIC are set out in annex 2 IHR (2005).

[3] WHO Covid-19 Emergency Committee, 'Statement on the Second Meeting of the IHR (2005) Emergency Committee Regarding the Outbreak of Novel Coronavirus (2019-nCoV)' (30 January 2020) https://www.who.int/news/item/30-01-2020-statement-on-the-second-meeting-of-the-international-health-regulations-(2005)-emergency-committee-regarding-the-outbreak-of-novel-coronavirus-(2019-ncov). Unless otherwise stated all web links given in this chapter last accessed between 29 April and 29 May 2025.

[4] WHO Covid-19 Emergency Committee, 'Statement of the Fifteenth Meeting of the IHR (2005) Emergency Committee on the Covid-19 Pandemic' (5 May 2023) https://www.who.int/news/item/05-05-2023-statement-on-the-fifteenth-meeting-of-the-international-health-regulations-%282005%29-emergency-committee-regarding-the-coronavirus-disease-%28covid-19%29-pandemic.

Once a PHEIC has been declared by the WHO, its Director-General and the Emergency Committee can recommend WHO Member States to take extensive medical and non-medical countermeasures to address the PHEIC.[5] During the Covid-19-PHEIC, recommendations for countermeasures were made by the Covid-19 Emergency Committee. They ranged from recommendations to conduct mass testing (including of healthy people)[6] and domestic and international contact tracing[7] (including through the use of digital technologies[8]);

---

[5] In line with IHR (2005), articles 15–17. All WHO recommendations to address the Covid-19-PHEIC at https://www.who.int/groups/covid-19-ihr-emergency-committee.

[6] See among many, WHO Covid-19 Emergency Committee, 'Statement on the Third Meeting of the International Health Regulations (2005) Emergency Committee Regarding the Outbreak of Coronavirus Disease (COVID-19)' (1 May 2020), recommendation to the WHO Secretariat and States Parties on surveillance https://www.who.int/news/item/01-05-2020-statement-on-the-third-meeting-of-the-international-health-regulations-(2005)-emergency-committee-regarding-the-outbreak-of-coronavirus-disease-(covid-19); 'Statement on the Eighth Meeting of the International Health Regulations (2005) Emergency Committee Regarding the Coronavirus Disease (COVID-19) Pandemic' (15 July 2021), recommendation 2 to State Parties; and 'Statement on the Tenth Meeting of the International Health Regulations (2005) Emergency Committee Regarding the Coronavirus Disease (COVID-19) Pandemic' (19 January 2022), recommendations 1 and 2 to State Parties.

[7] See among many, WHO Covid-19 Emergency Committee, 'Statement on the Second Meeting' (n 3), recommendation to the WHO and State Parties; 'Statement on the Fourth Meeting of the International Health Regulations (2005) Emergency Committee Regarding the Outbreak of Coronavirus Disease (COVID-19)' (20 August 2020), recommendation 4 to the WHO Secretariat and recommendations 4 and 8 to State Parties https://www.who.int/news/item/01-08-2020-statement-on-the-fourth-meeting-of-the-international-health-regulations-(2005)-emergency-committee-regarding-the-outbreak-of-coronavirus-disease-(covid-19); and 'Statement on the Ninth Meeting of the International Health Regulations (2005) Emergency Committee Regarding the Coronavirus Disease (COVID-19) Pandemic' (26 October 2021), recommendations 1 and 2 to State Parties https://www.who.int/news/item/26-10-2021-statement-on-the-ninth-meeting-of-the-international-health-regulations-(2005)-emergency-committee-regarding-the-coronavirus-disease-(covid-19)-pandemic.

[8] See among many, WHO Covid-19 Emergency Committee, 'Statement on Third Meeting' (n 6), recommendation to State Parties; and 'Statement on Seventh Meeting of the International Health Regulations (2005) Emergency Committee Regarding the Coronavirus Disease (COVID-19) Pandemic' (19 April 2021), recommendation 16 to the WHO Secretariat https://www.who.int/news/item/19-04-2021-statement-on-the-seventh-meeting-of-the-international-health

recommendations for controlling information through pre-, debunking and removal of alleged mis- or disinformation about Covid-19;[9] recommendations to detect and share genomic sequences of SARS-CoV-2 virus variants[10] and to 'strengthen mechanisms to link individual-level clinical, vaccination and genomic data to facilitate assessment of the impact of and vaccine effectiveness against VOC [variants of concern]';[11] to recommendations to vaccinate an increasing percentage of all countries' populations with emergency-listed or emergency authorised Covid-19 vaccines.[12] At the same time, the WHO

-regulations-(2005)-emergency-committee-regarding-the-coronavirus-disease-(covid-19)-pandemic.

9 Eg WHO Covid-19 Emergency Committee, 'Statement on Fifth Meeting of the IHR (2005) Emergency Committee regarding the Coronavirus Disease (Covid-19) Pandemic' (30 October 2020), recommendation 8 to State Parties https://www.who.int/news/item/30-10-2020-statement-on-the-fifth-meeting-of-the-international-health-regulations-(2005)-emergency-committee-regarding-the-coronavirus-disease-(covid-19)-pandemic; 'Statement on Ninth Meeting' (n 7), recommendation 9 to State Parties; and 'Statement on Eleventh Meeting of the International Health Regulations (2005) Emergency Committee regarding the Coronavirus Disease (COVID-19) Pandemic' (13 April 2022) recommendation 9 to State Parties https://www.who.int/news/item/13-04-2022-statement-on-the-eleventh-meeting-of-the-international-health-regulations-(2005)-emergency-committee-regarding-the-coronavirus-disease-(covid-19)-pandemic.

10 See among many, WHO Covid-19 Emergency Committee, 'Statement on Sixth Meeting of the International Health Regulations (2005) Emergency Committee regarding the Coronavirus Disease (COVID-19) Pandemic' (15 January 2021), recommendations 1–3 to the WHO Secretariat and recommendations 1, 2 and 11 to State Parties https://www.who.int/news/item/15-01-2021-statement-on-the-sixth-meeting-of-the-international-health-regulations-(2005)-emergency-committee-regarding-the-coronavirus-disease-(covid-19)-pandemic; 'Statement on the Eighth Meeting' (n 6), recommendation 4 to the WHO Secretariat and recommendation 4 to State Parties; and 'Statement on the Ninth Meeting' (n 7), recommendation 4 to State Parties.

11 WHO Covid-19 Emergency Committee, 'Statement on the Tenth Meeting' (n 6), recommendation 4 to State Parties; and 'Statement on the Eleventh Meeting' (n 9), recommendation 5 to State Parties.

12 See eg WHO Covid-19 Emergency Committee, 'Statement on the Eighth Meeting' (n 6), recommendation 3 to State Parties (10%); 'Statement on the Ninth Meeting' (n 7), recommendation 3 to State Parties (40%); 'Statement on the Tenth Meeting' (n 6), recommendation 3 to State Parties (70%); 'Statement on Twelfth Meeting of the International Health Regulations (2005) Emergency Committee Regarding the Coronavirus Disease (COVID-19) Pandemic' (12 July 2022), recommendation 3 to States Parties ('achieve the highest possible vaccination coverage among persons at highest risk of severe disease outcomes and

together with its public-private partners embarked on an unprecedented global programme to distribute and administer emergency-listed vaccines to the global population via its COVAX-facility.[13] This was enabled inter alia by the WHO's Emergency Use Listing (EUL) procedure[14] through which it de facto grants a global emergency authorisation for investigational medical products during a PHEIC.[15] Whilst lockdowns were never directly recommended by the WHO Covid-19 Emergency Committee, they were also not discouraged despite availability of longstanding knowledge of their ineffectiveness in preventing transmission whilst causing considerable socioeconomic damage and raising severe ethical and human rights concerns.[16]

---

among persons at highest risk of exposure, health workers, the elderly and other priority groups' including a 'booster dose') https://www.who.int/news/item/12-07-2022-statement-on-the-twelfth-meeting-of-the-international-health-regulations-(2005)-emergency-committee-regarding-the-coronavirus-disease-(covid-19)-pandemic; 'Statement on the Fourteenth Meeting of the International Health Regulations (2005) Emergency Committee Regarding the Coronavirus Disease (COVID-19) Pandemic' (30 January 2023), recommendation 1 ('achieve 100% [vaccination] coverage of high-priority groups') https://www.who.int/news/item/30-01-2023-statement-on-the-fourteenth-meeting-of-the-international-health-regulations-(2005)-emergency-committee-regarding-the-coronavirus-disease-(covid-19)-pandemic.

[13] 'COVAX' (*WHO*, 2020) https://www.who.int/initiatives/act-accelerator/covax.

[14] WHO, 'Emergency Use Listing Procedure' (9 August 2022) https://www.who.int/publications/m/item/emergency-use-listing-procedure.

[15] Obtaining an EUL from WHO was a precondition for a product to then be distributed globally via COVAX, see eg WHO, 'Product Eligibility under the COVAX Facility' (29 December 2020) https://portal-uat.who.int/prequal/sites/default/files/documents/Product-Eligibility_COVAX-Facility_Dec2020_0.pdf on file with the author. This indicates that EUL designations can have de facto regulatory consequences.

[16] Among many, Thomas Ingelsby et al, 'Disease Mitigation Measures in the Control of Pandemic Influenza' (2006) 4(4) Biosecurity and Bioterrorism: Biodefense Strategy, Practice and Science 366, 371; and WHO's own pre-Covid-19 guidance at WHO, 'Non-pharmaceutical Public Health Measures for Mitigating the Risk and Impact of Epidemic and Pandemic Influenza' (19 September 2019) https://www.who.int/publications/i/item/non-pharmaceutical-public-health-measuresfor-mitigating-the-risk-and-impact-of-epidemic-and-pandemic-influenza. For a more detailed discussion see also Silvia Behrendt and Amrei Müller, 'Do We Need to Protect the Entire World Population from Health Threats through One Global Biomedical Surveillance and Response System? A Human Rights-Based Comment on the Proposed WHO Treaty on Pandemic Preparedness and Response' (2021) 64 German Yearbook of International Law 41, 67–72.

WHO Member States around the world implemented the WHO-recommended countermeasures in the more than three years that the Covid-19-PHEIC lasted, and many continue to follow the WHO Director-General's advice – since August 2023 set out in the Standing Recommendations on Covid-19 – to inter alia continue surveillance activities, offer vaccination, and combat alleged mis- and disinformation about Covid-19.[17] In addition, numerous States declared a state of (health) emergency also under domestic law[18] and/or international[19] or European[20] human rights law, once the WHO had announced the Covid-19-PHEIC. Regional organisations like the European Union (EU) also started to operate in a health emergency mode,[21] enabled by Decision 1082/2013/EU on cross-border health threats adopted in 2013.[22]

This global, European, and domestic response to Covid-19 revealed two interconnected trends or processes that have shaped and continue to shape international (WHO), European (EU), and much of domestic pandemic/

---

[17] WHO Director-General, 'Standing recommendations for COVID-19 issued by the Director-General of the World Health Organization (WHO) in accordance with the International Health Regulations (2005)' (9 August 2023) annexed to UN Doc A78/INF./7 (14 May 2025) https://apps.who.int/gb/ebwha/pdf_files/WHA78/A78_INF7-en.pdf.

[18] See eg US Secretary of Health and Human Services Declaring a Public Health Emergency due to Covid-19 on 31 January 2020 (https://aspr.hhs.gov/legal/PHE/Pages/2019-nCoV.aspx; Magnus Lundgren et al, 'Emergency Powers in Response to COVID-19: Policy Diffusion, Democracy, and Preparedness' (2020) 38 Nordic Journal of Human Rights 305; Audrey Lebret, 'COVID-19 Pandemic and Derogation to Human Rights' (2020) 7 Journal of Law and Biosciences 1; and an early global overview offered by Christian Bjørnskov and Stefan Voigt, 'The State of Emergency Virus' (*VerfBlog*, 19 April 2020) https://verfassungsblog.de/the-state-of-emergency-virus/.

[19] List of derogations from the International Covenant on Civil and Political Rights (adopted 16 December 1966, entered into force 23 March 1976) 999 UNTS 171 (ICCPR) as per its article 4 can be found at https://treaties.un.org/Pages/ViewDetails.aspx?chapter=4&clang=_en&mtdsg_no=IV-4&src=IND.

[20] List of derogations from the European Convention on Human Rights (adopted 4 November 1950, entered into force 3 September 1953) 213 UNTS 221 (ECHR) as per its article 15 can be found at https://www.coe.int/en/web/conventions/full-list/-/conventions/treaty/005/declarations.

[21] Eg the early overview given by the European Commission 'Building a European Health Union: Reinforcing the EU's Resilience for cross-border health threats' (Communication) COM (2020) 724 final.

[22] Decision No 1082/2013/EU of the European Parliament and of the Council of 22 October 2013 on serious cross-border threats to health and repealing Decision No 2119/98/EC 2013 OJ L293/1 (in force until 25 December 2022, repealed by Regulation (EU) 2022/2371).

PHEIC preparedness and response law, policy, and institutions since the early 1990s: a securitisation and a public-private hybridisation trend. International, European, and domestic responses to SARS-CoV-2 acted (and continue to act) as a substantial catalyst for consolidating these trends. This book traces these trends – before, during, and in the aftermath of the Covid-19-PHEIC – and analyses some of the myriad effects they had and continue to have on various areas of law and the functioning of democratic (public) institutions. As these trends permeate, guide, and link the analyses in the chapters of this volume, an explanation is due as to how this volume understands both the 'securitisation' (Section 1.1) and the 'public-private hybridisation' (Section 1.2) trend.

1.1 The Securitisation of Global Public Health Law, Policy, and Institutions

The securitisation trend[23] of pandemic/PHEIC preparedness and response law, policy, and institutions finds its expression most clearly in the classifi-

[23] Eg Michael Baker and Andrew Forsyth, 'The New International Health Regulations: A Revolutionary Change in Global Health Security' (2007) 120 (1267) New Zealand Medical Journal U2872; Belinda Bennet and Terry Carney, 'Public Health Emergencies of International Concern: Global, Regional and Local Responses to Risk' (2017) 25(2) Medical Law Review 223; Stefan Elbe, 'Pandemics on the Radar Screen: Health Security, Infectious Disease and the Medicalisation of Insecurity' (2011) 59(4) Political Studies 848; Lawrence Gostin, 'Pandemic Influenza: Public Health Preparedness for the Next Global Health Emergency' (2004) 32(4) Journal of Law, Medicine & Ethics 565; Lawrence Gostin and Rebecca Katz, 'The International Health Regulations: The Governing Framework for Global Health Security' (2016) 94(2) Milbank Quarterly 264; Max Hardiman, 'The Revised International Health Regulations: A Framework for Global Health Security' (2003) 21(2) International Journal of Antimicrobial Agents 207; Tine Hanrieder and Christian Kreuder-Sonnen, 'WHO Decides on the Exception? Securitization and Emergency Governance in Global Health' (2014) 45(4) Security Dialogue 331; Rebecca Katz et al, 'Global Health Security Agenda and the International Health Regulations: Moving Forward' (2014) 12(5) Biosecurity & Bioterrorism 231; Alexander Kelle, 'Securitization of International Public Health: Implications for Global Health Governance and the Biological Weapons Prohibition Regime' (2017) 13(2) Global Governance 217; Hans Kluge et al, 'Strengthening Global Health Security by Embedding the International Health Regulations Requirements into National Health Systems' (2018) 3(1) BMJ – Global Health e000656; Guenael Rodier et al, 'Global Public Health Security' (2007) 13(10) Emerging Infectious Diseases 1447; Simon Rushton, *Security and Public Health* (Wiley 2019); and Simon Rushton and Yeremy Younde (eds), *Routledge Handbook of Global Health Security* (Routledge 2014).

cation of infectious disease outbreaks as *health emergencies* purportedly requiring the adoption and implementation of strict, blanket non-medical and medical *countermeasures*, and in the underlying doctrine of this approach: the Global Health Security (GHS) doctrine. Initiated and promoted primarily by the United States (US),[24] the GHS doctrine has dominated the WHO's approach – via global bio-surveillance for outbreak detection and building a rapid response apparatus – to what was originally referred to as 'new, emerging and re-emerging diseases' (EID) since the mid-1990s.[25]

Whilst there is no internationally agreed definition of the GHS doctrine,[26] its basic tenets that guide responses to infectious disease outbreaks are clear. In essence, coming from the biosecurity context, the doctrine understands pathogens (and (infected) persons and animals) as 'biological risks' that must be minimised, managed, and addressed through biomedical control measures enforced by a central authority. The doctrine thereby links two fields that have been separate before: health and national/international security,[27] leading it to combine biohazard and biowarfare mitigation strategies with public health. Or, more concretely: the GHS integrates classic rationales of security and defence policies and standard military operating procedures with the traditional medical field of communicable disease prevention and containment. This is achieved in particular by adopting a so-called 'all-hazards approach',[28] which requires (a) constant global biomedical surveillance networks to detect

---

24 For an overview of this process, see Lorna Weir, 'Inventing Global Health Security, 1994–2005', in Rushton and Younde (eds) (n 23) 18. Note also that the legal concept of 'health emergency' declared by an executive authority originates from US law. Under section 319 of the US Public Health Service (PHS) Act, the Secretary of the Department of Health and Human Services (HHS) may determine that: (a) a disease or disorder presents a public health emergency; or (b) that a public health emergency, including significant outbreaks of infectious disease or bioterrorist attacks, otherwise exists, see Administration for Strategic Preparedness and Response (ASPR), 'Declarations of a Public Health Emergency' (2023) https://aspr.hhs.gov/legal/PHE/Pages/default.aspx.

25 WHA Res 48.13 (12 May 1995) UN Doc WHA48.13.

26 Eg Richard Horton and Pamela Das, 'Global Health Security Now' (2015) 385(9980) Lancet 1805; Colin McInnes, 'The Many Meanings of Health Security', in Rushton and Younde (eds) (n 23) 7; for an overview of the ongoing conceptual debates also Preslava Stoeva, 'Dimensions of Health Security – A Conceptual Analysis' (2020) 4(10) Global Challenges (2020) 1, 2–4.

27 Weir (n 24) 18.

28 Micaela Frulli, 'The Challenge of Outlining a CBRN Definitional Framework' in Andrea de Guttry et al (eds), *International Law and Chemical, Biological, Radio-Nuclear (CBRN) Events – Towards an All-Hazards Approach* (Brill/Nijhoff 2022) 3, 5–7.

and alert domestic, regional, and global institutions to the appearance of new, emerging, or re-emerging pathogens; and (b) the adoption of rapid executive emergency medical and non-medical countermeasures that are coordinated, implemented broadly, and strictly enforced at national, regional, and/or at global level to combat infectious disease outbreaks. It is irrelevant whether these outbreaks are natural or the result of biowarfare/-terrorism or laboratory accidents.

Among the medical and non-medical countermeasures preferred by the GHS-doctrine are curfews, mass quarantines (also known as 'lockdowns'), mass testing, contact tracing, 'risk communication', which, among other things, involves information control,[29] and the fast-track development, production, and distribution of (emergency-licensed) diagnostics, therapeutics, and vaccines.[30]

When it comes to the institutional framework for the implementation of the GHS doctrine, it envisages dual-use (civilian and military) 'resilient national health systems'[31] and surveillance systems that serve to detect, prevent, and respond rapidly to threats of infectious disease outbreaks occurring naturally, as a result of biowarfare or due to accidental release of biohazards. Emergency contingency plans and 'surge capacities' shall support this.[32] At the international level, the WHO is to act as a global expert institution with global outbreak surveillance capacities and capacities to devise emergency medical and non-medical countermeasures against infectious disease outbreaks, and with

---

[29] See eg North Atlantic Treaty Organization (NATO), 'NATO's Approach to Countering Disinformation: A Focus on COVID-19' (17 July 2020) https://www.nato.int/cps/en/natohq/177273.htm.

[30] Brooke Courtney et al, 'Regulatory Underpinnings of Global Health Security: FDA's Roles in Preventing, Detecting, and Responding to Global Health Threats' (2014) 12(5) Biosecurity and Bioterrorism: Biodefense Strategy, Practice, and Science 239, 240–43; Adam Biggs and Lanny Littlejohn, 'A Hierarchy of Medical Countermeasures against Biological Threats' (2022) 187 (7/8) Military Medicine 830, 834; and Lois Joellenbeck et al (eds), *Giving Full Measure to Countermeasures: Addressing Problems in the DoD Program to Develop Medical Countermeasures against Biological Warfare Agents* (National Academies Press 2004), ch 3.

[31] WHO, 'National Civil-Military Health Collaboration Framework for Strengthening Health Emergency Preparedness' (2021) 16–17 https://apps.who.int/iris/bitstream/handle/10665/343571/9789240030343-eng.pdf; and Diane Meyer et al, 'A Checklist to Improve Health System Resilience to Infectious Disease Outbreaks and Natural Hazards' (2020) 5(8) BMJ – Global Health e002429.

[32] WHO, 'National Civil-Military Health Collaboration' (n 31) 11, 15–16.

an operative mandate to mobilise and deploy required resources at country level.[33]

The GHS doctrine was integrated into the IHR in 2005 as a result of a thorough revision process that had started in the mid-1990s.[34] To name but a few examples, it incorporated the GHS concept of classifying infectious disease outbreaks as 'health emergencies' – PHEICs – into the IHR,[35] giving the WHO Director-General the unique[36] executive authority to declare such a PHEIC. The Director-General also got the centralised power to issue recommendations to States for medical and non-medical measures – now regularly referred to using the military term[37] *countermeasures*[38] – to address the PHEIC.[39]

---

33 Eg Jonathan Duff et al, 'A Global Public Health Convention for the 21st Century' (2021) 6(6) Lancet e428, 37–9 and 61; WHO-EURO, which organised over '358 missions to 25 Member States, including 40 partner deployments through the Global Outbreak Alert and Response Network (GOARN) and deployment of emergency medical teams' see WHO, 'Two Years of COVID-19: What It Takes to Run an Emergency Response across 53 Countries' (*WHO News Release*, 21 January 2022) https://www.who.int/europe/news/item/21-01-2022-two-years-of-covid-19-what-it-takes-to-run-an-emergency-response-across-53-countries.

34 This process thoroughly revised an earlier version of the IHR from 1969. Documents relating to this process can be accessed at https://apps.who.int/gb/ghs/e/ (2004/05). See also sources listed at (n 23) above.

35 IHR (2005), articles 1 and 12, as well as the decision instrument in annex 2.

36 The authority to declare a quasi-'state of emergency' at the international level is not granted to any public official at an international organisation other than the WHO's Director-General. It can thus be qualified as unique executive authority and has also been referred to as a 'supersovereign power' of the WHO; see Lorna Weir and Eric Mykhalovskiy, *Global Public Health Vigilance. Creating a World on Alert* (Routledge 2010) 155 ff. For a substantial analysis of the unique authorities of the WHO Director-General, see also Silvia Behrendt, *The International Health Regulation and the Executive Authority of the World Health Organization during Public Health Emergencies of International Concern*, Dissertation no 3652, University of St Gallen (2009) 164 ff.

37 See eg 'countermeasures' defined by the US Department of Defense as: 'That form of military science that, by the employment of devices and/or techniques, has as its objective the impairment of the operational effectiveness of enemy activity'; see US Department of Defense, 'DOD Dictionary of Military and Associated Terms' (November 2021) 52 https://www.supremecourt.gov/opinions/URLs_Cited/OT2021/21A477/21A477-1.pdf.

38 Eg WHO, '10 Proposals to Build a Safer World Together. Strengthening the Global Architecture for Health Emergency Preparedness, Response and Resilience' (June 2022) https://cdn.who.int/media/docs/default-source/emergency-preparedness/who_hepr_june30draftforconsult.pdf.

39 IHR (2005), articles 15–18.

Overall, the IHR (2005) adopted an 'all-hazards approach', making it applicable[40] to control the international spread of disease regardless of whether these diseases are caused by naturally occurring pathogens or by the intentional or unintentional release of (natural or bio-engineered) biological agents or toxins.[41] The WHO developed programmes and procedures – most prominently the Health Emergency Programme in 2016,[42] as well as the *BioHub* system,[43] the Research and Development Blueprint for Emerging Pathogens (R&D Blueprint) Programme,[44] the EUL procedure, and the Infodemic Management programme[45] – that are guided and influenced by the GHS and which continue to grow. The WHO has worked to strengthen the global health-security interface.[46] The GHS has also driven the amendment process of the IHR (2005) resulting in the adoption of amendments by the 77th World Health Assembly (WHA) in May 2024,[47] as well as the negotiations of a new WHO Pandemic Agreement.[48]

---

[40] In 2005, this constituted a dramatic widening of the IHR's scope of application. The old version of the IHR (1969) (adopted 25 July 1967, entered into force 1 January 1971) 764 UNTS 3, after minor revisions in 1973 and 1981 respectively, regulated the management of only three diseases: cholera, bubonic plague, and yellow fever.

[41] IHR (2005), article 2 read in conjunction with article 1 (definition of 'disease').

[42] WHA Decision 69(9) (27 May 2016) UN Doc WHA.69(9).

[43] 'WHO *BioHub* System' (*WHO*, 2025) https://www.who.int/initiatives/who-biohub. Through the *BioHub* System, the WHO aims to collect biological materials with PHEIC or pandemic potential and their genetic sequence data.

[44] 'WHO R&D Blueprint for Epidemics' (*WHO*, 2025) https://www.who.int/teams/blueprint/who-r-and-d-blueprint-for-epidemics.

[45] 'Infodemic' (*WHO*, 2025) https://www.who.int/health-topics/infodemic#tab=tab_1.

[46] 'Strengthening the Global Health Security Interface' (*WHO*, 2025) https://www.who.int/activities/strengthening-the-global-health-security-interface.

[47] WHA Res 77.17 (1 June 2024) UN Doc WHA77.17, annex 'Amendments to the International Health Regulations (2005)' (IHR (2024)). Amendments will come into force in September 2025. The decision to amend the IHR (2005) was taken by the 75th WHA in May 2022, see: WHA Decision 75(9) (27 May 2022) UN Doc WHA75(9).

[48] The new Pandemic Agreement has not yet been adopted in April 2025. A draft version of 24 May 2024 is WHA, 'Proposal for the WHO Pandemic Agreement', draft text of 24 May 2024, appendix to the report of the WHO Director-General, 'Outcome of the Intergovernmental Negotiating Body (INB) to Draft and Negotiate a WHO Convention, Agreement or Other International Instrument on Pandemic Prevention, Preparedness and Response' (27 May 2024) UN Doc A77/10. The decision to negotiate a new Pandemic Agreement was taken

The GHS has also shaped EU and domestic health law, policy, and institutions in recent years. At the level of the EU, the EU Commission's powers to declare a public health emergency, activating a number of (legal) health emergency measures, had been put in place in 2013, and were expanded in response to Covid-19.[49] The Health Emergency Preparedness and Response Authority (HERA) as a new European Commission Directorate-General was established in September 2021.[50] The GHS is furthermore reflected in changes made in 2006 to the European legal framework on medical product authorisations, establishing a new process for fast-tracking the approval of vaccines and medicines: the conditional marketing authorisation. It provides for a time-limited conditional market authorisation for medicinal products based on incomplete pre-clinical and clinical data where the anticipated benefits to public health due to the immediate availability of the product in an emergency situation outweigh the anticipated risk, stemming from the fact that additional data is still required to establish the full efficacy and safety of the product.[51] The procedure can explicitly be invoked in regard to 'medicinal products to be used in emergency situations in response [ie as a medical countermeasure] to public health threats recognised either by the WHO' or under EU law.[52]

At the national level of the WHO Member States, the GHS first manifests itself in implementation legislation adopted to integrate the IHR (2005) into domestic legal orders.[53] Second, it is reflected in State obligations under the IHR (2005) to build domestic core bio-surveillance[54] and other core

---

by a Special Session of the WHA in December 2021, see: WHASS, Decision 2(5) (1 December 2021) UN Doc SSA2(5).

[49] Regulation (EU) 2022/2371 of the European Parliament and the Council of 23 November 2022 on serious cross-border threats to health and repealing Decision No 1082/2013/EU [2022] OJ L 314/26, articles 23–5.

[50] Commission Decision of 16 September 2021 establishing the Health Emergency Preparedness and Response Authority C (2021) 6712 final 2021 OJ CI393/3.

[51] Regulation (EC) No 507/2006 of 29 March 2006 on the conditional marketing authorisation for medicinal products for human use falling within the scope of Regulation (EC) No 726/2004 2006 OJ L92/6, articles 3 and 4.

[52] ibid, article 2.

[53] Hans Kluge et al, 'Strengthening Global Health Security by Embedding the International Health Regulations Requirements into National Health Systems' (2018) 3(1) BMJ – Global Health e000656; and Benjamin Mason Meier et al, 'Examining National Public Health Law to Realize the Global Health Security Agenda' (2017) 25(2) Medical Law Review 240.

[54] IHR (2005), article 5.

capacities;[55] and to establish National Focal Points (NFPs) for communication with the WHO.[56] All of these duties have been expanded and strengthened in the 2024 amendments to the IHR.[57] Diligent implementation of the WHO's recommendations for medical and non-medical countermeasures during the Covid-19-PHEIC has further consolidated the GHS-dominated approach at the national level. The involvement of the military in many European countries[58] in the implementation and enforcement of these countermeasures has made the GHS visible to affected populations. Furthermore, legal and institutional measures taken to implement WHO-recommended Covid-19 countermeasures have been made permanent, for example via domestic infection protection or public health acts[59] and through jurisprudence of domestic courts validating

---

[55] Annex 1 to the IHR (2005) lists core capacities concerning surveillance, reporting, notification, verification, response, and collaboration activities, as well as in regard to running designated airports, ports, and ground crossings that State Parties to the IHR shall build.

[56] IHR (2005), article 4.

[57] IHR (2024) (n 47). For more details see Amrei Müller and Silvia Behrendt, 'The 2024 Amendments to the International Health Regulations: A Commentary (Part II: Selected Substantive Amendments)' (*OpinioJuris*, 20 September 2024) https://opiniojuris.org/2024/09/20/the-2024-amendments-to-the-international-health-regulations-a-commentary-part-ii-selected-substantive-amendments/.

[58] See eg Volker Hartmann, '… eine enorm fordernde Aufgabe …'. Interview mit GStA Dr Holtherm, Leiter Abteilung 6, Gesundheitsschutz, Gesundheitssicherheit und Nachhaltigkeit im BMG, *Zeitschrift für Wehrmedizin und Wehrpharmazie* (30 December 2020) https://wehrmed.de/fuehrung-organisation/eine-enorm-fordernde-aufgabe.html; BigBrother Watch, 'Ministry of Truth. The Secretive Government Units Spying on Your Speech' (January 2023) 60–6 https://bigbrotherwatch.org.uk/wp-content/uploads/2023/01/Ministry-of-Truth-Big-Brother-Watch-290123.pdf; Theo Andres, 'Wie sich Gecko gegen den neuen "Feind" Omikron stemmen soll' (*Der Standard*, 18 December 2021) https://www.derstandard.at/story/2000132011624/wie-sich-gecko-gegen-den-neuen-feind-omikron-stemmen-soll; and Frank Bergmann, 'Dutch Government Official Admits Covid Pandemic was "Military Operation": "Ministry of Health Obeys NATO"' (*Slay*, 9 November 2024) https://slaynews.com/news/dutch-government-official-admits-covid-pandemic-military-operation-ministry-health-obeys-nato/.

[59] For an initial overview, eg Joelle Grogan, 'States of Emergency' (*VerfBlog*, 26 May 2020) https://verfassungsblog.de/states-of-emergency/; and contributions available on the website 'Lex Atlas: Covid-19. A Global Academic Project Mapping Legal Responses to Covid-19' https://lexatlas-c19.org. Concerning US health emergency laws, see Elizabeth Platt et al, 'Trends in US Public Health Emergency Laws 2021–2022' (2023) 113(3) American Journal of Public Health 288.

them.[60] Domestic laws may also allow for a reactivation of similar measures should the WHO declare a new PHEIC.

1.2 The Public-Private Hybridisation of Global Public Health Law, Policy, and Institutions

The public-private hybridisation trend incorporates two sides of a single dynamic:[61] first, the 'privatisation' of public institutions' obligations and rights as defined in public (international or domestic) law, or rather, their conferral to and/or exercise by private persons or entities. These can be public international organisations' obligations and rights, like the WHO's; or they can be domestic public institutions' obligations and rights. Second and conversely, the 'progressive "publicisation" of the rights and obligations of private persons' and private institutions, involving the 'invocation of public institutions' rights and obligations by those private persons'[62] or by those private institutions, positioning them in the sphere of 'public authority'.

In the area of global public health law, policies, and institutions, both developments can be observed. Many WHO work priorities are set, and WHO programmes and policies developed, shaped, and implemented via powerful public-private partnerships (PPPs),[63] in particular in the area of pandemic

---

60 Eg Stephanie Palmer and Stevie Martin, 'Public Health Emergencies and Human Rights: Problematic Jurisprudence Arising out of the Covid-19 Pandemic' (2020) 5 European Human Rights Law Review 488. See also Chapters 7–9 in the present volume.

61 As developed by Samantha Besson, 'What Can Public International Law Do against Privatisation?' (2024) 15(3) Transnational Legal Theory 341, 342.

62 ibid.

63 Eg Gian Luca Burci, 'Public/Private Partnerships in the Public Health Sector' (2009) 6 International Organizations Law Review 395; Lisa Clarke, 'The Exercise of Public Private Power over Global Health through Public-Private Partnerships and the Question of Responsibility under International Law' (2011) ASIL Proceedings 96; Lisa Clarke, 'Responsibility of International Organizations under International Law for the Acts of Global Health Public-Private Partnerships' (2011) 12(1) Chicago Journal of International Law 55; Jacob Levich, 'Disrupting Global Health: The Gates Foundation and the Vaccine Business' in Richard Parker and Jonathan Garcia (eds), *Routledge Handbook on the Politics of Global Health* (Routledge 2018) 207; Jens Martens and Karolin Seitz, 'Philanthropic Power and Development: Who Shapes the Agenda?' (*Global Policy Forum*, November 2015) 26–36 https://www.globalpolicy.org/sites/default/files/Philanthropic_Power_online_0.pdf; Mark Curtis, 'Gated Development: Is the Gates Foundation Always a Force for Good?' (*Global Justice Now*, June 2016) https://www.globaljustice.org.uk/wp-content/uploads/2016/06/gjn_gates_report_june_2016_web_final_version

preparedness, prevention, and response. Among the most prominent PPPs here are Gavi – the Vaccine Alliance,[64] CEPI – the Coalition for Epidemic Preparedness Innovations,[65] and, established and active during the Covid-19-PHEIC, the Access to Covid-19 Tools (ACT) Accelerator,[66] which includes the vaccine pillar COVAX.[67] Gavi, for example, is an observer in many WHO technical committees working on PHEIC/pandemic preparedness and response, such as the Strategic Advisory Group of Experts on Immunizations (SAGE)[68] and the Global Advisory Group on Vaccine Safety (GACVS).[69] CEPI is working with the WHO and its Member States towards developing (emergency) licensing and administering vaccines within just 100 days in the near future.[70] Other PPPs, such as the Global Health Security Agenda[71] and the Self-assessment State Party Annual Reporting Tool (SPAR-tool),[72] aim to assist States in building their bio-surveillance and other core capacities at the domestic level as required under the IHR (2005) and its 2024 amendments, and to assess States' efforts in this regard. The WHO Hub for Epidemic and Pandemic Intelligence,[73] established in 2021 in Berlin, is hosting PPPs oriented towards the collection of biodata. Among them is the International

_2.pdf; and, more generally on the process of privatisation of international organisations, see Melissa Durkee, 'International Lobbying Law' (2018) 127 Yale Law Journal 1742.

64 'Gavi' (2025) https://www.gavi.org.

65 'CEPI' (2025) https://cepi.net.

66 'What is the ACT-Accelerator?' (*WHO*, 2025) https://www.who.int/initiatives/act-accelerator/about.

67 'COVAX' (*WHO*, 2023) https://www.who.int/initiatives/act-accelerator/covax.

68 'Strategic Advisory Group of Experts on Immunizations' (*WHO*, 2025) https://www.who.int/groups/strategic-advisory-group-of-experts-on-immunization/about.

69 'Global Advisory Group on Vaccine Safety' (*WHO*, 2025) https://www.who.int/groups/global-advisory-committee-on-vaccine-safety/workingmechanisms.

70 'CEPI 2.0 and the 100 Days Mission' (*CEPI*, 2025) https://100days.cepi.net/.

71 'Global Health Security Agenda' (*GHSA*, 2025) https://globalhealthsecurityagenda.org. GHSA has been established in 2014 following a US initiative aiming to ensure implementation of IHR (2005) core capacities at domestic level. The WHO's role within the GHSA is that of an 'expert advisor'.

72 WHO, 'IHR 2005 States Parties Self-Assessment Annual Reporting Tool' (2nd edn, 2021) https://cdn.who.int/media/docs/default-source/health-security-preparedness/cap/spar/9789240040120-eng-new.pdf.

73 'The WHO Hub for Pandemic and Epidemic Intelligence' (*WHO*, 2025) https://pandemichub.who.int.

Pathogen Surveillance Network, cooperating inter alia with the Rockefeller Foundation[74] and the Chan Zuckerberg Biohub Network.[75]

There have also been considerable shifts in the WHO's funding structure in recent years. Member States' contributions, in particular to the non-earmarked budget, shrank continuously over the years, with private institutions such as the Bill and Melinda Gates Foundation (BMGF) and Gavi among the biggest contributors to WHO's 2020–24 budgets; and pharmaceutical companies also among the contributors.[76] It can also be noted that philanthropic foundations partnering with the WHO like the BMGF (and Gavi), the Wellcome Trust and the Rockefeller Foundation have considerable ties with the pharmaceutical industry.[77]

When it comes to private persons and institutions taking on classic public rights of public (international) organisations like the WHO, the granting of privileges and immunities to Gavi and other PPPs can be mentioned.[78]

Overall, this public-private hybridisation or blurring between the public and the private leads to a situation where the WHO, conceived originally as a *public* intergovernmental international organisation, has lost its character

---

74 'The Rockefeller Foundation and World Health Organization Announce Partnership to Expand Global Pandemic Preparedness in Era of Climate Change' (*Rockefeller Foundation*, 23 May 2023) https://www.rockefellerfoundation.org/news/the-rockefeller-foundation-and-world-health-organization-announce-partnership-to-expand-global-pandemic-preparedness-in-era-of-climate-change/.

75 'Chan Zuckerberg Biohub Network' (*WHO*, 2023) https://cdn.who.int/media/images/default-source/emergencies/the-international-pathogen-surveillance-network/partnership-profiles-chan-zuckerberg.jpg.

76 WHO, '2020–21 Budget: By Contributor' https://open.who.int/2020-21/contributors/contributor; '2022–23 Budget: By Contributor' https://open.who.int/2022-23/contributors/contributor; '2024–25 Budget: By Contributor' https://open.who.int/2024-25/contributors/contributor. For a discussion, see also Kristina Daugirdas and Gian Luca Burci, 'Financing the World Health Organization: What Lessons for Multilateralism?' (2019) 16(2) International Organizations Law Review 299.

77 Eg Tim Schwab, 'Covid-19, Trust, and Wellcome: How Charity's Pharma Investments Overlap with its Research Efforts' (2021) 372 British Medical Journal n556; Rohit Malpani, Brook Baker, and Mogha Kamal-Yanni, 'Corporate Charity – Is the Gates Foundation Addressing or Reinforcing Systemic Problems Raised by Covid-19?' (*Health Policy Watch*, 31 October 2020) https://healthpolicy-watch.news/gates-foundation/address-systemic-covid-19/; and Levich (n 63).

78 'GAVI Recognised as an International Institution' (*Gavi*, 23 June 2009) https://www.gavi.org/news/media-room/gavi-recognised-international-institution; and Davinia Abdul Aziz, 'Privileges and Immunities of Global Public-Private Partnerships: A Case-Study of the Global Fund to Fight AIDS, Tuberculosis and Malaria' (2009) 6 International Organizations Law Review 383.

as a public institution that acts in the collective public (health) interest of the world's States – also public institutions – and the people they (democratically) represent.[79] This also means that we may face more and more of an 'inversion of the hierarchical articulation and "relation" of the public and the private, whereby the public shall be instituted first and then organise the private rather than the reverse'[80] in the area of public health. Such inversion undermines the rule of law and its underlying principles, and leads to ever growing accountability gaps.[81]

Public-private hybridisation can also be observed at the level of the EU and the domestic level. At EU level, HERA, for example, brings together 'EU Member States, the industry and key stakeholders … to bolster systemic cooperation between actors on all fronts of the global health security architecture'.[82] This is reflected in its governance structure, which includes an Advisory Forum supported by two sub-fora on Joint Industrial Cooperation and on Civil Society.[83] When it comes to European Medicines Agency (EMA), its work has become highly dependent on the funding it receives via industry fees and charges for medicinal product approvals.[84]

At the domestic level, the public-private hybridisation plays out in the delivery and implementation of WHO supported medical and non-medical countermeasures via PPPs like the ACT-Accelerator, and PPPs like the Global Health Security Agenda aiming to foster and assess States' efforts to comply with their duties under the IHR (2005) and its 2024 amendments to build core capacities. Domestic medical agencies like the US Centre for Disease Control (CDC) are

---

79 See more generally (beyond the WHO), Letizia Lo Giacco, 'Private Entities Shaping Community Interests: (Re)Imagining the "Publicness" of Public International Law as an Epistemic Tool' (2023) 14(3) Transnational Legal Theory 270.

80 Besson (2024) (n 61) 343, with further references.

81 ibid.

82 'HERA – Overview' (*European Commission*, 2025) https://health.ec.europa.eu/health-emergency-preparedness-and-response-hera/overview_en.

83 'HERA Advisory Forum' (*European Commission*, 2025) https://health.ec.europa.eu/health-emergency-preparedness-and-response-hera/overview/hera-advisory-forum_en.

84 91.5% of EMA's 2025 budget derives from industry, see EMA, 'Funding' (2025) https://www.ema.europa.eu/en/about-us/how-we-work/governance-reporting/funding. In 1995, that figure was at only 20%, see Maryanne Demasi, 'From FDA to MHRA: Are Drug Regulators for Hire?' (2022) 377 British Medical Journal o1538. This, and EMA's policies in relation to experts, have led to criticism, see eg Leïla Miñano et al, 'Big Pharma Influence Hangs over Europe's Medicines Regulator' (*euobserver*, 17 June 2024) https://euobserver.com/Health%20&%20Society/ar6d0b9023.

accepting private funding through a non-profit called CDC Foundation with pharmaceutical companies among the funders,[85] and the US Food and Drug Administration (FDA) is funded inter alia through 'user fees' paid by pharmaceutical companies seeking approval for their products.[86] This applies also to other domestic public health institutions and medical regulators.[87] More indirectly, media reporting on PHEIC/pandemic preparedness and response and on global health more generally has been funded increasingly through philanthropic foundations like the BMGF.[88]

2. THE AIMS OF THE VOLUME

This volume has three overarching aims. First, it traces the two mentioned trends – the securitisation trend and the public-private hybridisation trend – and how they have been reiterated and consolidated over time in PHEIC/pandemic preparedness and response law, policy, and institutions at the international (WHO), the regional European (EU), and the domestic levels, and through the interaction of these levels. This includes tracing the extent to which these trends became apparent in the responses to the Covid-19-PHEIC, and the extent to which the Covid-19-PHEIC accelerated this consolidation process, inter alia by shaping the direction of post-Covid-19 reform processes of PHEIC/pandemic preparedness and response law, policy, and institutions at international, regional European, and domestic levels (some of which are ongoing at the time of writing in 2024 and early 2025). Contributions also look back to the time before the Covid-19-PHEIC in their examination of the two trends.

Second and relatedly, the book aims to analyse some of the myriad but under-researched effects that these two trends have had and continue to have on various areas of law and public institutions. The analysis is not limited to

---

85 'DCC Foundation' (2025) https://www.cdcfoundation.org; and Rebecca Strong, 'The Anatomy of BigPharma's Political Reach' (*Brownstone*, 8 April 2022) https://brownstone.org/articles/the-anatomy-of-big-pharmas-political-reach/.

86 'FDA User Fees Explained' (*FDA*, 2025) https://www.fda.gov/industry/fda-user-fee-programs/fda-user-fees-explained. Similar arrangements are made by EMA, see 'Fees Payable to European Medicines Agency' (*EMA*, 1 January 2025) https://www.ema.europa.eu/en/about-us/fees-payable-european-medicines-agency.

87 Demasi (n 84); and Strong (n 85).

88 Eg Alan MacLeod, 'Revealed: Documents Show that Bill Gates has Given $390 Million to Media Outlets' (*MintPress*, 15 November 2021) https://www.mintpressnews.com/documents-show-bill-gates-has-given-319-million-to-media-outlets/278943/.

one area of law. Contributions engage with questions about the extent to which these trends and their consolidation have been compatible with the protection of human rights and the (political) self-determination[89] of 'democratic societies'[90] as foreseen in international and European human rights treaties, as well as in domestic constitutions. They will also analyse questions concerning the extent to which WHO-led emergency responses to Covid-19 and the ongoing reforms towards consolidation of the securitisation and public-private hybridisation trends are compatible with the global, European and domestic regulatory frameworks of medicinal product authorisations, aspects of EU law, elements of the law of international organisations, and with private law principles.

The third aim of the book is to tentatively examine some of the possible legal and institutional approaches to better safeguard and protect human rights, the fundamental principles of medical law, of the law of international organisations, of EU law, and of private law at a time when the WHO's, the EU's, and domestic health emergency powers are growing and where the public-private distinction is further blurred. Questions on how to ensure accountability for violations, including alleged violations caused by medical and non-medical countermeasures recommended and implemented to address the Covid-19-PHEIC, may also be highlighted.

Concerning all three aims, the analyses offered in this book are both backward and forward looking, united in their focus on different aspects of the securitisation and the public-private hybridisation trends of PHEIC/pandemic preparedness and response law, policy, and institutions, and the broader legal and institutional effects of these trends. The chapters thus examine both the legal bases for, the lawfulness of and the broader institutional consequences of the medical and non-medical countermeasures adopted to address the Covid-19-PHEIC *and* the (legal) implications of the ongoing reform processes that will in all probability further consolidate the global health emergency mode in domestic, European, and international law to address future PHEICs or pandemics as well as the consolidation of the public-private hybridisation trend.

With these two trends in focus and its three aims, the book builds on and critically relates to (primarily legal) academic literature on global health

---

[89] See article 1 of the ICCPR and ICESCR respectively. Reinforced by political participation rights, eg ICCPR, article 15; interpreted by the UN Human Rights Committee (HRCttee), 'General Comment 25 – The Right to Participate in Public Affairs, Voting Rights and the Right of Equal Access to Public Service' (12 July 1996) UN Doc CCPR/C/21/Rev.1/Add.7.

[90] Eg ICCPR, articles 14(1), 21, and 22(2); ICESCR, articles 4 and 8(1)(a) and (c); ECHR, articles 8(2)–11(2), referring to 'democratic societies' protecting human rights.

emergencies and the securitisation of PHEIC/pandemic preparedness and response activities (and public health more generally),[91] as well as on the public-private hybridisation of (formally) public international, regional, and domestic (health) institutions and their public rights and obligations.[92] The emerging literature on the (legal) effects of WHO-recommended medical and non-medical countermeasures to the Covid-19-PHEIC[93] that were implemented by WHO Member States all over the world will also be engaged with by the authors. Moreover, the focus on the two trends and the three aims encourages analyses that raise (primarily legal) questions about the securitised, mechanistic, and almost exclusively biomedical and product-focused approach to PHEIC/pan-

---

91 See the literature listed (nn 23, 24, 26 and 30) above.

92 See the literature listed (nn 61, 63 and 77–9) above.

93 Eg Anna-Laure Beaussier and Lydie Cabane, 'Strengthening the EU's Response Capacity to Health Emergencies: Insights from EU Crisis Management Mechanisms' (2020) 11(4) European Journal of Risk Regulation 808; Karima Bennoune, '"Lest We Should Sleep": COVID-19 and Human Rights' (2020) 114 American Journal of International Law 666; Ronan Cormacain, 'Keeping Covid-19 Emergency Legislation Socially Distant from Ordinary Legislation: Principles for the Structure of Emergency Legislation' (2020) 8(3) Theory and Practice of Legislation 245; Sara Davies, 'Infectious Disease Outbreak Response: Mind the Rights Gap' (2017) 25(2) Medical Law Review 270; Dorota Anna Gozdecka, 'Human Rights during the Pandemic: COVID-19 and Securitisation of Health' (2021) 39(3) Nordic Journal of Human Rights 205; Joelle Grogan and Alice Donald (eds), *Routledge Handbook on Law and the COVID-19 Pandemic* (Routledge 2022); James Hodge et al, 'Covid's Constitutional Conundrum: Assessing Individual Rights in Public Health Emergencies' (2021) 88(4) Tennessee Law Review 837; James Maxeiner, 'America's Covid-19 Pre-existing Vulnerability: A Government of Men, Not Law' (2020) 8(2) Theory and Practice of Legislation 213; Kasey McCall-Smith, 'Good Better Best? Human Rights Impact Assessment in Crisis Lawmaking' (2022) (3) International Journal of Human Rights 1; Sébastien Platon, 'Reinventing the Wheel … and Rolling over Fundamental Freedoms? The Covid-19 Epidemic in France and the "State of Health Emergency"' (2020) 8(3) The Theory and Practice of Legislation 293; Eric Richardson and Colleen Devine, 'Emergencies End Eventually: How to Better Analyze Human Rights Restrictions Sparked by the COVID-19 Pandemic under the International Covenant on Civil and Political Rights' (2020) 42 Michigan Journal of International Law 105; Brigit Toebes, Lisa Forman, and Guilio Bartolino, 'Toward Human Rights-Consistent Responses to Health Emergencies' (2020) 22(2) Health and Human Rights 99; Pedro Villarreal, 'Public Health Emergencies and Constitutionalism before Covid-19: Between the National and International' in Richard Albert and Yaniv Roznai (eds), *Constitutionalism under Extreme Conditions* (Springer 2022) 217; and Eric Windholz, 'Governing during a Pandemic: From Parliamentary Sovereignty to Autocratic Technocracy' (2020) 8(2) Theory and Practice of Legislation 93.

demic preparedness and response promoted by much of the current literature and (reform) debate; as well as about the parallel public-private hybridisation trend. Analyses in this book thus go beyond the two dominating themes in much of the existing (legal) literature.[94] These dominating themes are: (a) pri-

[94] Eg Tolulope Adekola and Faith Majekolagbe, 'Human Rights Law, Intellectual Property and Vaccine Nationalism: Lessons for the Post-COVID-19 World' (2023) 29(2) Australian Journal of Human Rights 375; Dastan Bamwesigye et al, 'COVID-19 Vaccine Equity for the Global South: Vaccination Challenges and Opportunities for Small and Poor Countries' (2023) 10(1) European Journal of Economics, Law and Politics 56; Armin von Bogdandy and Pedro Villarreal, 'The Role of International Law in Vaccinating against COVID-19: Appraising the COVAX Initiative' (2021) 81 Zeitschrift für Öffentliches Recht und Völkerrecht 89; Kaitlin Fajber, 'Business as Usual? Centring Human Rights to Advance Global Covid-19 Vaccine Equity through COVAX' (2022) 24(2) Health and Human Rights Journal 219; Abbie-Rose Hampton et al, 'Equity in the Pandemic Treaty: Access and Benefit-Sharing as a Policy Device or a Rhetorical Device' (2023) 51(1) Journal of Law, Medicine & Ethics 217; Emily Harrison, 'Reimagining Vaccine Access for Health Equity' (2024) 52(2) Journal of Law, Medicine & Ethics 480; Nicole Hassoun, Kaushik Basu, and Lawrence Gostin, 'Pandemic Preparedness and Response: A New Mechanism for Expanding Access to Essential Countermeasures' (2024) 19(4) Journal of Law, Medicine & Ethics 474; Aruna Kashyap et al, 'Covid-19 Exposes Warped Global Health Power: The System Needs a Course Correction' (2021) 6 Business and Human Rights Journal 584; Tamar Luster et al, 'Promoting Vaccination from a Human Rights and Equity Perspective: Lessons from the Israeli "Green Pass"' (2021) 12 European Journal of Risk Regulation 308; Maxwell Smith et al, 'Should COVID-19 Vaccines Authorized for Emergency Use Be Considered "Essential" Medicines?' (2021) 23(1) Health and Human Rights Journal 145; Katrina Perehudoff and Jennifer Sellin, 'The Right to Science as a Guidepost for Fair Access to Covid-19 Vaccines: Investigating the Interpretative Role of the UN Committee on Economic, Social and Cultural Rights' (2022) 24(4) Health and Human Rights Journal 191; Ana Santos Rutschmann, 'The Covid-19 Vaccine Race: Intellectual Property, Collaboration(s), Nationalism and Misinformation' (2021) 64 Washington University Journal of Law and Policy 167; Sharifah Sekalala et al, 'Decolonising Human Rights: How Intellectual Property Laws Result in Unequal Access to the COVID-19 Vaccine' (2021) BMJ Global Health 1; Els Torreele and Joseph Amon, 'Virtual Roundtable: Equitable Covid-19 Vaccine Access' (2021) 23(1) Health & Human Rights Journal 273; German Velasquez, *Vaccines, Medicines and Covid-19. How Can WHO Be Given a Stronger Voice?* (Springer 2022). See also statements and documents by various UN human rights bodies, eg UN Human Rights Council (HRC), Res 46/14 (24 March 2021) UN Doc A/HRC/RES/46/14; CESCR, 'Statement on Universal Affordable Vaccination against Coronavirus Disease (COVID-19), International Cooperation and Intellectual Property' (23 April 2021) UN Doc E/C.12/2021/1; CESCR, 'Statement on Universal and Equitable Access to

oritising and ensuring global vaccine equity (and equal global distribution and administration of other emergency-listed PHEIC-/pandemic products) during future PHEICs/pandemics, and a corresponding global top-down, one-size-fits-all approach to implementation; and (b) calls to further centralise executive emergency powers at the WHO, and in particular in the hands of the WHO Director-General and the Emergency Committee that he can set up under the IHR.

Methodologically, the chapters rely on (doctrinal) legal analyses based on the interpretation and application of existing domestic and EU law as well as international treaty and customary law. Among the sources consulted by the authors are also documents and statements issued by domestic authorities, the WHO, other UN agencies or organs, the EU, the WHO's public-private partners, and by relevant civil society organisations and private persons or institutions on, and relating to, the securitisation trend and the public-private hybridisation trend. Statements and documents on the recent reform processes of PHEIC/pandemic preparedness and response law, policy, and institutions taking place at global, regional European, and domestic levels are also widely relied on. Most chapters furthermore include interdisciplinary elements and thus rely inter alia on public health literature, medical or security studies literature, political science or political philosophy literature, or on historical analysis.

3. THE STRUCTURE AND CONTENTS OF THE VOLUME

The edited collection is structured in three parts around the securitisation and public-private hybridisation trends of PHEIC/pandemic preparedness and response law, policy, and institutions and their myriad legal (and other) consequences. The parts span three levels of legal analysis as well as their interaction: the global level of the WHO, the regional European level of the EU, and the domestic level, albeit with a focus on a few European States.

Vaccines for the Coronavirus Disease (COVID-19)' (15 December 2020) UN Doc E/C.12/2020/2; and UN Independent Expert on Human Rights and International Solidarity, 'Report on International Solidarity in Aid of the Realization of Human Rights during and after the Coronavirus Disease (COVID-19) Pandemic' (13 April 2021) UN Doc A/HRC/47/31.

3.1 Part I – The WHO and Infectious Disease Management: Between Securitisation, Private Influence and Ensuring Equity

To set the scene, Part I approaches the WHO's activities in the area of infectious disease management from a historical perspective, tracing the securitisation trend as well as the growing influence of private entities through time. This includes an examination of the extent to which they have dominated the process of amending the IHR between 2022–24, or whether the concept of 'equity', strongly promoted by low-income countries in the negotiation process, counter-weighed these trends.

In Chapter 1 on 'The Pandemic Industry: Reinstituting Colonialism through Public Health', David Bell examines how the Constitution of the WHO, written in the aftermath of the Second World War, reflected experience with medical fascism and colonialism. Its broad definition of health, as 'a state of physical, mental and social well-being',[95] promoted a holistic view of individuals and society. However, recent decades have seen a reversal of many of these basic principles in international public health law and institutions like the WHO. The WHO has embraced the GHS doctrine guiding much of its work and become a de facto public-private partnership far removed from its original country-based model. The Covid-19 outbreak highlighted these changes. The WHO's response was centralised and restrictive, disregarding local context. Impoverishing, commodity-based approaches ran counter to prior public health guidance, benefiting private and corporate interests. An entire 'pandemic industry' is now normalizing these approaches. Bell concludes by observing that the return to a 'colonialist model' – today reflected in the securitisation and public-private hybridisation trends – puts decades of progress in securing human rights and access to adequate healthcare via local public health systems at risk.

Nithin Ramakrishnan and Sreenath Namboodiri pick up the 2022–24 negotiations of the amendments to the IHR in Chapter 2 on 'The Global Health Emergency Regime and the 2024 Amendments to the International Health Regulations', offering an analysis of their content. They examine the decision to amend the IHR (2005) against the background of the functioning of the WHO Global Health Emergency Regime prior to the amendments, and in light of responses to the Covid-19-PHEIC, taking account of the securitisation and public-private hybridisation trends. The authors evaluate proposals for amendments made by different developing and developed States during the negotiating process, and explore the potential changes they could bring to

---

95 Constitution of the World Health Organization (adopted 22 July 1946, entered into force 7 April 1948) 14 UNTS 185 (WHOC), preamble.

the emergency regime. Throughout, Ramakrishnan and Namboodiri place an emphasis on the question about the extent to which the 2024 amended IHR will secure equitable access to pandemic-related health products globally, thereby constituting a counterweight to continued securitisation and privatisation of global health.

3.2 Part II – Securitisation and Public-Private Hybridisation: The WHO and the EU

The chapters of Part II zoom in on selected developments at the level of both the WHO and the EU that reflect the securitisation of PHEIC/pandemic preparedness and response law, policies, and institutions and/or their public-private hybridisation. The chapters discuss these selected developments in detail and evaluate their implications for the protection of human rights, the regulation of medicinal product authorisations, EU (health) law, and private law principles.

In Chapter 3, on 'Safe and Effective Medical Countermeasures? The International Health Regulations, the WHO's Responsibilities for the Human Right to Health and Emergency Listed Vaccines', Amrei Müller and Silvia Behrendt focus on some of the legal questions about the most prominent medical countermeasure recommended by the WHO during the Covid-19-PHEIC, as informed by the GHS doctrine: the rapid development, emergency listing/authorisation, global promotion, distribution, and mass administration of investigational vaccines. The chapter describes the WHO's role in deploying this countermeasure, concentrating on the WHO's EUL procedure and its promotional activities. It then analyses the extent to which these activities are in line with the WHO's obligations under the IHR and its responsibilities for the human right to health. Müller and Behrendt place a special emphasis on the WHO's duties and responsibilities to ensure access to safe and efficacious medical products and to reliable health information; and to uphold the principle of free and informed consent to participation in medical or scientific experiments and to medical treatment.

In Chapter 4, on 'The Authority of the System of Global Health Governance', David McGrogan examines the justification for the exercise of authority by the WHO that aims to improve health security and to thereby contribute to the realisation of a more 'equal, just and resilient world'. Borrowing from the remarks of Alexandre Kojève on the subject of authority, published after his death, Chapter 4 makes the case that the system of global health governance justifies its authority on the basis of a claim to possess a project for responding to the future – and, particularly, future (pandemic or other health) risk. Following from this, the system justifies the almost unfettered powers of the WHO Director-General to declare a PHEIC and to make temporary and standing recommendations; the claim to be in a position to assess and control what type of information should be communicated in a given circumstance and hence what qualifies as 'expertise' via its infodemic management programmes; and the emphasis on a uniform approach to public health threats among States, under a centralised WHO coordinating mechanism. McGrogan ends with showing how Kojève's thinking on authority provides an opportunity to subject the WHO system of global health governance to critique and imagine other ways in which global health could be protected in line with other values, for example human rights and diversity in responses to infectious disease outbreaks in light of local contexts.

In Chapter 5 on 'Where is the Legal Basis for HERA's and the EU's Key Role in the Securitisation and Globalisation of Their Pandemic Preparedness and Response Policy?', Michael Geistlinger moves the analysis to the level of the EU. He explores how, on 16 September 2021, a new European Commission Directorate-General was launched on Health Emergency Preparedness and Response (HERA). In line with the GHS doctrine, HERA will anticipate threats and potential health crises and will ensure the development, production, and distribution of medicines, vaccines, and other medical countermeasures in the EU. The establishment of HERA, and other practices hastily developed by the Commission during the Covid-19-PHEIC, requires examination given the limited competences of the EU in health matters. Among these other practices are the EU Strategy for Covid-19 vaccines, the EU Conditional Marketing Authorisation of investigational Covid-19 vaccines, the introduction of the EU Digital Covid-Certificate, and the Emergency Support Instrument. The analysis shows that the EU, its Commission, and HERA are lacking a legal fundament in the Founding Treaties. This concerns both the activities they engage in and have set for themselves in the area of pandemic preparedness and prevention and when extending these activities beyond the EU, by negotiating the new WHO Pandemic Agreement and driving the 2022–24 revision process of the IHR.

In Chapter 6 on 'Private Law Aspects of Pandemic Preparedness, Prevention, and Response', Günter Reiner analyses the private law aspects of public health emergencies, uncovering various aspects of the public-private hybridisation of PHEIC/pandemic preparedness and response law, policy, and institutions at domestic, EU, and WHO levels. After introducing the major private law players in global health governance, Chapter 6 focuses on the private law instruments of public health emergencies by presenting and commenting on the typical design and clauses of private law contracts such as Advance (Vaccine) Purchase Agreements (APAs). This overview reveals the one-sided distribution of risk in favour of the manufacturers. A discussion of how WHO guidelines find direct entry into European and national German private law follows. The analysis concludes with an examination of the way in which the relevant public and private law actors of public health emergencies can be held accountable under private law for their decisions and influence by vaccine-injured individuals and other affected persons. A special focus is on the 'liability risk management' in favour of vaccine manufacturers.

3.3 Part III – Securitisation and Public-Private Hybridisation: The (European) Domestic Level

In Part III, the analysis moves to the (European) domestic level, examining securitised responses to infectious disease outbreaks in domestic law, policies, and institutions, including the effects of WHO-recommended medical and non-medical countermeasures to address PHEICs. With the help of case studies on Germany and Switzerland, and a comparative case study of France and Ireland, health emergency law and policies and their effects on other areas of domestic law, in particular the protection of human/constitutional rights, are examined. Their effects on the functioning of domestic legislatures, for example the suspension of normal legislative procedures via ruling by decrees, are also analysed. Another aspect analysed is the extent to which domestic courts reviewed medical and non-medical emergency countermeasures during the Covid-19-PHEIC, and with what effect.

In Chapter 7 on 'Governing during Covid-19: Comparative Insights on How Health Emergencies Tested Democracy', Marie-Luce Paris offers comparative insights into the legal response to the Covid-19-PHEIC in Ireland and France. After a presentation of the overall legal framework of health emergency legislation and the extraordinary processes it entailed for the institutions in both jurisdictions, the chapter examines how this emergency legislation disrupted decision-making processes, particularly in relation to democratic oversight and to courts' judicial review of violations of rights and freedoms. This, and the setting up of executive ad hoc bodies for crisis management with far-reaching mandates in both countries – like the Irish 'National Public Health Emergency Team' (NPHET) for Covid-19 and the French 'Health Defence Council' – reflect the centralisation and securitisation of health policies at the domestic level. Chapter 7 concludes with drawing insights from the experiences of Ireland and France, focusing on the robustness of their democratic systems, especially in the context of the WHO reform debate.

In Chapter 8 on '"Lockdowns", Rights Violations, Remedies and the New Global Health Security Order. Lessons to be Learnt from the German Experience?', Kai Ambos examines German law and policies in response to Covid-19-PHEIC and draws some lessons from this experience for the WHO's efforts to reform the international legal framework on pandemic preparedness and response. It first takes issue with the unexpected career of the 'lockdown' concept, often used interchangeably to capture the meaning of *Ausgangsbeschränkung* (exit restriction) and *Ausgangssperre* (exit prohibition). Second, a chronological overview and a preliminary assessment of the German Covid-19 countermeasures is offered. Exit restrictions are then analysed in more detail, given that they can be considered as paradigmatic interferences with a series of fundamental rights and that the ensuing rights restrictions can rarely be considered proportionate. Finally, the chapter discusses whether the German experience can offer any lessons for the envisaged new Global Health Security (Law) Order driving the WHO reform efforts.

In the last chapter, Chapter 9 on 'Top-Down versus Bottom-Up. WHO PHEIC Declarations and the Protection of Human Rights in Switzerland: A Libertarian Analysis', David Dürr highlights that the WHO's health emergency regime raises fundamental questions on how societies deal with the dilemma of ensuring public safety and individual liberty. The WHO's international scope leads to further questions on how that dilemma is to be addressed on different levels: the national, the regional, and the global level. Chapter 9 presents a libertarian bottom-up approach to this dilemma addressing it as consistently as possible from the perspective of individual human rights understood as natural phenomena. It derives from these not only defensive rights that individuals can invoke against internationally coordinated health measures but also criteria for legitimising such measures. One of the crucial elements in this respect is the human right to a fair trial. It does not only prohibit supra-individual interventions but subjects them to the judgement of an impartial instance. The extent to which such has happened in Switzerland during the Covid-19-PHEIC is evaluated, illustrating some of the deficits of the Swiss securitised response, especially when it comes to upholding the protection of human rights, effective judicial review, and democratic processes.

The volume closes with brief concluding remarks written by the editors, drawing together the findings from the nine chapters. It focuses on findings concerning the securitisation and public-private hybridisation trends permeating PHEIC/pandemic preparedness, prevention and response law, policies and institutions at the global WHO, the regional EU and the domestic levels, and its myriad legal (and other) effects. It also enters into a brief discussion as to whether, and if so how, the securitisation and public-private hybridisation trends could be reversed.

PART I

The WHO and infectious disease management: between securitisation, private influence and ensuring equity

1. The pandemic industry: reinstituting colonialism through public health

David Bell

1. INTRODUCTION: DEFINING AND MEASURING DISEASE

The Constitution of the World Health Organization (WHO) states that 'health is a state of physical, mental and social well-being, not merely the absence of disease or infirmity'.[1] When agreed in 1946, this broad view of human health sought to capture some of the sense of the time. The world was emerging from the throes of European fascism and, more gradually, colonialism. The definition touched on the hopes of a better world that the WHO, the United Nations, and other newly emerging international organisations supposedly enshrined.[2]

The WHO would be governed by the World Health Assembly (WHA),[3] with membership limited to nation States and making decisions based on a one-country-one-vote basis. While initially European-dominated, its membership expanded as more nations emerged from colonialist yokes. Over two decades, the WHA came to be dominated, at least through numbers, by lower- and middle-income States with their disproportionate burdens of endemic infectious disease. Financing came mainly from wealthier countries, proportional to gross domestic product, but was provided as core funding. The WHO then determined how it would be spent, based on disease burden, potential for health impact, and country interest. This inevitably led to an emphasis in the WHO's

[1] Constitution of the World Health Organization (adopted 22 July 1946, entered into force 7 April 1948) 14 UNTS 185 (WHOC), preamble.

[2] As expressed, eg, in the Charter of the United Nations (adopted 26 June 1945, entered into force 24 October 1945) 1 UNTS XVI (UN Charter); and the Universal Declaration of Human Rights (UDHR) UNGA Resolution 217A (10 December 1948) UN Doc A/RES/217 A.

[3] 'World Health Assembly' (*WHO*, 2024) https://www.who.int/about/governance/world-health-assembly. Unless otherwise stated all web links given in this chapter last accessed between 17 October 2024 and 7 April 2025.

programmes on the major preventable or treatable diseases such as malaria, tuberculosis, smallpox, and the outcomes of poor nutrition and sanitation.[4]

Disease burden is an important concept in public health. It normally involves an assessment of the number of years of life lost or impaired (by disability) from the disease. This is commonly rendered as Disability-Adjusted Life Years (DALYs).[5] A five-year-old child dying from malaria will likely lose about 70 years of life, whilst an 80-year-old dying from pneumonia will probably lose less than five. Therefore, although both are recorded as deaths, most human societies would maintain that the child's death is the most tragic. Resources should therefore be directed to improving the child's health before that of the elderly person. This is not a value judgement of a person's worth, but on their respective potential years of life remaining.

Other metrics involving life years, such as Quality-Adjusted Life Years (QALYs),[6] or years of well-being (WELLBYS),[7] reflect definitions of health incorporating the maintenance of good health resulting from interventions and a broader understanding of what constitutes a positive life experience, respectively. Understanding the concept of disease burden based on life years lost and how it relates to respiratory virus infections is essential to understanding the drivers behind the current pandemic preparedness agenda. These metrics were a basis for determining public health priorities prior to 2020 but were widely ignored in public messaging on the impact of Covid-19. This is important to understanding the way in which Covid-19 and the risk from disease outbreaks are being used to support the pandemic preparedness agenda including efforts to reform the relevant international legal framework at WHO level by amending the International Health Regulations (IHR, 2005)[8] and negotiating a

---

4 WHO, 'The First Ten Years of the World Health Organization' (1958) 157, 172–97 https://www.who.int/publications/i/item/9789241560146.

5 WHO, 'WHO Methods and Data Sources for Global Burden of Disease Estimates 2000–2019' (December 2020) 6–19 https://cdn.who.int/media/docs/default-source/gho-documents/global-health-estimates/ghe2019_daly-methods.pdf.

6 Robert Kaplan, 'Utility Assessment for Estimating Quality-adjusted Life Years' in Frank Sloan (ed), *Valuing Health Care: Costs, Benefits, and Effectiveness of Pharmaceuticals and Other Medical Technologies* (CUP 1995) 31–60.

7 Paul Frijters et al, 'The WELLBY: A New Measure of Social Value and Progress' (2024) 11 Humanities and Social Sciences Communications 736.

8 International Health Regulations (2005) (adopted 23 May 2005, entered into force 15 June 2007) 2509 UNTS 79 (IHR (2005)). Amendments to the IHR were adopted on 1 June 2024 by the 77th World Health Assembly (WHA): WHA Res 77.17 (1 June 2024) UN Doc WHA77.17, annex 'Amendments to the International Health Regulations (2005)' (IHR (2024)).

new WHO Agreement on Pandemic Preparedness, Prevention, and Response[9] discussed as a tool for increasing authoritarian control through the remainder of this chapter.

Briefly therefore, this chapter will describe how the WHO has changed, or been changed, to serve a purpose other than that for which it was formed. In Section 2, the potential for public health to be used as a means to manage populations beyond the strict area of disease mitigation will be discussed. Section 3 examines the pre-Second World War role of international public health in supporting such a broad agenda. The WHO in the early days after the Second World War was a very different organisation to that which exists now (Section 4), before tensions arose in recent decades between the return of the centrist or colonialist mindset that had dominated international public health thinking prior to the Second World War, and the post-War horizontal or decentralised mindset on which the WHO was ostensibly founded (Section 5). Section 6 highlights that the WHO-declared Covid-19 Public Health Emergency of International Concern (PHEIC)[10] and WHO-led global response to it emphasised the resurgence of the former, reflecting evolution within the WHO as funding models changed and parallel organisations with strong private sector influence arose beside it. What this chapter refers to as a growing 'pandemic industry' is building on this evolution, posing a significant threat to the understandings and protection of human rights and medical freedom that had underpinned post-War Western societies and many post-colonial States (Section 7). In conclusion, the chapter briefly discusses the need to return to an evidence- and human rights-based approach to public health, in particular in the area of responding to infectious disease outbreaks, a change that the WHO may or may not be fit to play a role in.

---

[9] The new Pandemic Agreement is still under negotiation at the time of writing in February 2025. A draft version of the Pandemic Agreement of 24 May 2024 has been submitted to the 77th WHA: WHA, 'Proposal for the WHO Pandemic Agreement', draft text of 24 May 2024, appendix to the report of the WHO Director-General, 'Outcome of the Intergovernmental Negotiating Body (INB) to Draft and Negotiate a WHO Convention, Agreement or Other International Instrument on Pandemic Prevention, Preparedness and Response' (27 May 2024) UN Doc A77/10.

[10] In accordance with IHR (2005), article 12; WHO Covid-19 Emergency Committee, 'Statement on the Second Meeting of the International Health Regulations (2005) Emergency Committee Regarding the Outbreak of Novel Coronavirus (2019-nCoV)' (30 January 2020) https://www.who.int/news/item/30-01-2020-statement-on-the-second-meeting-of-the-international-health-regulations-(2005)-emergency-committee-regarding-the-outbreak-of-novel-coronavirus-(2019-ncov).

2. DEFINING SCOPE AND POWER

While the definition of 'health' can be broad, influences on health can be similarly diverse. If health is considered (reasonably) to encompass physical, mental, and social well-being,[11] then potential risks to health encompass any threat to each of these aspects of life. Influences on each of these can also be extrapolated several layers beyond that of direct impacts. For instance, a warming climate may increase rainfall and humidity in certain regions, promoting the survival of mosquitoes.[12] This in turn may increase mosquito-borne diseases such as malaria or dengue fever. Thus, if human activities that burn hydrocarbons are considered to be a major contributor to global warming, they may then be construed to constitute a public health threat.

The term 'One Health' was originally used to denote, in particular, the relationship between animal health and human health. Controlling bovine tuberculosis will both reduce infections in humans and improve the food supply and therefore nutrition. 'One Health' has been increasingly extended to encompass concepts such as the proposed indirect impacts of burning hydrocarbons on human health outlined above. In using the broader health definition, the stress of concern for climate is also being considered to impact mental and social health.[13] Such broad approaches are now accepted within mainstream medical journals.[14]

This approach to health risk is not new – the idea of a holistic approach to improving and maintaining human well-being must be as old as humanity itself. Understanding of the influence of environmental factors on how we function may even have been stronger in the past, when people had closer connections to the natural environment. As a way of maintaining well-being most would accept it as common sense. We should not pollute rivers because drinking contaminated water makes us sick, and killing fish will leave us with less food.

The danger in such approaches lies in them being taken out of context (ie, in quite the opposite way to a holistic approach). While the earth has warmed over recent decades, malaria has declined,[15] and while globally insignificant increases consistent with warming have occurred in mountainous regions in

---

11 WHOC, preamble.

12 Shouro Dasgupta, 'Burden of Climate Change on Malaria Mortality' (2018) 221(5) International Journal of Hygiene and Environmental Health 782.

13 Paulo Cianconi et al, 'The Impact of Climate Change on Mental Health: A Systematic Descriptive Review' (2020) 11(47) Front Psychiatry 490206.

14 'One Health: A Call for Ecological Equity' (2023) 401(10372) Lancet 169.

15 WHO, 'World Malaria Report 2023' (30 November 2023) 8–10 https://www.who.int/publications/i/item/9789240086173.

Ethiopia and Papua New Guinea, the temperate countries most touted as at increasing risk are witnessing continued decline.[16] Malaria transmission is associated with climate, but it is associated even more strongly with poverty and health system access.[17] The implications of increasing poverty through actions intended to mitigate climate change are therefore obvious.

As long as public health remains a field of medicine aimed at supporting sovereign individuals in their decision-making, recommendations can be dealt with in local context and harm avoided. However, if public health becomes a set of rules dictated from a central authority, then the ability to manage the complexities necessary to ensure good outcomes in a heterogeneous world is lost. Centralisation also broadens the scope to use public health as a tool of authoritarian control, decreasing equality and social capital and thereby further promoting poor outcomes.[18] This danger is seen in the securitisation of public health – disease and well-being are declared issues of national or even global security (global health security),[19] allowing human rights to be abrogated in ways normally associated with war.

'One Health' definitions can thus be used to greatly inflate the potential harms of ecological influences on human well-being, justifying restrictive measures not just to allegedly prevent or reduce illness or mortality but to protect the perceived interests of governments through an appeal to a 'greater good'.[20] This requires the population to cede authority over their healthcare, and thus their bodies, to those deemed to have greater expertise or capacity to protect it. It requires a transition from an advisory and servanthood concept of public health officials as provided by the WHO's Constitution to a very different model that is much closer to public health's colonial and technocratic roots with self-appointed experts at the centre.[21]

---

16 ibid, 29–31.

17 Awash Teklehaimanot and Paola Mejia, 'Malaria and Poverty' (2008) 1136 Annals of the New York Academy of Sciences 32.

18 Michael Marmot et al, 'Health Inequalities among British Civil Servants: The Whitehall II Study' (1991) 337 Lancet 1387.

19 Committee on Global Health and the Future of the United States, 'Infectious Diseases, Pandemic Influenza, and Antimicrobial Resistance: Global Health Security Is National Security' in *Global Health and the Future Role of the United States* (National Academies Press 2017) 43–5. On the securitisation of global health policies and law, see also the introductory chapter to this volume.

20 David Bell, 'Pandemic Preparedness and the Road to International Fascism' (2023) 82 American Journal of Economics and Sociology 395.

21 WHOC, article 2(c); and Bell (n 20).

3. PUBLIC HEALTH AS A TOOL OF COLONIALISM AND SOCIAL CLEANSING

The 1851 International Sanitary Conference in Paris was the first international meeting of the modern era to concentrate on health cooperation between nations.[22] Portugal and the Netherlands still maintained slaves in colonial holdings, while others traded with North American states whose industries relied on slavery.[23] Epidemic disease was a threat to their own populations and to the productiveness of their colonies, but human rights could be subservient to economic opportunity. The conference discussed control of borders during outbreaks, and how to manage populations that cross them. Subsequent conferences led to the signing of a convention in Venice in 1892 concerning cholera, whilst a subsequent agreement would cover bubonic plague.[24] Understanding of the spread of disease and the role of pathogens grew rapidly at this time, exemplified by the work of the likes of Louis Pasteur in demonstrating the role of microscopic pathogens,[25] and John Snow in demonstrating how public health measures (disabling a water pump) could protect the population from them.[26] A health bureaucracy was born to implement responses built on this knowledge that could influence population health by modifying people's environment and their interactions with it.

The potential to control the welfare of individuals through medical care expanded over time to influence the welfare of whole populations. While it was long recognised that some diseases, such as leprosy, were spread within populations by individuals, the growing understanding of the link between pathogens and disease drove the case for controlling such individuals as a vehicle to protect the many. This was epitomised by the tragic case of Typhoid Mary, held for years against her will on potentially spurious justification.[27] Epidemics could be used to justify population control on a broad scale, and colonial structures made this far easier to implement. Colonial powers would

---

22 Norman Howard-Jones, *The Scientific Background of the International Sanitary Conferences 1851–1938* (WHO 1975) 409.

23 'Chronology: Who Banned Slavery When?' (*Reuters*, 9 August 2007) https://www.reuters.com/article/uk-slavery-idUSL1561464920070322.

24 Howard-Jones (n 22).

25 'Louis Pasteur' (*Biography.com*, 26 May 2021) https://www.biography.com/scientists/louis-pasteur.

26 SWB Newsom, 'Pioneers in Infection Control: John Snow, Henry Whitehead, the Broad Street Pump, and the Beginnings of Geographical Epidemiology' (2006) 64(3) Journal of Hospital Infection 210.

27 Filio Marineli et al, 'Mary Mallon (1869–1938) and the History of Typhoid Fever' (2013) 2 Annals of Gastroenterological Surgery 132.

pitch this extension of their wealth extraction programmes as a necessary altruism, a 'burden' to be borne by the colonialists.[28] Obviously, the colonised had little choice regarding others 'bearing this burden', and the burden proved advantageous to those who claimed to be bearing it. Parallels with today should not be lost.

With the establishment of a permanent office, the Office Internationale d'Hygiene Publique, in Paris in 1907 (and the International Sanitary Bureau in the Americas five years earlier), a permanent international health bureaucracy was born.[29] Based on a European model of centralised colonial power and a hierarchical view of human value or merit, the Paris Office set the pattern for the following century. It worked through a model within which Western governments and their corporate implementers considered themselves both entitled and empowered to tell the rest of humanity how to live, and the health standards they would follow.[30]

With greater wealth, a pervasive belief of better breeding or genetic heritage,[31] and access to the drivers of the chemical and physical sciences, this early global health bureaucracy had no reason to doubt the righteousness of its cause.[32] Party to colonial abuses against human rights and promotion of mass famine, they could still consider themselves part of an elite with a right to direct health policy across the colonial world.[33]

The First World War shook but did not remove the old colonialist order, and the League of Nations that formed afterwards still reflected a centralised colonialist view, in which European and North American powers should determine how much of the rest of humanity lived. One Asian nation, Japan, would be added. Though also a colonial power, Japan would later claim it

---

28 Rudyard Kipling, *The White Man's Burden* (The Kipling Society 1899).

29 Howard-Jones (n 22).

30 WHO, 'The First Ten Years' (n 4) 157, 172–97.

31 Garlan Allen, 'Eugenics and Modern Biology: Critiques of Eugenics, 1910–1945' (2011) 75(3) Annals of Human Genetics 314; and Omar Haque et al, 'Why Did So Many German Doctors Join the Nazi Party Early?' (2012) 33 International Journal of Law and Psychiatry 473.

32 James Corbett, 'A Brief History of Technocracy' (*International Forecaster Weekly*, 23 September 2017) https://theinternationalforecaster.com/topic/international_forecaster_weekly/a_brief_history_of_technocracy.

33 Kalim Siddiqui, 'The Political Economy of Famines during the British Rule in India: A Critical Analysis' (*The World Financial Review*, 30 June 2023) https://worldfinancialreview.com/the-political-economy-of-famines-during-the-british-rule-in-india-a-critical-analysis/; 'The Belgian Congo' (*History Guild*, 2022) https://historyguild.org/the-belgian-congo/; and Joseph Horan, 'The Colonial Famine Plot: Slavery, Free Trade, and Empire in the French Atlantic, 1763–1791' (2010) 55(S18) International Review of Social History 103.

was not accepted on equal terms.[34] The League of Nations formed its own International Health Organization, also concentrating on endemic and infectious diseases that still dominated healthcare in this pre-antibiotic world.[35]

Growing eugenics and technocracy movements were dominating public health approaches in many Western institutions, with the public health professions through the 1920s and 1930s claiming a role in improving society and cleansing it of attributes considered negative, such as certain physical and cognitive characteristics (eg, cerebral palsy and learning difficulties) and even the expression of disallowed political opinions.[36] This only came into wide disfavour when associated with the Nazi atrocities that were revealed toward the end of the Second World War. However, the attempted elimination of whole ethnic groups that the Nazis considered inferior, spearheaded by health professions,[37] could be seen as an extension of less physically brutal policies of ethnic cleansing and social control that epitomised the eugenics approach in other Western States,[38] and the broad subjugation of African and Asian populations by colonial powers.

4. A WINDOW FOR NEW IDEAS

The WHO was laid out on egalitarian principles in 1946, with each State having one vote in the WHA and in one of six regional assemblies.[39] The number of States grew rapidly as they emerged from colonialism, with the WHA structure ostensibly reflecting their equality with their former colonial masters. Funding of the WHO was dominated by 'core' contributions, agreed by the WHA and generally reflecting a country's gross domestic product,[40] leaving the assumed technical expertise of the organisation to decide how resources would be deployed.[41]

---

34 Michael McCarthy, 'A Brief History of the World Health Organization' (2002) 360(9340) Lancet 1111; and Howard-Jones (n 22).

35 Canadian Medical Association, 'An International Health Organization and the League of Nations' (1924) 14(6) Canadian Medical Association Journal 532; and Paul Weindling, *International Health Organisations and Movements, 1918–1939* (CUP 1995) 56.

36 Allen (n 31); and Corbett (n 32).

37 Alexander Mitscherlich and Fred Mielke, *Doctors of Infamy: The Story of the Nazi Medical Crimes* (Henry Schuman 1949) 21.

38 Allen (n 31); and Corbett (n 32).

39 WHOC, articles 44 and 59.

40 WHOC, article 57; and WHO Executive Board, 'Scale of Assessments for 2020–2021' UN Doc EB144.R6 (31 January 2019).

41 WHOC, articles 30 and 37.

Within this context, public health was being re-thought after the centralised prescriptive model of the eugenics and medical fascism of the Nazi and colonialist era, in which an elite of medical officers could dictate the medical management of individuals and populations. The Universal Declaration of Human Rights (UDHR) of 1948 attempted to express inalienable rights of each human being.[42] The 1947 Nuremberg Code,[43] while aimed at banning and preventing human experimentation, established principles of informed consent and non-coercion for medical research and treatment reflected in later agreements including the UDHR, the Declaration of Helsinki,[44] the International Covenant on Civil and Political Rights,[45] and the Convention on the Rights of Persons with Disabilities.[46]

Reflecting the context of many WHO Member States throwing off their colonial yokes, the WHO's Constitution emphasised equality and community involvement with a role for the WHO as an organisation of central coordination at a Member State's request.[47] An emphasis on primary care – the provision of readily accessible basic healthcare, including sanitation and nutrition, that had been shown to be the main driver of past health improvements in high-income countries, would dominate the public health agenda.[48] This culminated in the

---

42 UDHR (n 2).

43 Nuremberg Code 1947, reprinted in (1996) 313(7070) British Medical Journal 1448.

44 World Medical Association, 'Declaration of Helsinki: Ethical Principles for Medical Research Involving Human Participants' (June 1964), adopted by the 18th WMA General Assembly, articles 25–38 https://www.wma.net/policies-post/wma-declaration-of-helsinki/.

45 International Covenant on Civil and Political Rights (adopted 19 December 1966, entered into force 23 March 1976) 999 UNTS 171, article 7.

46 Convention on the Rights of Persons with Disabilities (adopted on 12 December 2006, entered into force 3 May 2008) 2515 UNTS 13, article 15; see also Convention on Human Rights and Biomedicine (1997), ETS No 164, article 16; Additional Protocol to the Convention on Human Rights and Biomedicine, concerning Biomedical Research (2005), CETS No 195, article 24; UNESCO Universal Declaration on Bioethics and Human Rights (2005), article 6(2); and UN Special Rapporteur on the Right to Health, 'Report on Informed Consent' (10 August 2010) UN Doc A/64/272.

47 WHOC, article 2.

48 Thomas Frieden, 'A Framework for Public Health Action: The Health Impact Pyramid' (2010) 100(4) American Journal of Public Health 590; and Leigh Shaw-Taylor, 'An Introduction to the History of Infectious Diseases, Epidemics and the Early Phases of the Long-run Decline in Mortality' (2020) 73(3) Economic History Review E1.

Alma-Ata Declaration, adopted by the International Conference on Primary Health Care in 1978.[49]

The importance of community and individual control over healthcare, and an economic and social status enabling this, was also recognised at domestic levels. For instance, it underlined the Whitehall Studies in the United Kingdom (UK) at this time, establishing the importance of personal autonomy and social capital on health and longevity.[50] Individual autonomy and self-determination conferred intrinsic benefits to health, while community involvement in the building of health systems and the development of health policies was accepted within the international public health sphere as a primary approach to ensuring both health and a respect for human rights and cultural diversity.

With the WHO focused primarily on diseases of highest burden in populations most in need of support, such as tuberculosis, malaria, and causes of infant mortality, international public health could broadly claim that its agenda and priorities were set by, or at least consistent with, those whom it aimed to serve and their human right to health. Through the Declaration of Alma-Ata, it also recognised the role of community involvement in ensuring this consistency.[51]

International public health would also be seen, however, as constantly under-resourced.[52] This created a dilemma that rewrote the script for the WHO and global health over the following decades. To address obvious gaps and achieve greater impact, more funding was required. However, the community-based primary care approach had less to offer for potential major private sector donors in terms of publicity or financial return on investment. The training of health workers in sanitation and the provision of better nutrition through local initiatives provides less scope for centralised profit than the sale of high-

49 International Conference on Primary Health Care, 'Declaration of Alma-Ata' (1978) S VI. VII(7) https://cdn.who.int/media/docs/default-source/documents/almaata-declaration-en.pdf.

50 Michael Marmot et al, 'Employment Grade and Coronary Heart Disease in British Civil Servants' (1978) 32(4) Journal of Epidemiology and Community Health 244 (known as 'Whitehall I'); Michael Marmot et al, 'Health Inequalities among British Civil Servants: The Whitehall II Study' (1991) 337 Lancet 1387; Sebastian Doerr and Boris Hofmann, *Recessions and Mortality: A Global Perspective* (Bank for International Settlements 2020); and 'Poverty and Health' (*World Bank Group*, 25 August 2014) https://www.worldbank.org/en/topic/health/brief/poverty-health.

51 Declaration of Alma-Ata (n 49).

52 WHO, 'The World Health Report 2000 – Health Systems: Improving Performance' (14 June 2000) 73–90 https://www.who.int/publications/i/item/924156198X.

value commodities such as drugs or vaccines. General improvement in health metrics is also harder to quantify than (health) commodity sales and distribution. To fuel growing private sector interest, a new emphasis emerged on the widescale distribution of commodities, providing a more quantifiable return on investment to justify interest and reporting needs of the multinational private sector.

5. PUBLIC-PRIVATE PARTNERSHIPS AND THE NEED FOR REWARD

Private philanthropy had long been present in international public health. Pasteur Institutes continued their work in former French colonies after independence, and the Wellcome Trust retained its presence in various former British (and non-British) colonies.[53] The Rockefeller Foundation had a role in the inauguration of the WHO, liaising behind the scenes and being the source for senior personnel, particularly in the Regional Office of the Americas, continuing as a funder today.[54] However, these organisations generally played a role subsidiary to the public sector. The Wellcome Trust and Pasteur Institutes concentrated on building research expertise within countries that could be argued to be building some form of independence in the host countries.

The rapid growth of the computing and software industries in the 1980s and 1990s began the concentration of a significant part of global commerce and wealth in a small number of corporations. Individuals dominating these companies gained wealth equivalent to many small and medium-sized emerging nations, accelerated during the bio-medicalised Covid-19 response.[55] Whether an initial interest in health 'philanthropy' led to interest in pharmaceutical investment, or an interest in maximising return on investment in the pharmaceutical industry stimulated interest in the international healthcare market, those with vast wealth (and the pharmaceutical corporations they were frequently invested in) developed and expanded an alliance with those developing international public health policy.

---

[53] The Institut Pasteur (2024) https://www.pasteur.fr/en/institut-pasteur; and 'Who We Are' (*Wellcome Trust*, 2022) https://wellcome.org/who-we-are.

[54] Anne-Emmanuelle Birn, 'Backstage: The Relationship between the Rockefeller Foundation and the World Health Organization, Part I: 1940s–1960s' (2014) 128(2) Public Health 129; and WHO, 'Contributors – 2024-25' https://open.who.int/2024-25/contributors/contributor.

[55] Giacomo Tognini, 'Meet The 40 New Billionaires Who Got Rich Fighting Covid-19' (*Forbes*, 6 April 2021) https://www.forbes.com/sites/giacomotognini/2021/04/06/meet-the-40-new-billionaires-who-got-rich-fighting-covid-19/?sh=4761285717e5.

The concept of public-private partnerships offered an apparent win-win for those controlling wealth and those seeking to implement what came to be known as 'global health' policy. Private funding flowed to the WHO, particularly from the Bill and Melinda Gates Foundation (BMGF, now the Gates Foundation),[56] whilst this Foundation itself, with budgets greater than the WHO, came to influence policy directly through the disbursement of its funds.[57] Private and non-State funding of the WHO, and increasingly the funding of Member States, became 'specified' rather than 'core', meaning funds were restricted to be spent on WHO projects specified by the funder. 'Specification' can determine disease emphasis, approach and geographical reach, and influence recruitment. The need to return to a situation where funding addresses global health priorities rather than letting priorities of the WHO's work be determined by funders was noted by former WHO Director-General, Margaret Chan, already in 2011.[58] Rather than an independent health agency, the WHO increasingly began to mimic a public-private partnership itself – a tool through which private individuals and corporations can leverage the WHO's wide legitimacy and (public) funding to further their own personal or financial interests. Specified and similar thematic contributions comprised approximately $6.7 billion of the $8.5 billion biennial budget in 2022–2023,[59] almost 75% of total funding. The privately owned BMGF ranked as the second largest contributor after the United States government.[60]

New public-private partnerships, growing alongside the WHO since the year 2000 and directly reflecting the interests of their private partners, have contributed to the shift in the centre of public health gravity from community to commodity interests. The Gavi Alliance (originally the Global Alliance for Vaccines and Immunization) developed under strong influence from BMGF to concentrate on the distribution of a single commodity type – vaccines.[61] CEPI, the Coalition for Epidemic Preparedness Innovations formed at the World Economic Forum (WEF) meeting in Davos in 2017, was focused only

---

56 WHO, 'Contributors – 2022–23' https://open.who.int/2022-23/contributors/contributor.

57 'Global Health Policy and Advocacy – Strategy Review' (*Bill and Melinda Gates Foundation*, December 2009) https://docs.gatesfoundation.org/documents/global-health-policy-strategy.pdf.

58 Margaret Chan, 'Dr Margaret Chan Introduces Proposed Reforms for WHO Priorities' (1 November 2011) https://www.who.int/director-general/speeches/detail/dr-margaret-chan-introduces-proposed-reforms-for-who-priorities.

59 WHO Contributors 2022–23 (n 56).

60 ibid.

61 'About our Alliance' (*GAVI – The Vaccine Alliance*, 2024) https://www.gavi.org/our-alliance/about.

on pandemics and epidemics,[62] a historically rare phenomenon[63] but seen as a potentially large market for vaccines in particular.[64] As with Gavi, BMGF was instrumental in setting it up, along with the Wellcome Trust, India and Norway. Unlike the WHO, Gavi, CEPI, and others, such as the commodity focused Unitaid,[65] include private actors directly on their boards of control.

As public-private partnership money increasingly flowed to global public health, the policy and programming approaches also became increasingly centralised and commoditised. Central bureaucracies have grown with these expanding international organisations as a burgeoning of global health schools, such as those of Johns Hopkins University and the University of Washington, often funded from the same sources, grew to staff them.[66]

The 40th anniversary of the Alma-Ata Declaration was marked by the Astana meeting of 2018.[67] Touted as a restatement of the primary care principles of the 1978 Alma-Ata Declaration, the 2018 Astana Declaration (uncritically) underlined the transformation of international public health to a plaything of corporate interests and their public-private partnerships based in the West. It reads somewhat like a string of fashionable terms interspersed with glossy pictures, mainstreaming a 'Health in All Policies' approach[68] and noting that primary healthcare will be equitable, safe, and gender sensitive.[69] However, it proposed nothing directly actionable or measurable towards reviving a focus of the WHO's work to promote the building of sustainable health systems, delivering primary care to people in low-income countries.[70] Much

62 'Preparing for Future Pandemics' (*CEPI*, 2024) https://cepi.net/.

63 WHO, 'Non-pharmaceutical Public Health Measures for Mitigating the Risk and Impact of Epidemic and Pandemic Influenza' (2019) 7 https://apps.who.int/iris/bitstream/handle/10665/329438/9789241516839-eng.pdf.

64 Richard Hatchett/CEPI, 'Developing Pandemic-Busting Vaccines in 100 Days' (*CEPI*, 2024) https://cepi.net/developing-pandemic-busting-vaccines-100-days.

65 'What We Do' (*UNITAID*, 2022) https://unitaid.org/.

66 Sandi Doughton, 'Historic Gift: Gates Foundation gives $279 Million to University of Washington' (*Seattle Times*, 25 January 2017) https://www.seattletimes.com/seattle-news/science/historic-gift-gates-foundation-gives-279-million-to-university-of-washington/; and 'History: Mike Bloomberg' (*Johns Hopkins Bloomberg School of Public Health*, 2022) https://publichealth.jhu.edu/about/history/mike-bloomberg.

67 Declaration of Alma-Ata (n 49); and Global Conference on Primary Health Care, 'Declaration of Astana' UN Doc WHO/HIS/SDS/2018.611 (25 and 26 October 2018) https://www.who.int/publications/i/item/WHO-HIS-SDS-2018.61.

68 ibid, article 5.

69 ibid, article 6.

70 ibid.

had changed from the days when community-centred care was the dominant theme in international public health in 1978. The Covid-19 outbreak and the WHO's declaration of the Covid-19-PHEIC that galvanised the world in early 2020, just two years after the adoption of the Astana Declaration, would bring this new paradigm fully into the open.

6. COVID-19: A REASON AND A PRECEDENT

In 2019, the WHO stated in its recommendations for management of pandemic influenza that 'under no circumstances' should contact tracing, border closures, entry or exit screening, or quarantine of exposed individuals be undertaken in an established pandemic.[71] The WHO envisioned, in severe epidemics, that it might be justified to close businesses for seven to ten days, explaining that such measures would cause considerable harm whilst providing small or no benefit, and disproportionately harm lower-income populations.[72]

A few months later, in early 2020, the WHO promoted the same measures they had warned against, lauding China for 'locking down' its population in Wuhan, closing businesses, and instituting contact tracing and other measures.[73] Such measures were then promoted through Europe, the Americas, and across the low-income populations of Africa and Asia among whom the WHO had predicted the most harm from such approaches.

Covid-19 mortality had been demonstrated by February 2020 to be mostly confined to the elderly,[74] whilst most populations in low-income countries are relatively young. Over half of the sub-Saharan African population is under 20 years of age,[75] at which age the median infection fatality rate from Covid-19 was and is expected to be 0.0003%.[76] These realities did not dissuade the

---

71 WHO, 'Non-pharmaceutical Public Health Measures' (n 63).

72 ibid, 41 and 55.

73 'WHO Lockdown Messaging: Why We All Copied China in Shutting down Economies' (*BizNews*, 15 October 2020) https://www.biznews.com/global-investing/2020/10/15/who-lockdown-messages.

74 Verity Robert et al, 'Estimates of the Severity of Coronavirus Disease 2019: A Model-based Analysis' (2020) 20 Lancet Infectious Diseases 669; Erratum #1 in 15 April 2020 Lancet Infectious Diseases; and Erratum #2 in 4 May 2020 Lancet Infectious Diseases.

75 'World Population Prospects (2022)' (*United Nations*, 2023) https://population.un.org/wpp/downloads?folder=Standard%20Projections&group=Most%20used; and David Bell and Kristian Schultz Hansen, 'Relative Burdens of the COVID-19, Malaria, Tuberculosis, and HIV/AIDS Epidemics in Sub-Saharan Africa' (2021) 105(6) American Journal of Tropical Medicine and Hygiene 1510.

76 Angelo Maria Pezzullo et al, 'Age-stratified Infection Fatality Rate of COVID-19 in the Non-elderly Population' (2022) 216 Environmental Research

WHO and partners from continuing to promote and condone these policies and advocate actions which they had previously noted could cause net harm.

The adverse impacts of lockdown policies became apparent early in the response to the Covid-19-PHEIC. UNICEF estimated 228,000 children under five years of age died from lockdown response measures in 2020 in six countries in South Asia, with another 400,000 additional teenage pregnancies.[77] Over 100 million people in low-income countries were considered to have moved into acute food insecurity,[78] whilst prolonged school closures were associated with increased abuse, child marriage, and child labour.[79] The health and economic impacts accruing to the hundreds of millions of children who lost educational opportunities, many permanently, will also be multi-generational.[80]

The burden of traditional infectious disease priorities of the WHO, including malaria and tuberculosis, has increased during the Covid response,[81] probably

---

114655.

[77] UNICEF, 'Direct and Indirect Effects of the COVID-19 Pandemic and Response in South Asia' (March 2021) 20 and 28 https://www.unicef.org/rosa/media/13066/file/Main%20Report.pdf.

[78] Food Security Information Network (FSIN), 'Global Report on Food Crisis 2023' (2023) 21 https://www.fsinplatform.org/sites/default/files/resources/files/GRFC2023-compressed.pdf; World Bank, 'Poverty and Shared Prosperity 2022: Correcting Course' (10 June 2022) 29 http://documents.worldbank.org/curated/en/099750110062235316.

[79] Sophie Cousins, '2.5 Million More Child Marriages Due to COVID-19 Pandemic' (2020) 396 (10257) Lancet 1059; UNICEF, 'COVID-19: A Threat to Progress against Child Marriage' (7 March 2021) https://data.unicef.org/resources/covid-19-a-threat-to-progress-against-child-marriage/; International Labour Organization (ILO) and UNICEF, 'COVID-19 and Child Labour: A Time of Crisis, a Time to Act' (2020) https://www.ilo.org/sites/default/files/wcmsp5/groups/public/@ed_norm/@ipec/documents/publication/wcms_747421.pdf; and UNICEF, 'COVID-19: Scale of Education Loss Nearly Insurmountable, Warns UNICEF' (23 January 2022) https://www.unicef.org/press-releases/covid19-scale-education-loss-nearly-insurmountable-warns-unicef.

[80] Chad Stone et al, 'A Guide to Statistics on Historical Trends in Income Inequality' (*Center on Budget and Policy Priorities*, 11 December 2024) https://www.cbpp.org/research/poverty-and-inequality/a-guide-to-statistics-on-historical-trends-in-income-inequality; 'Poverty and Health' (*World Bank*, 25 August 2014) https://www.worldbank.org/en/topic/health/brief/poverty-health; World Bank (n 78); and Melinda Moyer, 'The COVID Generation: How Is the Pandemic Affecting Kids' Brains?' (2022) 601(7892) Nature 180.

[81] WHO, 'World Malaria Report 2022' (8 December 2022) 19 https://www.who.int/publications/i/item/9789240064898; and WHO, 'Global Tuberculosis Report 2022' (27 October 2022) 5 https://www.who.int/publications/i/item/9789240061729.

setting back progress in fighting these diseases for many years. Economic deterioration will further limit national capacity and the capacity of donors to address them.[82]

The WHO's response in the form of medical countermeasures to the Covid-19-PHEIC is perhaps epitomised in the Covid-19 Vaccine Accelerator (COVAX) program,[83] aimed at mass-vaccinating low- and middle-income country populations globally against Covid-19.[84] While COVAX's aim of vaccinating 70 per cent of the population of each country was not achieved, roughly $10 billion (or three times the annual budget of the WHO) had been allocated to the programme by the time it was terminated in 2023.[85] The young populations of these countries are intrinsically low risk to Covid-19[86] and a wide survey conducted by the WHO in sub-Saharan Africa in 2021 demonstrated that two-thirds had already encountered and gained immunity to SARS-CoV-2, prior to the highly transmissible Omicron variant passing through Africa[87] and the roll-out of the experimental vaccines against Covid-19. It was also clear early in the programme that the vaccines would not substantially reduce transmission or prevent people from catching Covid-19.[88]

There was therefore no likelihood of a public health benefit from COVAX, yet this programme was funded and undertaken in the context of deteriorating malaria, tuberculosis, and other higher burden health issues.[89] The diversion

---

82 World Bank (n 78) 92–5.

83 'COVAX: Working for Global Equitable Access to COVID-19 Vaccines' (*WHO*, 2022) https://www.who.int/initiatives/act-accelerator/covax.

84 ibid.

85 'Access to COVID-19 Tools Funding Commitment Tracker' (*WHO*, 1 June 2023) https://www.who.int/publications/m/item/access-to-covid-19-tools-tracker.

86 United Nations (n 75); and Centers for Disease Control and Prevention, 'COVID-19 Risk Factor for Severe Diseases, Race, and Age' (28 June 2023) https://www.cdc.gov/coronavirus/2019-ncov/downloads/covid-data/hospitalization-death-by-age.pdf.

87 Hannah Lewis et al, 'SARS-CoV-2 Infection in Africa: A Systematic Review and Meta-analysis of Standardised Seroprevalence Studies, from January 2020 to December 2021' (2022) 7 BMJ Global Health e008793.

88 The vaccine manufacturers had never developed or tested their vaccines for preventing the transmission of Covid-19; see eg European Medicines Agency, 'Assessment Report – Comirnaty' EMA/707383/2020 Corr.2 (19 February 2021) 132.

89 WHO, 'Malaria Report 2022' (n 81) 19; WHO, 'Tuberculosis Report 2022' (n 81) 5; 'COVID-19 and Children' (*UNICEF*, September 2022) https://data.unicef.org/covid-19-and-children; and David Bell, 'One Health: Subverted, Corrupted, and Ruined' (*Brownstone Institute*, 4 June 2023) https://brownstone.org/articles/one-health-subverted-corrupted-and-ruined/.

of resources, financial and human, will clearly have exacerbated this crisis. The WHO and partners characterised this as 'vaccine equity', ensuring that all people on earth have equal access to a particular commodity, irrespective of disease risk, age, or local preference and priorities.[90]

In a prior era, the likely negative impact of COVAX would have prevented its implementation as financial and human resource diversion would have been hard to justify for a vaccine without transmission-blocking potential given to a population already generally immune and at intrinsic low risk due to young age. An assessment of disease burden in terms of life years lost would indicate resources were better spent on mitigating higher mortality diseases that target younger age groups.[91] However, in the era of Covid-19, the changes in the WHO and global health (associated with the rise of private and corporate funding and public-private partnerships) appear more than coincidental to the implementation of high-cost mass vaccination against Covid-19 in these populations.[92] The WHO strategy against infectious disease had moved from the community-based horizontal emphasis of the Alma-Ata Declaration to a homogenous, commodity-based approach emphasising centralised control.[93]

During the Covid-19 response, major sponsors of the WHO, including the BMGF and large pharmaceutical corporations (directly and through the Gavi Alliance),[94] greatly increased their wealth, later supplemented by (frequently mandated) vaccination campaigns.[95] Some leaders of these entities were prominent advocates for the use of (emergency authorised) vaccines, being put forward as 'public health experts' despite the obvious conflicts of interest involved.[96]

---

90 WHO, 'COVAX' (n 83).

91 Bell and Schultz Hansen (n 75).

92 WHO, 'Contributors 2022–23' (n 59).

93 Declaration of Alma-Ata (n 49), SIV, VIII; and David Bell et al, 'COVAX – Time to Reconsider the Strategy and its Target' (2023) 4 Health Policy Open 100096.

94 'About Us' (*Bill and Melinda Gates Foundation*, 2024) https://www.gatesfoundation.org/; WHO, 'Contributors 2022–23' (n 59).

95 Nabil Ahme et al, 'Inequality Kills: The Unparalleled Action Needed to Combat Unprecedented Inequality in the Wake of COVID-19' (*Oxfam*, 2022) https://oxfamilibrary.openrepository.com/bitstream/10546/621341/9/bp-inequality-kills-170122-en.pdf.

96 Matt Perez, 'Bill Gates Calls for National Tracking System for Coronavirus during Reddit AMA' (*Forbes*, 18 March 2020) https://www.forbes.com/sites/mattperez/2020/03/18/bill-gates-calls-for-national-tracking-system-for-coronavirus-during-reddit-ama/.

7. (RE-)INSTITUTING THE INTERNATIONAL COLONIALIST HEALTH STATE

Despite the harms arising from the change in the WHO priorities and policy that became concrete in the organisation's response to the Covid-19-PHEIC, there is little evidence of any serious review of the appropriateness of this approach in order to guide further policy development. The WHO and partner institutions, including the World Bank[97] are now prioritising the normalisation of these measures and working towards further centralising authority over global responses to PHEICs that the WHO Director-General can declare under the IHR, with the support of an Emergency Committee.[98] As part of this endeavour, an amendment process of the IHR (2005) was initiated in May 2022.[99] WHO Member States contributed draft amendments to the IHR in 2022–23.[100] These included amendments specifically aimed at changing the status of the recommendations issued under the IHR (2005) by the WHO Director-General on medical and non-medical countermeasures in response to a PHEIC from advisory to legally binding. Countries would 'undertake' to follow any future recommendations from the WHO Director-General once a PHEIC was declared.[101] Though such wording was dropped from the eventual texts amending the IHR agreed at the 77th WHA in May 2024,[102] the amendments that passed included those obliging countries to considerably expand surveillance for potential threats of infectious disease outbreaks upon which the WHO could base declarations of future PHEICs.[103] This also, in turn, considerably expands the potential for the WHO to recommend the (potentially global) use of specific 'relevant health products' to address a PHEIC.[104] In the

---

97 World Bank, 'Establishment of a Financial Intermediary Fund for Pandemic Prevention, Preparedness and Response' (17 June 2022) http://documents.worldbank.org/curated/en/733191656685369495.

98 IHR (2024), article 12.

99 WHA, Decision 75(9) (27 May 2022) UN Doc WHA75(9).

100 WHO, 'Article-by-Article Compilation of Proposed Amendments to the International Health Regulations (2005) Submitted in Accordance with Decision WHA75(9) (2022) of November 2022' https://apps.who.int/gb/wgihr/pdf_files/wgihr1/WGIHR_Compilation-en.pdf.

101 ibid, proposals to amend article 1(1) IHR.

102 IHR (2024), article 1; for a comment see Thi Thuy Van Dinh and David Bell, 'IHR Amendments Open Door to Perpetual Emergencies' (*Brownstone*, 7 June 2024) https://brownstone.org/articles/ihr-amendments-open-door-to-perpetual-emergencies/.

103 IHR (2024), annex 1.

104 IHR (2024) articles 1 and 13.

event the WHO considers any potential pathogen detected through this system to constitute a 'threat', it can declare a PHEIC and stimulate a market, whether or not an actual outbreak eventually occurs.

In parallel, a Special Session of the WHA had decided in December 2021 to negotiate a new Agreement on Pandemic Preparedness and Response to be adopted at the 77th WHA in May 2024.[105] However, the adoption of the Agreement was deferred by the 77th WHA for further discussion with the intent to put it to a vote of the WHA within 12 months, ie, in May 2025 at the 78th WHA.[106] The draft Pandemic Agreement available at the time of writing in November 2024 seeks to establish a Conference of the State Parties to the Pandemic Treaty under WHO auspices,[107] and increase funding for pandemic preparation and response,[108] including the ability for the WHO to require provision of goods and financial support when it declares a PHEIC under the IHR (including the newly defined 'pandemic emergency' in amended article 1(f) IHR (2024)).[109]

Both the planned Pandemic Agreement and the 2024 adopted IHR amendments expand the current definitions under which public health emergencies can be declared by the WHO Director-General to explicitly include threats rather than a requirement for demonstration of harm,[110] and to embrace a definition of 'One Health' that includes a broad range of animal, plant, and environmental influences as potential threats.[111] CEPI is working in parallel on an initiative aiming to adapt domestic, regional, and international regulatory and other mechanisms to enable the launch of '100 day vaccines' that can be developed to manufacture – as well as emergency authorised – within three months using mRNA technology.[112]

Put together, the agreed IHR amendments and proposed Pandemic Agreement seek to establish a centralised system in which intensive surveillance for viral variants and other (biological) threats is maintained in all

105 WHASS, Decision 2(5) (1 December 2021) UN Doc SSA2(5).

106 WHA, Decision 77(20) (1 June 2024) UN Doc WHA77(20).

107 Draft Pandemic Agreement (24 May 2024) (n 9), article 21.

108 ibid, article 20.

109 ibid, articles 1 and 9; and IHR (2024), articles 1 and 12.

110 Draft Pandemic Agreement (24 May 2024) (n 9), article 1; IHR (2024), articles 1, 12, and annex 2; and as indicated by WHO, 'Pandemic Prevention, Preparedness and Response Accord: Q&A' (*WHO*, 10 June 2022) https://www.who.int/news-room/questions-and-answers/item/pandemic-prevention--preparedness-and-response-accord.

111 Draft Pandemic Agreement (24 May 2024) (n 9), articles 1(b) and 5.

112 CEPI, 'Preparing for Future Pandemics' (n 62); and Ann Danaiya Usher, 'CEPI Launches 100-day Vaccine "Moonshot"' (2022) 339(10330) Lancet 1107.

Member States, with the WHO Director-General empowered to declare identified variants as global health threats and thus proclaim a PHEIC.[113] The cost estimate for implementing the proposed preparedness and prevention activities outlined in the 2024 IHR amendments and envisaged in the draft Pandemic Agreement is approximately $31.1 billion, including $10.5 billion in new funding.[114] The current total WHO annual budget is approximately $3.8 billion.[115]

Recommendations that can be issued by the WHO Director-General under article 18 IHR for potential application in a PHEIC include restrictions on cross-border movement and border closures, as seen in the Covid-19 response, and mandated vaccination. Both the 2024 amended IHR and the draft Pandemic Agreement include an expectation for countries to curtail information deemed 'misinformation',[116] (potentially) reducing the opportunity for public questioning of the WHO's recommendations on medical and non-medical countermeasures to address a PHEIC, or at least the dissemination of such questions. The WHO actively pursued such a policy during the Covid-19-PHEIC, though stopping short of mandating vaccination.[117] The advent of rapidly developed mRNA vaccines for outbreaks under the CEPI 100 day vaccine program,[118] that are excluded from normal clinical trial requirements such as product-specific medium term safety data in order to accelerate introduction, will provide a tool with which to offer a 'way out' of non-medical

113 IHR (2024), article 12; WHO Working Group on Strengthening WHO Preparedness and Response to Health Emergencies, 'Draft Report of the Member States Working Group on Strengthening WHO Preparedness and Response to Health Emergencies to the Special Session of the World Health Assembly' (12 November 2021) UN Doc A/WGPR/5/2; and WHO, 'Contributors 2022–23' (n 59).

114 World Bank 'Establishment of a Financial Intermediary Fund' (n 97); WHO, 'Contributors 2022–23' (n 59); and Garrett Brown et al, 'The Cost of Pandemic Preparedness: An Examination of Costings and the Financial Requests in Support of the Pandemic Prevention, Preparedness and Response Agenda' (May 2024) REPPARE Report, University of Leeds https://essl.leeds.ac.uk/downloads/download/234/the-cost-of-pandemic-preparedness-an-examination-of-costings-and-the-financial-requests-in-sup%3Eport-of-the-pandemic-prevention-preparedness-and-response-agenda.

115 WHO, 'Contributors 2022–23' (n 59).

116 IHR (2024), annex 1, section A(2)(c)(vi) and (3)(i).

117 'Combating Misinformation Online' (*WHO*, 2024) https://www.who.int/teams/digital-health-and-innovation/digital-channels/combatting-misinformation-online.

118 CEPI, 'Delivering Pandemic Vaccines in 100 Days' (May 2022) 20 https://static.cepi.net/downloads/2024-02/CEPI-100-Days-Report-Digital-Version_29-11-22.pdf.

restrictions like 'lockdowns' once imposed, consistent with vaccine mandates seen in many States in response to the Covid-19 outbreak,[119] but further raises concerns regarding restriction of information on their impact.

These 2024 IHR amendments and proposals for a new Pandemic Agreement are also consistent with position documents for the World Bank's pandemic Financial Intermediary Fund (FIF) and the G20 documents confirming them.[120] What is unusual is the speed with which this agenda is being brought into place, given the low frequency and impact of (global) infectious disease outbreaks, contrary to claims by the WHO and other agencies,[121] suggesting also that there will be many more outbreaks leading to PHEICs in the near future. Given the prior WHO advice against lockdown-type approaches,[122] it seems extraordinary that lockdown measures, and subsequent mass vaccination with experimental products, were so readily implemented with so little apparent dissent.

There were two streams of thought running through international public health over the past two decades. The first was consistent with the former WHO prioritisation of low-income community support and empowerment and the philosophy of 'do no harm' adopted after the Second World War, inter alia as a response to the abuse of public health by the Nazi regime, colonial powers, and eugenicists. A second stream, pushed by the progressive influence of private funders on the WHO, began to promote centralised and more prescriptive measures aimed at population behavioural control, favouring more uniform responses and a focus on health products and commodities. While the widescale use of lockdowns as a response began in China in early 2020, the WHO and some of its private funders were prominent in advocacy for its transfer to Europe, and then African and other low-income country settings.[123]

---

119 Usher (n 112).

120 World Bank, 'Establishment of a Financial Intermediary Fund' (n 97); and WHO, 'WHO Director-General's Opening Remarks at the Launch of the Pandemic Fund G20 Joint Finance Health Ministers Meeting' (13 November 2022) https://www.who.int/director-general/speeches/detail/who-director-general-s-opening-remarks-launch-of-the-Pandemic-FundG20-Joint-Finance-Health-Ministers-Meeting-13-november-2022.

121 Bell et al, 'Rational Policy over Panic. Re-evaluating Pandemic Risk within the Global Pandemic Prevention, Preparedness and Response Agenda' (July 2024) REPPARE Report, University of Leeds 9 https://essl.leeds.ac.uk/downloads/download/228/rational-policy-over-panic.

122 WHO, 'Non-pharmaceutical Public Health Measures' (n 63) 3.

123 Perez (n 96).

Thus, despite the prior recommendations of the WHO,[124] the lockdown concept had been discussed at meetings and tabletop exercises on pandemic preparedness in the West prior to 2020, including Event 201 sponsored by BMGF, the WEF, and others in 2019,[125] and through Rockefeller Foundation support years earlier.[126] The momentum in global health towards top-down, authoritarian approaches had been building for some time and the centralised control paradigm with a commodity-based approach (mass testing, and then mass vaccination) had clearly become the dominant paradigm within the higher echelons of global health power structures by the time the WHO declared the Covid-19-PHEIC in January 2020. The response directly benefited major backers of both the WHO and those advocating for the unprecedented, strict response measures, raising questions regarding the influence gained through the increasingly specified funding in the WHO's budget.[127]

A few centuries ago, the East India Companies, the great corporations of the United Kingdom and the Netherlands' imperial eras, worked with their respective governments to corral, control, and extract wealth from the populations they were colonising. They supported governments in enforcement, and governments gave them special privileges in return. The net result was a massive accumulation of wealth by these companies, their shareholders, and their home governments. This came at the expense of the populations they exploited. Wealth enabled greater power, which enabled greater wealth.

It seems difficult to miss the parallels put in place by these corporate authoritarian colonialist regimes and the direction we now see in the melding of international institutions and Western governments with the great Western-based pharmaceutical and tech corporations of today. International health public-private partnerships utilise public money in reaching far beyond borders to promote and facilitate the sale of health commodities produced by their private-sector partners. The pandemic prevention, preparedness, and response agenda provides both a tool to stoke population-wide fear and impose control,[128] and a vehicle for returning certain freedoms in return for compliance

---

124 WHO, 'Non-pharmaceutical Public Health Measures' (n 63) 3.

125 'Live Simulation Exercise to Prepare Public and Private Leaders for Pandemic Response' (*World Economic Forum*, 15 October 2019) https://www.weforum.org/press/2019/10/live-simulation-exercise-to-prepare-public-and-private-leaders-for-pandemic-response.

126 Zia Khan, 'Innovating for a Bold Future' (*The Rockefeller Foundation*, 2020) https://www.rockefellerfoundation.org/blog/innovating-for-a-bold-future/.

127 WHO, 'Contributors 2022–23' (n 59); and Tognini (n 55).

128 Gordon Rayner, 'Use of Fear to Control Behaviour in Covid Crisis was "Totalitarian", Admit Scientists' (*The Telegraph*, 14 May 2021) https://www.telegraph.co.uk/news/2021/05/14/scientists-admit-totalitarian-use-fear-control

with mandated and profitable medical policies, 'recommended' by the WHO to address PHEICs. Covid-19 demonstrated a centralisation of wealth perhaps unseen since the colonial eras through just such a mechanism.[129]

8. CONCLUSION

The analysis presented in this chapter revealed that public health emergencies are being promoted as a reason to change the way in which international health governance and individual sovereignty are viewed, under the pretext of promoting the public good in extraordinary situations. Examination of the trajectory of this agenda over recent decades suggests that the current push for top-down international pandemic preparedness and response policies, institutions, and law can be seen as the culmination of a fundamental change in international public health. Those advocating for this change appear among the main beneficiaries from the recent WHO-led response to the Covid-19-PHEIC, a time during which much of the global public were restricted and impoverished.

Through this broad public health agenda, society is returning to a more feudal or, at an international level, colonialist worldview. A self-appointed and wealthy technocracy, working through large corporations and in close collaboration with governments and international institutions they sponsor as well as through specially created public-private partnerships, is gaining powers to exercise increasingly restrictive control over the bulk of the population. The WHO and parallel institutions both declare the need for restrictions due to the existence of a PHEIC, and manage the response, including by 'recommending' specific experimental health products for global administration, that can benefit many of their sponsors. This impacts the human rights framework commonly thought unassailable after the Second World War, as discussed in other chapters of this edited volume. A broad collaboration will be required between health, legal, and civil society interests to understand and address the conflicts of interest that are seemingly underlying this. It will require a redefining of the limitations and public function of international bureaucracies,

-behaviour-covid/; and Laura Dodsworth, *A State of Fear. How the UK Government Weaponised Fear during the Covid-19 Pandemic* (Pinter & Martin 2021).

[129] Chase Peterson-Withorn, 'Nearly 500 People became Billionaires during the Pandemic Year' (*Forbes*, 6 April 2021) https://www.forbes.com/sites/chasewithorn/2021/04/06/nearly-500-people-have-become-billionaires-during-the-pandemic-year/?sh=19f5c4c525c0; Lucas Chancel et al, 'World Inequality Report 2022' (*World Inequality Lab*, 2022) https://wir2022.wid.world/; and 'Survival of the Richest' (*Oxfam*, 2023) https://www.oxfamamerica.org/explore/research-publications/survival-of-the-richest/.

and an open discussion on the centrality of individual self-determination over one's body and decisions concerning one's health as well as of (democratic) State sovereignty.

The public health basis on which this agenda is based is weak.[130] It reverses the post-colonial, anti-fascist emphasis on community-driven health policy that underpinned the WHO's beginnings. The world has followed this road previously, and the outcomes of that period, whilst still influencing the prosperity of former colonial and corporate masters, were quite different for the bulk of humanity. Recognition of the reality in which the world is currently heading, the perverse incentives that support this movement, and the historical parallels is essential if its direction is to be changed. This may need to come from quite different institutions than those setting and controlling the global health agenda today.

130 Bell et al (n 121) 111–12.

2. The Global Health Emergency Regime and the 2024 amendments to the International Health Regulations

Nithin Ramakrishnan and Sreenath Namboodiri[1]

1. INTRODUCTION

The Global Health Emergency Regime (hereafter emergency regime) is composed of diverse actors including States, international organisations (eg the World Health Organization (WHO) or the World Bank), public-private partnerships (eg the Global Fund, the Vaccine Alliance Gavi, or the Coalition for Epidemic Preparedness Innovations (CEPI)), civil society organisations, and private sectors entities.[2] The WHO and various legal instruments including the Constitution of the WHO (WHOC)[3] provide an international legal framework for managing their relations.[4] The core structure of this regime is made up of the national health systems and the International Health Regulations (IHR) 2005,[5] a legally binding instrument adopted under the auspices of the

---

[1] Views and arguments expressed in this chapter are solely those of the authors and not of the affiliated institutions.

[2] Lawrence Gostin, *Global Health Security – A Blueprint for the Future* (Harvard University Press 2021) 135.

[3] Constitution of the World Health Organization (adopted 22 July 1946, entered into force 7 April 1948) 9 UNTS 3 (WHOC).

[4] WHOC, article 18(g)–(h) and (k) describe WHA and non-governmental organisations (NGOs); article 33 provides for the Director-General to engage with NGOs; article 71 refers to arrangements for consultation and cooperation between NGOs and the WHO.

[5] International Health Regulations (adopted 23 May 2005, entered into force 15 June 2007) 2509 UNTS 79 (IHR (2005)).

WHO that enables interaction between these systems through the WHO.[6] The IHR (2005) obligates States Parties to build core capacities for surveillance and response to potential public health emergencies of international concern (PHEICs)[7] while also supporting international cooperation for emergency preparedness and response.[8] In other words, it is a 'pillar of global health security'.[9]

During the Covid-19 pandemic response, the provisions of the IHR (2005) proved insufficient,[10] and previous health emergencies like Ebola have also exposed the gaps in the IHR (2005) and its implementation.[11] The Review Committee on the Functioning of the IHR during the Covid-19 Response noted that:

> Despite being almost 20 years in the making, none of these elements [provided by IHR (2005)] have proved sufficient against SARS-CoV-2: since the beginning of 2020 we have been experiencing a prolonged crisis, unprecedented in our recent history. Millions of lives have been lost; countless more people are suffering from long-term complications of the acute disease and many others struggle with poor mental health resulting from months of anxiety, depression, deprivation and social isolation. Children have missed months of in-school education, adults have missed months of work, and existing inequities have been exacerbated.[12]

WHO Member States recognised equity as central to the breakdown of the global health architecture during the Covid-19 pandemic.[13] Despite unprec-

---

6 See generally, WHO, 'Strengthening Health Emergency Prevention, Preparedness, Response and Resilience' (2023) https://cdn.who.int/media/docs/default-source/emergency-preparedness/who_hepr_wha2023-21051248b.pdf?sfvrsn=a82abdf4_3&download=true. Unless otherwise stated all web links given in this chapter last accessed between 10 March 2025 and 15 May 2025.

7 IHR (2005), articles 5 and 13 read in conjunction with annex 1 to the IHR (2005).

8 IHR (2005), article 44.

9 WHO, 'Report of the Review Committee on the Functioning of the International Health Regulations (2005) during the COVID-19 Response' (5 May 2021) UN Doc A74/9 Add.1, para 135.

10 ibid, para 109 where the Review Committee noted that the IHR (2005) 'could be more relevant by providing guidance for the coordination of national and international response measures, beyond issuing temporary recommendations'; see also paras 82, 135–6.

11 WHO Executive Board, Decision 150(3) (26 January 2022) UN Doc EB150(3).

12 WHO, 'Report of the IHR Review Committee 2021' (n 9), para 136.

13 WHO, 'Report of the Member States Working Group on Strengthening WHO Preparedness and Response to Health Emergencies to the Special Session

edented developments of health products such as vaccines and diagnostics (against Covid-19),[14] universal and equitable access failed. Acknowledging the importance of providing incentives for the implementation of IHR (2005) and assistance to respond[15] to health emergencies as well as the need for amendments,[16] the 150th Session of the WHO Executive Board in 2022 urged Member States to consider potential amendments to the IHR (2005).[17]

This chapter examines recent negotiations for amending the IHR (2005) and the amendments adopted during the 77th World Health Assembly (WHA) in 2024 (IHR (2024)),[18] and how these amendments possibly alter the global health emergency regime's functioning. The chapter also advances a perspective that the amendments will improve this functioning considerably, despite several shortcomings and challenges remaining. The amendments establish a legal framework to promote equity and to hold the WHO better accountable for its work on health emergencies. It describes how the negotiations unfolded based on the authors' first-hand observations of the negotiations and interactions with the negotiators.

To achieve this, the chapter has six sections starting with an overview of the IHR (2005) pre-amendment and its coordination failures (Section 2). Subsequently, the structural problems in the implementation of the IHR (2005) from the perspective of developing countries are provided (Section 3). Section 4 describes the process of amending the IHR (2005), including challenges arising from the parallel negotiations of a new WHO Pandemic Agreement and from the WHO Secretariat's approach to international health law. Section 5 discusses selected proposals for amendments to the IHR (2005) submitted by different States; and an overall assessment of the outcomes of the negotiations, the legal changes to the global health emergency regime, and implementation challenges is offered in Section 6. Section 7 concludes.

Before proceeding further, a preliminary observation on the concept of health equity needs to be taken, to better understand the context in which it is

---

of the World Health Assembly' (23 November 2021) UN Doc SSA2/3, para 8(a).

14 It must be noted that this chapter is without prejudice to arguments of critics with regard to global mass vaccination strategies with rapidly developed and WHO Emergency Use Listed products being promoted as an effective strategy to address infectious disease outbreaks.

15 WHO, 'Report to Special Session of the WHA' (n 13), para 8(d).

16 WHO, 'Interim Report to the Executive Board at its 150th Session of the Working Group on Strengthening WHO Preparedness and Response to Health Emergencies' (19 January 2022) UN Doc EB150/16, para 11(b)(1).

17 WHO Executive Board, Decision 150(3) (n 11), operative para 2.

18 WHA Res 77.17 (1 June 2024) UN Doc WHA77.17, annex 'Amendments to the International Health Regulations (2005)' (IHR (2024)).

used in this chapter. While health equity as a concept has a broad meaning,[19] in international health law and in the area of law on health emergencies, in the context of negotiations of the 2024 IHR amendments as discussed here, the word 'equity' is used to refer to a scenario in which both developed and developing countries have adequate access to financial, economic, technical, knowledge, and other resources required for health emergency prevention, preparedness, and response. This chapter focuses primarily on equitable access to adequate health products, and sometimes on access to healthcare in general, promoted through several legal and policy actions. In other words, this chapter is not dismissive of the need for a de-verticalised public health approach focused on universal healthcare and health promotion strategies.

2. THE INTERNATIONAL HEALTH REGULATIONS BEFORE THE 2024 AMENDMENTS: AN OVERVIEW

The IHR (2005) is an international legal instrument aiming to help countries collaborate[20] against 'the international spread of diseases'[21] and protect life and livelihood. With 196 State Parties, including all WHO Member States, it has been operational since 2007.

First introduced in 1969,[22] replacing the WHO's 1952 Sanitary Regulations (ISR), the IHR (1969) showed a shift in the international approach[23] from a sanitary or quarantine-based approach towards a broader public health approach to infectious disease management. However, it lacked in many

---

[19] Commission on Social Determinants of Health 'Closing the Gap in a Generation: Health Equity through Action on the Social Determinants of Health. Final Report of the Commission on Social Determinants of Health' (*WHO*, 2008) https://www.who.int/publications/i/item/9789241563703.

[20] IHR (2005), article 2 read in conjunction with article 44. Several other provisions provide for coordination and collaboration among States and the WHO, eg articles 14 and 43.

[21] WHO, 'Frequently Asked Questions about International Health Regulations 2005' (*WHO*, 2020) https://www.who.int/news-room/questions-and-answers/item/emergencies-international-health-regulations-and-emergency-committees (accessed 26 July 2020).

[22] International Health Regulations (adopted 25 July 1969, entered into force 1 January 2007) 764 UNTS 3 (IHR (1969)).

[23] David Fidler, 'From International Sanitary Conventions to Global Health Security: The New International Health Regulations' (2005) 4(2) Chinese Journal of International Law 325.

practical aspects,[24] for instance, in posing obligations on States regarding the actual delivery of access to healthcare. The IHR (1969) was revised between 1995 and 2005, following repeated calls for revision since 1993. This period also marked the strengthening of the Global Health Security (GHS) doctrine in international health law.

While the IHR (1969) covered only specific quarantinable diseases, the IHR (2005) mandates States Parties to report[25] 'all events which may constitute' a PHEIC within 24 hours of risk assessment[26] to the WHO. The IHR (2005) also aims to provide internationally coordinated public health responses to such events, in particular to those that constitute a PHEIC.[27] A PHEIC is defined as an extraordinary event determined to constitute a public health risk through international disease spread potentially requiring a coordinated international response. States must establish core surveillance and response capacities to prevent and respond to PHEICs at the domestic level and, in this regard, State duties of international collaboration and assistance are also provided for in the IHR (2005).[28] Further, the WHO can collect information on health events from other sources (eg the press or non-governmental organisations (NGOs) etc)[29] and request the respective State Party to verify such information. The IHR (2005) also maintains communication channels between IHR State Focal Points and the WHO IHR Contact Point for all these exchanges of information on public health events and for offers and acceptances of collaboration between States and the WHO.[30]

---

[24] Julie Fischer and Rebecca Katz, 'Moving Forward to 2014: Global IHR (2005) Implementation' (2013) 11(2) Biosecurity and Bioterrorism 153; see also Sara Davies, Adam Kamradt-Scott, and Simon Rushton, *Disease Diplomacy: International Norms and Global Health Security* (Johns Hopkins University Press 2015).

[25] This obligation includes sharing information on the source of the risk, conditions affecting disease spread, health measures, challenges faced and support needed in responding to a potential PHEIC.

[26] IHR (2005), article 6.

[27] IHR (2005), article 15 provides for the WHO to issue temporary recommendations, while article 42 requires immediate implementation of health measures during a PHEIC. Article 13 describes public health responses.

[28] IHR (2005), articles 5 and 13 read in conjunction with annex 1 to the IHR (2005) establish capacity-building obligations, while article 44 read in conjunction with articles 5 and 13 provides for international collaboration and assistance in this regard.

[29] IHR (2005), article 9 allows the WHO to take into account reports from sources other than States. The WHO shall assess these reports according to established epidemiological principles.

[30] IHR (2005), article 4 establishes such Focal Points.

Despite the advances of the IHR (2005) provisions relating to State duties on 'international collaboration and assistance',[31] most of the provisions remained largely hortatory in practice,[32] giving the donors – developed countries and the public-private partnerships (PPPs) with and through which the WHO works – control over the determination of priorities for cooperation and investment[33] as well as over coordination mechanisms for implementation.[34] This has resulted in significant disparities in the development of surveillance capacities in countries around the world, while PHEIC response capacities lag behind, in particular in developing countries.

Hence, the IHR (2005) and the way in which it has been implemented have been criticised for continuing colonial legacies[35] by ensuring 'health security' for developed countries while also providing profiting opportunities to their pharmaceutical industries. Notably, the 73rd WHA adopted a resolution to promote equal access to Covid-19 treatment for all without referring to the IHR (2005) as the legal basis for the same.[36] This is despite the fact that articles

---

31 Key provisions include IHR (2005), articles 44, 5(3), and 13(5).

32 Shinya Murase, *Epidemics and International Law* (Institute De Droit International 2021) 120, noting that 'States need not offer assistance as a matter of a legal duty'; see also Margherita Cinà et al, 'The Stellenbosch Consensus on the International Legal Obligation to Collaborate and Assist in Addressing Pandemics: Clarifying Article 44 of the International Health Regulations' (2020) 19(1) International Organizations Law Review 158, 172, on 'the absence of assistance' in the text of article 44; Lawrence Gostin and Robert Archer, 'The Duty of States to Assist Other States in Need: Ethics, Human Rights, and International Law' (2007) 35 Journal of Law, Medicine & Ethics 526, 527, on transnational cooperation by States tending to be 'ineffectual and inconsistent' unless aligned with self-interest and referring to IHR (2005) as a specific instance (530–1).

33 Lawrence Gostin and Rebecca Katz, 'The International Health Regulations: The Governing Framework for Global Health Security' (2016) 94(2) The Milbank Quarterly 264, 291 and 302, explaining the impact of donors, and on the use of funding conditionalities.

34 Erin Banco, Ashleigh Furlong, and Lennart Pfahler, 'How Bill Gates and Partners Used Their Clout to Control the Global Covid Response—With Little Oversight' (*Politico*, 14 September 2022) https://www.politico.com/news/2022/09/14/global-covid-pandemic-response-bill-gates-partners-00053969.

35 Adam Kamradt-Scott, *Managing Global Health Security: The World Health Organization and Disease Outbreak Control* (Palgrave Macmillan 2015) 152.

36 WHA, Res 73.1 (19 May 2020) UN Doc WHA73.1. Although Res 73.1 refers to the IHR (2005) as part of its call on WHO Member States to engage in 'cooperation and collaboration at all levels', it fails to consider vaccine development and equitable deployment as a commitment under the IHR. Their call merely refers to States' duties to share public information relating to the Covid-19 response.

13(5) and 42–4 would have provided valid legal bases for promoting equitable access to health products.[37] This omission promotes a false impression that duties to cooperate under the IHR (2005) are legally inconsequential.

3. THE GLOBAL HEALTH EMERGENCY REGIME AND ITS PROBLEMS

Today more than 200 international health initiatives, organised across public, private, and (public-private) multi-stakeholder agencies, inhabit the global health landscape.[38] Most of these agencies also participate in the health emergency regime, often 'partnering' with the WHO as PPPs. This creates critical challenges in terms of coordination and leadership. Even though the WHO is constitutionally mandated to be the 'directing and coordinating' authority of international health work,[39] this expectation is neither adequately supported by financial resources over which the WHO can freely dispose[40] nor by relevant subsequent legal frameworks like the IHR (2005). Whilst the IHR (2005) gives the WHO a central role, in, for example, declaring PHEICs and recommending countermeasures, most of the public health responses to emergencies are in fact developed and implemented by other international agencies and actors, 'partnering' with the WHO. These 'partners', however, operate outside the framework of the IHR (2005). Despite articles 14 and 44(3) IHR (2005) and article 71 WHOC, the WHO's engagement with these 'partners' has done very little to make them accountable to the WHA.

Instead, the WHO Health Emergencies Programme plays a pivotal role in managing the relationship between these numerous actors and WHO 'partners' in emergency management, prevention and mitigation, preparedness

---

37 UN Human Rights Council, 'Report of the Independent Expert on Human Rights and International Solidarity, Obiora Chinedu Okafor, on International Solidarity in Aid of the Realization of Human Rights during and after the Coronavirus Disease (COVID-19) Pandemic' (13 April 2021) UN Doc A/HRC/47/31, paras 26, 29, 31, and 33.

38 Gostin (n 2) 135, quoting Steven Hoffman, Clarke Cole, and Mark Pearcey, 'Mapping Global Health Architecture to Inform the Future' Chatham House Research Paper (January 2015) https://www.chathamhouse.org/sites/default/files/field/field_document/20150120GlobalHealthArchitectureHoffmanColePearcey.pdf.

39 WHOC, articles 2(a) and 2(g).

40 Devi Sridhar et al, 'Global Rules for Global Health: Why We Need an Independent, Impartial WHO' (2014) 348 British Medical Journal g3841.

and readiness, and response and recovery.[41] However, this programme itself is established outside the IHR (2005) through a WHA resolution.[42] Another similar example is the Standing Committee (2022) of the WHO's Executive Board to provide guidance to Member States on (Covid-19) emergency prevention, preparedness, and response.[43]

This has become a structural concern in the functioning of the global health emergency regime. The non-State actors and WHO 'partners' operating outside the IHR (2005) framework often follow a charity or philanthropic approach rather than responding to legally binding commitments to cooperate under the IHR (2005). This makes international collaboration for emergency prevention, preparedness, and response unpredictable and uncertain. It is altogether a different question whether some of these non-State actors do in fact engage in charitable or philanthropic work or whether their activities are driven by other motives.[44]

In addition, the WHO's extensive reliance on voluntary funding for health emergency preparedness and response[45] exacerbates these structural concerns and poses risks to the WHO's integrity and independence.[46] The current model makes the WHO susceptible to forum capturing by powerful Member States and powerful private or public-private 'partners' and donors.[47]

Overall, keeping the de facto key actors and WHO 'partners' of the health emergency regime outside the IHR (2005) framework[48] and depriving the WHO of full budgetary authority reduces the influence of the WHO and, in particular, the WHA – where *all Member States are involved in decision-making* – over them and the emergency preparedness and response programmes.

---

41 WHO, 'Emergency Response Framework: Internal WHO Procedures' (2024) https://iris.who.int/bitstream/handle/10665/375964/9789240058064-eng.pdf.

42 WHA, Decision 69(9) (27 May 2016) UN Doc WHA69(9).

43 WHO Executive Board, Decision 151(2) (30 May 2022) UN Doc EB151(2).

44 Jacob Levich, 'Disrupting Global Health. The Gates Foundation and the Vaccine Business' in Richard Parker and Jonathan Garcia (eds), *The Routledge Handbook of Global Public Health* (Routledge 2018) 207.

45 Gostin (n 2) 11

46 Independent Panel for Pandemic Preparedness and Response, 'COVID-19: Make It the Last Pandemic' Report (12 May 2021) 48 https://theindependentpanel.org/wp-content/uploads/2021/05/COVID-19-Make-it-the-Last-Pandemic_final.pdf.

47 Devi Sridhar and Ngaire Woods, 'Trojan Multilateralism: Global Cooperation in Health' (2013) 4 Global Policy 325.

48 Nithin Ramakrishnan and KM Gopakumar, 'Proposal for a Pandemic Treaty Raises Concerns' (*Third World Network*, 2021) 11 https://twn.my/title2/books/pdf/Proposal%20for%20a%20WHO%20treaty.finaledited.pdf.

This undermines the efficacy of the WHO's mandate by making it prone to coordination failure and unaccountability. It also leads to the fragmentation of financial resources, limiting funds available to the WHO to support comprehensive preparedness and responses based on the true priorities of the recipient Member States and their people.[49]

The WHO's structural vulnerability thus creates four key problems in the context of health emergencies, which shall be discussed in more detail in the following: donor-led priority setting (especially in the area of surveillance); the absence of explicit legally binding guarantees securing equitable access to safe and high-quality health products during PHEICs; lack of accountability; and a 'do first, legislate later' approach favouring the mentioned powerful actors and WHO 'partners' operating outside the IHR (2005) framework.

3.1 Policy and Action Follow Donor Priorities

The critical problem with health emergency actors operating outside the IHR legal framework is that it provides a free hand to them – as donors of voluntary contributions to determine the areas of priority, allocation of resources (investments), and coordination.[50] This approach has generated commitments to build or strengthen surveillance capacities, early detection, and reporting – donor priorities – with no similar commitment on strengthening core health systems and access to health services and health products for health emergency response. While priorities and resources concentrate on surveillance systems, mechanisms supporting broader public health purposes and responses to health emergencies lack financing. Recent studies[51] reviewing the IHR core capacities during Covid-19 show a considerable achievement in the capacity to detect epidemic or health emergency outbreaks, while the

---

[49] ibid, 11–15 regarding fragmentation and diffusion of accountability; see also Rebecca Katz and Mackenzie Moore, *The Outbreak Atlas* (Vanderbilt University Press 2024) 165, arguing that governing in an outbreak relies on a 'web of agreements, policies, plans, and guidelines' and that 'it can get complicated fast especially when trying to figure out who is in charge of what'. Also, David Fidler and Lawrence Gostin, 'The New International Health Regulations: An Historic Development for International Law and Public Health' (2006) 34 Journal of Law, Medicine & Ethics 85, 88, on the IHR (2005)'s silence on how the financial demands of achieving the core capacity objectives will be met; and Gostin and Katz, (n 33) on donor impact on funding.

[50] Gostin and Katz (n 33).

[51] Nirmal Kandel et al, 'Health Security Capacities in the Context of COVID-19 Outbreak: An Analysis of International Health Regulations Annual Report Data from 182 Countries' (2020) 395 Lancet 1047.

same level of achievement is absent in the response and prevention capacities. However, this was foreseeable since scholars have cautioned against this since as early as 2006.[52]

According to a WHO and World Bank analysis, approximately 43 per cent of financing flows for pandemic prevention, preparedness and response go to 'surveillance, collaborative intelligence and early warning'.[53] Work in the area of 'live saving, safe, and scalable health interventions and resilient health systems', and on 'public health and social measures and engaged, resilient communities' receives only 19 and 18 per cent, respectively. Financial flows for 'prioritized research, and equitable access to relevant health products and essential supplies' are even lower at 12 per cent.

This skewed, donor-driven approach means that developing countries have no legal certainty of health service and product delivery during emergencies like Ebola or Covid-19, despite the recognition that the economic consequences of such emergencies vary significantly[54] between developed and developing countries. More generally, both the implementation of surveillance and response activities under the IHR arguably suffer from funding shortages,

---

52 Philippe Calain, 'From the Field Side of the Binoculars: A Different View on Global Public Health Surveillance' (2006) 22 Health Policy and Planning 13, 13, arguing that the multiplication of supra-national public health surveillance initiatives in developing countries reflects a focus on the exclusive interests and priorities of donor countries or institutions.

53 WHO and World Bank, 'Analysis of Pandemic Preparedness and Response (PPR) Architecture, Financing Needs, Gaps and Mechanisms' (22 March 2022) Report Prepared for the G20 Indonesia, Joint Finance & Health Task Force, 21 https://thedocs.worldbank.org/en/doc/5760109c4db174ff90a8dfa7d025644a-0290032022/original/G20-Gaps-in-PPR-Financing-Mechanisms-WHO-and-WB-pdf.pdf. While these estimates on total financial flows may not directly establish a correlation between donor control and capacity building priorities on surveillance, the priorities of the World Bank's Pandemic Fund, established following the above estimates, show recurrent focus on surveillance capacities.

54 UNDP, 'Breaking the Gridlock: Reimagining Cooperation in a Polarized World' *(United Nations Development Programme*, 2024) 30, noting that 'the recovery has been highly unequal. For 2023 all OECD countries are projected to have reached or surpassed their pre-2019 HDI values, in contrast to only 49 percent of the Least Developed Countries (LDCs)' https://hdr.undp.org/system/files/documents/global-report-document/hdr2023-24reporten.pdf.

both at the level of the WHO and at national levels. IHR Review Committees[55] have consistently flagged this.[56]

3.2 No Duty to Cooperate in Guaranteeing Equitable Access to Health Products and Technologies during Emergencies

As mentioned above, the international health emergency response operates through multiple multi-stakeholder arrangements outside the IHR (2005) legal framework, including the Global Outbreak Alert and Response Network (GOARN), the United Nations Inter-Agency Standing Committee (UNIASC), Global Health Clusters (GHC), and the Global Preparedness Monitoring Board (GPMB). During the Covid-19-PHEIC, additional mechanisms like the Access to COVID-19 Tools Accelerator (ACT-A) and the Covid-19 Technology Access Pool (C-TAP) emerged and are currently being transformed into regular platforms with a broader scope.

The peripheral role of the WHO in these public-private networks indicates a clear fragmentation of international health response to public health emergencies. After the initial grading of the outbreak information by concerned departments in the WHO, the information is passed on to the IHR Emergency Committee set up by the WHO Director-General under articles 12(2), 48, and 49 IHR (2005) to advise on whether the event constitutes a PHEIC, as well as on temporary or standing recommendations to address the PHEIC.[57] Information is also shared with the UN Emergency Relief Coordinator for coordinating international response.[58] Afterwards, the WHO and IHR States Parties are most often dependent on these public-private networks of the WHO over whom they have no administrative control for technical support

---

55 Three of them predated the IHR Review Committee on the Covid-19 Pandemic Response in 2021. They are (i) the Review Committee on the Functioning of the IHR and on Pandemic (H1N1) 2009; (ii) the Second Extensions for Establishing National Public Health Capacities and on IHR Implementation; and (iii) the Role of the IHR in the Ebola Outbreak and Response. All reports at https://www.who.int/teams/ihr/ihr-review-committees.

56 WHO, 'Report of the IHR Review Committee 2021' (n 9), para 147; but see, REPPARE Policy Brief, 'The Cost of Pandemic Preparedness: Unclear and Unaffordable?' (May 2024) https://essl.leeds.ac.uk/downloads/download/235/the-cost-of-pandemic-preparedness-unclear-and-unaffordable-reppare-policy-brief.

57 IHR (2005), articles 15–17.

58 WHO, 'Emergency Response Framework' (n 41); see also Inter-Agency Standing Committee, 'Humanitarian System-wide Scale-Up Activation Protocol for the Control of Infectious Disease Events – Reference Document' (4 April 2019) https://interagencystandingcommittee.org/sites/default/files/migrated/2019-04/190404_iasc_infectious_disease_scale-up_activation_protocol_web.pdf.

in the implementation of WHO temporary and standing recommendations. Moreover, these networks do not owe legally enforceable commitments to WHO Member States under the IHR (2005).

Two WHO initiatives can provide crucial insights into these issues – ACT-A[59] and C-TAP,[60] which were convened by the WHO together with other global public, private, and public-private health organisations and foundations.[61] They were established to accelerate and ensure the equitable distribution of vaccines, therapeutics, and diagnostics. ACT-A operated through four pillars, with Covid-19 Vaccines Global Access (COVAX) serving as the vaccine pillar. C-TAP was created in May 2020 to promote equitable access to technologies to respond to Covid-19. This voluntary platform was created within the WHO's Access to Medicines and Health Products Division, once more with multiple external partners.[62] The gaps in the functioning of the COVAX and C-TAP can reveal how and why the global health emergency architecture failed in delivering equitable access to health products, for instance, vaccines.

COVAX aimed to deliver 2 billion vaccine doses against Covid-19 by 2021 but managed only 958 million, with 640 million in the last quarter. It missed the 40 per cent vaccination target in 92 countries, with 36 below 10 per cent. Advance purchase agreements entered into by developed countries with vaccine manufacturers reduced supply availability for COVAX and developing countries, while funding shortfalls diminished COVAX's procurement position, compromising equitable access to vaccines. According to the United Nations Development Programme (UNDP) estimates, equitable distribution could have saved 670,000 lives.[63] The limited number of COVAX's

---

59 'Access to COVID-19 Tools Accelerator (ACT-A)' (*WHO*, 2020) https://www.who.int/initiatives/act-accelerator.

60 'Covid-19 Technology Access Pool (C-TAP)' (*WHO*, 2020) https://www.who.int/initiatives/covid-19-technology-access-pool.

61 Participants included the WHO, CEPI, Gavi, Global Fund, UNITAID, FIND, Wellcome Trust, the World Bank, and the Gates Foundation.

62 Participants included UNDP, UNITAID, UNAIDS, MPP, and the Open COVID Pledge.

63 UNDP (n 54) 94 states: 'The inequity in access to Covid-19 vaccines is a moral stain on the international community, contributing to a longer and deadlier pandemic than might have happened with more equitable access to vaccines. More than 2 billion people were vaccinated within 8 months in 141 countries, averting 2.4 million excess deaths. But a counterfactual with equitable distribution of vaccines, with vaccination in each country proportional to its population, would have saved roughly 670,000 more lives.' Moving beyond modelling, reliable calculations are, however, difficult to carry out. See eg, for opposite results concerning vaccines against Covid-19, Emmanuel Okoro et al, 'Paradoxical Increase in Global COVID-19 Deaths with Vaccination Coverage: World Health Organization

manufacturing partners restricted production capacity, resulting in a shortage of vaccines for States counting on COVAX.[64] Developed countries and donors prioritised product delivery over promoting diversified production across WHO regions.

Despite support from Costa Rica and 43 other countries (mostly developing nations), the C-TAP initiative to diversify manufacturing received minimal attention from developed countries and non-State donors. Major donors like the Gates Foundation prioritised downstream product absorption and subsequent distribution over intellectual property (IP) sharing that could have enabled local production of vaccines.[65] This led to inadequate funding, human resources, and political support, limiting C-TAP's success during the Covid-19-PHEIC, with only four IP holders providing licences to date (April 2025).

As a result, the two major initiatives failed to deliver. Developed countries allocated more funds to ACT-A, reinforcing donor-driven policies that failed to ensure equitable access. Without legal commitments for private sector licensing, C-TAP lacked funding, political support, and visibility.[66]

3.3 Lack of Accountability

Many organisations involved in global health emergency prevention and response programmes are multi-stakeholder in nature, with each of the stakeholders operating under their independent and respective mandates established by their own governing bodies. This fragmentation[67] creates challenges in terms of transparency and accountability to WHO Member States and the WHO's governing bodies. Since responsibilities are shared among various

---

Estimates (2020–2023)' (2025) International Journal of Risk & Safety in Medicine (*online*, 23 April 2025). However, the focus of this chapter is not on the efficacy of vaccines, but rather on the need for equitable access to safe and effective vaccines, once such vaccines are developed.

64 Andrea Taylor, 'What Have We Learned in One Year of COVAX?' (*The Launch and Scale Speedometer Initiative*, 23 April 2021) https://launchandscalefaster.org/blog/what-have-we-learned-one-year-covax.

65 'COVID-19: Bill Gates hopeful world "completely back to normal" by end of 2022' (*Sky News*, 25 April 2021) via *YouTube* at 00:02:36 to 00:04:06 https://youtu.be/0-Ic4EN0io4?si=it0hI8QNZ5gpgArC&t=156.

66 Julia Hochberger, 'Make Pooling Work to End Pandemics: A Qualitative Analysis of the Covid-19 Technology Access Pool' (*WEMOS*, 2022), https://www.wemos.org/wp-content/uploads/2023/04/Make-pooling-work-to-end-pandemics_Nov-2022.pdf.

67 Lawrence Gostin et al, 'The Legal Determinants of Health: Harnessing the Power of Law for Global Health and Sustainable Development' (2019) 393 (10183) Lancet 1857.

public, private, and public-private actors without any concrete legal commitments to provide equitable access, seldom can anyone be held responsible. This compromises accountability. The case of ACT-A is an example[68] here – ACT-A's complex partnership model[69] dilutes the coordinating capacity of the WHO and allows for the diffusion of accountability.[70]

An external evaluation report on ACT-A found that 'accountability and transparency were not sufficiently promoted'.[71] The report identified that prioritising speed has led to unclear roles of the various actors involved and too complex structures. This has compromised the principles of accountability and transparency in the operations of ACT-A. It also shows that multi-stakeholder agencies are not reliable mechanisms through which States' duties under the IHR to cooperate effectively in responding to PHEICs can be discharged. These agencies do not only lack accountability but also direct responsibilities or duties to protect the right to life of people under the IHR (2005), the WHOC, or international human rights law.

3.4 A 'Do First, Legislate Later' Approach is Shaping Legal Norms in Favour of Powerful States, Private Entities, and the WHO's PPPs

Work on infectious diseases, especially with potential for international spread, has been central to the WHO's work since its inception. With the adoption of the resolution on GHS in 2001,[72] the WHO at the Secretariat level has gained greater autonomy to take measures, and initiate programmes and partnerships with little Member State oversight (eg by the WHA) or consultation. This has also led to a convenient strategy for the Secretariat of promoting an approach that can be referred to as 'do first, legislate later'.[73]

---

68 Suerie Moon et al, 'Governing the Access to COVID-19 Tools Accelerator: Towards Greater Participation, Transparency, and Accountability' (2022) 399(10323) Lancet 487.

69 WHO, 'What is the Access to COVID-19 Tools (ACT) Accelerator, How is it Structured and How Does it Work?' (29 April 2021) 3 https://www.who.int/publications/m/item/what-is-the-access-to-covid-19-tools-(act)-accelerator-how-is-it-structured-and-how-does-it-work.

70 One of the present authors raised this concern of fragmentation and accountability in July 2021, see (n 48).

71 WHO, 'External Evaluation of the Access to COVID-19 Tools Accelerator (ACT-A)' (10 October 2022) 10, https://www.who.int/publications/m/item/external-evaluation-of-the-access-to-covid-19-tools-accelerator-(act-a).

72 WHA Res 54.4 (21 May 2001) UN Doc WHA54.4.

73 Kamradt-Scott (n 35) 82.

Practices promoted by the Secretariat and its 'partnerships', including with private actors and foundations, are later tabled in the WHO's governing bodies like the WHA or the Executive Board for endorsement. This situation creates problems at three levels. First, governing bodies and Member States have insufficient time to properly review operating procedures or evaluate their appropriateness. This leads to a general welcoming of these initiatives without proper scrutiny, which passively legitimises their practices even when they do not correspond to Member States' priorities or are not optimal or efficient. Secondly, such endorsement then shapes standards or legal norms, by guiding or influencing the negotiations for subsequent instruments such as resolutions, decisions, or treaties.[74] Thirdly, Member States' oversight is limited to overseeing frameworks that are pre-designed by the WHO Secretariat and its close 'partners',[75] leaving little room for initiatives driven by all Member States collectively and inclusively.

During the Covid-19 response, multiple multi-stakeholder agencies emerged outside existing legal frameworks, including the WHO *BioHub* Facility,[76] the WHO Hub for Pandemic and Epidemic Intelligence (Berlin Hub),[77] the Health Technologies Access Pool (H-TAP), the interim-Medical Counter-Measures (i-MCM) Platform,[78] and the World Bank's Pandemic Fund.[79] There were other initiatives like the Universal Health Preparedness Review for

---

[74] A significant example is the 'One Health Joint Plan of Action' developed by the Quadripartite with the help of the 'One Health High Level Panel'. This plan of action significantly influenced the notion of surveillance capacities as debated in the IHR amendment process as well as the development of the Pandemic Agreement. See FAO, UNEP, WHO, and WOAH, 'One Health Joint Plan of Action (2022–2026): Working Together for the Health of Humans, Animals, Plants and the Environment' (*WHO*, 14 October 2022) https://www.who.int/publications/i/item/9789240059139.

[75] For instance, neither the IHR (2005) amendment process nor the development of the WHO Pandemic Agreement process called for building their own monitoring framework at the Member State level. They chose to rely on existing monitoring mechanisms developed by the WHO Secretariat, such as Universal Health Preparedness Review https://www.who.int/emergencies/operations/universal-health---preparedness-review.

[76] 'WHO BioHub System' (*WHO*, 2025) https://www.who.int/initiatives/who-biohub.

[77] 'The WHO Hub for Pandemic and Epidemic Intelligence' (*WHO*, 2025) https://pandemichub.who.int/.

[78] 'Interim Medical Countermeasures Network' (*WHO*, 2025) https://www.who.int/initiatives/i-mcm-net.

[79] 'The Pandemic Fund' (*World Bank*, 2025) https://www.thepandemicfund.org/.

independent monitoring and measuring of preparedness.[80] All these initiatives skipped detailed consultations and negotiations by Member States both in the Working Group on the Amendments of the International Health Regulations (WGIHR) and in the Intergovernmental Negotiating Body (INB). Their terms of reference were not based on a consensus among all Member States, and their work can potentially continue quite independently until WHO Member States actively intervene.

Interestingly, in January 2023 the WHO Director-General came up with his own view on the reform and restructuring of the global health emergency architecture, giving significant importance to these PPPs and agencies established by the Secretariat.[81] Notably, the Director-General treated the IHR and the planned WHO Pandemic Agreement as two distinct elements alongside other elements of this architecture,[82] which included the work of these PPPs and agencies. This clearly indicated limited interest in bringing them within a legal framework of operation and accountability. The Director-General's proposal faced criticism by Member States during both the meetings of the Executive Board (EB) and the WHA that year, including calls for an examination of such proposals during the negotiation processes of the amendments of the IHR (2005) and the development of the WHO Pandemic Agreement.[83]

In summary, fragmentation and ad hoc approaches, and lack of predictable financing, legal certainty, and accountability remain major structural concerns in the global health emergency architecture. This compromises the delivery of health services and medical products equitably. Developing countries aimed to address these concerns by amending the IHR (2005). However, the amendments adopted in May 2024 remained limited and targeted given the parallel negotiations for a proposed new WHO Pandemic Agreement.

---

80 'Universal Health and Preparedness Review' (*WHO*, 2025) https://www.who.int/emergencies/operations/universal-health---preparedness-review.

81 WHO, 'Strengthening the Global Architecture for Health Emergency Preparedness, Response and Resilience: Ten Proposals to Build a Safer World Together', Report of the WHO Director-General (5 January 2023) UN Doc EB152/12.

82 KM Gopakumar and Nithin Ramakrishnan, 'WHO: DG's Proposals for Global Health Emergency Architecture Skip Critical Issues' (*TWN Info Service on Health Issues*, 30 January 2023) https://twn.my/title2/health.info/2023/hi230107.htm.

83 Third World Network, 'WHO: EB Members Express Reservations on DG's Proposals on Global Health Emergency Architecture' (*TWN Info Service on Health Issues*, 31 January 2023) https://twn.my/title2/health.info/2023/hi230108.htm.

4. THE LAUNCH OF NEGOTIATIONS TO AMEND THE IHR AND THE SHADOW OF AN UPCOMING (PROPOSED) PANDEMIC AGREEMENT

The described structural concerns about the global health emergency regime and the deficiencies of the global response to Covid-19 thus drove the reforms of the international legal framework on health emergencies at the WHO, at least from the perspective of developing countries – both the 2024 amendments to the IHR and the negotiation of a new Pandemic Agreement. However, in 2020 and 2021, there was a major question to answer as to whether the problems could be best addressed through amending the IHR (2005) or by negotiating a new legal instrument – the Pandemic Agreement.

The European Union (EU) and a few other developed countries favoured the latter approach, particularly because they intended to focus the scope of application of the new Pandemic Agreement primarily on 'pandemic emergencies' – understood as particularly grave PHEICs. This would have helped the EU and its allies to limit their possible obligations to cooperate towards facilitating equitable access to health products and services to times of yet to be defined 'pandemic emergencies'.[84]

President Charles Michel of the European Commission, as early as November 2020, made the call for a new Pandemic Agreement for pandemic emergencies. In March 2021, the WHO Director-General and the European Commission issued a joint statement calling for this new treaty,[85] even though the WHA was still awaiting the review reports of various Committees[86] on the WHO's and its Member States' Covid-19 response.[87] Civil society organisations and

---

84 Third World Network, 'A Pandemic Treaty: In Whose Interest? EC Envisages a Framework Convention with Binding and Non-binding Provisions' (*TWN Info Service on Health Issues*, 3 October 2021) https://twn.my/title2/health.info/2021/hi211001.htm.

85 'WHO Director-General's Remarks at the Press Conference with President of the European Council to Discuss the Proposal for an International Pandemic Treaty' (*WHO*, 30 March 2021) https://www.who.int/director-general/speeches/detail/who-director-general-s-remarks-at-the-press-conference-with-president-of-the-european-council-to-discuss-the-proposal-for-an-international-pandemic-treaty.

86 Eg 'Report of the IHR Review Committee 2021' (n 9); WHO, 'The Report of the Independent Oversight and Advisory Committee for the WHO Health Emergencies Programme' (5 May 2021) UN Doc A74/16; and WHO, 'The Report of the Independent Panel for Pandemic Preparedness and Response' (n 46).

87 Nithin Ramakrishnan, KM Gopakumar, and Sangeeta Shashikant, 'WHO: Should Members Pursue a Pandemic Treaty in the Midst of a Global Pandemic?'

academic commentators raised questions on the timing.[88] However, most of the review reports that were published later in May 2021 incorporated the European Commission's call for a new legal instrument.

At the 74th WHA in May 2021, several countries proposed launching negotiations for a new WHO Pandemic Agreement, but disagreement about its necessity led to the establishment of the Working Group on Strengthening WHO Preparedness and Response to Health Emergencies (WGPR).[89] This group was tasked with examining the potential benefits of a new WHO legal instrument and reporting to a Special Session of the WHA before year-end 2021.[90] Notably, there were minimal plans to amend the IHR (2005) at this stage.

Following the WGPR's recommendations, WHO Member States decided to launch negotiations for a new WHO instrument on Pandemic Prevention, Preparedness, and Response at the Special Session of the WHA in December 2021. The INB, a Member State-driven body, was established for this purpose.[91]

At the same time, the US circulated proposals to amend the IHR (2005),[92] some of which were considered and adopted with modifications during the 75th WHA in May 2022.[93] The proposals were one-sided, aimed at accelerating surveillance and information sharing,[94] and thus merely onerous to

(*TWN Info Service on Health Issues*, 12 May 2021) https://twn.my/title2/health.info/2021/hi210507.htm.

88 Nicoletta Dentico, Remco van de Pas, and Priti Patnaik, 'The Politics of a WHO Pandemic Treaty in a Disenchanted World', G2H2 Report (December 2021) https://g2h2.org/wp-content/uploads/2021/11/The-Politics-of-a-WHO-Pandemic-Treaty-final.pdf.

89 WHA, Res 74.7 (31 May 2021) UN Doc WHA74.7.

90 WHA, Decision 74(16) (31 May 2021) UN Doc WHA74(16).

91 WHASS, Decision 2(5) (1 December 2021) UN Doc WHASSA2(5).

92 WHA, 'Proposals for Amendments to the International Health Regulations', proposed by the USA (12 April 2022) annex to UN Doc A75/18 https://apps.who.int/gb/ebwha/pdf_files/WHA75/A75_18-en.pdf; and Nithin Ramakrishnan, 'WHO: US Proposal on IHR Amendment Pursues Health Security Agenda' (*TWN Info Service on Health Issues*, 8 December 2021) https://www.twn.my/title2/health.info/2021/hi211204.htm.

93 WHA Res 75.12 (28 May 2022) UN Doc WHA75.12.

94 Nithin Ramakrishnan and KM Gopakumar, 'WHO: U.S. Pushes Onerous IHR Obligations on Developing Countries' (*TWN Info Service on Health Issues*, 16 December 2021) https://twn.my/title2/health.info/2021/hi211209.htm; and Silvia Behrendt and Amrei Müller, 'The Far-reaching US Proposals to Amend the International Health Regulations at the Upcoming 75th World Health Assembly: A Call for Attention' (*EJIL:!Talk*, 18 March 2022) https://www.ejiltalk.org/the

developing countries. They promised them nothing in return. This prompted several developing countries to consider making counter proposals, fearing that the inequities and structural gaps in the IHR (2005) would be reinforced should the US-proposed amendments be adopted by the WHA. This pushed further demands for IHR (2005) amendments in the WGPR meetings.

In January 2022, the EB Decision 150(3)[95] urged Member States to take all appropriate measures to consider potential amendments to the IHR (2005), including on questions of equity. And, following the adoption of Decision 75(9)[96] by the 75th WHA in May 2022, the WGPR was transformed into the WGIHR, focusing solely on amending the IHR (2005). The Decision also mandated the WGIHR to coordinate its work with that of the INB, creating a feedback loop between the two parallel negotiations.[97]

For developing countries, the most challenging aspect of the IHR (2005) amendment negotiations was the position of negotiating blocs like the EU and its developed country allies, who argued that securing equitable access to health products fell outside the scope of the IHR (2005) and article 21 of the WHOC. Their aim was to restrict equity considerations to 'pandemic emergencies' only, the regulation of which was to fall under the scope of the new Pandemic Agreement.[98] Nonetheless, out of fear that the US would not ratify the new Pandemic Agreement in the future, the definition of a 'pandemic emergency' as a particularly aggravated form of a PHEIC[99] was to be included not only in the new Pandemic Agreement but also in article 1 IHR as amended in 2024.[100]

Overall, throughout the negotiations in the WGPR, WGIHR, and the INB, from 2021–24, the EU showed reluctance to undertake legally binding

-far-reaching-us-proposals-to-amend-the-international-health-regulations-at-the-upcoming-75th-world-health-assembly-a-call-for-attention/.

95 WHO EB, Decision 150(3) (n 11).

96 WHA, Decision 75(9) (27 May 2022) UN Doc WHA75(9).

97 ibid, operative para 2(d).

98 Third World Network, 'WHO: EU Says "no" to Equity in Health Emergencies in the WGPR Recommendations' (*TWN Info Service on Health Issues*, 23 May 2022) https://twn.my/title2/health.info/2022/hi220507.htm.

99 IHR (2024), article 1.

100 Thus, even though the 2024 final amendments of the IHR do not create any additional duties for the WHO or States Parties once the WHO Director-General declares a 'pandemic emergency' (and not only an 'ordinary' PHEIC), States that decide not to become Parties to the new Pandemic Agreement will still need to comply with their obligations under the IHR (2024) during a 'pandemic emergency'.

commitments on health emergency prevention, preparedness, and response,[101] favouring only a Framework Convention expanding surveillance and information-sharing obligations while maintaining soft law approaches to equitable health product access.

Many proponents of the Pandemic Agreement, including the WHO Secretariat, viewed the WGIHR process as potentially undermining the INB process. The worry was that if the WGIHR comprehensively addressed demands for securing equitable access to health products through amending the IHR (2005), the new Pandemic Agreement would lose purpose in the eyes of developing countries.[102] Consequently, key elements relating to equitable access to health products were initially deemed outside the scope of the IHR (2005),[103] despite the IHR Review Committee's recommendation that any new Pandemic Agreement should strengthen and be compatible with article 57 IHR (2005).[104]

An artificial distinction emerged between 'technical' provisions (on surveillance and information sharing) and 'political' provisions (on public health response requiring equitable access to health products deemed necessary to address a PHEIC).[105] However, developing countries persisted[106] and successfully argued that the IHR (2005) required the inclusion of equity-related

---

[101] Third World Network, 'EU Says "no"' (n 98); and Gerardo Fortuna and Marta Iraola Iribarren, 'Pandemic Treaty Delay Leaves "Mixed Feelings", says Charles Michel' (*Euro News*, 4 June 2024) https://www.euronews.com/health/2024/06/04/pandemic-treaty-delay-leaves-mixed-feelings-says-charles-michel.

[102] Gian Luca Burci et al, 'Governing Pandemics Snapshot' (*Health Policy Watch*, 27 July 2023) https://healthpolicy-watch.news/governing-pandemics-snapshot/, raising the question about what role would remain for the new Pandemic Agreement if the IHR (2005) were expanded to encompass the issues of health equity.

[103] Priti Patnaik, 'Choice Facing Countries: Expand Scope or Preserve Core Functions? [Amendments to the International Health Regulations]' (*Geneva Health Files*, 17 Feb 2023) https://genevahealthfiles.substack.com?utm_source=navbar&utm_medium=web.

[104] WHO, 'Report of the IHR Review Committee (2021)' (n 9), para 117, box 3.

[105] Burci et al (n 102), arguing proposals from the global south were political in nature.

[106] Kerry Cullinan, 'WHO IHR Negotiators Agree on Special Session on Equity' (*Health Policy Watch*, 12 February 2024) quoting an EU negotiator arguing that issues of equitable access cannot be addressed in isolation in any one of the processes https://healthpolicy-watch.news/who-ihr-negotiators-agree-on-special-session-on-equity/.

amendments.[107] A general narrative was created which viewed acceptance of such amendments by developed countries as a trust-building measure towards continued constructive negotiations of the Pandemic Agreement with the participation of developing countries.[108] However, developed countries then worked to dilute amendments aimed at securing equitable access to health products[109] by reducing details of those proposals. At the same time, they promoted such details and similar ideas in the INB to be included into the new Pandemic Agreement with a narrow scope of application to 'pandemic emergencies'. At one point, there was pressure to abandon demands for an IHR (2005) financial mechanism in favour of one proposed under the Pandemic Agreement.[110]

Access and benefit sharing (ABS) for pathogens and genetic sequence data (GSD) – a critical preparedness component – was also deliberately excluded from WGIHR negotiations due to challenges created by the parallel processes.[111] While the US proposed GSD sharing and African countries counter-proposed an ABS system in the WGIHR, no formal decision materialised on these issues in the 2024 IHR amendments adopted by the 77th WHA. African countries also proposed an ABS system in the INB to be included into the new Pandemic Treaty. Time pressure to conclude negotiations of the amendments to the IHR before May 2024 further constrained WGIHR deliberations.

Further, in early 2024, the INB Bureau and WHO Secretariat proposed a 'signal light' approach whereby the Pandemic Agreement would be adopted at the 77th WHA without details on key components like the financial

---

107 Priti Patnaik and Tessa Jager, '"Equity" in the IHR, Makes it to the Negotiating Table' (*Geneva Health Files*, 11 March 2024) https://genevahealthfiles.substack.com/p/equity-who-ihr-geneva-ip-access-tech-pheic-amend.

108 Priti Patnaik and Tessa Jager, '"Equity" Stands a Chance in the International Health Regulations. Without Financing, Compliance at Stake' (*Geneva Health Files*, 23 April 2024) https://genevahealthfiles.substack.com?utm_source=navbar&utm_medium=web.

109 Nithin Ramakrishnan and KM Gopakumar, 'WHO: Developed Countries Push to Dilute WGIHR Bureau's Half-hearted Equity Text' (*TWN Info Service on Health Issues*, 11 March 2024) https://www.twn.my/title2/health.info/2024/hi240305.htm.

110 Third World Network, 'WHO: Bureau Rejects Secretariat's Proposal to Delete Equity-related IHR Amendment Proposals' (*TWN Info Service on Health Issues*, 8 February 2024) https://twn.my/title2/health.info/2024/hi240203.htm.

111 Priti Patnaik and Nishant Sirohi, 'Countries Split between Retaining Existing Scope on Surveillance vs Widening Commitments on Equity in the Amendments to IHR [A wrap from WG-IHR3]' (*Geneva Health Files*, 21 April 2023) https://genevahealthfiles.substack.com/p/exclusive-countries-split-between?utm_source=publication-search.

mechanism, the Global Supply Chain Network, and the Pathogen Access and Benefit Sharing (PABS) system.[112] These details would be negotiated post-WHA77 or by the Conference of Parties to the new Pandemic Agreement. For the PABS system in particular, this two-stage process envisaged options like a future annex to the Pandemic Agreement on ABS, a protocol or an entirely separate instrument loosely linked to the new Pandemic Agreement. In early 2024, when delegations rushed to conclude negotiations before the start of the 77th WHA in May 2024 to enable the WHA to adopt the new Pandemic Agreement, they quickly welcomed this approach. This rush resulted in the adoption of greater compromise language on equity-related provisions in both processes.

Earlier in 2022, the tensions between the two processes had already led to the unprecedented referral of all State proposals for the amendment of the IHR (2005) to an IHR Review Committee for technical recommendations – a step not taken with previous amendments. Not only did the 75th WHA take a decision in this regard, the Director-General expanded the Committee's mandate to include suggestions for the 'reformulation of text proposals' for amendments of the IHR made by the States Parties to the IHR (2005).[113] The Secretariat's terms of reference for the IHR Review Committee included tasks to determine whether certain proposals for amendments would require a reopening of the IHR (2005) and, if so, the Committee was requested to identify which provisions would require amending to maintain the IHR's integrity.[114] The Review Committee, despite acknowledging that cooperation towards securing equitable access to pandemic health products fell within the scope of the IHR (2005), largely aligned with developed countries' views,[115] casting doubt on developing countries' equity-related proposals without, however, offering

[112] Nithin Ramakrishnan, 'WHO: Draft Resolution on WHO Pandemic Instrument opens Floodgates to Endless Negotiations' (*TWN Info Service on Health Issues*, 28 April 2024) https://twn.my/title2/health.info/2024/hi240408.htm.

[113] WHO, 'Terms of Reference for the IHR Review Committee regarding amendments to the International Health Regulations (2005)' (23 October 2022) 4 https://cdn.who.int/media/docs/default-source/international-health-regulations/terms-of-reference_ihr-amendments-rc_for-web_rev-221024.pdf; and Nithin Ramakrishnan and KM Gopakumar, 'WHO: DG Aims to Control IHR Amendment Content through IHR Review Committee' (*TWN Info Service on Health Issues*, 6 October 2022) https://twn.my/title2/health.info/2022/hi221001.htm.

[114] ibid.

[115] WHO, 'Report of the Review Committee regarding amendments to the International Health Regulations (2005)' (6 February 2023) UN Doc A/WGIHR/2/5 paras 53 and 55.

practical recommendations on how such equitable access can be secured in health emergency responses. The WHO Secretariat and its technical experts also expressed concerns about potential uncertainties that may unfold were the amendments to the IHR (2005) to strengthen equity adopted,[116] such as withdrawal of some States from the IHR.

Despite all these pressures, the WGIHR successfully adopted an unqualified mandate for the WHO to work on equitable access to health products during PHEICs by amending article 13 IHR.[117] Negotiations about the PABS system were, however, shifted to the INB for inclusion into the new Pandemic Agreement.

5. IHR AMENDMENT PROPOSALS FROM STATES

Following the adoption of Decision 74.9 by the 74th WHA, 16 States Parties, including 4 on behalf of four different groups of States, ie the EU, the Member States of the WHO African Region, the Eurasian Economic Union, and MERCOSUR, submitted amendment proposals by 30 September 2022. These included proposals by Armenia, Bangladesh, Brazil, Czech Republic on behalf of the Member States of the EU, Eswatini on behalf of the WHO African Region Member States, India, Indonesia, Japan, Malaysia, Namibia, New Zealand, Republic of Korea, Russian Federation on behalf of the Member States of the Eurasian Economic Union, Switzerland, the United States of America, and Uruguay on behalf of MERCOSUR. All the proposed amendments are publicly available except for the proposals from Japan.[118]

Overall, a clear distinction in the focus was visible in the proposals coming from the developed countries on the one hand and developing countries on the other hand. The former once more wished to focus on information sharing and early warnings, while the latter clearly sought to improve upon coordinated public health responses through promoting equitable access to health products and technologies required to prevent and address health emergencies due to infectious disease outbreaks. In addition, some of the proposals made by developed countries aimed to legitimise the work and role of the WHO's 'partners' and agencies like PPPs, foundations, corporations, and other private entities; while developing countries' proposals often aimed to make them

[116] Cullinan (n 106), quoting Dr Mike Ryan on everyday rapid risk assessments on potential epidemics pursuant to IHR (2005).

[117] IHR (2024), article 13(8).

[118] WHO, 'Proposed Amendments to the International Health Regulations (2005) submitted in accordance with decision WHA75(9) (2022)' (September 2022) ('Compilation of Proposed IHR Amendments (2022)') https://apps.who.int/gb/wgihr/pdf_files/wgihr1/WGIHR_Submissions_Original_Languages.pdf.

accountable to the WHA. Complementing the discussions in Section 4, a presentation and analysis of selected proposals for the amendment of the IHR by both developed and developing countries follow.

5.1 Selected Proposals of Developed Countries

It was the US proposal of December 2021[119] that kickstarted the IHR amendment process. Many of these proposals focused on altering the information sharing regime under the IHR (2005) and on accelerating the process of amending the IHR (2005) and the entry into force of the amendments. Some of the key proposals were as follows:[120]

- Adding an early warning system in article 5(5) IHR (2005) for health events of unknown causes;
- Establishing specific timeframes in article 6(1) IHR (2005) within which States should notify the WHO about a health event: 48 hours for event assessment by national authorities and 24 hours for WHO notification;
- Including 'genetic sequence data' under information-sharing requirements;
- Removing the obligation in article 9(1) IHR (2005) to consult with concerned States before sharing information with other States and actors;
- Modifying article 10 IHR (2005) to require the WHO to offer collaboration to a State reporting an event within 24 hours of receiving the information, with States required to respond within 48 hours;
- Transforming article 11 IHR (2005) from a restrictive to an enabling clause, empowering the WHO to share information with other States; and
- Establishing a new Compliance Committee under a new chapter IV of the IHR (2005).

The US had included very few proposals on securing access to relevant health products – and only in the form of provisions to address the unhindered movement of essential medical products and supplies. There was no provision about States having large capacities and resources for the development and production of health products to share the same with States having no or insufficient capacities.

The EU's proposals from September 2022 for IHR amendments were similar in approach. They focused on extracting epidemiological and clinical data

119 US IHR amendment proposals (2021) (n 92); and Ramakrishnan (n 92). The US proposals circulated in December 2021 were later made part of formal submission to the WGIHR in September 2022.

120 'Compilation of Proposed IHR Amendments (2022)' (n 118), US proposals.

from everywhere on the planet, as well as microbial and genomic data in cases where public health events occur due to infectious pathogens.[121] The EU also proposed setting up an expert committee to support the effective implementation of the IHR without addressing equitable access to health products.[122] Both US and EU proposals emphasised compliance and implementation mechanisms that would primarily hold developing countries accountable for information sharing (or failing to do so), without comparable accountability for equitable distribution of health products or preventing hoarding during emergencies.

Another interesting proposal from a developed country was to amend article 4 on relevant domestic authorities to establish an additional National IHR Authority and to include the need for national legislation to provide a legal framework for the activities of such new IHR authorities. This was one of Switzerland's key proposals, which received significant support from the WHO Secretariat and its technical experts. The proposal also aimed to establish a network of IHR National Authorities across different States Parties that would bypass domestic political oversight of emergency communications.[123]

5.2 Selected Proposals of Developing Countries

Many proposals of developing countries, unlike those of the EU and US, sought to ensure equity in health emergency preparedness and response in a comprehensive manner. They sought to address issues such as health systems strengthening and capacity building including for surveillance, equitable access to health products, technologies and know-how, international financial assistance, implementation oversight, regulation of unilateral measures, and actions of non-State actors, each targeting the realisation of equity in health emergency preparedness and response. These equity proposals had the backing of a total of 55 developing countries at the time of submission and first compilation in September 2022.[124]

---

121 ibid, amendments proposed to article 6 by the EU.

122 ibid, proposal for a new article 54bis by the EU.

123 KM Gopakumar and Nithin Ramakrishnan, 'WHO: WGIHR Bureau's Push for two New National Institutions for IHR Implementation Raises Concerns' (*TWN Info Service on Health Issues*, 5 February 2024) on the WHO Secretariat's recommendation to create a National IHR Authority outside the Ministry of Health at the country level https://www.twn.my/title2/health.info/2024/hi240202.htm.

124 'Compilation of Proposed IHR Amendments (2022)' (n 118); see also Nithin Ramakrishnan and KM Gopakumar, 'WHO: Developing Countries Focus on Equity in IHR Amendment Proposals' (*TWN Info Service on Health Issues*, 11 January 2023) https://twn.my/title2/health.info/2023/hi230102.htm.

Developing countries like India, Bangladesh, and the States of the African Region sought to amend article 2 IHR (2005) not only to incorporate rights and duties to secure equitable access to health products during PHEICs but also to address other concerns of equity such as interference with livelihood due to the imposition of health emergency countermeasures and general health systems strengthening. India, Bangladesh, Malaysia, and the WHO Member States of the African Region also proposed to include new principles of equity, solidarity, common but differentiated responsibilities and respective capabilities, prioritisation of establishment and strengthening of health systems capacities, and peaceful purposes in article 3 IHR on guiding implementation principles of the IHR.[125]

These countries were also keen on altering the approaches to IHR (2005) core capacities and international collaboration and assistance in building, developing, and maintaining those capacities. Bangladesh, for example, proposed amendments to incorporate duties on building broader health systems capacities among core capacities in annex 1 to the IHR (2005). In its 2005 version, annex 1 lists only health emergency capacities. With a proposal to amend article 3 listing the above-mentioned additional guiding principles for the implementation of the IHR, Bangladesh further attempted to prioritise broader obligations to strengthen health systems in the IHR. The argument brought forward by Bangladesh was that without strengthening basic health systems capacities generally, emergency capacities focusing on surveillance, risk assessment, and information sharing cannot function effectively to prevent or contain outbreaks.[126]

Malaysia, India, Indonesia, and the WHO Member States of the African Region also sought the improvement of capacity building provisions in the IHR (2005) and proposed the incorporation of duties to engage in wide-ranging health systems capacity building and strengthening as IHR core capacities within annex 1.[127] Bangladesh and Malaysia called for explicit commitment from the developed countries to assist the developing countries in this regard.[128]

---

125 'Compilation of Proposed IHR Amendments (2022)' (n 118), proposals for amendments of article 3 by India, Bangladesh, Malaysiam and the WHO Member States of the African Region.

126 See 'justification', contained in the 'Compilation of Proposed IHR Amendments (2022)' (n 118), on the amendment being proposed by Bangladesh, which reiterates Bangladesh's stress on strengthening wider health systems capacities from the beginning of various negotiation processes post Covid-19 pandemic.

127 ibid, proposals to amend annex 1 by Malaysia, India, Indonesia, and the African Region respectively.

128 ibid, proposals to amend article 44 by Bangladesh and Malaysia.

The 47 Member States of the WHO Africa Region made a compelling, clear, and straightforward amendment proposal which would have enabled access to health products, technologies, and know-how required for a public health response to a PHEIC to all countries on an equitable basis. So did Bangladesh. Both proposed to have an additional article 13A to establish obligations for States Parties and the WHO to cooperate towards ensuring such equitable access to the health products and technologies.[129] The new article 13A proposed by the States of the African Region was titled 'Access to Health Products, Technologies and Know-How for Public Health Response'. The proposal under this new provision would require:

(a) the WHO Director-General (DG) to:
    (i) make an immediate assessment about availability and affordability of required health products for public health response, and
    (ii) make recommendations including an allocation mechanism to avoid any potential shortage.
(b) States Parties to:
    (i) cooperate with each other and the WHO in complying with such recommendations made by the WHO DG and to take measures to ensure equitable access to health products and technologies,
    (ii) include in their intellectual property legislations a provision for waiving or suspending intellectual property rights protection during a PHEIC,
    (iii) share the rights over products developed in the course of research partially or wholly funded by public sources,
    (iv) share regulatory dossiers with developing countries to kick-start local production in their territories, and
    (v) to ensure non-State actors and manufacturers do not act contrary to the IHR 2005, recommendations, and actions taken pursuant to the IHR provisions.

Bangladesh also proposed a new article 13A, which was titled 'WHO-led International Public Health Response'. Bangladesh envisaged the WHO as the central and coordinating authority for international public health responses to PHEICs and proposed something similar to the African Group, beginning with an assessment of availability and affordability of the health products needed to address PHEICs, such as vaccines, diagnostics, and therapeutics by the WHO. Bangladesh further proposed:

---

129 ibid, proposals for a new article 13A by the African Region and by Bangladesh.

(1) The WHO to develop an allocation mechanism in cases of expected shortages and in doing so identify and prioritise recipients of the health products and determine the required quantity of health products to meet the needs of those recipients;
(2) The WHO to develop and maintain databases that contain all sorts of information required by potential manufacturers in order to start manufacturing in their facilities;
(3) States Parties with production capacities to diversify production, including to developing countries upon request of WHO; and
(4) States Parties to ensure that the manufacturers operating from their territories shall supply the WHO the requested quantities of health products in a timely manner.

India, Malaysia, Indonesia, and Russia meanwhile sought to address issues relating to the equitable access to health products on their own terms, for example, by proposing their incorporation in amended articles 15 and 16 on temporary and standing recommendations to be issued by the WHO Director-General during a PHEIC.[130] Though limited in nature, they clearly complemented the proposals made by Bangladesh as well as the States of the African Region. Interestingly, the African Group and Bangladesh proposed to include increased reporting obligations for the WHO on its activities and initiatives in the area of PHEIC prevention, preparedness, and response, including on activities and initiatives undertaken in partnership and collaboration with various private and external agencies.[131] The African Group specifically proposed that all WHO activities relating to health emergency preparedness and response, including those undertaken through collaborations and partnerships, should be regulated by and carried out in accordance with the IHR (2005).[132] If engaging with the private sector or PPPs, the proposal demanded to duly apply the WHO's Framework for Engaging with Non-State Actors (FENSA) to any such engagement.[133]

Bangladesh, Malaysia, Eswatini for the States of the African Region, and Brazil for the Member States of MERCOSUR proposed amendments to address the gaps relating to international financing. Their proposals sought to include specific mention of international financial assistance to prevent the

130 ibid, proposals for amendments of articles 15 and 16 IHR by India, Malaysia, Indonesia, and Russia.

131 ibid, proposal on a new para 6 of article 12 by the African Group; and a proposal for a new article 13A by Bangladesh respectively.

132 ibid, proposal by the African Group for a new para 6 of article 12, calling for reporting obligations.

133 ibid, proposal for new para 7 of article 12 by the African Group.

international spread of disease.[134] In amendment proposals for paragraph 3 of article 13, Member States of MERCOSUR, for example, proposed that the WHO should cooperate with Member States in seeking support and international financial assistance to facilitate the containment of health risks at source.

Bangladesh further suggested having a dedicated international financial mechanism to support the implementation of health emergency preparedness and response under an amended article 44. The WHO Member States of the African Region and Malaysia, on the other hand, suggested establishing a new financial mechanism under a new article 44A. This fund, which was proposed to provide grants and concessional loans to developing countries, was envisaged to be operational under the guidance of, and be accountable to States Parties of the IHR. African States wanted States Parties to decide on and review the policies, programme priorities, and eligibility criteria set by the new financial mechanism on a periodic basis.

The 47 States of the African Region and Namibia in particular, as well as India and Malaysia, also called for access and benefit sharing of genetic resources, including pathogens and sequence information.[135] While India and Malaysia proposed to include obligations concerning access and benefit sharing capacities in the annexes to the IHR (2005), the States of the African Region and Namibia indicated that there shall be no sharing of genetic sequence information without the guarantees on fair and equitable sharing of benefits derived therefrom.[136] This was Africa's counterproposal to the US proposal to share GSD under an amended article 6 IHR (2005). The African Region in its proposal sought to incorporate an explicit paragraph 3 into an amended article 6 which aimed at securing the sharing of GSD through a prior-established WHO Member State-approved mechanism ensuring fair access and equitable benefit sharing.

5.3 Other IHR Amendment Proposals

There were other proposals placed for the consideration of the WGIHR, including some changes in definitions and additions of new definitions of

134 ibid, proposed amendments by Bangladesh, Malaysia, Eswatini for the African Region, and Brazil for the Member States of MERCOSUR to articles 44, a new article 44bis, and article 13 respectively.

135 ibid, proposed amendments by the African Region and Namibia to articles 6; and Indian and Malaysian proposals to include requirements for access and benefit sharing in annex 1 and in a newly proposed annex 10 to the IHR respectively.

136 ibid, proposed amendments to article 6 by the African Region.

health products, technologies, etc.[137] There were also proposals to modify the powers of the WHO Director-General to issue temporary and standing recommendations and expand the explicit scope of such recommendations to include securing equitable access to health products and technologies required for addressing health emergencies.[138] Similarly, there were proposals to expand the functions of the conveyance operators.[139]

Some other proposals included suggestions to amend the annexes and to change the composition and procedures of the Emergency Committee, as well as the inclusion of a new procedure for addressing excessive unilateral health measures taken by States Parties in addition to the medical and non-medical countermeasures recommended by the Director-General under IHR.[140] Some other proposals included addressing the dispute settlement process.[141]

6. WGIHR OUTCOMES

Several amendments were finally adopted by the 77th WHA in May 2024, seeking to bring the above-discussed differing interests of developed countries on the one hand and developing countries on the other hand into an acceptable balance.[142] The adopted amendments and their purported purpose are provided in a nutshell in Table 2.1.

Apart from the initial proposals, the WGIHR also took into consideration addressing 'pandemic emergencies' by, as indicated above,[143] amending the IHR (2005) accordingly.[144] To draft a definition of a 'pandemic emergency' relevant for both the amended IHR and the new Pandemic Treaty, WHO Member States, via a joint meeting of the WGIHR and INB, decided to allocate the work relating to the definition and determination of 'pandemic

---

137 ibid, proposed amendments to article 1; see also WHO, 'Article-by-Article Compilation of Proposed Amendments to the International Health Regulations (2005) submitted in accordance with decision WHA75(9) (2022)' (September 2022) https://apps.who.int/gb/wgihr/pdf_files/wgihr1/WGIHR_Compilation-en.pdf.

138 ibid, proposed amendments to articles 15 and 16.

139 ibid, proposed amendment to article 24

140 ibid, amendment proposals to annexes 1–4, 6, and 8 as well as to articles 48, 49, and 43.

141 ibid, amendment proposals to article 56.

142 IHR (2024); Nithin Ramakrishnan, 'WHO: Member States Term Amendments to International Health Regulations as "Historic"' (*TWN Health Info Service on Health Issues*, 7 June 2024) https://twn.my/title2/health.info/2024/hi240602.htm.

143 See text accompanying Third World Network nn 84, 98–100 above.

144 INB, 'Report of the 8th Meeting' (11 March 2024) UN Doc A/INB/8/6.

emergencies' to the WGIHR with a view to including this definition in the IHR as amended in 2024. The understanding was that the determination of a 'pandemic emergency' by the WHO Director-General under the amended IHR would trigger certain provisions of the WHO Pandemic Agreement, for example, article 12(6) on the PABS system. However, there is no specific provision in the IHR as amended in 2024 which will be applicable only during 'pandemic emergencies'.

In brief, the amendments adopted in May 2024 included the following shown in Table 2.1.[145]

Most of these amendments are compromise texts, on which most of the Parties could agree. This means amendments are not ideal texts addressing all the problems discussed in Sections 3 and 4 above. However, they do not weaken the IHR in its version of 2005; rather, they strengthen it in various ways, in particular in relation to ensuring equitable access to pandemic-related health products. There are provisions which are carefully planted in the text, making duties of States and the WHO in relation to equitable access to health products in emergencies more explicit, creating relevant institutional structures and financing provisions. If they are implemented with careful oversight and planning, any remaining gaps in the text of the IHR (2024) could be adequately addressed through the work of the States Parties Committee for the Implementation of the International Health Regulations (2005) – a (yet to be constituted) new Member State-led body under the IHR (2004).

6.1 Potential Changes and Implications for Global Health Emergency Regime

The 2024 IHR amendments can be broadly understood as an attempt to shift from a surveillance-centric emergency regime preferred by developed countries and private and public-private donors to the WHO to a regime with more focus on comprehensive preparedness and response. It must be noted that the expansion of capacities on surveillance and enhancement of quality of information sharing and risk assessment continues as the focus of the health emergency regime post-Covid-19.[146] The main feature of the amendment is that it attempts to change this focus, through several steps.

---

[145] IHR (2024); Nithin Ramakrishnan and KM Gopakumar, 'WHO: IHR 2005 Amendments Adopted, Includes Equity-Related Provisions' (*TWN Info Service on Health Issues*, 7 June 2024) https://twn.my/title2/health.info/2024/hi240601.htm.

[146] Pandemic Fund, 'Call for Proposals' (19 December 2024) https://www.thepandemicfund.org/call-for-proposals. The first, second, and third cycles of the pandemic fund prioritise: (1) early warning and disease surveillance systems, and (2) laboratory systems, alongside 'One Health' workforce.

Table 2.1 *2024 IHR amendments*

Article	Amendments in brief
1	amended to incorporate definitions for a 'pandemic emergency', 'National IHR Authority', 'relevant health products'
2	scope of the IHR (2005) amended to explicitly mention preparedness aspects
3	principles guiding implementation of the IHR amended to include the promotion of equity and solidarity
4	amended to specifically obligate Parties to establish a National IHR Authority
5	'core capacities to prevent' included within the obligation to build capacities related to surveillance
6	amended to mandate the WHO to immediately notify other intergovernmental organisations if the matter concerns their respective competencies
10	amended to increase the level of expectations of the WHO offering to collaborate with States to assess the potential for the international spread of disease from health events, and the control measures adopted to address events
11	amended to include application of the provision in 'pandemic emergencies'
12	amendments introduced defining a process for the determination of 'pandemic emergencies'
13	amendments to mandate the WHO and obligate States Parties to promote equitable access to health products, including through the scaling up and diversification of production
15 and 16	scope of temporary and standing recommendations amended to include 'pandemic emergencies' as well as to incorporate an explicit reference to 'relevant health products'
17	availability and accessibility of 'relevant health products' as a factor to be considered while developing and issuing recommendations
18	amendment to mandate the WHO to actively take into account the need for facilitating international travel particularly for health workers and maintaining international supply chains particularly for medical products and food supplies
24	amendments made to explicitly mention that functions of conveyance operators related to health measures apply both on board and upon disembarkation

Article	**Amendments in brief**
27	quarantine measures for vessels are incorporated alongside isolation measures
35	amendments to ensure that health documents can be issued in digital and non-digital formats, and that they have to conform with annex 6 to the IHR and their authenticity should be verifiable. The WHO is also mandated to develop and update technical guidance as to the issuance and ascertainment of authenticity of health documents
43	amended to give an additional role to the WHO Director-General to facilitate consultations between States Parties taking additional health measures and with States that are affected by such measures
44	amendments introduce certain elements such as preparedness, facilitation of access to 'relevant health products' and financing into larger picture of general duties on collaboration and assistance
44 bis	a new article added to establish a coordinating financial mechanism, with a mandate to mobilise international financial assistance both by relying on existing and new financial resources
48 and 49	amended to include 'pandemic emergencies' into the work of Emergency Committees as well as subject the work of the Committees to the WHO Advisory Panel Regulations
54 bis	new provision included for the establishment of the States Parties Committee for the Implementation of the International Health Regulations (2005)
19 to 23, 28, 38, 45, 50, 53	some amendments to improve language consistency
Annex 1	revising the list of the core capacities
Annex 2	clusters of cases of severe acute respiratory disease of unknown or novel cause
Annexes 3, 4, 6, and 8	amendments to reflect changes in articles 28 and 35

First, access to health services and 'relevant health products' needed to address PHEICs are now established as IHR core capacities. National implementation will be overseen by national IHR authorities with potential financial assistance from the new Coordinating Financial Mechanism (CFM). The States Parties Implementation Committee will review international compliance and address gaps.[147] Both bodies must prioritise nationally determined needs over donor priorities, as constitutionally mandated in articles 44(2ter)(b) and 44bis(1)(b) IHR (2024).

Second, WHO and States Parties are specifically mandated to facilitate equitable access to health products such as vaccines, diagnostics, and treatments during PHIECs and 'pandemic emergencies'.[148] In other words, it has become an obligation on the WHO to deliver on these aspects, and States Parties with adequate resources to support these WHO activities globally. The WHO Director-General has been mandated to periodically conduct reviews, updates, and assessments of public health needs in relation to pandemic prevention, preparedness, and response and in relation to product availability/accessibility, and coordinate mechanisms to facilitate equitable access based on these assessments and publish such assessments.[149] Amended article 13 of IHR (2024) addresses preparedness by mandating the WHO to support scaling up and geographically diversifying 'relevant health product' production through networks, research collaboration, and technology sharing. The WHO Secretariat must report on these activities to the Implementation Committee.

Third, the new States Parties Committee for the Implementation of the IHR will oversee both preparedness and response activities within States. States Parties must collaborate with the WHO and engage private sector actors to support response activities, particularly regarding equitable access to health products during emergencies.[150]

6.2 Challenges to Implementation of Amendments to IHR 2005

Despite promising advancements in the 2024 amended IHR, at least three significant challenges remain.

First, State obligations contain caveats that weaken their legal force. The new article 13(9) IHR (2024) that requires States Parties to support the WHO's

---

147 Nithin Ramakrishnan, 'IHR 2005 Amendments: Setting the Legal Framework for Equity' (2024) *MMS Bulletin* #169 https://www.medicusmundi.ch/de/advocacy/publikationen/mms-bulletin/pandemic-preparedness/kapitel-i/ihr-2005-amendments-setting-the-legal-framewo.

148 IHR (2024), articles 13 and 44.

149 IHR (2024), article 13(8)(a).

150 IHR (2024), article 54bis.

activities promoting equitable access to health products includes qualifying language like 'subject to applicable law and available resources'. Similarly, the newly added paragraph 4 of annex 1 on international cooperation towards building core capacities merely echoes the language of article 44 IHR (2024) with the phrase 'to the extent possible'.

Second, the 2024 amendments lack direct financial obligations owed by developed countries to developing countries. While the CFM[151] can seek new funding sources and potentially create dedicated funds, its primary functions involve:

- Conducting needs and gap analyses;
- Promoting harmonisation of existing instruments;
- Identifying available financing sources;
- Advising States Parties on accessing resources; and
- Leveraging voluntary contributions.

Initially, the CFM will likely depend on external donors' financial resources provided by developed countries and private actors or PPPs, potentially compromising its ability to serve developing countries' national priorities. To be effective, the CFM may eventually need to establish dedicated funds that respond directly to developing countries' needs.

Third, concurrent negotiations for a new Pandemic Agreement appear to emphasise surveillance-based approaches[152] rather than equity, potentially repeating shortcomings of the IHR (2005). If developed countries prioritise surveillance-centric prevention, resources may be diverted from comprehensive health system strengthening, universal health coverage, and equitable access to 'relevant health products' to address PHEICs.

Overcoming these challenges requires active involvement from States Parties in the Implementation Committee and the CFM, complemented by civil society oversight to ensure balanced attention to preparedness, response, and comprehensive prevention of PHEICs and 'pandemic emergencies' beyond surveillance.

---

151 IHR (2024), article 44bis.

152 Third World Network, 'WHO: INB Bureau Pressures Global South to Align with G7's One Health and Prevention Agenda' (*TWN Info Service on Health Issues*, 6 December 2024) https://twn.my/title2/health.info/2024/hi241201.htm.

7. CONCLUSION

The amendments adopted to the IHR in May 2024 have the potential to change the global health emergency architecture in a more comprehensive and systematic manner. Negotiations in the WGPR and the WGIHR have created significant awareness and increased visibility on the IHR and its focus on surveillance. Developing countries have clearly communicated this message to the international community that a 'surveillance-only approach' is no longer acceptable for them.

If implemented diligently, the amendments will improve global equitable access to 'relevant health products' during PHEICs and 'pandemic emergencies' through effective cooperation between the WHO, its Member States, and WHO's numerous private and public-private partners. This has the potential to re-balance the global health emergency architecture.

PART II

Securitisation and public-private hybridisation: the WHO and the EU

3. Safe and effective medical countermeasures? The International Health Regulations, the WHO's responsibilities for the human right to health and emergency listed vaccines

Amrei Müller and Silvia Behrendt

1. INTRODUCTION

Under the International Health Regulations (IHR) (revised 2024),[1] the Director-General of the World Health Organization (WHO) can declare a public health emergency of international concern (PHEIC)[2] and, with the amendments adopted in 2024, also something called a 'pandemic emergency',[3] understood as a particularly serious PHEIC with a wide geographical spread to multiple States. Once the Director-General has made such a declaration, s/he can issue, with the advice of an Emergency Committee that s/he sets up,[4] temporary and standing recommendations for medical and non-medical countermeasures that all WHO Member States shall adopt to address the PHEIC.[5] With the 2024 amendments, these recommendations can directly

[1] International Health Regulations (2005) (adopted 23 May 2005, entered into force 15 June 2007) 2509 UNTS 79 (IHR (2005)). The 77th World Health Assembly (WHA) adopted far-reaching amendments to the IHR: WHA Res 77.17 (1 June 2024) UN Doc WHA77.17, annex 'Amendments to the International Health Regulations (2005)'. This chapter relies on the IHR as amended in 2024 (IHR (2024)), even though the amendments have not yet entered into force at the time of writing in August 2024.

[2] IHR (2024), articles 1 and 12.

[3] IHR (2024), article 1.

[4] IHR (2024), articles 48 and 49.

[5] IHR (2024), articles 15–17.

include recommendations for the (global) administration of 'relevant health products',[6] ie health products that are 'needed', in the opinion of the Director-General/Emergency Committee, to respond to the respective PHEIC because they allegedly 'prevent or reduce the international spread of [the] disease'[7] causing the PHEIC.

In the most prominent PHEIC that the Director-General has declared in recent years, the Covid-19-PHEIC lasting for more than three years,[8] the rapid development, emergency 'listing', global distribution, and mass administration of investigational modified-RNA-based or adenovirus-derived DNA-based vaccines was by far the most prominent medical countermeasure that the WHO recommended and pro-actively promoted in order to address the Covid-19-PHEIC, and still recommends and promotes at the time of writing in autumn 2024.[9] Recommendations centring on investigational vaccines also dominated and continue to dominate the medical countermeasures against the 2022[10] and

---

[6] IHR (2024) articles 13, 15–18, and 44, as well as to annex 1 A(2) and A(3)(h).

[7] IHR (2024), article 15(2).

[8] WHO Covid-19 Emergency Committee, 'Statement on the Second Meeting of the IHR (2005) Emergency Committee Regarding the Outbreak of Novel Coronavirus (2019-nCoV)' (30 January 2020); and 'Statement of the Fifteenth Meeting of the IHR (2005) Emergency Committee on the Covid-19 Pandemic' (5 May 2023). Both Statements https://www.who.int/groups/covid-19-ihr-emergency-committee. Unless otherwise stated all web links given in this chapter were last accessed between 7 March and 29 May 2025.

[9] WHO, 'Standing Recommendations for Covid-19 Issued by the Director-General of the WHO in Accordance with the IHR (2005)' (9 August 2023) annexed to UN Doc A78/INF./7 (14 May 2025) https://apps.who.int/gb/ebwha/pdf_files/WHA78/A78_INF7-en.pdf.

[10] The first m-pox-PHEIC lasted from 22 July 2022 to 11 May 2023; see WHO Mpox Emergency Committee, 'Statement on the Second Meeting of the IHR Emergency Committee Regarding the Multi-Country Outbreak of Mpox' (22 July 2022), declaring the Mpox-PHEIC; and 'Statement on the Fifth Meeting of the IHR Emergency Committee on the Multi-Country Outbreak of Mpox' (11 May 2023), ending the Mpox-PHEIC https://www.who.int/groups/monkeypox-ihr-emergency-committee. Standing Recommendations for mpox were issued by the Director-General on 21 August 2023, which recommended to 'make mpox vaccines available for primary prevention (pre-exposure) and post-exposure vaccination for persons and communities at risk of mpox, taking into account recommendations of the WHO Strategic Advisory Group of Experts on Immunization (SAGE)', para G(20) https://cdn.who.int/media/docs/default-source/documents/ihr/mpox-standing-recommendations-082023.pdf.

2024 Mpox-PHEICs[11] and the 2019 Ebola-PHEIC in the Democratic Republic of the Congo (DRC).[12]

Given the focus of the 2024 IHR amendments and the general direction that the WHO's work around pandemic preparedness, prevention, and response has taken – driven not least by the Global Health Security (GHS) doctrine,[13] fuelled by considerable investments[14] and new WHO-sponsored initiatives involving public-private partnerships (PPPs)[15] – it is expected that the global administration of investigational vaccines will play the central role in WHO-recommended countermeasures against future PHEICs. At the same time,

---

[11] A second mpox-PHEIC was declared on 14 August 2024 and is ongoing in 2025, see WHO Mpox Emergency Committee, 'Statement on the First Meeting of the IHR Emergency Committee Regarding the Upsurge on Mpox 2024' (19 August 2024) https://www.who.int/news/item/19-08-2024-first-meeting-of-the-international-health-regulations-(2005)-emergency-committee-regarding-the-upsurge-of-mpox-2024. The Statement recommends States affected by mpox outbreaks to prepare a vaccination strategy. The declaration of the mpox-PHEIC was preceded by a call from the WHO Director-General on mpox vaccine manufacturers to submit their dossiers to the WHO for emergency listing to kick-start the EUL procedures for their unlicensed vaccines, see WHO, 'WHO Invites Mpox Vaccine Manufacturers to Submit Dossiers for Emergency Evaluation' (*News Release*, 9 August 2024) https://www.who.int/news/item/09-08-2024-who-invites-mpox-vaccine-manufacturers-to-submit-dossiers-for-emergency-evaluations.

[12] WHO Ebola Emergency Committee, 'Statement on the Meeting of the IHR (2005) Emergency Committee for Ebola Virus Disease in the Democratic Republic of the Congo' (17 July 2019) https://www.who.int/news/item/17-07-2019-statement-on-the-meeting-of-the-international-healthregulations-(2005)-emergency-committee-for-ebolavirus-disease-in-the-democratic-republic-of-the-congo-on-17-july-2019; and 'WHO Prequalifies Ebola Vaccine, Paving the Way for Its Use in High-risk Countries' (*WHO News Release*, 12 November 2019) https://www.who.int/news/item/12-11-2019-who-prequalifies-ebola-vaccine-paving-the-way-for-its-use-in-high-risk-countries; WHO R&D Blueprint, 'A WHO Strategic Research Agenda for Filovirus. WHO-AFIRM Strategy 2021–2031' (June 2022) https://cdn.who.int/media/docs/default-source/blue-print/afirm-roadmap_2021_2031.pdf.

[13] See introduction to this volume.

[14] See eg Garrett Brown et al, 'The Cost of Pandemic Preparedness: An Examination of Costings and the Financial Requests in Support of the Pandemic Prevention, Preparedness and Response Agenda', REPPARE Report 2024, University of Leeds https://essl.leeds.ac.uk/downloads/download/234/the-cost-of-pandemic-preparedness-an-examination-of-costings-and-the-financial-requests-in-support-of-the-pandemic-prevention-preparedness-and-response-agenda.

[15] Eg CEPI's mission to develop, test, and globally administer new vaccines within 100 days, see 'CEPI 2.0 and the 100 Days Mission' (*CEPI*, 2024) https://cepi.net/cepi-20-and-100-days-mission.

since the 2024 IHR amendments expanded the definition of a PHEIC, it is likely that the world will face more WHO-declared PHEICs in the future.[16]

Overall, the biomedical focus on emergency-authorised vaccines has been welcomed by a broad coalition of State and non-State actors,[17] including human rights and public international law scholars.[18] Support broadly unites around the idea of ensuring global 'vaccine equity',[19] accepting that outbreaks of infectious diseases must indeed be addressed primarily by the rapid global mass administration of 'relevant health products' and, in particular, vaccines; and that every human being, no matter where they live, what their age, health,

---

16 Further, Amrei Müller and Silvia Behrendt, 'The 2024 Amendments to the International Health Regulations: A Commentary (Part II: Selected Substantive Issues)' (*Opinio Juris*, 20 September 2024) https://opiniojuris.org/2024/09/20/the-2024-amendments-to-the-international-health-regulations-a-commentary-part-ii-selected-substantive-amendments/.

17 See eg Statement by Kristalina Georgieva (Managing Director of the International Monetary Fund), Tedros Ghebreyesus (WHO Director-General), David Malpass (President of the World Bank Group), and Ngozi Okonjo-Iweala (Director-General of the World Trade Organization), 'A New Commitment to Vaccine Equity and Defeating the Pandemic' (31 May 2021) https://www.who.int/news-room/commentaries/detail/a-new-commitment-for-vaccine-equity-and-defeating-the-pandemic; 'EU and WHO to Collaborate to Protect Vulnerable Populations from Vaccine-preventable Diseases by Ensuring Immunization Equity' (*WHO News Release*, 19 April 2024) https://www.who.int/europe/news/item/19-04-2024-eu-and-who-collaborate-to-protect-vulnerable-populations-from-vaccine-preventable-diseases-by-ensuring-immunization-equity; and the numerous international organisations, PPPs, NGOs, philanthropic organisations, and corporations that signed the Declaration on Vaccine Equity in January 2021 https://www.who.int/campaigns/vaccine-equity/vaccine-equity-declaration.

18 Eg Armin von Bogdandy and Pedro Villarreal, 'The Role of International Law in Vaccinating against COVID-19: Appraising the COVAX Initiative' (2021) 81 Zeitschrift für öffentliches Recht und Völkerrecht 89; Els Torreele and Joseph Amon, 'Virtual Roundtable: Equitable Covid-19 Vaccine Access' (2021) 23(1) Health & Human Rights Journal 273; Kaitlin Fajber, 'Business as Usual? Centring Human Rights to Advance Global Covid-19 Vaccine Equity through COVAX' (2022) 24(2) Health & Human Rights Journal 219; Nancy Jecker, 'Achieving Global Vaccine Equity: The Case for an International Pandemic Treaty' (2022) 95(2) Yale Journal of Biology and Medicine 271; Alexandra Phelan et al, 'Legal Agreements: Barriers and Enablers to Global Equitable Covid-19 Vaccine Access' (2020) 396 Lancet 800; and Siva Thambisetty et al, 'Addressing Vaccine Inequity during the Covid-19 Pandemic: The TRIPS Intellectual Property Waiver Proposal and Beyond' (2022) 81(2) Cambridge Law Journal 384.

19 IHR (2024) amendment to article 3(1), which included 'equity and solidarity' as principles that should guide the implementation of the IHR (2024).

immunisation or other status is, shall have 'equal'[20] access to such vaccines. This shall inter alia contribute to realising the human right to health (HRH), which, according to the UN Committee on Economic, Social and Cultural Rights (CESCR), includes a right to access immunisation against major infectious diseases.[21]

Whilst this securitised, bio-medicalised, and product-focused approach can rightly be questioned from a medical, public health and health economic perspective,[22] this chapter focuses on selected *legal* questions that arise around this approach's compatibility with the WHO's obligations under the IHR and some of its responsibilities for the HRH.

The analysis proceeds in three steps. Section 2 briefly describes the WHO's programmes for the emergency 'listing' and promotion of investigational vaccines to address PHEICs. The extent to which these WHO activities around emergency vaccines are compatible with selected WHO obligations under the IHR and some of its responsibilities for the HRH are examined in Section 3. Section 4 concludes.

2. WHO'S PROGRAMMES ON EMERGENCY LISTING AND PROMOTION OF VACCINES AS MEDICAL COUNTERMEASURES

The medical countermeasure preferred by the GHS doctrine – the rapid development, emergency authorisation/listing and subsequent administration of investigational vaccines – forms the centrepiece of the WHO's pandemic

---

[20] It should, however, be noted that such a one-dimensional understanding of 'equality' or 'equity' – treating everyone identically, with no regard to their personal circumstances and differences – has long been rejected in equality and non-discrimination human rights jurisprudence, eg UN HRCttee, 'General Comment No 18: Non-Discrimination (Thirty-seventh session, 1989)' (10 November 1989), paras 7–8; and Paul Taylor, *A Commentary on the International Covenant on Civil and Political Rights* (CUP 2020) 732–45.

[21] International Covenant on Economic, Social and Cultural Rights (adopted 16 December 1966, entered into force 3 January 1976) 993 UNTS 3 (ICESCR), article 12(2)(c); and CESCR, 'General Comment No 14: The Right to the Highest Attainable Standard of Health' (11 August 2000) UN Doc E/C.12/2000/4, paras 16, 36, and 44.

[22] Eg David Bell et al, 'COVAX – Time to Reconsider the Strategy and its Target' (2023) 4 Health Policy OPEN 100096; and David Bell et al, 'Rational Policy over Panic: Re-examining Pandemic Risk within the Global Pandemic Prevention, Preparedness and Response Agenda', 2024 REPPARE Report, University of Leeds https://essl.leeds.ac.uk/downloads/download/228/rational-policy-over-panic.

preparedness and response activities. The WHO has built an entire infrastructure across departments to promote the rapid deployment of this countermeasure. This includes the World Health Emergency Programme (WHE) but also the Regulation and Prequalification (RPQ) Department for research and development (R&D), emergency listing, and the promotion and distribution of investigational vaccines against newly emerging or re-emerging pathogens the existence of which constitute (or may constitute) a PHEIC. The 2024 IHR amendments strengthen and expand this infrastructure further. Due to space constraints, the following focuses on two vaccine-related aspects of this infrastructure: the Emergency Use Listing (EUL) procedure (Section 2.1) and the WHO's promotion of EUL vaccines during PHEICs (Section 2.2).

2.1 The Emergency Use Listing (EUL) Procedure

The WHO's EUL procedure is one through which the WHO de facto issues manufacturers with time-limited global emergency authorisations for their unlicensed vaccines, medicines, and in-vitro diagnostics that are deemed relevant to address the diseases underlying WHO-declared PHEICs. It is based on a risk-benefit assessment in an emergency situation, where available data on the medical product 'must provide an indication that the use of the product will provide *a benefit* to the target population'.[23] The procedure thereby de facto mirrors, at global level, parallel programmes of medical regulators in high-income countries granting such emergency authorisations[24] based on the assumption that, in an emergency situation, the likely benefits of making available the unlicensed product outweigh the unknown risks, deduced from preliminary quality, efficacy, and safety data.[25] If the WHO, through its expert committees, issues a positive EUL for an unlicensed product of a

---

[23] 'Q&A for Guidelines on Emergency Use Listing Procedure' (*WHO*, July 2020) 1 (emphasis added) https://cdn.who.int/media/docs/default-source/medicines/regulatory-updates/qa-eul-general-july-2020.pdf.

[24] For an overview of these domestic procedures: WHO/ICMRA, 'Deep Dive Report on the Review of Provisions and Procedures for Emergency Authorisation of Medical Products for Covid-19 among ICMRA members' (July 2021) https://icmra.info/drupal/sites/default/files/2021-12/eua_deep_dive_report.pdf (accessed 26 August 2024).

[25] ibid, 6. Examples are the European Medicines Agency's (EMA) processes to grant 'conditional marketing authorisation', or the US Food & Drug Administration's (FDA) processes to issue 'emergency use authorisation' for unlicensed medical products.

certain manufacturer, it de facto endorses the product as 'safe and effective'[26] for global use.[27]

The EUL procedure is referred to here as a procedure for the *global de facto emergency authorisation* of medical products since it indeed has de facto global regulatory effects, if not *de jure*.[28] In practice, it enables global procurement and distribution of unlicensed products by UN agencies (eg UNICEF), by WHO's PPPs like Gavi,[29] and by WHO Member States,[30] often through pre-fixed purchase agreements activated by default once an EUL has been issued for a medical product. EUL vaccines moreover have their own WHO labelling[31] which allows them to be put on domestic markets (usually without undergoing a thorough authorisation process by national regulatory agencies) especially in low-income countries which lack the relevant regulatory capacities. During the Covid-19-PHEIC, an EUL for the respective investigational Covid-19 vaccines was a pre-condition for their global distribution via Covid-19 Vaccines Global Access (COVAX).[32] Also, the WHO's Covid-19 Emergency Committee has,

---

26 Eg the WHO's invitation on Mpox Vaccine Manufacturers to Submit Dossiers for Emergency Evaluation (n 11). The WHO advertised, and continues to advertise, all vaccines against Covid-19 which it granted an EUL as 'safe and effective', see below text accompanying (nn 79–99).

27 This is, however, misleading. Unlicensed products have not undergone thorough safety and efficacy testing, and can therefore, by definition, not be classified and advertised as 'safe and effective'.

28 The WHO is indeed keen to point out that vaccines (and other medical products) recommended via the EUL procedure are not WHO-endorsed global emergency use authorisations, but recommendations ('listings') to provide guidance. WHO, 'Emergency Use Listing Procedure' (9 August 2022) 8 https://extranet.who.int/prequal/sites/default/files/document_files/EUL-v9August2022.pdf. Also below, text accompanying (nn 74–7).

29 WHO, 'Manufacturing, Safety and Quality Control of Vaccines' (8 December 2020) https://www.who.int/news-room/feature-stories/detail/manufacturing-safety-and-quality-control.

30 WHO, 'EUL Procedure' (n 28) 7; reiterated recently in the WHO's invitation on Mpox Vaccine Manufacturers to Submit Dossiers for Emergency Evaluation (n 11).

31 See eg labels for EUL vaccines distributed by COVAX during the Covid-19-PHEIC: WHO, 'Model Packaging for Carton and Label for Vials for COVID-19 Vaccines' (4 November 2020) https://www.who.int/teams/regulation-prequalification/eul/covid-19/covid-19-model-packaging.

32 WHO, 'Product Eligibility under the COVAX Facility' (29 December 2020) https://extranet.who.int/pqweb/sites/default/files/documents/Product-Eligibility_COVAX-Facility_Dec2020_0.pdf; Gavi et al, 'COVAX Global Supply Forecast' (8 September 2021) 3 https://www.who.int/docs/default-source/coronaviruse/act-accelerator/item-6_covax-supply_presented.pdf.

in its temporary recommendations, called on States to recognise the WHO's EUL Covid-19 vaccines 'in the context of international travel',[33] promote their administration through the introduction of digital Covid-19 vaccine passports that can be 'implemented on [internationally] interoperable digital platforms'[34] for international travel, and advised States to follow a strategy of mass vaccination of the entire global population with these products.[35]

---

33 WHO Covid-19 Emergency Committee, 'Statement on the Eighth Meeting of the International Health Regulations (2005) Emergency Committee Regarding the Coronavirus Disease (COVID-19) Pandemic' (15 July 2021), recommendation 8 to State Parties; 'Statement on Ninth Meeting of the International Health Regulations (2005) Emergency Committee Regarding the Coronavirus Disease (COVID-19) Pandemic' (26 October 2021), recommendation 8 to State Parties; and 'Statement on the Tenth Meeting of the International Health Regulations (2005) Emergency Committee Regarding the Coronavirus Disease (COVID-19) Pandemic' (19 Jan 2022), recommendation 8 to State Parties. All Statements https://www.who.int/groups/covid-19-ihr-emergency-committee.

34 WHO Covid-19 Emergency Committee, 'Statement on the Sixth Meeting of the International Health Regulations (2005) Emergency Committee Regarding the Coronavirus Disease (COVID-19) Pandemic' (15 January 2021), recommendations 9 and 10 to the WHO Secretariat; 'Statement on the Seventh Meeting of the International Health Regulations (2005) Emergency Committee Regarding the Coronavirus Disease (COVID-19) Pandemic' (19 April 2021), recommendation 16 to WHO Secretariat; 'Statement on the Eighth Meeting of the International Health Regulations (2005) Emergency Committee Regarding the Coronavirus Disease (COVID-19) Pandemic' (15 July 2021), recommendation 3 to WHO Secretariat. All Statements https://www.who.int/groups/covid-19-ihr-emergency-committee.

35 WHO Covid-19 Emergency Committee, 'Statement on the Fifth Meeting of the International Health Regulations (2005) Emergency Committee Regarding the Coronavirus Disease (COVID-19) Pandemic' (30 October 2020), recommendation 9 to State Parties; 'Statement on the Sixth Meeting of the International Health Regulations (2005) Emergency Committee Regarding the Coronavirus Disease (COVID-19) Pandemic' (15 January 2021), recommendations 5 and 6 to State Parties; 'Statement on the Seventh Meeting of the International Health Regulations (2005) Emergency Committee Regarding the Coronavirus Disease (COVID-19) Pandemic' (19 April 2021), recommendations 1–5 and 18 to State Parties; 'Statement on the Eighth Meeting of the International Health Regulations (2005) Emergency Committee Regarding the Coronavirus Disease (COVID-19) Pandemic' (15 July 2021), recommendations 3 and 9 to State Parties; 'Statement on Ninth Meeting of the International Health Regulations (2005) Emergency Committee Regarding the Coronavirus Disease (COVID-19) Pandemic' (26 October 2021), recommendation 3 to State Parties; 'Statement on the Tenth Meeting of the International Health Regulations (2005) Emergency Committee Regarding the Coronavirus Disease (COVID-19) Pandemic' (19 January 2022),

What is more, the EUL procedure is intrinsically linked[36] to the WHO's Research and Development Blueprint for Emerging Pathogens (R&D Blueprint) Programme aiming to accelerate the development of medical countermeasures during a PHEIC even before such PHEICs occur. This happens by preventively commissioning and supporting manufacturers to carry out R&D on pathogens with PHEIC – or pandemic potential, and in particular on priority pathogens that made it onto a list of such priority pathogens that is regularly updated by the R&D Blueprint programme.[37] The WHO's PPPs are involved here too with the Coalition for Epidemic Preparedness Innovation (CEPI) promising to develop, produce, test, authorise, and administer safe and effective vaccines within 100 days in the near future.[38]

Overall, the purpose of the EUL procedure is thus to expedite the availability of medical countermeasures, prior to and/or during PHEICs as declared by the Director-General 'when the community/public health authorities may be willing to tolerate *less certainty* about the efficacy and safety of products, given the morbidity and/or mortality of the disease and the lack or paucity of treatment, diagnosis/detection or prevention options'.[39] Whilst there are three product streams under the EUL procedure – for in vitro diagnostics, medicines, and vaccines – which are regulated in an almost identical fashion, the following description concentrates on vaccines.

2.1.1 Product eligibility for the EUL procedure

Manufacturers can submit an unlicensed and thus investigational (ie experimental) vaccine to the EUL procedure if the vaccine meets four eligibility criteria. First, the disease underlying or causing the emergency context must be 'serious or immediately life threatening' and have 'the potential of causing an outbreak, epidemic or pandemic'.[40] It appears that the WHO assumes that this criterion is met by default once it has declared a PHEIC under the IHR, even though the definition of a PHEIC in article 1 IHR does not include a severity

recommendations 3 and 9 to State Parties. All Statements https://www.who.int/groups/covid-19-ihr-emergency-committee.

36 WHO, 'EUL Procedure' (n 28) 9.

37 'Research Prioritization for Pandemic and Epidemic Intelligence: Technical Brief' (*WHO*, 23 May 2024) https://www.who.int/publications/i/item/9789240094529; 'Research and Development (R&D) Roadmaps' (*WHO*) https://www.who.int/teams/blueprint/r-d-roadmaps.

38 CEPI (n 15).

39 WHO, 'EUL Procedure' (n 28) 7 (emphasis added).

40 ibid, 8.

threshold for the underlying disease that spreads internationally.[41] A second eligibility criterion is that there must not be any existing medical product or treatment licensed for the same purpose that addresses the disease in question.[42] Third, the product must be 'manufactured under a functional Quality Management System (QMS)';[43] and fourth, the applicant manufacturer must commit to completing the development of the vaccine by finalising outstanding clinical trials and other tests, and later transfer their EUL product into the WHO's (regular) prequalification programme.[44]

2.1.2 Three phases of the EUL procedure

The EUL procedure is divided into three distinct phases: the pre-emergency, emergency, and post-listing phase. Two distinct WHO expert committees are attached to these different phases,[45] namely the Product Evaluation Group-Vaccines (PEG-V)[46] and the Technical Advisory Group-Vaccines (TAG-EUL-V).[47]

During the pre-emergency phase, the PEG-V, composed of ten experts[48] selected from the WHO's RPQ Department roster, takes the responsible lead. The experts undertake a 'risk-based assessment of the scientific data for a … [vaccine], including quality, safety/efficacy/performance and programmatic aspects'[49] within a timeframe of approximately three months.[50] Through this process, they assess the vaccine against predefined targets developed by the above-mentioned WHO R&D Blueprint strategy.

In the emergency phase (which starts once the WHO Director-General declares a PHEIC), the TAG-EUL-V is responsible for publishing a

---

41 IHR (2024), article 1; Silvia Behrendt and Amrei Müller, 'The Proposed Amendments to the International Health Regulations: An Analysis' (*OpinioJuris*, 27 February 2023) https://opiniojuris.org/2023/02/27/the-proposed-amendments-to-the-international-health-regulations-an-analysis/.

42 WHO, 'EUL Procedure' (n 28) 8.

43 ibid.

44 ibid.

45 ibid, 9.

46 ibid, 11 and annex 1, 21.

47 The TAG-EUL-V (where the 'V' stands for the 'vaccines' pillar of the EUL procedure) consists of 6 experts from various fields, see ibid, 27; and WHO, 'Technical Advisory Group for Emergency Use Listing (established December 2020)' https://extranet.who.int/prequal/vaccines/technical-advisory-group-emergency-use-listing-established-december-2020.

48 WHO, 'EUL Procedure' (n 28) 23.

49 ibid, 11.

50 ibid, 19.

recommendation within just five days[51] as to whether the unlicensed vaccine under consideration should be 'emergency listed'.

The post-listing phase starts once the unlicensed vaccine has been publicly listed. In this phase, the WHO will monitor the efficacy/quality/safety of the EUL vaccine, taking into consideration 'reports on safety surveillance, efficacy/performance monitoring, quality complaints and other relevant data that may impact the validity of the listing status'.[52] Such information will come from surveillance mechanisms in countries in which the EUL vaccines are administered, as well as from the manufacturers. The WHO may seek the advice of the TAG-EUL once more on quality and safety questions post-listing.[53] In addition, so-called 'post-EUL commitments' are attached to any granted EUL which are 'a series of recommendations or conditions that must be addressed by the EUL-holder within the timelines discussed and agreed [between the WHO and the manufacturer] at the time of the EUL recommendation'.[54] These commitments build on the previous PEG-V reports and recommendations concerning the respective unlicensed EUL vaccines. The detailed PEG-V and TAG-V reports, particularly those on the 'post-EUL commitments', are not available for public scrutiny.

2.1.3 Data requirements

Annex 5 to the 2022 document setting out the WHO's EUL procedure specifies what data an applicant must submit relating to the unlicensed vaccine. First to note is that data requirements are negotiable between the WHO and the applicant, and the WHO 'highly encourages'[55] applicants to contact the WHO as early as possible on these matters. Limited non-clinical (pre-clinical) and clinical data are required. Non-clinical data demonstrating 'acceptable safety, immunogenicity, and efficacy' in the 'most appropriate animal model' must be provided.[56]

If such data is not available, the applicant must give a justification for this and provide a plan for the submission of such data. Clinical (human) data should demonstrate the 'appropriate dose and initial acceptable safety and immunogenicity'; and some preliminary clinical data showing 'some efficacy'

51 ibid.
52 ibid, 16.
53 ibid.
54 WHO, 'Post EUL Submission Procedure' (30 March 2022) 1 https://extranet.who.int/prequal/sites/default/files/document_files/Post-EUL-Submissions-Procedure_VAX2022.pdf.
55 WHO, 'EUL Procedure' (n 28), annex 5, 40.
56 ibid, 41.

should also be submitted 'if available'.[57] If such clinical efficacy data is not available, WHO committees 'will consider whether the preponderance of evidence from the non-clinical, and early human studies justifies considering the immunogenicity data as a potential surrogate that is thought to be reasonably predictive of clinical efficacy'.[58] Moreover, safety and immunogenicity data concerning '*other* vaccines made by the manufacturer using the same product *platform*' can be submitted in support.[59] It is thus clear that data from phase 3 clinical trials is not required, let alone data from controlled long-term human and post-marketing pharmacovigilance studies as vaccines submitted for EUL have by definition not received a regular market authorisation. The WHO also encourages manufacturers to discuss their plans to collect and analyse information on safety and efficacy of an EUL vaccine when the listing is in effect and 'for a reasonable time' thereafter in pre-submission meetings,[60] and the results of such discussions presumably flow into the above-mentioned 'post-EUL commitments' attached to a granted EUL.

In general, an EUL for an unlicensed product is granted for 12 months with a possibility of extension,[61] but it shall end in any event once the PHEIC that the product shall address ends.[62]

2.1.4 WHO Secretariat's/Director-General's control over the EUL procedure

Every aspect of the EUL procedure is under the control of the WHO Secretariat. The exclusive and final decision-making authority on all its aspects thus rests with the Director-General without there being adequate legal and institutional safeguards against arbitrariness. The Secretariat decides which dossiers submitted by manufacturers for consideration for an EUL are accepted.

The Secretariat also retains full control over the appointment of experts and the recommendations they issue when assessing an investigational vaccine for an EUL. The experts of the PEG-V and TAG-V are chosen by the Secretariat from a pre-existing expert roster, after experts have passed the WHO's internal (but lacking transparency) conflict of interest procedures.[63] It does not seem that the names of the PEG-V experts involved in EUL assessments are

57 ibid, 42.

58 ibid.

59 ibid (emphasis added).

60 ibid, 42.

61 ibid, 15. There is no indication of how long and how often an EUL can be extended.

62 ibid, 15.

63 WHO, 'Declarations of Interests' https://www.who.int/about/ethics/declarations-of-interest.

disclosed anywhere,[64] whilst the list of the current six members of the TAG-V is publicly available.[65] It is within the discretion of the Secretariat to terminate the membership of an expert on the PEG-V during an ongoing assessment without providing reasons for the removal.[66] Moreover, the Director-General is the final authority to decide on any contentious issue and conflicts arising between WHO experts and officers and the applicant manufacturer, and the Director-General's decisions are 'final and binding on the parties'.[67]

Finally, it remains within the discretion of the Secretariat to decide when an EUL product requires market withdrawal due to safety concerns.[68] However, current WHO documents on the EUL procedure do not define criteria as to when an EUL must be withdrawn, for example concerning the number of serious adverse events (including deaths) after vaccination with an EUL vaccine.

2.1.5 Publication of reports

In principle, the EUL procedure foresees that any EUL is accompanied by a public report prepared by the PEG-V and TAG-V.[69] It is, however, challenging to find any reports on the WHO's website. There is no central place on the WHO website displaying all reports on EUL products. If reports are available, their scope and quality appear limited. For example, one of the few available reports concerns *Pfizer/BioNTech* (Tozinameran) – an EUL vaccine against Covid-19 – which is a rudimentary summary of the European Medicines Agency (EMA) emergency regulatory assessment, neither containing critical analysis, nor are the names of WHO-nominated experts involved in the assessment provided.[70] Otherwise, neither minutes of the meetings between WHO committees and pharmaceutical industry applicants, nor agreements as to which data requirements the manufacturer must fulfil according to annex

---

[64] Eg WHO, 'Recommendation for an Emergency Use Listing of Tozinameran (Covid-19 mRNA Vaccine (Nucleoside Modified)) submitted by *BioNTech* Manufacturing GmbH' (26 January 2021) https://extranet.who.int/prequal/sites/default/files/document_files/TAG-EUL_PublicReport_BioNTech_DEC20.pdf.

[65] WHO, 'Technical Advisory Group for Emergency Use Listing' (n 47).

[66] WHO, 'EUL Procedure' (n 28) 24. The document is silent on the Secretariat's corresponding authority to terminate an expert membership of the TAG-V during an ongoing assessment.

[67] ibid, 17. A similar absence of any due process guarantees for applicants wishing to challenge the outcome of the WHO's panels under the Prequalification Programme has been criticised in academic literature, eg Connor Fuchs, 'Process is Due: The World Health Organization Prequalification of Medicines' (2019) 68 Emory Law Journal 634.

[68] WHO, 'EUL Procedure' (n 28) 15.

[69] ibid.

[70] WHO, 'Recommendation for EUL of *Tozinameran*' (n 64).

5 to the WHO's document outlining the EUL procedure, nor the terms of each granted EUL, nor pharmacovigilance data or (serious) adverse events reporting are made public as part of the EUL procedure.[71]

2.1.6 Financing

It remains unclear how the EUL procedure is financed. According to the WHO Secretariat, any fees for EULs are regularly waived to avoid that such fees become a roadblock for pharmaceutical corporations with unlicensed products in their R&D pipelines that are potentially urgently needed to respond to a PHEIC. If EUL products transition into standard authorisation procedures, the WHO requests the manufacturers to pay the applicable fees.[72] There is, however, no public data available on how much manufacturers of Covid-19 vaccines (eg *Pfizer/BioNTech* or *Moderna*), whose products have later attained regular authorisations, paid in fees under WHO's regular prequalification[73] scheme, and/or whether they paid a fee for the successful EUL of their vaccines ex post.

2.1.7 Liability

It appears that the WHO excludes 'any and all liability and responsibility for any injury, death, loss, damage or other prejudice of any kind whatsoever that may arise as a result of or in connection with the procurement, distribution and use of any unlicensed product included in the list' of EUL vaccines as well as 'for any loss, damage, liability or other prejudice of any kind whatsoever that may arise as a result of or in connection with any assessment and recommendation under the EUL procedure' made by the WHO.[74] The WHO furthermore highlights that the organisation, its officials, and/or experts involved in the EUL procedure enjoy privileges and immunities under international law exempting them from any national courts' jurisdiction.[75] This is problematic

---

[71] The WHO may share some of this information 'with relevant authorities of any interested Member States … and interested UN agencies', see: WHO, 'EUL Procedure' (n 28) 15.

[72] The authors' e-mail exchange with WHO Secretariat (2 February 2023); and 'WHO: Bureau's Text Suggestion for "Pre-Qualification" Raises Concerns of Vaccine Supply Concentration' (*Third World Network*, 12 February 2024) https://www.twn.my/title2/health.info/2024/hi240204.htm.

[73] From the WHO's website on prequalified vaccines it is, however, not clear if all EUL vaccines against Covid-19 ever entered the prequalification scheme. WHO, 'Pre-Qualified Vaccines' https://extranet.who.int/prequal/vaccines/prequalified-vaccines.

[74] WHO, 'EUL Procedure' (n 28), annex 8, 65.

[75] ibid, 17.

given the de facto regulatory effects that the EUL procedure has on a global scale, that the WHO widely advertises its investigational EUL vaccines as 'safe and effective',[76] as well as the fact that EUL vaccines distributed globally through the WHO's PPP consortia like COVAX during the Covid-19-PHEIC have indeed caused serious adverse events, including deaths.[77]

2.2 WHO's Promotion of EUL Vaccines during PHEICs

The foregoing points to the fact that the WHO pro-actively promoted the administration of EUL Covid-19 vaccines during the Covid-19-PHEIC and does so during the ongoing 2024 mpox-PHEIC.[78] The WHO will likely do so in future PHEICs, given the 2024 IHR amendments concerning 'relevant health products' that the Director-General/Emergency Committee can now directly recommend to States to administer to their populations in order to address a PHEIC.

The Covid-19-PHEIC already saw the WHO advertising, as 'safe and effective', the vaccines against Covid-19 that it had granted an EUL.[79] In synchronicity with many others,[80] the WHO also reasserted that 'no one is safe until

[76] Below text accompanying (nn 78–99). This is particularly problematic because at the same time the WHO 'explicitly disclaims any warranty of the fitness of any listed unlicensed product for a particular purpose, including in regard to its safety and/or efficacy and/or performance' (WHO, 'EUL Procedure' (n 28), annex 8, 64).

[77] This is confirmed by scientific literature on Covid-19 EUL vaccines, listed eg below (n 163).

[78] See (n 10) and (n 11). The 2024 mpox-PHEIC is ongoing at the time of writing in autumn 2024.

[79] Eg WHO, 'Covid-19 Advice for the Public: Getting Vaccinated' https://www.who.int/emergencies/diseases/novel-coronavirus-2019/covid-19-vaccines/advice; 'Safety of Covid-19 Vaccines' (31 March 2021) https://www.who.int/news-room/feature-stories/detail/safety-of-covid-19-vaccines; and 'Vaccine Efficacy, Effectiveness and Protection' (14 July 2021) https://www.who.int/news-room/feature-stories/detail/vaccine-efficacy-effectiveness-and-protection.

[80] Eg COVAX, 'No one is Safe until Everyone is Safe' https://www.who.int/initiatives/act-accelerator/covax; GAVI/Seth Berkley, 'No one is Safe until Everyone is Safe' (*Gavi*, 29 October 2021) https://www.gavi.org/vaccineswork/no-one-safe-until-everyone-safe; and various religious leaders and heads of international organisations, 'No-one is Safe until Everyone is Safe – Why We Need a Global Response to Covid-19' (*UNHCR*, 24 May 2021) https://www.unhcr.org/news/news-releases/statement-no-one-safe-until-everyone-safe-why-we-need-global-response-covid-19.

everyone is safe',[81] indicating that the Covid-19-PHEIC would only end if as many people as possible worldwide would get vaccinated.[82] Guidance to generate acceptance and demand for EUL Covid-19 vaccines,[83] as well as for future EUL and fully licensed vaccines, was and continues to be developed by the WHO,[84] heavily relying on behavioural science.

At the same time, shortly after the Covid-19-PHEIC was declared, the Director-General also claimed that '[w]e are not just fighting an epidemic; we're fighting an infodemic. Fake news spreads faster and more easily than this virus, and is just as dangerous.'[85] This was the beginning of the implementation of the so-called WHO infodemic programme.[86] It included regular calls of the Covid-19 Emergency Committee on States to counter alleged mis- and disinformation about Covid-19 and in particular vaccines,[87] and 2023 standing

---

[81] Eg WHO, 'No one is Safe from Covid-19 until Everyone is Safe' https://www.who.int/news-room/photo-story/photo-story-detail/No-one-is-safe-from-COVID19-until-everyone-is-safe. Whether the phrase makes sense is another question. One would expect that either vaccines are indeed 'safe and effective' and are thus protecting those who have been vaccinated, regardless of whether other people are also vaccinated; or they are not, in which case nobody will be effectively protected from catching Covid-19.

[82] Eg the global Covid-19 vaccination strategy set out by the WHO Strategic Advisory Group of Experts on Immunization (SAGE) in October 2021, summarised in WHO, (2021) 50(96) Weekly Epidemiological Record 613, 623–5.

[83] WHO, 'Generating Acceptance and Demand for Covid-19 Vaccines' https://www.who.int/initiatives/act-accelerator/covax/covid-19-vaccine-country-readiness-and-delivery/acceptance-and-demand; and WHO Technical Advisory Group on Behavioural Insights and Sciences for Health, 'Behavioural Considerations for Acceptance and Uptake of Covid-19 Vaccines' (15 October 2020) https://iris.who.int/bitstream/handle/10665/337335/9789240016927-eng.pdf.

[84] WHO, 'Demand for Immunization' https://immunizationdata.who.int/global/wiise-detail-page/demand-for-immunization; and WHO/UNICEF, 'Behavioural and Social Drivers for Vaccination. Tools and Practical Guidance for High Uptake' (2022) https://iris.who.int/bitstream/handle/10665/354459/9789240049680-eng.pdf.

[85] WHO Director-General, 'Speech at Munich Security Conference' (*WHO*, 15 February 2020) https://www.who.int/director-general/speeches/detail/munich-security-conference.

[86] WHO, 'Infodemic' https://www.who.int/health-topics/infodemic#tab=tab_1.

[87] Among others, WHO Covid-19 Emergency Committee, 'Statement on the Third Meeting of the International Health Regulations (2005) Emergency Committee Regarding the Coronavirus Disease (COVID-19) Pandemic' (1 May 2020); 'Statement on the Fourth Meeting of the International Health Regulations (2005) Emergency Committee Regarding the Coronavirus Disease (COVID-19)

recommendations for Covid-19 continue to demand that States actively address 'vaccine [against Covid-19] misinformation, disinformation, acceptance and demand issues'.[88] The 2024 IHR amendments provide this practice with a firmer legal basis for future PHEICs.[89]

The WHO, in cooperation with governments and big technology corporations,[90] deploys various strategies to control alleged mis- and disinformation on EUL vaccines as part of its infodemic management programmes, some preventive, others reactive.[91] The *preventive* strategy is referred to as 'pre-bunking', aiming to 'immunise' and regularly 'boost' the population against possible future mis- or disinformation.[92] This is done by providing targeted advance information, explaining the alleged strategies and techniques employed by those who purportedly spread mis- or disinformation[93] or by

---

Pandemic' (1 August 2020), recommendation 6 to States Parties; 'Statement on the Eighth Meeting of the International Health Regulations (2005) Emergency Committee Regarding the Coronavirus Disease (COVID-19) Pandemic' (15 July 2021), recommendation 9 to States Parties; 'Statement on the Eleventh Meeting of the International Health Regulations (2005) Emergency Committee Regarding the Coronavirus Disease (COVID-19) Pandemic' (13 April 2022), recommendation 9 to States Parties; and 'Statement on the Fifteenth Meeting of the International Health Regulations (2005) Emergency Committee Regarding the Coronavirus Disease (COVID-19) Pandemic' (5 May 2023), recommendation 5 to States Parties. All statements https://www.who.int/groups/covid-19-ihr-emergency-committee.

88 WHO, 'Standing Recommendations for Covid-19' (n 9), para D(13).

89 IHR (2024), amendments to annex 1, section A(2)(c)(vi) and (3)(i).

90 See eg the monthly meetings of the WHO's Tech Task Force, a standing group of representatives from over 40 major technology companies including Amazon, Facebook/Meta, Google/YouTube, Microsoft, and TikTok, which collaborate with the WHO to ensure application of global principles to identify alleged misinformation. WHO, 'WHO and NAM Encourage Digital Platforms to Apply Global Principles for Identifying Credible Sources of Health Information' (24 February 2022) https://www.who.int/news/item/24-02-2022-who-and-nam-encourage-digital-platforms-to-apply-global-principles-for-identifying-credible-sources-of-health-information; or WHO, 'Digital Channels' https://www.who.int/teams/digital-health-and-innovation/digital-channels.

91 For an overview of 'pre-emptive' and 'responsive' strategies, see Emily Vraga and Leticia Bode, 'Addressing Covid-19 Misinformation on Social Media Pre-emptively and Responsively' (2021) 27(2) Emerging Infectious Diseases 396.

92 Eg Sander van der Linden et al, 'Inoculating against Fake News about COVID-19' (2020) 11 Frontiers in Psychology 1; and Robert McPhedran et al, 'Psychological Inoculation Protects against the Social Media Infodemic' (2023) 13(5780) Nature Scientific Reports 1.

93 Cecilie Traberg et al, 'Prebunking against Misinformation in the Modern Digital Age' in Tina Purnat et al (eds), *Managing Infodemics in the 21st Century*

pre-classifying certain sources pre-emptively as unreliable and untrustworthy[94] in order to build resilience and even 'herd immunity'[95] against alleged misinformation.

The *reactive* strategies include debunking or removing alleged vaccine misinformation from the public sphere. Debunking can be done by adding disclaimers and corrections to articles and social media posts, often through fact checks,[96] or by re-directing to allegedly trustworthy sources like the WHO's website or the social media accounts of 'Dr Tedros' (the current Director-General),[97] or by downranking (ie reducing the reach by suspending algorithmic amplification) of certain accounts or pieces of alleged misinformation.[98] Removing alleged vaccine misinformation involves outright censorship and de-platforming of social media accounts, banning specific people – including scientists and doctors – from posting anything on social media or appearing otherwise in public debates.[99] How exactly the WHO determines what

(Springer 2023) 99, 102–4; and Emily Vraga et al, 'To Debunk or Not to Debunk? Correcting (Mis)Information' in Purnat et al (eds), ibid, 85 and 92.

94 Eg by consistently classifying a source as spreading (usually undefined) 'conspiracy theories' with the effect that readers categorise any information coming from the source as wrong or misleading; see eg United Nations Interregional Crime and Justice Research Institute (UNICRI), 'Stop the Virus of Disinformation. The Risk of Malicious Use of Social Media during COVID-19 and the Technology Options to Fight it' (November 2020) 27 https://unicri.it/sites/default/files/2021-01/misuse_sm_0.pdf.

95 Traberg et al (n 93) 106–7; and Toby Pilditch et al, 'Psychological Inoculation can Reduce Susceptibility to Misinformation in Large Rational Agent Networks' (2022) 9(8) Royal Society Open Science 1.

96 Eg the International Fact Checking Network (https://www.poynter.org/coronavirusfactsalliance/), which, between January 2020 and August 2023 allegedly carried out 170,000+ fact checks on information around Covid-19 in 110+ countries, in 40+ languages; Jane Singer, 'Closing the Barn Door? Fact-Checkers as Retroactive Gatekeepers of the Covid-19 "Infodemic"' (2023) 100(2) Journalism & Mass Communication Quarterly 332.

97 John Zarocostas, 'How to Fight an Infodemic' (2020) 395 Lancet 676, 676.

98 Nandita Krishnan et al, 'Research Note: Examining How Various Social Media Platforms Have Responded to COVID-19 Misinformation' (2021) 2(6) Harvard Kennedy School Misinformation Review 1; and Joseph Bak-Coleman et al, 'Combining Interventions to Reduce the Spread of Viral Misinformation' (2022) 6 Nature Human Behaviour 1372.

99 Eg Queenie Wong, 'Facebook Removed More Than 20 Million Posts for Covid-19 Misinformation' (*CNET*, 18 August 2021) https://www.cnet.com/news/social-media/facebook-removed-more-than-20-million-posts-for-covid-19-misinformation; Nicole Wetsman, '*YouTube* will Remove Videos with Covid-19 Vaccine Misinformation' (*The Verge*, 14 October 2020) https://www.theverge.com/2020

amounts to medical mis- or disinformation, and for how long, remains unclear to the outsider.

3. THE WHO'S OBLIGATIONS UNDER THE IHR, ITS RESPONSIBILITIES FOR THE HRH AND EUL VACCINES AS MEDICAL COUNTERMEASURES

An examination follows of the extent to which the described WHO activities concerning vaccines are compatible with the WHO's obligations under the IHR and its responsibilities for the HRH. Since not all IHR obligations and responsibilities for the HRH can be discussed here, after a few general remarks (Section 3.1), the focus is on obligations and responsibilities to ensure access to safe and efficacious medicinal products of good quality (Section 3.2), to reliable health information (Section 3.3) and to strictly upholding the principle of free and informed consent (Section 3.4).

3.1 General Remarks: Sources of WHO's Obligations and Responsibilities

The first point to recall is that the WHO is directly bound by the IHR. The IHR is a multilateral treaty binding all State Parties to it. At the same time, the IHR was adopted (and recently amended) as a constitutional regulation by the World Health Assembly (WHA) in line with the procedures set out in articles 21 and 22 of WHO's Constitution (WHOC).[100] This qualifies the IHR as unique 'secondary' WHO law of a *sui generis*[101] and *lex specialis* character that is firmly grounded in and interconnected with the WHOC and inseparable from the comprehensive WHO governance system. Thus, whilst the WHO is not a party to the IHR, it is directly bound by these regulations, including via WHA resolution 58.3, which bestowed it with the obligation to implement the IHR.[102]

/10/14/21515796/youtube-covid-vaccine-misniformation-policy; and '*YouTube* to Remove all Anti-Vaccine Misinformation' (*BBC News*, 29 September 2021) https://www.bbc.com/news/technology-58743252.

100 Constitution of the World Health Organization (adopted 22 July 1946, entered into force 7 April 1948) 14 UNTS 185 (WHOC).

101 Eg Andrea Spagnolo, '(Non) Compliance with the International Health Regulations of the WHO from the Perspective of the Law of International Responsibility' (2018) 17(3) Global Jurist 1, 3.

102 WHA Res 58.3 (23 May 2005) UN Doc WHA58.3, paras 2 and 6(4).

Second, the WHO has responsibilities for human rights,[103] including the HRH which is the focus of the current analysis. These responsibilities flow from the IHR itself, requiring the WHO – and in particular the Director-General/Emergency Committees – to implement the IHR with 'full respect for the dignity, human rights and fundamental freedoms of persons'.[104] This demands an interpretation and application of the IHR in conformity with international human rights law (IHRL),[105] supported also by the strong references to the HRH in the WHOC.[106] Customary responsibilities for the HRH binding international organisations like the WHO are also emerging.[107]

The nature of the WHO's responsibilities for human rights (including for the HRH) is, however, different from States' human rights duties (or obligations),[108] which States, having ratified international or regional human rights treaties,

---

103 'Responsibilities for human rights' discussed here shall not be confused with secondary (remedial) responsibilities that arise once (primary) responsibilities for human rights have been violated by international organisations, in accordance with the 'Draft Articles on the Responsibilities of International Organisations' (DARIO), adopted by the International Law Commission at its sixty-third session in 2011. The terminology 'responsibilities for human rights' is chosen here to distinguish them from human rights duties/obligations of States which differ in their nature and scope from international organisations' responsibilities for human rights. For a full explanation of these differences, see Samantha Besson, 'The Bearers of Human Rights Duties and Responsibilities for Human Rights: A Quiet (R)evolution' (2015) 32(1) Social Philosophy & Policy 244.

104 IHR (2024), article 3(1).

105 Eg Gian Luca Burci and Riikka Koskenmaki, 'Human Rights Implications of Governance Responses to Public Health Emergencies: The Case of Major Infectious Disease Outbreaks' in Andrew Clapham and Mary Robinson (eds), *Realizing the Right to Health* (Springer 2009) 346, 351; and Andraz Zidar, 'WHO International Health Regulations and Human Rights: From Allusion to Inclusion' (2015) 19(4) International Journal of Human Rights 505.

106 WHOC, preamble; IHR (2024), article 3(2) also cross-refers to the WHOC. International organisations are bound by their constituent instrument, even if they are not parties to this instrument; see eg ICJ, *Reparations for Injuries Suffered in the Service of the United Nations* (Advisory Opinion) 1949 ICJ Reports 174, 180.

107 ICJ, *Interpretation of the Agreement of March 1951 between the WHO and Egypt* (Advisory Opinion) 1980 ICJ Reports 73, para 37; DARIO (n 103), articles 2(b) and 10; and International Law Commission commentaries to DARIO (2011) 63 https://legal.un.org/ilc/texts/instruments/english/commentaries/9_11_2011.pdf.

108 The terms 'obligation' and 'duty' are used as synonyms in this chapter. For the full explanation of the notion of 'responsibilities for human rights', see Besson (n 103).

owe to individuals under their jurisdiction.[109] The content and scope of the WHO's responsibilities for human rights are determined in relation to States' human rights duties. As highlighted by the CESCR, the WHO's responsibilities for human rights have a more negative dimension *not to undermine* the ability of States to implement their human rights duties through a functioning domestic (democratic) institutional framework and owed to everyone coming under the respective State's jurisdiction;[110] and a more positive dimension to (pro-actively) *enable and assist* States of jurisdiction to do so.[111] The CESCR has furthermore highlighted that 'it is particularly incumbent on … actors [including international organisations like the WHO] in a position to assist' to support States to 'fulfil their *core obligations*',[112] adding that core obligations, 'when grouped together establish an international *minimum threshold* that all developmental policies should be designed to respect'.[113] Whilst this statement was made for the context of 'national and international development policies', there is no reason why this should not also apply to WHO policies and recommendations issued in relation to PHEICs/pandemic emergencies.

---

109 Eg European Convention on Human Rights (adopted 4 November 1950, entered into force 3 September 1953) 213 UNTS 221 (ECHR), article 1; and International Covenant on Civil and Political Rights (adopted 16 December 1966, entered into force 23 March 1976) 999 UNTS 171 (ICCPR), article 2(1).

110 CESCR, 'General Comment 14' (n 21), para 64; more generally concerning these more negative responsibilities for human rights of international organisations, eg CESCR, 'General Comment No 22: The Right to Sexual and Reproductive Health' (2 May 2016) UN Doc E/C.12/GC/22, para 52; 'General Comment No 4: The Right to Adequate Housing' (1991) contained in UN Doc E/1992/23, para 19; General Comment No 7: The Right to Adequate Housing: Forced Evictions' (1997) contained in UN Doc E/1998/22, paras 17–18; and the 'Maastricht Principle on Extraterritorial Obligations of States in the Area of Economic, Social and Cultural Rights' (29 February 2012), principle 16 https://www.icj.org/wp-content/uploads/2012/12/Maastricht-ETO-Principles-ENG-booklet.pdf.

111 CESCR, 'General Comment 14' (n 21), para 64. Generally, concerning these more positive responsibilities of international organisations, eg CESCR, 'General Comment No 15: The Right to Water' (20 January 2002) UN Doc E/C.12/2002/11, para 60; 'General Comment No 2: International Technical Assistance Measures' (2 February 1990) contained in UN Doc E/1990/23, para 8(a); and 'General Comment No 21: Right of Everyone to Take Part in Cultural Life' (21 December 2009) UN Doc E/C.12/GC/21, paras 75–6.

112 CESCR, 'General Comment 14' (n 21), para 45 (emphasis added); and 'General Comment 15' (n 111), para 38.

113 CESCR, 'Statement on Poverty and the ICESCR' (10 May 2001) UN Doc E/C.12/2001/10, para 17.

Third, the WHO's activities described above concerning emergency listing and promotion of investigational vaccines during (and before) PHEICs arguably have their legal basis in the WHOC, for example the WHO's role in 'promoting and conducting research in the field of health'[114] and to 'develop, establish and promote international standards with respect to … biological, pharmaceutical and similar products',[115] reinforced by the functions of the WHA in the area of medical R&D.[116] Resolutions of the WHA have further endorsed these activities.[117] They do not, however, authorise the WHO to promote international emergency standards and recommend medicinal products for global use whose efficacy and safety have not been fully established, in contravention to the WHO's duties under the IHR and its responsibilities for the HRH.

3.2 Ensuring Access to Safe and Efficacious Medical Products of Good Quality

Among the relevant responsibilities of the WHO for the HRH are those that require the WHO not to undermine States' abilities to comply with their direct human rights duties to ensure access to medicinal products of 'good quality',[118] and rather, to pro-actively support States in complying with these duties. Medical products of good quality are products that are 'safe and efficacious' having undergone 'ethically and medically validated clinical trials'[119] and produced in accordance with good manufacturing practices (GMP).[120]

---

114 WHOC, article 2(n).

115 WHOC, article 2(u); also articles 2(s) and (t).

116 WHOC, article 18(k), establishing that among the functions of the WHA is to 'promote and conduct research in the field of health by the personnel of the Organization, by the establishment of its own institutions or by co-operation with official or non-official institutions of any Member with the consent of its Government'.

117 See (n 129) and (n 130) below.

118 CESCR, 'General Comment 14' (n 21), para 12(d).

119 UN Special Rapporteur on the Right to Health, 'Report of the Special Rapporteur on the Right of Everyone to the Enjoyment of the Highest Attainable Standard of Physical and Mental Health, Anand Grover, on Access to Medicines' (1 May 2013) UN Doc A/HRC/23/42, para 61.

120 The WHO has developed standards concerning GMP (https://www.who.int/teams/health-product-policy-and-standards/standards-and-specifications/gmp). Due to space constraints, this chapter cannot, however, discuss the extent to which it may be justified under the IHR and IHRL for the WHO to promote EUL products during a PHEIC that do not comply with these GMP and thus limit the safety and efficacy of these EUL products.

The Director-General's/Emergency Committees' duties under the IHR similarly require that any temporary or permanent recommendations they issue on medical countermeasures to address a PHEIC, including those on the global administration of 'relevant health products', must indeed be effective in 'prevent[ing] and reduc[ing] international spread of [the] disease'[121] that led to the declaration of the PHEIC. Moreover, whilst the Director-General/Emergency Committees may issue recommendations concerning persons that advise States to 'review proof of' or 'require' vaccination,[122] such recommendations must be based on 'scientific principles' and 'available scientific evidence',[123] in compliance with 'international standards and instruments'[124] and be made 'on the basis of risk assessment appropriate to the circumstances' to ensure that they are 'not more intrusive to persons than reasonably available alternatives that would achieve the appropriate level of health protection'.[125]

The reference to 'international standards' guarantees that medical products recommended as countermeasures by the Director-General adhere to internationally accepted guidelines for the development of drugs set by the WHO[126] and specifically the International Council for Harmonisation of Technical Requirements for Pharmaceuticals for Human Use (ICH).[127] This implies that these medical products have to undergo the standard four stages of clinical trials to identify potential risks such as carcinogenicity, genotoxicity, and reprotoxicity in line with ICH guidelines.

Overall, this means that the WHO must ensure that any vaccine it recommends for administration as a medical countermeasure is indeed safe, efficacious, and of good quality, proven in 'ethically and medically validated clinical trials' following these 'international standards' and 'scientific principles', and that no other medical or non-medical countermeasures are available that are less intrusive to persons than vaccines achieving a similar level of health protection.

121 IHR (2024), articles 15(2), 16(2), and 18.

122 IHR (2024), article 18(1).

123 IHR (2024), article 17(c).

124 IHR (2024), article 17(e).

125 IHR (2024), article 17(d) IHR.

126 Eg WHO, 'Clinical Trial Oversight (CT): Indicators and Factsheets' (March 2022) https://cdn.who.int/media/docs/default-source/medicines/regulatory-systems/gbt-blood/08_gbt-md_rev_vi-md_ver_1_ct_20220301_clean.pdf.

127 ICH Efficacy Guidelines, https://www.ich.org/page/efficacy-guidelines; and Bhavna, Abhijeet Ojha, and Samir Bhargava, 'International Council for Harmonisation (ICH) Guidelines' in Javed Ali and Sanjula Baboota (eds), *Regulatory Affairs in the Pharmaceutical Industry* (Academic Press 2022) 47.

The above-described WHO recommendations for the *global* administration of EUL vaccines that have not undergone the full cycle of medical trials to ensure their safety and efficacy according to ICH standards, and which are therefore investigational, as well as their global promotion as 'safe and effective', are hard to square with these responsibilities for the HRH and IHR obligations. This is even more so because the EUL procedure if not de jure then de facto gives the WHO the powers of a global medical regulator[128] for vaccines (and other medical products) to address WHO-declared PHEICs. As discussed above, an EUL granted for a vaccine or other medical product opens de facto global market admission for the EUL product and triggers global procurement chains without, however, ensuring that the relevant 'international standards' for 'ethically and medically validated clinical trials' are complied with.

If the EUL procedure is seen in isolation, however, some may argue that the WHA empowered the WHO Secretariat in 2022 to develop '*new* guidance as needed on best practices in clinical trials' including provisions 'for application during a PHEIC',[129] thereby specifying the WHO's role in 'developing, establishing and promoting international standards with respect to … biological, pharmaceutical and similar products'[130] set out in the WHOC.

Whilst it will be hard to justify the WHO's own 'new' powers to act as a de facto global medical regulator for EUL products that it created for itself under the EUL procedure, one could accept the argument that the WHA indeed requested the WHO to develop reference standards regarding the authorisation of investigational vaccines during some PHEICs to purportedly address an extraordinary situation of a global health emergency that potentially threatens the lives of a considerable part of the world's population if there are indeed no viable alternatives.

However, if this is accepted, a number of issues must be urgently addressed and clarified concerning the EUL procedure. This is needed to ensure that any limitations[131] that this procedure constitutes to the WHO's responsibilities and obligations to ensure access to safe and effective medicinal products under the HRH and IHR, involving modifications to the normal procedures of 'ethically

---

128 See text accompanying (nn 28–35) above.

129 WHA Res 75.8 (27 May 2022) UN Doc WHA75.8, para 3.2 (emphasis added).

130 WHOC, article 2(u), also, articles 2(s) and (t); and WHA Res 67.21 (24 May 2014) UN Doc WHA67.21; and WHA Res 67.20 (24 May 2014) UN Doc WHA67.20, both reinforcing the WHO's function to set norms and standards particularly through strengthening the role of the WHO Expert Committee of Biological Standardisation.

131 Note that no derogations are permitted from the rights set out in the ICESCR. It does not contain a derogation clause equivalent to that of the ICCPR, article 4.

and medically validated clinical trials' in line with 'international standards' in highly exceptional cases, are fully justified. After all, the consequence of such limitations is that WHO-recommended unlicensed EUL vaccines whose efficacy and safety has not been proven are administered to healthy persons as preventive but intrusive medical interventions, potentially on a global scale. This poses numerous risks to the health and lives of individuals, with the scope and severity of these risks largely unknown, constituting clear interferences not only with the right to access safe and effective medical products but also other components of the HRH, and even with the right to life since deaths are not excluded as severe adverse events from EUL products. In line with the ICESCR's limitation clause article 4, these limitations must have a 'legal basis', a legitimate aim, and their proportionality – effectiveness/suitability, necessity and the 'no excessive burden' requirement[132] – must be ensured.

3.2.1 Legal basis

First, concerning the 'legal basis', for the context of international organisations like the WHO, it can be argued that even though they are not strictly speaking legally binding for the WHO, States, or individuals, the documents and guidelines that the WHO and its relevant expert committees have adopted to 'regulate' the EUL procedure constitute such 'legal bases' defining limitations to the WHO's responsibilities not to undermine States' abilities to comply with their HRH duties to secure access to safe and efficacious medical products. However, IHRL defines certain qualitative minimum standards that a 'legal basis' must fulfil, usually concerning *domestic* law that defines limitations to States' human rights duties: 'law' must be accessible and sufficiently clear (foreseeable),[133] and must have a democratic (usually parliamentary) origin. This is not the place to discuss the full implications of adapting these criteria to 'regulations' made by international organisations like the WHO, recognising that, at least in theory, international organisations have limited legislative powers compared to States. However, it can be argued that general rules of (international) law principles[134] would indeed require sufficient precision, in

132 See in general about the IHRL proportionality test, Yutaka Arai-Takahashi, 'Proportionality' in Dinah Shelton (ed), *The Oxford Handbook of International Human Rights Law* (OUP 2013) 446.

133 Eg HRCttee, 'General Comment No 34: Freedoms of Opinion and Expression' (29 July 2011) UN Doc CCPR/C/GC/34, para 21; and HRCttee, 'General Comment No 27: Freedom of Movement' (2 November 1999) UN Doc CCPR/C/21/Rev.1/Add.9, para 13.

134 Eg requirements of clarity, publicity, certainty, equality, transparency, and fairness, as discussed eg by Arthur Watts, 'The International Rule of Law' (1993) 36 German Yearbook of International Law 15; and Ruti Teitel, 'Humanity's Law:

particular in the current case, where WHO 'regulations' of the EUL procedure can indeed, if followed and implemented by States, severely interfere with individuals' HRH and right to life. In their current form, EUL regulations remain vague – for example, on the requirements for non-clinical and clinical trial data evidencing (even preliminary) safety and efficacy[135] – leaving the Director-General and the expert committees that advise him/her, as well as the applicant pharmaceutical companies, almost unfettered discretion.[136] Moreover, whilst demanding a democratic origin of WHO 'regulations' is challenging,[137] it can reasonably be asked if centralising the powers of shaping ('making'), implementing *and* 'adjudicating' EUL regulations primarily in the hands of the Director-General, advised by small expert committees, who have a narrow biomedical and technocratic perspective on EUL vaccines, guarantees a balanced outcome, or at least is sufficient to prevent abuse. At the very least, all WHO Member States should have an opportunity to thoroughly reflect, comment on, and discuss the EUL procedure and the extent to which it can limit the enjoyment of individuals' HRH and right to life, carefully considering requirements of necessity and proportionality as discussed in the following. Moreover, transparency and accessibility requirements would demand that all guidelines issued, decisions made, EUL terms agreed with pharmaceutical corporations, etc, by expert committees should be open to scrutiny by the public, including in particular the wider scientific and medical community.

3.2.2 Legitimate aims

Second, regarding legitimate aims, limitations to the right to access safe and effective medicinal products in the form of modifications to regular procedures of 'ethically and medically validated clinical trial' in line with international standards must 'promote general welfare',[138] which can arguably include the

Rule of Law for the New Global Politics' (2002) 35 Cornell International Law Journal 355.

[135] See text accompanying (nn 55–60) above.

[136] HRCttee, 'General Comment 34' (n 133), para 21; and 'General Comment 27' (n 133), para 13, indicate that leaving those who 'execute' laws 'unfettered discretion' is a sign of these laws' insufficient precision.

[137] The 'democratisation' of international organisations must, however, be promoted, even if 'democratic' decision-making at the level of international organisations will look different from what is and can be done at the domestic level. For a discussion, see Samantha Besson, 'Democratic Representation within International Organisations: From International Good Governance to International Good Government' (2022) 19 International Organizations Law Review 489.

[138] ICESCR, article 4.

aim of protecting (public) health[139] during a PHEIC. Given, however, that such limitations constitute far-reaching interferences with the HRH and the right to life, involving also largely unknown risks, it must be ensured that the legitimate aim of 'promoting general welfare' in this context is interpreted narrowly.

This would mean that not all declarations of a PHEIC that currently, by default, activate the EUL procedure for vaccines can also by default be seen as achieving the aim of 'promoting general welfare'/'protecting (public) health'. This is so in particular because the threshold to declare a PHEIC is low[140] and the criteria according to which such declarations can be made are very flexible, leaving the Director-General wide discretion that is not subject to independent review. Therefore, to ensure that the activation of the EUL procedure and WHO recommendations for the global use of EUL vaccines actually 'promote general welfare'/'protect public health', a clear 'severe' and 'life-threatening' disease benchmark should be established[141] that triggers the EUL procedure in highly exceptional circumstances. The eligibility criteria guiding applicants who wish to secure an EUL for their unlicensed vaccines point already in this direction.[142] Only if the EUL procedure for vaccines addresses a truly severe emergency health hazard, for the treatment of which no licensed medical products are available, can it be seen as serving the legitimate aim of 'promoting general welfare'/'protecting public health'. In this context, due to the low infection fatality rate (IFR) of Covid-19 it is questionable whether the Covid-19-PHEIC should have triggered the EUL procedure.[143]

3.2.3 Proportionality

Third, when it comes to proportionality of limitations, the modifications to 'ethically and medically validated clinical trial' in the form of the EUL

---

[139] Justified eg by reading article 4 ICESCR in light of limitation clauses in other international human rights treaties, eg ICCPR, articles 12(3), 18(3), 19(3), 21, and 22(2).

[140] Müller and Behrendt (n 16).

[141] It can, of course, be argued that the definitions of a PHEIC/pandemic emergency in the IHR themselves should include such a severity threshold to prevent the undue proliferation of such declarations and their far-reaching legal and practical consequences. However, by adopting the 2024 IHR amendments to article 1, WHO Member States decided against such an approach.

[142] Above (n 40).

[143] Angelo Pezzullo et al, 'Age-stratified Infection Fatality Rate of COVID-19 in the Non-elderly Population' (2022) 114655 Environmental Research 216, concluding that the median IFR was 0.0003% at 0–19 years, 0.002% at 20–29 years, 0.011% at 30–39 years, 0.035% at 40–49 years, 0.123% at 50–59 years, and 0.506% at 60–69 years.

procedure must first of all be effective and suitable, that is, there must be evidence that vaccinations with EUL products are *effective* in 'prevent[ing] or reduc[ing] the international spread of [the respective] disease',[144] and thus suitable to achieve the legitimate aims of 'promoting general welfare'/protecting public health in an extraordinary health emergency. Whilst the modifications permit that efficacy does not need to be established through fully finished 'ethically and medically validated clinical trials' following regular international standards, there must be some medical and epidemiological evidence showing that the spread of the severe disease that should be addressed by an EUL vaccine can in fact be prevented effectively by a vaccine. Not every severe disease can technically be prevented, or its spread reduced, through vaccinations. For example, apart from the question as to whether Covid-19 (given its low IFR) can be classified as a severe disease, concerning the WHO-recommended EUL vaccines against Covid-19, it was clear from the beginning that these vaccines were designed neither to prevent nor to reduce the spread of Covid-19,[145] and their recommendation as a medical countermeasure could therefore not 'prevent or reduce the international spread' of Covid-19 as required under the IHR. Moreover, more work is to be done to clearly specify what exact data from pre-clinical tests and clinical trials is required for an EUL vaccine to be considered effective and suitable to achieve the defined legitimate aims. The current formulation that there needs to be 'a benefit'[146] of an EUL vaccine and that clinical data showing 'some efficacy' must be provided only 'if available'[147] appears too vague.

A second requirement of proportionality concerns the question about the least restrictive means being relied on to limit the right to access safe and effective medical products, ie the question as to whether there are any alternative measures that are less restrictive whilst being equally effective to achieve the legitimate aim of 'promoting general welfare'/'protecting public health' during the PHEIC. As indicated above, this requirement is directly specified in the IHR, which obliges the Director-General/Emergency Committee to only issue recommendations concerning EUL vaccines when 'on the basis of risk assessment appropriate to the circumstances' there are no other medical or non-medical countermeasures available that are less intrusive to persons than vaccines achieving the 'appropriate level of health protection'.[148]

---

144 IHR (2024), article 15(2).

145 EMA, 'Assessment Report – *Comirnaty*' (19 February 2021) EMA/707383/2020 Corr.2, 139 https://www.ema.europa.eu/en/documents/assessment-report/comirnaty-epar-public-assessment-report_en.pdf.

146 Above (n 23).

147 Above (n 57).

148 IHR (2024), article 17(d).

Since the administration of EUL vaccines is by definition highly intrusive, in particular because their effectiveness and safety has not been proven and will involve numerous unknown risks, and because they are generally given to healthy persons, the EUL procedure for vaccines should only be considered once other less intrusive alternatives, such as non-medical countermeasures or the use of safe and effective, fully licensed repurposed drugs for treatment, have been carefully considered. This has not been done consistently during the Covid-19-PHEIC, and one may argue that it has even been prevented;[149] and the current EUL documents do not explicitly require this, apart from asking the expert committees involved to consider whether it is 'reasonable' to consider an investigational vaccine for an EUL because it addresses a 'serious or immediately life threatening disease'.[150] In addition, clear requirements must be set out in the documents on the EUL procedure about the pre-clinical test and clinical trial data that manufacturers of EUL vaccines are to provide to preliminarily assess the safety and efficacy of these vaccines in relation to any other possibly less intrusive countermeasure, even if no data from completed 'ethically and medically validated clinical trials' following regular 'international standards' are available to prove full safety and effectiveness.

A last requirement of proportionality is that no excessive burden (proportionality in the strict sense) can be placed on individuals affected by the restriction of their right to access safe and effective medicinal products that States impose due to WHO recommendations. That is, the severity of the limitation must not be excessive as compared to the benefits to be obtained from the limiting measure, which, in the current case, is the reliance on the EUL procedure for vaccines and WHO recommendations for the (potentially global) use of such experimental vaccines. This requires a very careful (qualitative) balancing of the health benefits anticipated from the investigational EUL vaccine against the anticipated risks to the enjoyment of the HRH and the right to life arising from the administration of a preventive medical intervention whose effectiveness has not been proven and that lacks a clear safety profile (especially long term). In this exercise, it must be recognised that the anticipated benefits and risks are (highly) uncertain and are likely not distributed equally among all persons.

Blanket WHO recommendations to globally vaccinate all persons with investigational EUL vaccines, no matter where they live, what their age is, or what their health, socioeconomic or other status is during the Covid-19-PHEIC,

---

149 See the video report by Dr Tess Lawrie concerning *Ivermectin*: 'Dr Tess Lawrie Provides an Exclusive Insight into Her Conversation with Dr Andrew Hill' (*World Council for Health*, 20 December 2021) https://worldcouncilforhealth.org/multimedia/tess-lawrie-andrew-hill/.

150 Above (n 40).

appear highly problematic in this context, and blanket, indiscriminate measures are rarely considered proportionate limitations to human rights.[151] Once more, the EUL documents must also urgently specify, through a fully open debate involving all States as well as scientists and medical professionals beyond the narrow membership of relevant small WHO expert committees, what minimal pre-clinical and clinical data concerning the expected safety and efficacy of the EUL vaccine must be provided to meaningfully support such qualitative balancing with preliminary medical-scientific evidence. The broad discretion left to the expert committees and the Director-General must be limited, and, given the far-reaching consequences of potentially *global* administration of EUL vaccines, much broader participation in, and review of, decisions must be secured. Moreover, it should be highlighted that the 'no excessive burden' requirement clearly demands that no limitations to the right to access safe and effective medicinal products (or to other related components of the HRH like the right to bodily integrity, and even to other human rights, like the right to life) are permitted that fully extinguish this right/these rights. In the terminology of article 4 ICESCR, any limitation must 'be compatible with the nature of [... the HRH]', a requirement that is often interpreted as a requirement to exclude limitations that touch on the minimum core content of the HRH[152] (and corresponding core responsibilities for that core content of the WHO).[153] Among this core content of the HRH relevant for the current context is the right not to be subjected to medical or scientific *experimentation* without prior free and informed consent,[154] as well as not to be subjected to medical *treatment* without free and informed consent,[155] and the related right to access

151 Eg *Hirst v UK* (No 2) App no 74025/01 (ECtHR, 6 October 2005) para 82; *Söyler v Turkey* App no 29411/07 (ECtHR, 17 September 2013), paras 46–7; and *Scoppola v Italy* (No 3), App no 126/05 (ECtHR, 22 May 2012), para 120.

152 Eg Jacob Weinrib, 'The Essence of Rights and the Limits of Proportionality', in Geneviève Cartier and Mark Walters (eds), *The Promise of Legality: Critical Reflections upon the Work of TRS Allan* (forthcoming https://ssrn.com/abstract=4321570); Amrei Müller, 'The Minimum Core Approach to the Right to Health' in Sabine Klotz et al (eds), *Healthcare as a Human Rights Issue* (transcript 2017) 55.

153 Above (nn 112–13).

154 CESCR, 'General Comment 14' (n 21), para 8 and strongly reinforced by article 7 ICCPR. Also, UN Special Rapporteur on the Right to Health, 'Report on Informed Consent' (10 August 2009) UN Doc A/64/272, para 19.

155 CESCR, 'General Comment 14' (n 21), paras 8 and 34; UN Special Rapporteur on HRH, 'Informed Consent' (n 154), para 19.

reliable health information[156] enabling the making of self-determined decisions over one's own body and health.[157] These rights are discussed below.[158]

In the context of WHO-recommended, experimental EUL vaccines and the significant interference with the HRH that they constitute, the strict proportionality test also puts a heightened responsibility on the WHO to ensure that strict continuous safety/pharmacovigilance monitoring and reporting of the EUL vaccine is carried out by States and pharmaceutical companies under the EUL procedure. This would include defining clear thresholds for the number of severe adverse events for withdrawing an EUL and removing the investigational products from the (global) market. Whilst the WHO runs its database *VigiAccess* recording adverse events caused by medical products, including EUL vaccines, it is unclear why the high number of adverse events reported occurring in relation to Covid-19 EUL vaccines, many of them serious, have never been acted upon.[159] Similarly, strict proportionality would require the WHO to ensure that the clinical trials testing investigational EUL vaccines finish the full cycle of regular 'ethically and medically validated clinical trials' following 'international standards' to fully establish their safety and efficacy, including in the long term and very long term, as indeed required by the EUL

---

156 CESCR, 'General Comment 14', (n 21) para 44(d), and paras 11, 12(b), 34, 35, and 37; UN Special Rapporteur on HRH, 'Informed Consent' (n 154), paras 22–3; and Carlos Diaz and Javier Vasquez, 'The Right to Receive and Impart Information as a Cross-Cutting Issue in the Protection of the Right to Health' (2012) 6(2) Health Law & Policy Brief 1.

157 UN Special Rapporteur on HRH, 'Informed Consent' (n 154), para 9; and Trudo Lemmens and Candice Helfer, 'Access to Information and the Right to Health: The Human Rights Case for Clinical Trial Transparency' (2012) 38(1) American Journal of Law and Medicine 63, 105.

158 Text below accompanying (nn 167–86).

159 The WHO's EUL vaccines against Covid-19 have not been withdrawn despite an unprecedented number of adverse events having been reported to the US' *Vaccine Adverse Event Reporting System* (VAERS) (https://openvaers.com/covid-data), the EU's *EudraVigilance* (https://www.adrreports.eu/en/index.html), and the WHO's *VigiAccess System* (https://www.vigiaccess.org) since the global roll-out of these vaccines in late 2020. This seems to indicate that benchmarks relied on in earlier years are no longer applied. Eg in 1967, when almost 25% of the US population at the time (about 45 million US citizens) had been vaccinated against swine flu, the campaign was discontinued after reports of 25 deaths and 362 reports on serious neurological disorders after vaccination; see Kenrad Nelson, 'Influenza Vaccine and Guillain-Barre Syndrome – Is there a Risk?' (2012) 175(11) American Journal of Epidemiology 1129; and Richard Krause, 'The Swine Flu Episode and the Fog of Epidemics' (2006) 12(1) Emerging Infectious Diseases 40.

documents.[160] The limitation to the right to access safe and effective medical products by permitting WHO-recommended experimental products to be administered must be kept to an absolute minimum in light of a severe health hazard, given the severe – but also unknown – consequences this can have for human health and life. The quick unblinding of control groups by *Pfizer* and *Moderna* during the Covid-19-PHEIC[161] made it impossible to ever establish the safety and effectiveness of the EUL vaccines against Covid-19. This is an unfortunate reality given the numerous severe adverse events connected to these products recorded[162] and documented in emerging scientific literature.[163]

---

[160] Above (n 44).

[161] See WHO, 'Covid-19 Vaccine Trial Designs in the Context of Authorized Covid-19 Vaccines and Expanding Global Access: Ethical Considerations' (29 November 2021) https://iris.who.int/bitstream/handle/10665/349693/WHO-2019-nCoV-Policy-brief-Vaccine-trial-design-2021.1-eng.pdf.

[162] At the time of writing in late August 2024, concerning all Covid-19 vaccines, VAERS records 1,644,278 adverse event reports (https://openvaers.com/covid-data accessed 26 August 2024) and *EudraVigilance* records 2,295,557 reports (https://impfnebenwirkungen.net/ema/tabellen/ (accessed 26 August 2024).

[163] Among many, eg Joseph Fraiman et al, 'Serious Adverse Events of Special Interest Following mRNA COVID-19 Vaccination in Randomized Trials in Adults' (2022) 40 Vaccine 5798; K Faksova et al, 'Covid-19 Vaccines and Adverse Events of Special Interest: A Multinational Global Vaccine Data Network (GVDN) Cohort Study of 99 Million Vaccinated Individuals' (2024) 42 Vaccine 2200; Peter Parry et al, '"Spikeopathy" Covid-19 Spike Protein is Pathogenic, from both Virus and Vaccine mRNA' (2023) 11(8) Biomedicines 2287; Stephanie Seneff et al, 'Innate Immune Suppression by SARS-CoV-2 mRNA Vaccinations: The Role of G-quadruplexes, Exosomes, and MicroRNAs' (2022) 164 Food and Chemical Toxicology 113008; Peter Rhodes and Peter Parry, 'Gene-Based Covid-19 Vaccines: Australian Perspectives in a Corporate and Global Context' (2024) 253 Pathology – Research and Practice 155030; Gianmarco Stati et al, 'Concern about the Effectiveness of mRNA Vaccination Technology and its Long-Term Safety: Potential Interference on miRNA Machinery' (2023) 24(2) International Journal of Molecular Sciences 1404; Fadi Nahab et al, 'Factors Associated with Stroke after Covid-19 Vaccination: A Statewide Analysis' (2023) 14 Frontiers in Neurology 1199745; Raquel Angues and Yolanda Bustos, 'SARS-CoV-2 Vaccination and the Multi-Hit Hypothesis of Oncogenesis' (2023) 14(12) Cureus e50703; Miki Gibo et al, 'Increased Age-Adjusted Cancer Mortality after the Third mRNA-Lipid Nanoparticles Vaccine Dose during the Covid-19 Pandemic in Japan' (2024) 16(4) Cureus e57860; Vladimir Uversky et al, 'IgG4 Antibodies Induced by Repeated Vaccination May Generate Immune Tolerance to the SARS-CoV-2 Spike Protein' (2023) 11 Vaccine 991; and Dimitrios Bitounis et al, 'Strategies to Reduce the Risks of mRNA Drug and Vaccine Toxicity' (2024) 23(4) Nature Reviews Drug Discovery 281.

The EUL procedure should exclude such practice for the future, and the WHO must not disregard its own regulations.

The difficulty of recording and tracking adverse events caused by EUL vaccines in low-resource settings might also be one of the reasons why COVAX's high-profile campaign titled 'No-Fault Compensation Program'[164] was unsuccessful. The programme was established to compensate eligible injured individuals who experienced serious adverse events from the 2 billion EUL vaccine doses against Covid-19 delivered in 146 countries.[165] However, as of 31 May 2024, only 16 persons received compensation through the COVAX claims initiative.[166]

3.3 Ensuring Access to Reliable Health Information

It is the WHO's responsibility for the HRH not to undermine States' abilities to comply with their human rights duties to ensure individuals' right to 'seek, receive and impart information and ideas concerning health issues'[167] by recommending EUL vaccines without giving full information about their experimental character and the limited data available on their efficacy and safety, but instead promoting and advertising them as 'safe and effective' and fit for the widest possible global administration.

The UN Special Rapporteur on the HRH noted that the right to access safe and effective medical products of good quality includes a right to access available clinical trial data, including negative results.[168] This can be achieved through public trial registries and regular results reporting.[169] Though there has been fierce resistance by the pharmaceutical industry against such public registries and results reporting, invoking the confidentiality of commercial data and patents,[170] stifling inter alia WHO initiatives in this area,[171] it

164 COVAX AMC (2021) https://covaxclaims.com.

165 UNICEF, 'COVAX Information Centre' (*UNICEF*, 2023) https://www.unicef.org/coronavirus/covax.

166 COVAX No-Fault Compensation Programme, 'Application and Claims Data' (31 May 2024) https://covaxclaims.com/wp-content/uploads/2024/02/COVAX-Compensation-Program-Data.pdf.

167 CESCR, 'General Comment 14' (n 21), para 12(b); and Diaz and Vasquez (n 156) 3.

168 UN Special Rapporteur on HRH, 'Access to Medicines' (n 119), para 63.

169 ibid; and Lemmens and Helfer (n 157).

170 For a comprehensive refutation of such arguments, eg Lemmens and Helfer (n 157) 81–9.

171 WHO, 'International Clinical Trial Registry Platform' https://www.who.int/clinical-trials-registry-platform; and Lemmens and Helfer (n 157) 75–7.

is clear that only public availability of clinical trial data can ensure rigorous and independent scrutiny by scientists and medical professionals. This contributes to enhanced evaluation of the safety and efficacy of medical products, to protecting individuals from potential harm and, overall, to improving evidence-informed medicine.[172] This appears particularly important against the background of the well-documented, serious problems with (even regular) clinical trials – ranging from their biased design, organisation, and analysis, to data that is reported through manipulative publication practices in academic journals – resulting in misleading understandings of the efficacy and safety of many medical products.[173] The WHO's responsibility for the HRH to access health information by publishing trial data and regularly reporting results from ongoing clinical trials involving EUL vaccines (the use of which it recommends to address a PHEIC) is even more stringent than concerning fully tested and fully licensed medical products. This stringency is due to the experimental character and unknown safety and efficacy profile of these EUL vaccines. In addition, decisions, the terms of the EULs, reasons why they were granted, and discussions of WHO expert committees concerning EUL vaccines must be published in their entirety. Publication will permit scientists and medical professionals beyond the narrow WHO expert groups appointed by the Director-General to scrutinise the data, to alert to emerging safety concerns, and, not least, to enable medical professionals and individuals to make fully informed decisions about their reasonable use in the circumstances of the world facing a severe health hazard.

Moreover, it can be noted that the WHO's responsibility not to undermine States' abilities to comply with their duties flowing from the right to access health information includes a negative responsibility to 'refrain from … censoring, withholding or intentionally mis-representing health-related information'.[174] Advertising and promoting EUL vaccines as 'safe and effective' during the Covid-19-PHEIC appears highly problematic in light of this responsibility. And, though space constraints do not permit examination of this in detail, the WHO's infodemic programme appears incompatible with these responsibilities for the HRH.[175]

---

172 Lemmens and Helfer (n 157) 89.

173 ibid, 92–93; Katherine Fierlbeck et al (eds), *Transparency, Power and the Pharmaceutical Industry* (2021 University of Toronto Press); and Peter Gotzsche, *Deadly Medicines and Organised Crime: How Big Pharma Has Corrupted Health Care* (Radcliffe Publishing 2013).

174 CESCR, 'General Comment 14' (n 21), para 34; and Diaz and Vasquez (n 156) 3.

175 See above text accompanying (nn 85–99).

3.4 Upholding Free and Informed Consent

The UN Special Rapporteur on the HRH highlights: 'reliable information about medicines must be accessible to patients and health professionals so they can take well-informed decisions and use medicines safely'.[176] This draws a clear connection between the right to seek, receive, and impart health-related information and the right not to be subjected to medical treatment or medical or scientific experimentation without free and informed consent. The WHO has a stringent responsibility not to encourage States – for example, by recommending the indiscriminate administration of investigational EUL vaccines to an increasing percentage of all countries' populations[177] – to violate *their* respective highly stringent human rights duties owed to the people under the respective States' jurisdiction to respect, protect, and fulfil these elements of the HRH as well as the prohibition of torture or inhuman or degrading treatment. The stringency of these State duties and WHO responsibilities flow from the fact that these rights form part of the absolute minimum core of the HRH: the right not to be subjected to non-consensual medical or scientific experimentation is an absolute right that can neither be limited nor derogated from,[178] and the right not to be subjected to medical treatment without free and informed consent can be restricted in strictly limited circumstances only.[179] The IHR also reiterates in articles 23(3) and (4) that no vaccinations (or other health measure) 'shall be carried out on travellers without their prior express informed consent' and that they shall be 'informed of any risk associated with vaccination or with non-vaccination'.[180]

---

176 UN Special Rapporteur on HRH, 'Access to Medicines' (n 119), para 49.

177 Above (n 35).

178 See ICCPR, article 7 read in conjunction with ICCPR, article 4; HRCttee, 'General Comment No 29: States of Emergency' (31 August 2001) UN Doc CCPR/C/21/Rev.1/Add.11, para 7; and HRCttee, 'Concluding Observations – USA' (18 December 2006) UN Doc CCPR/C/USA/CO/3/Rev.1, para 31.

179 Summarised by the HRCttee: 'non-consensual … treatment may only be applied, if at all, in exceptional cases as a measure of last resort where absolutely necessary for the benefit of the person concerned, provided that he or she is unable to give consent, and for the shortest possible time without any long-term impact and under independent review' in, 'Concluding Observations – USA' (23 April 2014) UN Doc CCPR/C/USA/4, para 18.

180 Note that even though IHR (2024), article 31(2) appears on first sight to provide an exception to this rule, and permit 'compelling' travellers to undergo vaccinations if they do not consent, article 23(3) highlights that article 31(2) still must be applied 'in accordance with … international obligations of the State Party'. This includes the stringent obligations under IHRL not to subject individuals

Free and informed consent can only be given after individuals have been informed objectively about the purpose and nature of a medical procedure, its benefits, risks, and adverse effects, about reasonable alternatives, and what will happen if the treatment is not carried out.[181] This must be done without any coercion, deception, inducement, or exerting any kind of other pressure.[182] When participating in medical experiments, the information process must be a continuous one, ie participants must continuously receive information about new risks, possible negative consequences, and uncertainties,[183] and consent must be given in writing.[184] Free consent also includes the right to refuse medical treatment or participation in medical experiments[185] and to withdraw consent at any time.[186]

Thus, if the WHO decides to recommend the (global) administration of an EUL vaccine, it must explicitly inform people about the experimental character

---

to medical treatment or medical or scientific experimentation without free and informed consent.

[181] Convention on Human Rights and Biomedicine (adopted 4 April 1997, entered into force 1 December 1999) ETS 164 (1997) (Oviedo Convention), article 5; and the Explanatory Report to the Oviedo Convention, para 35 https://rm.coe.int/1680a8e4d0; UNESCO Universal Declaration on Bioethics and Human Rights (2005), article 6 https://unesdoc.unesco.org/ark:/48223/pf0000146180; CESCR, 'General Comment No 25: On Science and Economic, Social and Cultural Rights' (30 April 2020) UN Doc E/C.12/GC/25, para 71; CEDAW, 'Views: Communication No 4/2004' (*AS v Hungary*) (29 August 2006) UN Doc CEDAW/C/36/D/4/2004, para 11.3; and UN Special Rapporteur on HRH, 'Informed Consent' (n 154), para 15.

[182] Eg Nuremberg Code (1947), principle 1; article 5 Oviedo Convention and Explanatory Report (n 181), para 35; UNESCO Declaration (n 181), article 15(2); UN Special Rapporteur on HRH, 'Informed Consent' (n 154), paras 13 and 36; CESCR, 'General Comment No 22: Right to Sexual and Reproductive Health' (2 May 2016) UN Doc E/C.12/GC/22 para 58; CEDAW, *AS v Hungary* (n 181), para 11.3.

[183] Additional Protocol to Oviedo Convention, concerning Biomedical Research (adopted 25 January 2005, entered into force 1 September 2007) CETS 195 (2005), article 24; UN Special Rapporteur on HR, 'Informed Consent' (n 154), para 35.

[184] Oviedo Convention, article 16(v); UNESCO Declaration (n 181), article 6(2); and UN Special Rapporteur on HRH, 'Informed Consent' (n 154), para 35.

[185] Oviedo Convention, article 5; UNESCO Declaration (n 181), articles 6(1) and (2); CESCR, 'General Comment 25' (n 181), para 44; UN Special Rapporteur on HRH, 'Informed Consent' (n 154), para 28; and John Tasioulas and Effy Vayena, 'Getting Human Rights Right in Global Health' (2015) 385 (9978) Lancet 42, 42, referring to a human right not to participate in medical experiments.

[186] Article 16(v) Oviedo Convention and Explanatory Report (n 181), para 38; and UN Special Rapporteur on HRH, 'Informed Consent' (n 154), para 35.

of this product, highlight that clinical studies on the effectiveness and safety are ongoing, and that, consequently, the safety of and short- and long-term risks to health and life involved with taking these products are unknown. If such information – in constantly updated form – is not provided to both healthcare professionals and patients, no free and fully informed consent to such vaccinations can be given. During the Covid-19-PHEIC, by advertising the EUL vaccines as safe and effective, not informing about their experimental character and their unknown risk profile (as well as incoming reports about severe adverse effects), and by stifling open scientific debate about a global vaccination campaign with experimental products through its infodemic management programme, the WHO arguably violated its responsibilities for the HRH. By recommending EUL vaccines and certificates of vaccinations for international travel, and by promoting nudging and other techniques informed by behavioural science aimed at generating acceptance of and demand for EUL vaccines, the WHO supports and continues to support States in exerting indirect coercion on individuals to take investigational medical products.

In no case can the WHO recommend making EUL vaccines – or even fully licensed vaccines – mandatory; that is, recommend administration by direct or indirect coercion, given the high stringency of its responsibilities not to undermine States' compliance with their human rights duties not to subject individuals to medical treatment, or medical or scientific experiments, without their free and informed consent. In fact, during the Covid-19-PHEIC, when numerous States made experimental EUL vaccines mandatory or indirectly coerced people into taking them, the WHO should have issued clear statements that this amounts to a violation of both the IHR and States' stringent human rights duties.

4. CONCLUDING REMARKS

The chapter examined the most prominent medical countermeasure – emergency listed vaccines – that are regularly recommended by the WHO to address PHEICs. This is a medical countermeasure preferred by the GHS doctrine that dominates WHO law, programmes and institutions in the area of pandemic preparedness, prevention and response, and has been further ingrained into the revised IHR (2024). At the centre of promoting this prominent medical countermeasure is the WHO's EUL procedure through which the WHO issues de facto global emergency authorisations for unlicensed vaccines, enabling their global procurement by UN agencies, the WHO's PPPs, and Member States, and their administration to the (global) population. The analysis revealed that the EUL procedure, in its current form, is hardly compatible with the WHO's obligations under the IHR – including those under the revised IHR (2024) – and its responsibilities for human rights, in particular for the HRH but also for other human rights such as the right to life and the right not to be subjected to torture or inhumane or degrading treatment.

The chapter would therefore like to end with a call on all WHO Member States as well as on the WHO, its Director-General, its Secretariat, and its expert committees to meticulously review the EUL procedure as well as the WHO's practice to recommend investigational EUL vaccines for global administration as 'safe and effective' countermeasures to a WHO-declared PHEIC, for their compliance with the relevant legal requirements. As they constitute a strong interference with various aspects of the HRH and other human rights, they can be justified only if their concise legal basis, their legitimate aim, and their proportionality – their effectiveness and suitability, their compliance with the 'least restrictive means test', and their proportionality *stricto sensu* – are guaranteed. Other components of the WHO law and regulation, policies, and institutions adopted and built to prepare for, prevent, and respond to future PHEICs – among them the R&D Blueprint Programme, the WHO global biomedical surveillance programmes, the Infodemic Management Programme, etc – must also be carefully analysed for their compatibility with the WHO's obligations under the IHR and its responsibilities for human rights.

Last but not least, State duties under IHRL to ensure access to effective remedies for any individual whose rights may have been violated by WHO-recommended emergency measures, as well as the WHO's responsibilities for ensuring such access, deserve more attention in future research and the design of WHO programmes on the prevention, preparedness, and response to PHEICs.

4. The authority of the system of global health governance

David McGrogan

1. INTRODUCTION

The incorporation of the aims and methodology of global health security into the work of the World Health Organization (WHO) since 2005 makes it appropriate to describe a system of 'global health governance' as having emerged.[1] This is because what has come into being represents, to use Rosenau's definition of 'global governance', a 'system of rule' within which 'the pursuit of goals through the exercise of control has transnational repercussions'.[2] In short, the WHO, chiefly through the operationalisation of the doctrine of global health security through repeated amendments to the International Health Regulations (IHR),[3] now aims to 'fundamentally improve global public health protection

[1] On global health security, see Michael Baker and Andrew Forsyth, 'The New International Health Regulations: A Revolutionary Change in Global Health Security' (2007) 120 New Zealand Medical Journal 1267; Lorna Weir, 'Inventing Global Health Security, 1994–2005' in Simon Rushton and Jeremy Younde (eds), *The Routledge Handbook of Global Health Security* (Routledge 2014) 18. On 'global health governance' see Lawrence Gostin et al, 'Reimagining Global Health Governance in the Age of COVID-19' (2020) 110 (11) American Journal of Public Health 1615.

[2] James Rosenau, 'Governance in the Twenty-First Century' (1995) 1 Global Governance 13, 13.

[3] International Health Regulations (2005) (adopted 23 May 2005, entered into force 15 June 2007) 2509 UNTS 79 (IHR (2005)). The IHR were amended most recently in May 2024 with the adoption of Res 77.17 by the 77th World Health Assembly: WHA Res 77.17 (1 June 2024) UN Doc WHA77.17, annex 'Amendments to the International Health Regulations (2005)' (IHR (2024)). The amendments are due to come into effect in September 2025. The following analysis refers to the amended IHR (2024).

and help create a more equal, just and resilient world'.[4] This requires it, necessarily, to *govern*: it must purposefully achieve objectives through the '"control" or influence' of others – chiefly, State Parties to the WHO Agreements.[5]

This makes it important to examine the basis for the *authority* which this system of global health governance seeks to exert. This is for the obvious reason that authority lies at the heart of the subject of government. As the Council of the Club of Rome put it long ago, 'governance' denotes a 'command' mechanism.[6] Even if a less severe word is used – such as 'control' or 'steering'[7] – the principle is the same; to govern, somebody must frame goals, issue directives, and pursue policies.[8] And somebody else must follow them. This implies a relationship of authority between the former over the latter. And since the system of global health governance seeks to exert authority in this sense (over States, and ultimately therefore over populations), an inquiry into the basis of its authority becomes necessary.

This chapter sets out such an inquiry. It suggests that the justification for exercising authority upon which the system of global health governance relies is strongly reminiscent of what Alexandre Kojève referred to as the 'Aristotelian' theory. The system stakes its claim to govern on the basis of being able to anticipate the future – chiefly, future threats, but also of course the potential for a 'more equal, just and resilient world' – and having the capacity to indeed act upon the future by literally, as it were, 'projecting' a project.[9] The chapter shows that, while Kojève's remarks on the subject are brief, they are thought-provoking and insightful, and help us to understand something important about the way in which global health governance, as it were, 'governs'. This is that, when the authority of governing (ie the authority upon which mechanisms of 'command', 'control', or 'steering' rest) justifies itself in 'Aristotelian' terms, it necessarily takes on three inferred characteristics. The first of these is that the possessor of authority must be capable to 'lead' from its position of clear-sightedness and expertise – its operating modality must be the issuing of commands or orders to those subject to it in the interests of a particular project,

4 WHO, 'Report of Review Committee regarding Amendments to the International Health Regulations (2005)' UN Doc A/WGIHR/2/5 (6 February 2023) 6.

5 Lawrence Finkelstein, 'What Is Global Governance?' (1995) 1 Global Governance 367, 368.

6 Alexander King and Bertrand Schneider, *The First Global Revolution – A Report by the Council of the Club of Rome* (Pantheon 1991) 181.

7 Rosenau (n 2) 14.

8 ibid.

9 Alexandre Kojève, *The Notion of Authority: A Brief Presentation* (François Terré (ed) and Hager-Weslati (translator), Verso 2014) 19.

unfettered by other concerns. The second is that the possessor of authority must lay an exclusive claim to be 'clear-sighted', and therefore relies on the understanding that those who are governed are 'blind'. And the third is that it must position itself as transcending, and coordinating, an otherwise undifferentiated group of equals – it relies not on the existence of a pre-existing or natural hierarchy, but on its having the capacity to marshal and corral others derived precisely from its 'clear-sightedness'.[10]

This, the chapter shows, has corresponding consequences that are readily apparent in the manner in which the system of global health governance operates, and which make it highly apposite to analyse that system's justification of its authority in 'Aristotelian' terms. Such an approach, as we shall see, has considerable explanatory power in helping us to understand why the system has taken the form which it has. But it also allows us to raise a fundamental question lying at the heart of the effort to govern global health, and through doing so expose the system itself to critique: to what extent is the governance of global health as it is currently constituted necessary to 'fundamentally improve global public health protection', and to what extent does the manner in which it currently operates merely reflect and derive from the basis on which its authority is purportedly justified? In asking this question, new avenues for investigation are revealed.

Section 2 of this chapter describes the emergence of a framework of global health governance, and Section 3 observes in particular certain salient features of that framework's mode of operation. Sections 4 and 5 provide an analysis of the form of authority that is implied by this framework, drawing on Kojève's writings, and Section 6 makes the case that this helps us to reveal a critique that, in problematising the way in which the system of global health governance justifies its own authority, opens up possibilities for reimagining how it indeed 'governs'. The chapter closes with some brief concluding reflections.

2. THE SYSTEM OF GLOBAL HEALTH GOVERNANCE

The emergence of a system of global health governance has taken place fairly rapidly within the last 20 years. Although the WHO has been in existence since 1948, and although there were international legal instruments designed to prevent the spread of disease prior to its formation,[11] it is only after the 2005 revisions to the IHR entered into force in 2007 that it might be said that

[10] ibid.

[11] Gian Luca Burci, 'Health and Infectious Disease' in Thomas Weiss and Sam Daws (eds), *The Oxford Handbook of the United Nations* (OUP 2007) 582, 583.

a system for *governing* 'global health security' came into being – with governance here being understood, as we have seen, as a 'system of rule' for 'the pursuit of goals through the exercise of control'. At that time, what took place was a transformation from what would more aptly be described as a system of rules (which had originally been called the International Sanitary Regulations) providing for the restriction of transport and sharing of information in respect of a short list of defined diseases, to a comprehensive 'all hazards' framework designed to achieve 'global health security' through global action coordinated by the WHO as a central authority.[12]

This framework is aptly referred to as one of 'governance' in the sense outlined above for two reasons. The first is its establishment of a 'crucial governance activity'[13] – the power which the Director-General of the WHO is granted by the IHR (2024) to declare a public health emergency of international concern (PHEIC).[14] Although this power only results, strictly speaking, in the making of 'temporary' or 'standing' recommendations, it relies upon a system of mandatory requirements that can be properly said to represent a mechanism of control. These include the establishment of National IHR Focal Points (NFPs) in each jurisdiction which are 'at all times' accessible to communicate with designated WHO IHR Contact Points[15] so as to establish a system of 'surveillance' by which to notify the WHO of any events that may constitute a PHEIC.[16] And they also include the maintenance of certain 'core capacities' so as to 'respond promptly and effectively' to inter alia a PHEIC,[17] which are designed to ensure that PHEICs can be detected promptly and responded to rapidly in terms chiefly of 'prevent[ing] … spread'.[18] The result is a globally coordinated mechanism through which 'events' are detected by national surveillance systems, analysed accordingly, and then communicated to the WHO itself for a decision on whether to declare the existence of a PHEIC; and through which a security response comes into being so as to isolate and limit the event in question.

---

12 Lawrence Gostin and Rebecca Katz, 'The International Health Regulations: The Governing Framework for Global Health Security' (2016) 94(2) Milbank Quarterly 264. On the 'securitisation' of global health governance see also the introduction to this volume.

13 Lawrence Gostin, Mary DeBartolo, and Eric Friedman, 'The International Health Regulations 10 Years On: The Governing Framework for Global Health Security' (2015) 386 Lancet 2222, 2222.

14 IHR (2024), article 12.

15 IHR (2024), article 4.

16 IHR (2024), articles 5 and 6.

17 IHR (2024), article 13.

18 IHR (2024), annex 1A, 6(a).

And the second reason why it is apt to refer to this framework as a system of governance is of course that it is designed to achieve a specific goal – ie 'the goal of [universal] protection of all people of the world from the international spread of disease' and thereby 'fundamentally improve global public health protection'.[19] The system exerts control, in other words, purposively to achieve objectives. And it does so in light of a particular overarching ideal, which is, as we have seen, that 'a more equal, just and resilient world' can be created by the global elimination of threats to public health, achieved through centralised, coordinated, and planned security responses. This is evident throughout the material produced by the WHO itself, and is frequently expressed in speeches, press releases and so on – the two most recent, at the time of writing, being the Director-General's closing remarks at the 'signature event' of the WHO Investment Round for 2024, in which the threats of 'pandemics … noncommunicable diseases … antimicrobial resistance [and] health impacts of climate change' were described as requiring the existence of 'a clear plan' from the WHO,[20] and his opening remarks at the launch of the Global Preparedness Monitoring Board, on the very same day, in which he emphasised 'constant preparedness' through coordination by the WHO.[21]

It is appropriate, then, to say that since 2007 a global 'system of rule' has emerged for achieving the goal of the 'protection of all people of the world from the international spread of disease', and that there has thereby come into being a system of global health governance which seeks to exert 'command', 'control' or 'steering' so as to realise that objective. And this, of course, immediately raises the question of how this system of global health security exerts authority. How is it that its efforts to 'command', 'control' or 'steer' find effect and thereby 'structure the behaviour' of those who are its subjects, particularly in light of the fact that accession to the IHR (2024) and the planned

[19] IHR (2024), article 1(3).

[20] Tedros Adhanom Ghebreyesus, 'WHO Director-General's Closing Remarks at the Signature Event on the WHO Investment Round, World Health Summit' (14 October 2024) https://www.who.int/director-general/speeches/detail/who-director-general-s-closing-remarks-at-the-signature-event-on-the-who-investment-round---world-health-summit---14-october-2024. Unless otherwise stated all web links given in this chapter last accessed on 10 December 2024.

[21] Tedros Adhanom Ghebreyesus, 'WHO Director-General's Opening Remarks at the Launch of the Global Preparedness Monitoring Board' (14 October 2024) https://www.who.int/director-general/speeches/detail/who-director-general-s-opening-remarks-at-the-launch-of-the-global-preparedness-monitoring-board---14-october-2024.

WHO Agreement on Pandemic Prevention, Preparedness, and Response[22] is itself voluntary, and there is no particular enforcement mechanism to ensure compliance?[23] This question will be addressed concretely in Sections 3 and 4; before that, certain features of that system – particularly as they have found expression in the most recent amendments to the IHR – are important to map out, because they help us to sketch the contours of what follows.

3. THE SYSTEM OF GLOBAL HEALTH GOVERNANCE: SALIENT FEATURES

We have seen, then, that since 2007 a system of global health governance has been created, and we have noted certain elements in its composition. But here the chapter will further identify three salient features of its operations that have become more pronounced through the most recent round of amendments to the IHR,[24] which will come into effect in 2025. These are, first, that the power of the Director-General to declare a PHEIC and to make temporary and standing recommendations is almost unfettered; second, that the 'system' increasingly relies on a claim to be in a position to assess and control what type of information should be communicated in a given circumstance and hence what qualifies as 'expertise'; and, third, that global health governance has come to emphasise a uniform approach to public health threats among State Parties, under a centralised coordinating mechanism. Each of these will now be described in further detail.

First, then, the power to declare a PHEIC, which as we have seen can be called the system's 'crucial governance activity', is exceptionally loosely defined and constrained. Under the IHR (2024) as amended, a State Party is to notify the WHO pursuant to article 6 when its national surveillance system has identified an event involving a list of certain diseases or when the 'decision instrument' (contained in annex 2), essentially a simple algorithm, suggests that an event should be notified. But the circumstances under which

[22] Negotiations of the Pandemic Agreement are ongoing at the time of writing in December 2024. A draft version of the Pandemic Agreement of 24 May 2024 is available: WHA, 'Proposal for the WHO Pandemic Agreement', draft text of 24 May 2024, appendix to the report of the WHO Director-General, 'Outcome of the Intergovernmental Negotiating Body (INB) to Draft and Negotiate a WHO Convention, Agreement or Other International Instrument on Pandemic Prevention, Preparedness and Response' (27 May 2024) UN Doc A77/10.

[23] Michael Zürn, 'From Constitutional Rule to Loosely Coupled Spheres of Liquid Authority: A Reflexive Approach' (2017) 9(2) International Theory 261, 277.

[24] See (n 3).

the algorithm will result in a notification outcome are very wide-ranging – they could include events which are not deemed to have serious consequences for public health, but which are merely 'unusual or unexpected' and likely to spread internationally. And an event deemed to have serious consequences for public health is defined similarly broadly – it might include situations in which 'no or very few human cases have yet been identified' or even simply where cases have been reported 'among health staff'.[25]

The procedure by which a Director-General's power to declare a PHIEC, once notified, is exercised is similarly loosely defined – the Director-General is simply given the discretion to make the determination after convening a meeting of an Emergency Committee by selecting 'a number of experts' from a roster, who are supposed to make a 'brief summary report' after a meeting which may include 'teleconferences, videoconferences or electronic communications'.[26] Perhaps the only clearly defined element of this procedure (apart from the fact that membership of the Committee must be appointed from a roster) is that the State Party within whose territory the event in question is occurring is given the right to nominate 'at least one' expert.[27] And the scope of the response which the Director-General puts into effect is, likewise, very broad – 'temporary recommendations' which may include inter alia quarantine, isolation, contact tracing, requirements to vaccinate, or requirements for medical examinations.[28]

In addition to being very widely defined, this 'crucial governance activity' is also almost unconstrained in its exercise. The Director-General is given effectively sole, and legally untrammelled, discretion to declare a PHEIC, with no possibility for appeal or review. To be sure, this power is to be exercised after an Emergency Committee has 'provide[d] its views',[29] but the Committee itself is composed of experts 'selected by the Director-General', as we have seen, from a roster, with a duration of membership likewise determined by the Director-General, and its meetings are convened under an agenda provided by the Director-General and at dates and times he or she selects.[30] The Director-General is additionally given the power to 'appoint one or more technical experts' to advise the Committee. And, in any event, the Director-General

25 IHR (2024), annex 2.
26 IHR (2024), articles 48 and 49.
27 IHR (2024), article 48(2).
28 IHR (2024), article 18.
29 IHR (2024), article 48(1).
30 IHR (2024), article 49.

may simply ignore the Committee's advice, since he or she makes the 'final determination'.[31]

Moreover, there is no means by which a State Party may dispute such a determination. A postponement of a meeting of an Emergency Committee at the request of the 'State Party concerned' is expressly prohibited,[32] and at best, after a PHEIC has been declared, the State Party in question only has recourse to 'propos[ing] to the Director-General' its termination.[33] Much the same applies with respect not just to the identification of a PHEIC but also the temporary recommendations that are issued. And much the same also applies with respect to the identification and response to a so-called 'pandemic emergency', namely a PHEIC with a high risk of geographical spread, the requirement of 'coordinated international action', and so on.[34]

The result is a governing power that is almost entirely unfettered except in respect of its voluntariness. We have already noted that, in respect of the system of global health governance, compliance – both in the sense of signing the IHR (2024) to begin with, and in the sense of complying with temporary recommendations – is voluntary (and, indeed, since there is no enforcement mechanism in the IHR (2024), there is nothing stopping State Parties from simply refusing to cooperate even with ostensibly mandatory requirements). This is a matter to which we will briefly return in Section 4. For the time being, though, it suffices to note that in its idealised form in which compliance is taken for granted, the system presupposes an exceptionally broad executive function.

The second feature of the system of global health governance that is important to emphasise is its claim to not just possess expertise, but to have the sole power to marshal and deploy it. Obviously, as it is constituted, it can be

---

[31] IHR (2024), article 49(5); see eg the declaration of the first m-pox PHEIC on 23 July 2022 by the WHO Director-General where the m-pox Emergency Committee could not reach consensus that such a PHEIC indeed existed: WHO m-pox Emergency Committee, 'Second meeting of the International Health Regulations (2005) (IHR) Emergency Committee regarding the multi-country outbreak of monkeypox' (23 July 2022) https://www.who.int/news/item/23-07-2022-second-meeting-of-the-international-health-regulations-(2005)-(ihr)-emergency-committee-regarding-the-multi-country-outbreak-of-monkeypox (accessed 1 May 2025).

[32] IHR (2024), article 49(4).

[33] IHR (2024), article 49(7).

[34] IHR (2024), article 1. The concept of 'pandemic emergency' has been introduced by amendments to article 1 IHR adopted in May 2024. It is not yet clear what the legal import of the classification of a 'pandemic emergency' is, and is presumably to be clarified if the WHO Pandemic Agreement (n 22) comes into being.

described readily as an instance of 'government by experts'[35] in the sense that it relies on a claim to possess the competence and knowledge to make assessments regarding risks to global health security and the expertise to make recommendations accordingly.[36] This will be readily apparent in the basic structure of its mode of governance, wherein surveillance by States Parties (itself, of course, informed by technical expertise) reveals 'events' which are then transmitted to the Director-General, advised by the expert Emergency Committee, for resolution.

But also readily apparent is the way in which the IHR (2024) has evolved to centralise control over expertise within the structure of the WHO itself, through the creation of a new 'core capacity' requirement for States Parties regarding 'risk communication' and the addressing of 'misinformation and disinformation' at both local and national levels.[37] While none of these terms are defined in the IHR (2024) itself, their appearance within the latest amendments to the Regulations alludes to the existence of a broader agenda for so-called 'infodemic management' being implemented by the WHO. This stems from a consultation and subsequent conference convened by the Organization under the auspices of a new Information Network for Epidemics (EPI-WIN), which took place over the course of the middle of 2020 and which gave rise to a 'Public Health Research Agenda for Managing Infodemics'.[38] The novel concept of an 'infodemic' is defined as an 'overabundance of information – some accurate and some not – that occurs during an epidemic'[39] and which 'spreads between humans in a similar manner to an epidemic', thereby 'mak[ing] it hard for people to find trustworthy sources and reliable guidance when they need it'.[40] And 'infodemic management', it obviously follows, is the deployment of 'coordinated and integrated methods' to 'manage the flow of information' and thereby 'reorient existing knowledge and expertise towards strategies that

---

35 Eg Stephen Turner, *Liberal Democracy 3.0: Civil Society in an Age of Experts* (Sage 2003).

36 The literature on this form of governance, especially in relation to international organisations, is vast; see eg Andrea Liese et al, 'The Heart of Bureaucratic Power: Explaining International Bureaucracies' Expert Authority' (2021) 47(3) Review of International Studies 353 for a thorough overview.

37 IHR (2024), annex 1A, articles 2(c) and (2)(v) and article 3(i).

38 WHO, 'WHO Public Health Research Agenda for Managing Infodemics' (*WHO*, 2 February 2021) https://iris.who.int/bitstream/handle/10665/339192/9789240019508-eng.pdf?sequence=1.

39 ibid, 1.

40 ibid.

result in positive health-seeking or self-protective behaviours in individuals and communities'.[41]

The result has been a series of policy statements and initiatives asserting the importance of a 'health authority-led infodemic management strategy', most notably – for obvious reasons – in relation to Covid-19,[42] but increasingly in general terms as a way of elaborating on the content of the IHR themselves vis-à-vis the 'risk communication' core capacity. These include training modules and instruction manuals,[43] and a taxonomy for 'social listening' to allow analysts to 'monitor and report narrative[s]' among the population based on different 'topics of conversation'.[44] And the link between infodemic management and the 'risk communication' core capacity is becoming more evident; recent training materials on 'Preparedness and Resilience for Emerging Threats'[45] designed for use by 'cross-sectoral stakeholders … involved in preparedness and response planning for respiratory pathogen pandemics',[46] make it abundantly clear that 'risk communication' indeed requires 'infodemic management' so as to 'ensure that scientific knowledge is synthesized, shared and applied by communities, decision makers, and other stakeholders in a way that is accessible, understandable and meaningful to everyone'.[47] What emerges is a vision of the WHO's role as being, in part, to coordinate and implement that vision in the interests of its broader goals and objectives, and channelled through the legal instrument of the IHR (2024). And this is in turn of course suggestive of a form of government which functions not through merely possessing its own expertise but precisely through being the overarching means

---

41 ibid, 3–4.

42 WHO, 'COVID-19 Infodemic Management' (14 September 2022) https://iris.who.int/bitstream/handle/10665/362668/WHO-2019-nCoV-Policy-Brief-Infodemic-2022.1-eng.pdf?sequence=1.

43 See eg, WHO, 'How to Build an Infodemic Insights Report in Six Steps' (2023) https://www.who.int/publications/i/item/9789240075658.

44 WHO, 'Public Health Taxonomy for Social Listening on Respiratory Pathogens' (2023) 4 https://iris.who.int/bitstream/handle/10665/373534/9789240081017-eng.pdf?sequence=1&isAllowed=y. For a list of initiatives, see WHO, 'New Infodemic Management Tools to Support Pandemic Planning and Preparedness for Pandemic Influenza and Respiratory Pathogen Disease Events' (25 October 2023) https://www.who.int/news/item/25-10-2023-new-infodemic-management-tools-to-support-pandemic-planning-and-preparedness-for-pandemic-influenza-and-respiratory-pathogen-disease-events.

45 WHO, 'Preparedness and Resilience for Emerging Threats – Module 1: Planning for Respiratory Pathogen Pandemics' (2023) https://iris.who.int/bitstream/handle/10665/376312/9789240084674-eng.pdf?sequence=1.

46 ibid, xi.

47 ibid, 40–1.

through which expertise is identified, sanctioned, and marshalled so as to realise outcomes – and which functions, indeed, through a claim to have the sole capacity to oversee that process.

The third salient feature of the system of global health governance is that it presents itself as a transcendent coordinating power which ensures that the mass of States Parties acts in unison – or at least in very similar ways. We have already noted that the system relies on a surveillance and notification model, wherein IHR NFPs notify events to the WHO itself for a determination as to whether a PHIEC exists. This, naturally, has resulted in attempts made by the WHO itself to direct and standardise the work of the NFPs, even to the extent of drawing up a 'toolkit' for implementation in legislation.[48] But the most recent IHR (2024) amendments cement considerably the extent to which the WHO coordinates the activities of States Parties, not merely at the level of surveillance but at the level of implementation of the IHR (2024) *tout court*. The Regulations as amended require not just the creation of IHR NFPs but also National IHR Authorities – separate institutions whose role is to 'coordinate the implementation of [the IHR] within the jurisdiction of the State Party'.[49] And while the detail of how these new National IHR Authorities will function is not yet clear at the time of writing, it is apparent that their existence is designed to ensure that implementation of the IHR (2024) is 'more uniform across all State Parties'.[50] This is suggestive, obviously, of a strengthened role for the WHO itself in determining how core capacities are to find expression in domestic legislation and policy, and would appear to be a response to World Health Assembly (WHA) Resolution WHA74.7 of 2021.[51] This Resolution was made in response to a report by an IHR Review Committee, convened by the Director-General on 'Strengthening Preparedness for Health Emergencies',[52]

---

48 WHO, 'International Health Regulations – Toolkit for Implementation in National Legislation: The National IHR Focal Point' (2009) https://cdn.who.int/media/docs/default-source/documents/emergencies/ihr-toolkit-for-implementation-in-national-legislation3cceba0c-4580-48a4-9d4e-2b17a2146b66.pdf?sfvrsn=60aea14d_1&download=true.

49 IHR (2024), article 4.

50 Department of Health and Social Care, 'Letter from Andrew Gwynne MP, Parliamentary Under-Secretary of State for Public Health and Protection, to the Rt Hon the Lord Goldsmith KC, Chair of the House of Lords International Agreements Committee dated 31 October 2024' (*Parliament.uk*, 2024) https://committees.parliament.uk/publications/45570/documents/225518/default/.

51 WHA Res 74.7 (31 May 2021) UN Doc WHA74.7.

52 WHO, 'Strengthening Preparedness for Health Emergencies: Implementation of the International Health Regulations (2005)' (5 May 2021) UN Doc A74//9 Add.1.

one of whose chief findings was that '[the IHR] could be more relevant [*sic*] by providing guidance for the coordination of national and international response measures, beyond issuing temporary recommendations'.[53] The report's first 'key message' was that '[l]ack of compliance of States Parties with certain obligations under the IHR, particularly on preparedness, contributed to the COVID-19 pandemic becoming a protracted global health emergency'.[54] And this fed into the text of Resolution WHA74.7 itself, which begins by reaffirming the WHO's role as 'the directing and coordinating authority on international health work';[55] further acknowledges the 'key leadership role of WHO within the United Nations system in preparing for and in catalysing and coordinating a comprehensive, early, effective, transparent, sustainable response to health emergencies';[56] and then calls on the Director-General to 'strengthen' the pandemic preparedness system particularly through 'support[ing] implementation by States Parties of the [IHR]', and especially with respect to core capacities.[57] The implication is that a 'key learning [*sic*]'[58] from the Covid-19 period was that the WHO itself must take a more active role in ensuring that core capacities are realised within States Parties.

In summary, then, the system of global health governance operates in a complex fashion, but it is nonetheless possible to identify within it the three features just described. The first of these is that its power of command, or 'control' or 'steering', is largely unfettered at least in formal terms, and that it can be exercised to cover an extremely wide remit. The second is that the system presents itself not just as possessing expertise but as possessing the sole, supreme capacity to determine how expertise is gathered and deployed. And the third is that it relies on an understanding of its role as being that of coordinating the activities of an otherwise uncoordinated group of agents (ie the States Parties). These characteristics, as will now be shown, help us to better analyse the basis of the authority which the system seeks to exert, and, in due course, will be shown to also help us problematise its structure.

4. THE NATURE OF THE AUTHORITY OF GLOBAL HEALTH GOVERNANCE

Authority is a comparatively new subject of interest amongst international lawyers, since the notion of international institutions possessing 'authority'

53 ibid, 48.
54 ibid, 60.
55 WHA (n 51) 21.
56 ibid, 22.
57 ibid, 29.
58 Department of Health and Social Care (n 50).

is a recent development in historical terms.[59] And it has become the subject of intense debate, stemming from the fact that there appears to be something genuinely novel or different about the way in which authority is exercised in the international sphere versus how it might be understood as operating in the domestic context.[60] This is because, if authority is exercised at all in respect of global governance, then it is exercised in a dispersed, disorganised, and frequently informal 'bricolage'[61] of international governance mechanisms that have emerged particularly since the end of the Cold War, rather than in the form of a central organising body. Any theory of the way in which authority operates in this realm must, then, it is commonly assumed, be able to account for its 'liquidity' and for the fact that it encompasses, within the rubric of both the governing and the governed, such a range of different actors, organisations, and circumstances.[62]

Here, licence is taken to analyse the matter in an entirely different way, by drawing on the thought of Alexandre Kojève, which has been entirely absent from these discussions.[63] Kojève's writing on authority is highly abstract and the result is admitted oversimplification. But approaching the matter of authority in global governance through a reading of his work nonetheless helps us to identify important overarching themes that can be lost when examining the topic in concrete detail, and which – as we shall see later – allow us to think about the subject in a fresh and useful way. Here, then, with Kojève the analysis places emphasis on authority in the phenomenological sense, meaning the

---

[59] Obviously, authority is one of the oldest concepts in political philosophy and has been endlessly discussed; see eg Richard Friedman, 'On the Concept of Authority in Political Philosophy', in Joseph Raz (ed), *Authority* (NYU Press 1990) 56.

[60] See eg, Ole Jacob Sending, *The Politics of Expertise: Competing for Authority in Global Governance* (University of Michigan Press 2015); Frank Biermann and Rakhyun Kim (eds), *Architectures of Earth System Governance: Institutional Complexity and Structural Transformation* (CUP 2020); and Michael Barnett and Martha Finnemore, *Rules for the World: International Organisations in Global Politics* (Cornell University Press 2004).

[61] Philip Cerny, *Rethinking World Politics: A Theory of Transnational Neopluralism* (OUP 2010) 179.

[62] Eg Michael Zürn, *A Theory of Global Governance: Authority, Legitimacy and Contestation* (OUP 2018); David Lake, 'Rightful Rules: Authority, Order and the Foundations of Global Governance' (2010) 5(3) International Studies Quarterly 587; Nico Krisch, 'Liquid Authority in Global Governance' (2017) 9(2) International Theory 237; and Oren Perez, 'Transnational Networked Authority' (2022) 35 Leiden Journal of International Law 265.

[63] This is likely for the good reason that Kojève's writings on authority were not published until after his death and were not translated into English until 2014.

way in which it appears to those subject to it – not in the interests of providing a thoroughgoing and systematic theory of its operation, but so as to capture its essential features in respect of the way in which the system of global health governance justifies its own exercise of governing. It goes without saying that 'the system' is by no means monolithic, and has come into being under a range of pressures and incentives. But, as we shall see, to speak of the authority of 'the system' as such, in this phenomenological sense, provides insights.

Kojève defines 'authority' as the 'possibility that an agent has of acting on others … without those others reacting against him, despite being capable to do so' – or, alternatively, the possibility of acting without having to make compromises.[64] It is a relationship in which one agent, who possesses authority, is able to order or command others, who do not – and in which those other agents consciously and voluntarily obey.[65] The moment that force or coercion intrudes into the relationship, the necessary implication is that those who are subject to the order or command in question are resisting – which means in turn that no authority is being exerted over them.[66] And, likewise, the moment that a purported authority enters into a discussion or negotiation, it is therefore persuading or making compromises – which is to say it is not exerting authority at all.[67]

The fact that authority is relational, and that it definitionally requires both the absence of force or coercion and also the absence of compromise or persuasion, means that it is always contingent on being obeyed. The moment it ceases to be obeyed, it disappears. And this in turn means that it is always, implicitly, forced to provide a continual justification for why it should be unquestioningly obeyed – '[e]very authority raises the question of knowing *why* it exists, that is to say, *why* it is "recognised" by people submitting to acts that ensue from it without reacting against them'.[68] This means that authority must always have a '"cause", a "reason" or a "justification" for its existence';[69] if it at any point comes to lack such a justification, then people will, naturally, cease to voluntarily obey it.[70]

64 Kojève (n 9) 8–9. Kojève was well known for his eccentric deployment of italics and capitalisations. In order to avoid confusion, unless otherwise noted, these have not been replicated in the main body of the text of this chapter.

65 ibid, 8.

66 ibid, 10.

67 ibid, 8–9.

68 ibid, 14 (emphasis in original).

69 ibid, 13.

70 This puts Kojève in opposition to theorists who see authority as being essentially irrational, eg Joseph Raz, *The Authority of Law* (2nd edn, OUP 2009) 3.

Kojève then sets out a taxonomy of different modes of authority and different theories of its functioning, which is to say, different justifications for its existence. But the most interesting of his observations for our purposes is his identification of a particular theory or justification which he labels 'Aristotelian'.[71] This, he tells us, is a theory of authority which justifies the exertion of command on the basis of it deriving from a claim to be able to anticipate the future, whereas the one who is commanded only notices his or her short-term needs. Kojève goes on:

> It is, therefore, if we like, the authority of the 'intelligent' over the 'unthinking', of the 'civilised' over the 'barbarian', of the 'ant' over the 'grasshopper', of the 'clear-sighted' over the 'blind'.[72]

Where this justification for authority is recognised, Kojève tells us, the one who obeys does so because he 'realises that he sees less well and less far', and therefore 'allows himself to be led or guided' by the one who possesses authority, submitting without protest or discussion – which is to say going 'blindly'.[73] And the possessor of authority meanwhile leads because he sees further than all others: 'it was he alone who thought out a project, while the others did not manage to get beyond the level of immediate facts'.[74]

From this, we see emerging a form of authority which justifies itself on the basis of its far-sightedness and its ability to make preparations for what it sees: it has 'information about the future', 'contrive[s] plans and projects', and '[has] a broader and more profound view of things'[75] than the 'uneducated' subordinates; it 'see[s] to the bottom of things' while they only 'see the surface' and their 'daily needs'.[76] And it is for this reason that they submit to it. The analogy that Kojève here uses is that of a group of children, at play in a field; ostensibly equals, one of them sooner or later asserts him- or herself as leader by proposing – to use Kojève's example – a raid on an orchard to steal apples. He has thereby put himself in a position of authority by seeing '*further* than the others' and because it was 'he alone who thought out a *project*';[77] the others follow along accordingly.

---

[71] Kojève (n 9) 18.

[72] ibid, 19; the reference to the ant and grasshopper would appear to be an allusion to Aesop.

[73] ibid.

[74] ibid, 19.

[75] ibid, 20.

[76] ibid.

[77] ibid, 18 (emphasis in original).

It will be immediately seen that, even put in this very simple fashion, Kojève's description of the 'Aristotelian' justification for authority provides us with a useful way to conceptualise the authority which the system of global health governance exerts. The system, like any other form of governance, needs to exert authority (because it needs subjects to comply with or obey its commands, or efforts at 'control' and 'steering'), and therefore it must have a '"cause", a "reason" or a "justification" for its existence' so that the subjects do not 'react against' it. And that cause, reason, or justification comes in the form of a claim to be, precisely, 'far-sighted'. The system governs on the basis that its existence, and its governance, is necessary to anticipate the emergence of risks that are, necessarily, yet to emerge, and to apply its expertise to 'think out a project' in order to respond. And this is based on a relationship between the system and those subordinate to it wherein the former commands on the basis of its 'seeing to the bottom of things', and the latter obeys because it is caught up in 'immediate facts' and 'daily needs' and is in this sense therefore 'blind'.

It will also be immediately seen that this places the 'voluntariness' of compliance by the subjects, which was raised in both Sections 2 and 3, in its proper context – and shows it, to some extent, to be a red herring. As Kojève demonstrates conceptually, compliance with authority as such is always voluntary and is therefore contingent on it; where compliance is not forthcoming or is somehow coerced, or elicited through persuasion, then authority does not (strictly speaking) exist.

And it will also be then seen that this is all entirely in keeping with the underlying rationale for global health governance that was identified in Section 2, wherein the globalised threats of 'pandemics … noncommunicable diseases … antimicrobial resistance [and] health impacts of climate change' are said to require the existence of 'a clear plan' and 'constant preparedness', and hence the apparatus of the system of governance itself as the coordinating mechanism for a global project of surveillance and response. And in light of this, it will also be seen that it is apt, and useful, to describe the justification for the authority which the system exerts as being 'Aristotelian' in the sense which Kojève used the term.

This superficial connection having been made, however, the next section will make it more concrete by demonstrating its analytical power. This will require a further elucidation of how this analysis helps us to understand why the three salient features of the system of global health governance that were earlier identified have developed. And this will then lead us to a position in which we can open the system's operations and structure to critique.

5. JUSTIFYING GLOBAL HEALTH GOVERNANCE IN THE 'ARISTOTELIAN' MODE

It will be recalled that in Section 3 we saw that the system of global health governance is defined by exerting a power of command, or 'control' or 'steering', that is largely unfettered; by a claim to sole possession of the capacity to determine how expertise is gathered and deployed; and by the adoption of a position of coordinator for the activities of an otherwise uncoordinated mass. It is now important to elucidate how these features derive from aspects of the 'Aristotelian' justification for authority which are fundamental to it.

First, Kojève emphasises that the 'Aristotelian' justification for authority presupposes that said authority will be exerted by a leader, which is to say somebody who takes charge on the basis, as we have seen, of the possession of a 'project'. Two corollaries follow from this. The first is that this justification for authority rests on the continued existence of such a project; it lasts only as long as the project itself continues.[78] And the second is that the leader precisely 'leads' – he is not merely prescient in the sense of being able to anticipate the future, but also because he issues commands or orders and hence is prescient in the sense of knowing the contours of the project in advance of those who obey.[79]

It follows from these corollaries that the leader must be in a position of maximal freedom in relation to the development of the project in question, and also in relation to its ongoing implementation. He must exert mastery over it. And the implications for the system of global health governance are here obvious. As we have seen, it is a salient feature of that system that its 'crucial governance activity' – the declaration of a PHIEC and corresponding recommendations – is almost unfettered; absent of oversight, appeal, or procedural review; and exercised with regard to a very broad and loosely defined range of events. And, clearly, this is entirely what one would expect in circumstances in which authority is derived from an 'Aristotelian' justification in the terms which it has here been laid out. Authority in this sense, to repeat, is that of the leader, who leads through having a project over which he exerts total command, and whose prescience or far-sightedness extends not just to the 'facts' that lie in the future but to the manner in which the very project will be implemented and the substance of the commands which the subordinates will obey.

Second, Kojève's 'Aristotelian' justification for authority is contingent upon a claim to possess sole expertise. To repeat, such a justification does not merely suggest that the leader who exerts authority is expert, though obviously this

---

78 ibid, 19.

79 ibid, 20.

is required. Rather, it is reliant on the existence of a relationship between the 'clear-sighted' and the 'blind' – and it therefore necessarily constructs the one who leads as the former and those who are led as the latter – because this is the entire basis on which this justification for authority rests. Reactions against authority are 'renounced' because those who are led 'realise' that they see 'less well and less far'.[80] And since this is the core, as it were, of the 'Aristotelian' justification, it is indispensable to authority that is exercised in that mode that the leader should be in a position to always assert his own special 'clear-sightedness'.

And so it is that we find the system of global health governance being predicated, as it is, precisely on a claim to being 'clear-sighted' and a construction of those subject to it as 'blind'. The State Parties, seeing only 'immediate facts', follow an algorithm to identify 'events', which are then transmitted to the 'clear-sighted' for an assessment and a planned response. The subjects see only the 'surface' and their 'daily needs'; the expert apparatus of the WHO sees 'to the bottom of things'. And necessarily, then, the system of global health governance must exercise control over what it refers to as 'information'. It must present itself as having absolute oversight over the task of, as we have seen, 'manag[ing] the flow of information' – of 'ensur[ing] that scientific knowledge is synthesized, shared and applied by communities, decision makers, and other stakeholders in a way that is accessible, understandable and meaningful to everyone'. It must determine what qualifies as 'trustworthy sources and reliable guidance' – and, correspondingly of course, what is to be disqualified on the basis of its being 'disinformation' or 'misinformation' (or even just part of an 'overabundance of information').

And, third, Kojève's 'Aristotelian' justification for authority rests on the ability to coordinate and hence direct or lead an otherwise uncoordinated group or 'band' – a mass of ostensible equals who otherwise are directionless or lacking in a project or plan. Here, Kojève's own analogy of the group of children at play will come immediately to mind; in it, the children are of course equal in the sense that they do not have a pre-existing or 'natural' hierarchy. They are merely an undifferentiated and purposeless grouping. It is only when one steps forward and presents himself as a leader, with an idea for what to do, that they are given form and impetus. Authority here, in other words, derives from having the capacity precisely to lay out a project for which no prior plan exists, and to thereby corral subordinates together into a shared enterprise.

It is therefore entirely to be expected that, since the system of global health governance justifies its authority in 'Aristotelian' terms, its emphasis should be on the fact that the WHO constitutes a 'directing and coordinating authority'

---

80 ibid, 19.

for the community of State Parties – that, as it were, it should take on the role of the child who presents his or her playmates with the project of raiding the apple orchard. It is through the coordination of the 'blind' by the 'clear-sighted' that the 'Aristotelian' justification for authority finds expression – and it is therefore through the coordination of subordinates in the interests of the 'protection of all people of the world from the international spread of disease' that, likewise, the system of global health security governance operates. And the increasing drive to standardise and make uniform the implementation of the IHR (2024) and responses to the Director-General's temporary recommendations and other measures during a PHEIC must be understood then in exactly those terms – as a manifestation of the impetus for authority, conceived in the 'Aristotelian' mode, to display itself in the form of a power of an all-encompassing direction and coordination that brings an orderless grouping together for a common purpose.

It will be readily apparent, then, that the salient features of the system of global health governance that were earlier identified reflect features of the 'Aristotelian' justification for authority and thereby give force to the notion that the system indeed relies for its authority, and justifies itself to those who are subject to it, within that rubric. And it now, then, falls to be explained how this allows the operation of the system to be fully analysed and exposed to critique.

6. REIMAGINING GLOBAL HEALTH GOVERNANCE

Describing the system of global health governance in the way it is presented here reveals it in a fresh light. Its essential features as sketched out are thereby shown to be ineluctable consequences of the theory of authority which justifies the system's position of governance. The system anticipates the future and 'thinks out a project' in response to it – to 'fundamentally improve global public health protection' – and in respect of a mass of subjects who would otherwise lack order or leadership. And this, in turn, allows it to justify and rationalise its own exertion of authority, and thereby persuade those subject to it not to 'react' against it. It is, then, reliant on an 'Aristotelian' justification for its existence. And since this is the case, the features hitherto identified in its composition necessarily follow.

This observation is useful analytically in explaining why it is that the system has taken on the shape which it has. But the argument in this final section will also suggest that it allows us to open up the fundamental predicates of the system itself to critique. This is because it naturally leads us to a further question. As we have seen, since the justification for the system of global health governance's authority is essentially 'Aristotelian' in nature, it is inescapable that it should have developed, broadly, the features which it has. Given that is the case, then, it is apt to ask to what extent we are to understand those features as being actually necessary in respect of the goal of 'fundamentally improv[ing] global public health protection', as opposed to being merely ineluctable epiphenomena of governing on an 'Aristotelian' basis. In other words, is it truly inevitable that the system of global health governance should have taken on the form that it has – or might there in fact be different ways to 'fundamentally improve global public health protection' and thereby 'help create a more equal, just and resilient world'?

On the one hand, the underlying rationale for the system of global health governance having emerged in the first place is the subject of broad consensus in the literature. Here, we see time and again being emphasised the fact that in a 'globalised world [*sic*]'[81] the threat of infectious disease (something that has always been, and presumably always will be, within the experience of humanity) takes on a special and newfound character in light precisely of the fact that it is indeed 'globalised'. The 'accelerated pace of globalisation', as the story goes, 'amplifies ... risks' from both existing pathogens and new biological agents, since 'a disease is just a plane trip away', and 'an outbreak anywhere [can be] a threat everywhere'.[82] This linkage between increased infection threat and globalisation has led to a generalised acceptance that protecting health security 'requires international cooperation within a robust global regime'.[83] And this, it is said, means that 'traditional approaches' have to be 're-evaluated to fit the increasingly interconnected, polarised, and complex communities we live in'.[84]

And, clearly, this paints a compelling case for the system taking on the shape which it has. Since risks have become globalised and amplified, and since this requires new approaches so as to realise international cooperation, then what follows must take the form of 'detection systems, skilled and properly equipped personnel, authorities, [and] methods and tools to coordinate different governing bodies, which possess varying levels of preparedness, capacity and resources in a timely manner to prevent additional events', achieved

---

81 Harley Feldbaum and Kelley Lee, 'Public Health and Security' in Alan Ingram (ed), *Health, Foreign Policy and Security: Towards a Conceptual Framework for Research and Policy* (UK Global Health Programme Working Paper No 2, Nuffield Trust 2004) 19.

82 Thomas Frieden et al, 'Safer Countries through Global Health Security' (2014) 383(9919) Lancet 764, 764.

83 Simon Rushton, 'Global Health Security: Security for Whom? Security from What?' (2011) 59(4) Political Studies 779, 785.

84 Saskia Popescu and Jessica Malaty Rivera, 'Building Harm Reduction into Global Health Security and Pandemic Prevention' (2024) 384 British Medical Journal 1.

through a 'harmonised approach by affected governments, organisations, and communities'.[85] And so, in essence, we see the architecture of the system as described herein emerging by sheer necessity, almost as common sense.

But, on the other hand, the three features of the system as it has emerged and which have been identified in this contribution are also revealed, by viewing them through Kojève's lens, to have a self-justificatory aspect that belies their genuine necessity. First, as we have seen, the 'Aristotelian' justification for authority relies on the existence of a project over which the person exerting authority leads and has mastery – the implication being that, as long as the project is thought to have a reason to continue, his position of authority will remain assured. It follows that as soon as the project ceases to have such a reason to continue, his position of authority will be extinguished. In light of this, it naturally follows that the system of global health governance should display the first of the salient features which we indeed have identified in it – exercising as it does exclusive executive power over its project, and retaining a grasp on the ongoing importance of that project particularly through retaining almost unfettered discretion in identifying PHEICs and an unchallenged capacity to resolve them. But it remains an open question as to whether it is necessary for the system to do this in respect of the goal of 'fundamentally improv[ing] global public health protection', or whether it is necessary for it to do so merely in order to justify its continued exercising of authority.

Second, we have also seen that the 'Aristotelian' justification for authority relies on a construction of the leader as 'clear-sighted' and those subject to its authority as 'blind'. It 'sees to the bottom of things' while they only see 'immediate facts'. And we have seen that this manifests itself in the system of global health governance in particular in an insistence on its having the capacity to govern the 'flow' of information, and to marshal the requisite expertise to identify 'mis- and disinformation' and even circumstances of 'overabundance' of information. Again, are we, then, to understand the recent incorporation of the 'risk communication' core capacity into the IHR (2024) as something which is genuinely necessary for the goal of 'fundamentally improv[ing] global public health protection', or are we to understand it simply as a characteristic of a system of governance which conceives of its own authority in the 'Aristotelian' mode, and which therefore must insist on its own superior capacity to deploy expertise? It is perhaps plausible that 'too much information including false or misleading information' can '[cause] confusion and risk-taking behaviours that can harm health', as the WHO's infodemic webpage puts it.[86] But

85 Rebecca Katz and Erin Sorrell, 'Preparedness and Resilience in Public Health Emergencies' in Rushton and Younde (eds) (n 1) 201, 206.

86 'Infodemic' (*WHO*, 22 December 2020) https://www.who.int/health-topics/infodemic#tab=tab_1.

we might also be nonetheless led to question whether the 'use of risk- and evidence-based analysis and approaches' to 'manage infodemic[s]' through a centralised response is the appropriate means to resolve that problem, given that it is also reflective of an ineluctable rhetorical claim that authority justified in 'Aristotelian' terms must necessarily make. We might also ask whether the desire to 'manage infodemic[s]' will bring the imperatives of the system into conflict with other values – such as freedom of expression, freedom of conscience, and freedom of science – which we consider to be important.

And third, we have noted that the 'Aristotelian' justification for authority derives from the purported capacity to coordinate, direct, and lead an otherwise disordered or unstructured mass or group. And we have seen this exemplified in the way in which the system of global health governance increasingly insists on a 'uniformity' of approach in implementing the IHR (2024) and temporary recommendations of the Director-General, on the basis of the WHO's constituting of a 'directing and coordinating authority' in respect of the goal of 'fundamentally improv[ing] global public health protection'. And this, similarly, poses to us a question. Is it in fact the case that globalised coordination of responses to events posing a serious risk to public health ought to result in 'uniformity', or is this merely the result of a particular claim being necessary in order to contribute to a certain justification for authority? Might it in fact be the case that a diversity of approaches, conducted in light of local conditions and differing values and perspectives, would result in a more effective way of responding to such events?

It is one thing, in other words, to accept that the goal of 'fundamentally improv[ing] global public health protection' is in the first place necessary and in the second place that its realisation necessarily gives rise to a globalised response. But it is another to accept that the globalised response in question must take on the features which it has. And interrogating the justification for authority upon which the system rests, in phenomenological terms, thereby gives us the opportunity to reflect on whether there are other possibilities available and whether indeed 'global public health protection' might be 'fundamentally improved' in other ways. Does the system in fact need to rely on the existence of an almost unfettered and open-ended executive function in order to achieve what it is designed for? Does it need to rely on a claim to be able to identify what kind of information, and in what volume, it is permissible to spread in relation to public health? And does it need to emphasise 'uniformity' and centralised coordination at the expense of dispersed and decentralised decision-making? For reasons of space no answers are offered here. But the path to further inquiry lies open – and it is the phenomenological analysis of the justification for the system's authority that has allowed us to open it.

7. CONCLUSION

It would of course be difficult to argue that the effort to govern global health security is illegitimate even in light of the problematisation offered here. Clearly, global cooperation in the sharing of information and best practices with respect to threats to public health is not only sensible but an inevitable feature of modern life. But we can nonetheless make the case that the way in which the system of global health governance is constituted is not necessarily inevitable in respect of the goals which the system is designed to achieve, and that it could be constructed to operate in different ways. And, as it has here been shown, the way in which this case can be made is through a thoroughgoing critique and reimagining of how the system of global health governance justifies its own authority.

As currently constituted, that justification comes in the 'Aristotelian' sense as a claim, as we have seen, to represent the rule of the 'clear-sighted' over the 'blind'. And this leads the system to adopt the features which have here been identified. This connection, between the justification for authority and the shape which the governing mechanism takes, has the appearance of inevitability. But this, as demonstrated here, is an inevitability that arises not because there is no other way to realise the system's objective of 'fundamentally improv[ing] global public health protection', but out of the nature of the claim which the system makes in order that its authority be recognised.

It follows that there is nothing intrinsically inevitable about the system of global health governance's turn towards greater centralisation, uniformity, and control, and certainly not in respect of global public health protection and improvement. Other modes of realising that goal can be imagined which might function to provide better oversight of the decision-making processes of the Director-General and Emergency Committee, that do not bring the system itself into conflict with fundamental values in respect of free expression and the open-ended process of scientific inquiry, and which are more permissive of a plurality of approaches to public health management. The analysis provided here is offered as a preliminary step towards that re-imagination – and an invitation to further reflection on the appropriate basis on which the effort to govern global health can be justified.

5. Where is the legal basis for HERA's and the EU's key role in the securitisation and globalisation of their pandemic preparedness and response policy?

Michael Geistlinger

1. INTRODUCTION

The major result of the Covid-19 pandemic on the European Union (EU) level was the launching of a new European Commission Directorate-General, called Health Emergency Preparedness and Response (HERA), modelled on the US's Public Health Emergency Preparedness (PHEP) Program.[1] HERA was launched on 16 September 2021 based on Communication from the Commission to the European Parliament, the European Council, the Council, the European Economic and Social Committee and the Committee of the Regions Introducing HERA, the European Health Emergency Preparedness and Response Authority, the next step towards completing the European Health Union,[2] and on the Decision of the European Commission establishing the Health Emergency Preparedness and Response Authority of 16 September

[1] 'Public Health Emergency Preparedness (PHEP) Program and Guidance' (*US Center for Disease Control and Prevention*, 16 August 2024) https://www.cdc.gov/readiness/php/phep/index.html (accessed 28 April 2025). Unless otherwise stated all web links given in this chapter last accessed on 27 February 2025.

[2] Commission, 'From the Commission to the European Parliament, the European Council, the Council, the European Economic and Social Committee and the Committee of the Regions Introducing HERA, the European Health Emergency Preparedness and Response Authority, the next step towards completing the European Health Union' (Communication) COM (2021) 576 final.

2021.[3] HERA intends to complement and bring added value to the work of the European Centre for Disease Prevention and Control (ECDC) and the European Medicines Agency (EMA) 'in both preparedness and crisis times, thus becoming a crucial pillar of the European Health Union'.[4] In fact, with HERA the EU has established and institutionalised a permanent and perpetual health crisis mode expecting new crises to come. This expectation is not limited to naturally occurring pandemics, but, as can be seen from the introductory part of the Communication, also includes 'man-made threats such as bioterrorism'.[5] It refers to allegedly

> the most devastating outbreaks of infectious diseases ever, including Influenza, Ebola and the Zika epidemics. Global population growth, climate change and the consequential pressure on land use, food production and animal health are driving the rise and increasing the frequency of emerging pathogens. Modern travel allows viruses and other pathogens to spread across the world in a matter of hours.[6]

These factors, making a new major health crisis almost inevitable in the view of the European Commission, will hardly change quickly, if at all. It will thus serve as a perfect legitimisation for the European Commission to uphold the crisis mode. Besides, it is obvious that the perpetuation of a crisis mode is in the interests of all those who economically profited from the Covid-19 pandemic.

Instead of referring to a provision in the Founding Treaties of the EU, the Communication on HERA just mentions the European Health Union, a political construct developed to gain political support during the Covid-19 pandemic. The European Commission's Decision on HERA in the broadest possible manner refers to the Treaty on the Functioning of the European Union (TFEU)[7] without specifying the relevant articles. The Communication on HERA indicates that HERA shall be a crucial pillar of this European Health Union side by side with the ECDC and EMA.

The ECDC has its legal fundament in Regulation (EC) No 851/2004 establishing a European Centre for Disease Prevention and Control.[8] This

---

3 Commission Decision of 16 September 2021 establishing the Health Emergency Preparedness and Response Authority C (2021) 6712 final 2021 OJ CI393/3.

4 COM (2021) 576 final (n 2) 3.

5 ibid, 1.

6 ibid.

7 Consolidated version of the Treaty on the Functioning of the European Union [2012] OJ C326/47.

8 Regulation (EC) No 851/2004 of the European Parliament and of the Council of 21 April 2004 establishing a European Centre for Disease Prevention and Control 2004 OJ L142/1.

Regulation does not indicate a legal basis in the Founding Treaties of the EU either. The Regulation was amended by Regulation (EU) 2022/2370,[9] which intended to address 'some important gaps in the effectiveness of the Centre's response to the COVID-19 pandemic, such as regarding complete and comparable data, the level of transparency and communications to the public' which the Ombudsman had identified.[10] Not surprisingly, this Regulation also remains silent as to its legal base in the Founding Treaties.

Only in regard to the EMA and in particular its reinforced role in crisis preparedness and management for medicinal products and medical devices based on the respective Regulation (EU) 2022/123, specific reference has been made to the TFEU, and in particular to article 114 and article 168(4)(c) thereof as the legal basis for the operation of the EMA.[11] This Regulation recognises managing the 'unprecedented experience of the COVID-19 pandemic' as forming part of the Union's competences pursuant to articles 9 and 168 TFEU and article 35 of the Charter of Fundamental Rights of the European Union (ChEU),[12] to ensure a high level of human health protection in the definition and implementation of all Union policies and activities.[13] The same provisions of the TFEU and ChEU enumerated above are also understood as providing a legal basis for the establishment and operation of HERA.

The following will clarify the ideology behind HERA, its framework, mission, and expanding powers and practice, including at the international level through its interaction with the WHO (Sections 2–4). It will then be shown that none of the provisions mentioned above and no other provisions in the Treaty of European Union (TEU) and TFEU justify the creation of HERA and its activities (Section 5). Section 6 concludes.

---

[9] Regulation (EU) 2022/2370 of the European Parliament and of the Council of 23 November 2022 amending Regulation (EC) No 851/2004 establishing a European Centre for Disease Prevention and Control 2022 OJ L314/1.

[10] ibid, preamble, point (4).

[11] Regulation (EU) 2022/123 of the European Parliament and the Council of 25 January 2022 on a reinforced role for the European Medicines Agency in crisis preparedness and management for medicinal products and medical devices 2022 L20/1.

[12] Charter of Fundamental Rights of the European Union [2012] C326/391.

[13] ibid, preamble, points (1)–(3).

2. THE EUROPEAN HEALTH UNION AS AN IDEOLOGICAL BASIS AND FRAMEWORK OF HERA

A better understanding of the ideological background and framework of HERA can be reached by looking at the roof, the European Health Union itself, carried by the three pillars of the EMA, the ECDC, and HERA. The respective Communication from the Commission on Reinforcing the EU's Resilience for Cross-border Health Threats of 11 November 2020[14] was the EU's immediate answer to unilateral action taken by the EU Member States at the beginning of the Covid-19 crisis.[15] The Communication states that 'European citizens' expected the EU 'to have a more active role in protecting their health, particularly in protecting them from health threats that transcend national borders'.[16] Taking advantage of the Covid-19 crisis in her 2020 State of the Union address, the Head of the Commission called for building such a Health Union, pointing to the increased need for coordination at EU level during the then ongoing pandemic and during 'other future health emergencies'.[17] This should happen by expanding and building new blocks of the Health Union, allegedly fulfilling the EU's obligation to ensure a high level of human health protection as defined in the ChEU. An enlarged Health Union was meant to strengthen the existing structures and mechanisms for better EU-level protection, prevention, preparedness, and response against human health hazards, to recommend a reinforced framework for cross-border cooperation against all health threats, and finally, to strengthen the EU's role in international coordination and cooperation to prevent and control cross-border health threats and improve global health security.[18] This statement was made irrespective of the fact that the EU framework for the Health Union had existed since 2013 but had not proved helpful and was not even relied on during the Covid-19 pandemic.

With reference to article 168(5) TFEU, the Communication was accompanied by the above-mentioned legislative proposals upgrading the ECDC and extending the mandate of the EMA,[19] as well as by a proposal for enhancing

---

[14] Commission, 'To the European Parliament, the Council, the European Economic and Social Committee and the Committee of the Regions Building a European Health Union: Reinforcing the EU's Resilience for Cross-border Health Threats of 11 November 2020' (Communication) COM (2020) 724 final.

[15] ibid, 1.

[16] ibid.

[17] ibid, 2.

[18] ibid, 3.

[19] Concerning ECDC, Regulation (EC) No 851/2004 (n 8) and Regulation (EU) 2022/2370 (n 9); concerning EMA, Regulation (EU) 2022/123 (n 11).

the Union Civil Protection Mechanism.[20] This third legislative proposal was based on articles 196 and 322(1)(a) TFEU. It followed a Decision adopted a year earlier which explicitly referred only to article 196 TFEU. That Decision, amending Decision 1313/2013/EU on a Union Civil Protection Mechanism, had been adopted on 13 March 2019.[21] The Communication's further proposal of amendment of this Mechanism has not yet been adopted at the time of writing in September 2024.

The Communication on Building a European Health Union proposed to enforce the coordination of health measures at EU level as 'central not only to an effective practical response by the authorities but also to ensure that citizens understand that action is evidence-based and grounded in consensus'.[22] At the European Commission, this should happen through the EU Health Security Committee and the Early Warning and Response System (EWRS) and at the Council through the EU Integrated Political Crisis Response (IPCR) arrangements.

The Communication on Building a European Health Union further intends to provide access to medical countermeasures (in response to a health emergency) and to support the development, production, procurement, and purchase of necessary vaccines, therapeutics, diagnostics, as well as personal protective equipment and medical devices.[23] Instead of monitoring Member States' preparedness and response planning primarily based on Member States reporting, the Communication proposed to strengthen coordination mechanisms for preparedness, via the development of a binding EU health crisis/pandemic preparedness and response plan and an EU audit process on national level capacities.[24] This includes proposals for building national capacities for epidemiological surveillance[25] and measures concerning laboratory findings, testing, and contact tracing.[26] The EWRS was proposed to also include a system for the assessment of needs for, or shortages of, medical countermeasures as well as a system for coordinating requests and/or offers for cross-border

[20] Commission, 'Proposal for a Decision of the European Parliament and of the Council amending Decision No 1313/2013/EU on a Union Civil Protection Mechanism' COM (2020) 220 final.

[21] Decision (EU) 2019/420 of the European Parliament and of the Council of 13 March 2019 amending Decision No 1313/2013/EU on a Union Civil Protection Mechanism 2019 OJ L77I/1.

[22] COM (2020) 724 final (n 14) 5.

[23] ibid, 8–12.

[24] ibid, 12 ff.

[25] ibid, 14–16.

[26] ibid, 16 ff.

emergency assistance.[27] Last but not least, the Communication addresses international cooperation and collaboration.[28]

Close to the end of the Communication on Building a European Health Union, in chapter 10, the Communication announces the establishment of HERA and discloses the original intent and doctrine behind this initiative. HERA was thought to address weaknesses brought to light by the Covid-19 crisis in view of the expectation that Covid-19 was not the only global or pan-European health crisis of the century, and that others will follow. HERA's mission was intended 'to enable the EU and its Member States to rapidly deploy the most advanced medical and other measures in the event of a health emergency, by covering the whole value chain from conception to distribution and use'.[29] Its role shall cover the anticipation of specific threats; the identification of promising potential countermeasures; the generation and dissemination of knowledge on these countermeasures; the monitoring of production capacity and development facilities, raw material requirements and availability, securing the functioning of supply chains; the support of the development of cross-cutting technologies and solutions; as well as the development of specific countermeasures, including through clinical trials and data sharing infrastructure. HERA shall ensure sufficient production capacity and arrangements for stockpiling and distribution of medical countermeasures. It shall plan, coordinate and assemble ecosystems of public and private capabilities meeting the need that arises.[30]

However, the Communication on Building a European Health Union does not lose a word on the legal basis allowing the European Commission to establish HERA. The European Commission considers it self-evident that a Commission service as Directorate-General, consisting of a Head, a Coordination Committee, a Board, and an Advisory Forum,[31] using significant tools and funding,[32] is justified by the TFEU.

---

[27] ibid, 17 ff.

[28] ibid, 18–20.

[29] ibid, 20.

[30] ibid, 21.

[31] Commission Decision of 16 September 2021 (n 3), articles 1 and 3.

[32] 'Crisis Management' (*European Commission*, 2024) https://health.ec.europa.eu/health-emergency-preparedness-and-response-hera/funding_en.

3. HERA'S MISSION AND ACTIVITIES SINCE ITS ESTABLISHMENT

According to the Communication on Building the European Health Union, HERA should have become operative only in 2023.[33] However, it became operative on 8 December 2021 and is considered 'the core of the new European Health Union and Pandemic Preparedness and Response system'.[34] HERA calls itself 'a central pillar of the European Health Union'.[35] It places itself at the centre of both the allegedly improved EU reaction to Covid-19 and of the EU's efforts to become the leader in strengthening global preparedness for future health emergencies.[36]

HERA links its activities to the definition of 'serious cross-border threats to health' set out in the respective EU Regulation:

> [A] 'serious cross-border threat to health' means a life-threatening or otherwise serious hazard to health of biological, chemical, environmental or unknown origin, as referred to in Article 2(1), which spreads or entails a significant risk of spreading across the national borders of Member States, and which may necessitate coordination at Union level in order to ensure a high level of human health protection.[37]

It also refers to the EU Global Health Strategy.[38] The EU Global Health Strategy was published by the Directorate-General for Health and Food Safety and Directorate-General for International Partnerships on 30 November 2022.[39] By referring to that Strategy, which in the opinion of HERA 'deepens the EU in the centre of international efforts, strengthens EU's leadership and reasserts its responsibility to strengthen global preparedness for future health

---

33 COM (2020) 724 final (n 14) 21.

34 'Keynote speech of Peter Piot, Special Advisor on Covid-19 to the European Commission President, on the occasion of the first anniversary of HERA' (*European Commission*, 8 December 2022) 1 https://health.ec.europa.eu/system/files/2023-01/hera_ev_20221208_keynote_piot.pdf.

35 HERA, 'State of Health Preparedness Report' (2022) 5 https://health.ec.europa.eu/publications/state-health-preparedness-report_en (HERA Report 2022).

36 ibid, 5 ff.

37 Regulation (EU) 2022/2371 of the European Parliament and the Council of 23 November 2022 on serious cross-border threats to health and repealing Decision No 1082/2013/EU 2022 OJ L314/26, article 3(1).

38 HERA Report 2022 (n 35) 6 (fn 9).

39 European Commission, 'EU Global Health Strategy: Better Health for All in a Changing World' (30 November 2022) https://health.ec.europa.eu/publications/eu-global-health-strategy-better-health-all-changing-world_en.

emergencies', HERA considerably expands its own mandate. The EU Global Health Strategy addresses health as a global good that is 'impacted by the triple planetary crisis of climate change, biodiversity and pollution'.[40] In addition, this Strategy includes fostering 'digitalisation as enabler' as the fourth, supporting 'a stronger, effective and accountable WHO' as the fourteenth, steering 'the new global health governance by filling gaps and ensuring coherence of action' as the fifteenth and ensuring 'a stronger EU role in international organisations and bodies' as the sixteenth of its 20 guiding principles.[41] Also, other principles, in particular principles seventeen – twenty, twelve, and thirteen, go well beyond the definition of a 'serious cross-border threat to health'.[42]

By means of reference to Regulation and Strategy, HERA provided itself with super-powers in the area of health which cannot be recognised in the Commission's Decision on HERA's establishment.[43] Article 2 of that Decision reads as follows:

> Mission and tasks
>
> 1. HERA shall work to improve preparedness and response to serious cross-border threats in the area of medical countermeasures, in particular by:
>   (a) strengthening health security coordination within the Union during preparedness and crisis response times, and bringing together Member States, the industry and the relevant stakeholders in a common effort
>   (b) addressing vulnerabilities and strategic dependencies within the Union related to the development, production, procurement, stockpiling and distribution of medical countermeasures
>   (c) contributing to reinforcing the global health emergency preparedness and response architecture
> 2. HERA shall be responsible for the following tasks:
>   (a) assessment of health threats and intelligence gathering relevant to medical countermeasures;

---

40 ibid, 4.

41 ibid, 3.

42 ibid, 3, principle 17: 'Expand partnerships based on equal footing, co-ownership, mutual interest and strategic priorities'; principle 18: 'Strengthen engagement with key global health stakeholders'; principle 19: 'Enhance EU finance for global health with maximum impact'; principle 20: 'Assess progress and ensure the accountability of the EU's global health action through permanent monitoring and assessment'; principle 12: 'Link effectively all policies and measures that have an impact on global health within the Commission, EU agencies and EU financing institutions'; principle 13: 'Better link and coordinate policies and measures of the EU and its Member States to speak with one voice and deliver effective action worldwide'.

43 Commission Decision of 16 September 2021 (n 3).

(b) promoting advanced research and development of medical countermeasures and related technologies;
(c) addressing market challenges and boosting the Union's open strategic autonomy in medical countermeasures production;
(d) swift procurement and distribution of medical countermeasures;
(e) increasing stockpiling capacity of medical countermeasures;
(f) strengthening knowledge and skills in preparedness and response related to medical countermeasures.

These tasks shall be exercised in close cooperation with Member States

The first year's report on HERA's activities discloses in figure 1 that HERA's mission to ensure availability and access to medical countermeasures by reinforcing the whole value chain encompassed activities in the area of health threat assessment and intelligence gathering, advanced research and clinical trials, medical countermeasures development, and medical countermeasures distribution and stockpiling.[44]

Whereas the ten early lessons the EU Commission drew from the Covid-19 pandemic were primarily linked to the ECDC – the EU FAB facilities for a network of producers of vaccines, the EMA, the EU Structured Dialogue on the security of the supply chains of medicines, VACCELERATE for vaccines, EU-RESPONSE for therapeutics, the Clinical Trials Information System (CTIS), EU4Health, the Covid-19 Vaccines Global Access (COVAX), the European External Action Service (EEAS), and Foreign Information Manipulation and Interference (FIMI)[45] – HERA quickly became involved in these EU activities too. For example, an EU FAB was launched by the Commission in cooperation with the European Health and Digital Executive Agency (HaDEA), financed by HERA's annual work plan for 2022. The objective was 'to ensure that sufficient and agile manufacturing capacities for different vaccine types are kept operational and can be activated quickly in case of a public health emergency'.[46] The respective factsheet explained already at that time that HERA 'is … supporting Europe's world-leading industrial capacities and establishing a network of vaccine manufacturers in the EU and EEA to quickly manufacture vaccines when and where needed'.[47]

[44] HERA Report 2022 (n 35) 7.

[45] ibid, 7–10. EU FAB is an EU mechanism created to ensure that manufacturing capacities for vaccines are operational and can be activated quickly in case of a public health emergency.

[46] European Commission, 'HERA and EU FAB' (2022) https://health.ec.europa.eu/system/files/2022-05/2022_eufab_factsheet_en_0.pdf.

[47] ibid, 1.

The State of Play and Planned Actions on Medical Countermeasures discloses that on 8 July 2022, the HERA Advisory Forum and the HERA Board were briefed on the European Commission's identification of a list of three priority health threats: pathogens with high pandemic potential covering mainly respiratory ribonucleic acid (RNA) viral families; chemical, biological, radiological, and nuclear (CBRN) threats originating from accidental or deliberate release; and anti-microbial resistance (AMR), referred to as the silent pandemic.[48] The second of these priority health threats extends well beyond the Covid-19 pandemic spectrum and expands the scope of HERA's activities even to those of the European Atomic Energy Community (EURATOM). A first annual assessment of these priority health threats by HERA was envisaged for early 2023.[49]

In order to detect threats to health, the European Commission through HERA has started to develop the Medical Countermeasures Intelligence Platform (HERA MCMI platform), an intelligence gathering and threat assessment tool in place since 2023.[50]

HERA supports epidemiological surveillance through a network of laboratories and research institutes and granting EUR 17 million to Member States for consolidating and modernising their wastewater surveillance capacities.[51] This shows a considerable overlap in the powers of HERA and the ECDC, which once more appears to undermine the rationality of HERA. HERA INVEST shall become the European Commission's tool for expanding investment in the development of innovative medical countermeasures.[52] HERA is intended 'to develop and implement a strategic research and innovation agenda identifying the main research gaps, the key emerging health and bio-technologies needed for pandemic preparedness and response solutions', thereby taking on the preparatory work to establish the European partnership for pandemic preparedness. It shall boost 'horizon scanning capacities of emerging innovations and technologies for vaccines, therapeutics and other medical countermeasures' and consolidate EU clinical trial networks.[53]

The silent expansion of HERA's activities from improving preparedness and response to serious cross-border threats to regular health management can be best seen from its planned actions on vaccines. To support research and development of new vaccines for infectious diseases with pandemic or epidemic potential beyond Covid-19 may well be accommodated in its tasks under

48 HERA Report 2022 (n 35) 11.
49 ibid, 11–12.
50 ibid, 12–13.
51 ibid, 13–14.
52 ibid, 14–15.
53 ibid, 15.

the European Commission's Decision. However, HERA informs in its first annual report that the next steps it shall take will include investing 'up to EUR 80 million in second generation COVID-19 vaccines, with the aim of obtaining pan-coronavirus vaccines and vaccines targeting both COVID-19 and influenza that elicit broader, stronger and longer lasting immune responses'. In addition, HERA plans to finance projects 'to develop alternative models for testing vaccine candidates and analysing host-pathogen interactions to enable the targeted development of vaccines' and to support 'research projects aiming at improving our understanding of vaccine-induced immunity to develop vaccines with broader and longer lasting immune response'.[54]

Similarly, concerning therapeutics, the support of 'the development of and access to broad-spectrum antivirals targeting viruses with high epidemic or pandemic potential' and the planned measures concerning anti-microbials[55] can be seen as covered by its mandate from the Commission. But plans to develop a roadmap to support pre-clinical and clinical research for novel and re-purposed antivirals clearly cross the border between pandemic preparedness and regular health research.

Whilst HERA puts its planned next steps in the area of diagnostics into the context of preparedness for pandemics, they could also all be seen as measures supporting the development of medical diagnostics not necessarily linked to potential pandemics. This applies, for instance, to activities to 'support the development of smart in-vitro diagnostics to detect and characterise pathogens with pandemic potential', to 'explore and develop regulatory pathways for diagnostics to ensure both an appropriate level of control and speedy access to the market in the event of an emergency', and to 'support the development of rapid point-of-care diagnostics for Antimicrobial Resistance (AMR), including diagnostics allowing for differential diagnosis, species identification and antimicrobials susceptibility testing (AST)'.[56]

HERA's initiatives to build resilient supply chains for pharmaceuticals are by their very nature ambiguous. They can be linked to pandemic preparedness, but also to safeguarding the regular supply of pharmaceutical products.

---

[54] ibid, 16.

[55] ibid, 17: 'Establish pull incentives, and assess the feasibility of establishing EU multi-country pull incentives for antimicrobials, to support the development of high priority, high quality and safe medicines to prevent and/or address identified public health threats'; 'Map existing medical countermeasures to combat AMR and those in development'; 'Strengthen the coordination of the AMR medical countermeasures pipeline including basic research, pre-clinical and clinical development'.

[56] ibid, 18.

They also disclose the industries interested in, or possibly profiting from, these initiatives.[57]

The creation of an EU FAB, which 'consists of a network of vaccine manufacturing sites with an "ever-warm" capacity to produce 500–700 million vaccine per year to ensure that vaccines are rapidly available once a crisis hits' and signing contracts with suppliers in 2023, investing EUR 160 million annually, can be classified as 'pandemic-preparedness' activities. However, they can also be seen as a massive financial support instrument in the interests of industries that already profited from the Covid-19 pandemic.[58] HERA does not even try to create an explicit link between the planned measures in this field to pandemic- or other crisis-preparedness.[59]

HERA obviously follows the proposal of the Special Advisor on Covid-19 to the European Commission President, Peter Piot, to replace the term Covid-19 'booster' vaccinations by 'seasonal vaccinations' similar to seasonal influenza vaccinations,[60] and included influenza in its list of 'pandemic' diseases, having concluded on 28 July 2022 'a joint reservation contract for 85 million doses

---

[57] ibid, 19. These initiatives are: 'Revise the pharmaceutical legislation to enhance security of supply and address shortages through measures such as stronger obligations for supply and transparency, earlier notification of shortages, enhanced transparency of stocks and stronger EU coordination and mechanisms to monitor, manage and avoid shortages'; 'Develop a medical countermeasure supply chain risk management framework through MCMI platform, to improve the visibility, agility, and resilience of end-to-end supply chain networks for medical countermeasures'; 'Increase the resilience of supply chains of crisis-relevant medical countermeasures, raw materials, intermediate ingredients and Active Pharmaceutical Ingredients (APIs)'; 'Map and assess supply chains criticalities of a targeted list of crisis relevant medical countermeasures through qualitative and quantitative exchanges with manufacturers and suppliers, including within the JICF (Joint Industrial Cooperation Forum) and through the monitoring scheme for trade flows of critical components for vaccines and therapeutics'.

[58] ibid, 19–20.

[59] ibid, 20: 'Consider investment decision to expand EU flexible manufacturing capacity following the results of a study due to be finalised in early 2023'; 'Support actions for leveraging investments into state of the art production capabilities in the EU, including via the Health Important Project of Common European Interest (IPCEI) being developed by Member States and the industry'; 'Support actions for increased awareness and training in public procurement practices'; 'Continue to support the ramp up and or launch manufacturing facilities in the EU and promote industrial partnerships through matchmaking events.'

[60] Piot (n 34) 2: 'By the way, I suggest we no longer use the term "booster" for such repeat vaccinations, but simply seasonal vaccination as we do for influenza vaccination'.

of pandemic influenza vaccines'.[61] The contract was concluded for Adjupanrix with the global biopharma company GlaxoSmithKline (GSK) based in the United Kingdom. HERA's announcement of the deal reveals its understanding of what amounts to a 'pandemic' when it states: 'An influenza pandemic would be a global epidemic caused by a new influenza strain to which there is little to no pre-existing immunity in the human population. While it is difficult to predict an influenza pandemic, it is important to be prepared.'[62] The contract is just the beginning, as HERA aims to develop 'dynamic purchasing systems to facilitate access to main medical countermeasures such as PPE (Personal Protective Equipment; pilot project ongoing), medical devices and laboratory materials'.[63]

The broad understanding of cross-border health threats also impacts HERA's stockpiling initiatives. HERA argues that EU citizens must be protected 'from ongoing and emerging health threats stemming from pathogens with high pandemic potential, chemical, biological, radiological and nuclear (CBRN) threats, underlying threats such as antimicrobial resistance (AMR) or other unknown threats'.[64] As a consequence, in 2022, EUR 580 million was allocated 'to support Member States in the establishment of "rescEU" stockpiles of CBRN relevant medical countermeasures such as antidotes against nerve agents, vaccines and therapeutics against specific biological threats, and different countermeasures for radio-nuclear events'. HERA used the M-pox outbreak of May 2022 for direct procurement of medical countermeasures and announced to 'launch a second call to procure and stockpile CBRN relevant medical countermeasures and other medical items, with the intention to disburse over EUR 1.2 billion for the establishment of further stockpiles between 2022 and 2026'.[65]

Summarising HERA's activity report for the first year of its existence shows that HERA excellently picked up a proposal in the literature to provide for 'a five-prong bundled model for health emergency preparedness',[66] and even went well beyond the suggested five prongs.

---

61 HERA, 'European Health Union: HERA Signs Joint Procurement Contract for Pandemic Influenza Vaccine' (28 July 2022) https://ec.europa.eu/commission/presscorner/detail/en/ip_22_4363.

62 ibid.

63 HERA Report 2022 (n 35) 21.

64 ibid, 5.

65 ibid, 21 ff.

66 Eg Simone Villa et al, 'HERA: A new Era for Health Emergency Preparedness in Europe?' (2021) 397(10290) Lancet Correspondence 2145.

4. HERA AND THE WHO'S PANDEMIC AGREEMENT AND THE AMENDMENTS OF THE INTERNATIONAL HEALTH REGULATIONS

In the last chapter of its activity report, HERA focuses on international coordination and global activities. In this context, it is worth emphasising the European Commission's contribution – through HERA – to a new WHO Pandemic Agreement that is still being negotiated at the time of writing and in the form of its proposals for amendments of the International Health Regulations (IHR) 2005,[67] some of which were adopted by the 77th World Health Assembly (WHA) in May 2024.[68] Using both instruments, HERA is preparing to cement its own broad field of operation.

4.1 The Negotiations of a WHO Pandemic Agreement

As for the WHO Pandemic Agreement (original title: Treaty on Pandemic Preparedness and Response), the initial Zero Draft of 1 February 2023[69] was based on a Decision adopted during a Special Session of the WHA on 29 November – 1 December 2021.[70] The WHO established an Intergovernmental Negotiation Body (INB) which includes the 194 Member States of the WHO. The Zero Draft followed a Conceptual Zero Draft of 25 November 2022[71] and has been circulated among the Member States and other interested parties on 31 January 2023, offering the possibilities to submit statements or proposals. The INB Bureau set a deadline of 22 May 2023 for finalising a text for the redaction group, which started to meet in June 2023 to continue negotiations. The final draft of the Pandemic Agreement should have been submitted to the 77th WHA in May 2024 for adoption. This, however, has not happened and a Decision was made to continue negotiations of the Agreement until the 78th WHA in May 2025.[72]

---

[67] International Health Regulations (2005) (adopted 23 May 2005, entered into force 15 June 2007) 2509 UNTS 79 (IHR (2005)).

[68] WHA Res 77.17 (1 June 2024) UN Doc WHA77.17, annex 'Amendments to the International Health Regulations (2005)' (IHR (2024)).

[69] INB, 'Zero Draft of the WHO CA+ for the Consideration of the Intergovernmental Negotiation Body at its Fourth Meeting' (1 February 2023) UN Doc A/INB/4/3 (Zero Draft Pandemic Agreement (1 February 2023)).

[70] WHASS Decision 2(5) (1 December 2021) UN Doc SSA2(5).

[71] INB, 'Conceptual Zero Draft for the Consideration of the Intergovernmental Negotiation Body at its Third Meeting' (25 November 2022) UN Doc A/INB/3/3.

[72] WHA, Decision 77(20) (1 June 2024) UN Doc WHA77(20).

Already the Zero Draft was a fully elaborated international treaty based on article 19 of the WHO Constitution.[73] The EU, holding an informal observer status at the WHO, supported the rapid elaboration and conclusion of the WHO Pandemic Agreement from the very beginning. Based on a Decision of the European Council of 25 February 2021, the Council of the EU on 20 May 2021 decided to support the launch of negotiations for an international treaty on the fight against pandemics in the framework of the WHO and authorised the European Commission to negotiate the WHO Pandemic Agreement on behalf of the EU.[74] Whereas the initial Commission Recommendation and Council Decision had been prepared by the Directorate-General for Health and Food Safety, HERA's first annual report discloses that it is now HERA that has taken the lead in shaping the Commission's position in the WHO Pandemic Agreement negotiations, at least on material questions. The Commission is active in the negotiations side by side with the EU Member States that are also members of the WHO.

The EU textual proposals in the Zero Draft of the WHO Pandemic Agreement[75] date from 28 March 2023.[76] The most important EU proposal for

---

[73] Constitution of the World Health Organization (adopted 22 July 1946, entered into force 7 April 1948) 14 UNTS 185 (WHOC).

[74] Council of the EU, 'EU Supports Start of WHO Process for the Establishment of Pandemic Treaty: Council Decision' (*Council of the EU Press Release*, 20 May 2021) https://www.consilium.europa.eu/en/press/press-releases/2021/05/20/eu-supports-start-of-who-process-for-establishment-of-pandemic-treaty-council-decision/?utm_source=dsms-auto&utm_medium=email&utm_campaign=EU+supports+start+of+WHO+process+for+establishment+of+Pandemic+Treaty%3a+Council+decision; Commission, 'Recommendation for a Council Decision authorising the opening of negotiations on behalf of the European Union for the conclusion of an international agreement on pandemic preparedness and response as well as for the negotiations of complementary amendments to the International Health Regulations (2005)' COM (2021) 766 final 2; and Commission, 'Annex to Recommendation for a Council Decision authorising the opening of negotiations on behalf of the European Union for the conclusion of an international agreement on pandemic preparedness and response as well as for the negotiations of complementary amendments to the International Health Regulations (2005)' COM (2021) 766 final 2.

[75] Zero Draft Pandemic Agreement (1 February 2023) (n 69).

[76] European Commission, 'Outline of EU Textual Proposals in the Zero Draft of the WHO Convention, Agreement or Other International Instrument on Pandemic Prevention, Preparedness and Response ("WHO CA+")' (28 March 2023) https://www.eeas.europa.eu/sites/default/files/documents/2023/EU%20proposals%20integrated%20into%20the%20ZD%2028%20March.pdf (EU Textual Proposals Zero Draft Pandemic Agreement (28 March 2023)).

amendment of the Zero Draft related to the definition of a 'pandemic' in article 1. The Zero Draft definition read as follows:

> 'Pandemic' means the global spread of a pathogen or variant that infects human populations with limited or no immunity through sustained and high transmissibility from person to person, overwhelming health systems with severe morbidity and high mortality, and causing social and economic disruptions, all of which require effective national and global collaboration and coordination for its control.[77]

The EU proposed to replace this definition with the notion of a 'pandemic situation' which:

> means a manifestation of a disease, irrespective of origin or source, that is spreading or is likely to spread over a wide geographical area, often worldwide, that is affecting or is likely to affect a large number of persons, and is creating or is likely to create a severe social disruption and economic loss.[78]

The EU's proposal, if accepted in the ongoing negotiations, would imply a considerable material expansion of an already wide definition proposed by the WHO and, in addition, the opening up for a 'regional pandemic' given the reference to 'wide geographical area, often worldwide' in the EU's proposal.

The report of the WHO Director-General to the 77th WHA with another draft version of the Pandemic Agreement of 24 May 2024 (Draft Pandemic Agreement (24 May 2024)) attached[79] prefers the terms 'pandemic emergencies' or 'pandemics', without, however, defining these terms. However, a parallel report on the amendments of the IHR (2005) of the WHO Director-General to the 77th WHA[80] indicates the intention to define the term 'pandemic emergency' in the amended IHR. And indeed, the amendments to article 1 of the IHR (2005) adopted by the 77th WHA on 1 June 2024[81] define a 'pandemic emergency' as follows:

---

[77] Zero Draft Pandemic Agreement (1 February 2023) (n 69), article 1(1)(b).

[78] EU Textual Proposals Zero Draft Pandemic Agreement (28 March 2023) (n 76), article 1(1)(b).

[79] 'Proposal for the WHO Pandemic Agreement', draft text of 24 May 2024, appendix to the report of the WHO Director-General, 'Outcome of the Intergovernmental Negotiating Body (INB) to Draft and Negotiate a WHO Convention, Agreement or Other International Instrument on Pandemic Prevention, Preparedness and Response' (27 May 2024) UN Doc A77/10 (Draft Pandemic Agreement (24 May 2024)).

[80] 'Bureau's Proposed Text' of 20 May 2024, appendix to the report of the WHO Director-General, 'Working Group on the Amendments of the International Health Regulations' (27 May 2024) UN Doc A77/9.

[81] IHR (2024), article 1.

> 'Pandemic emergency' means a public health emergency of international concern that is caused by a communicable disease and: (i) has, or is at high risk of having, wide geographical spread to and within multiple States; and (ii) is exceeding, or is at high risk of exceeding, the capacity of health systems to respond in those States; and (iii) is causing, or is at high risk of causing, substantial social and/or economic disruption, including disruption to international traffic and trade; and (iv) requires rapid, equitable and enhanced coordinated international action, with whole-of-government and whole-of-society approaches.

The definition clearly shows the influence of the EU's preferred approach and comes closer to the EU's proposal than to the one contained in the Zero Draft version of the WHO Pandemic Agreement.

This EU-preferred definition of a 'pandemic emergency' is related to EU proposals to include a definition for 'countermeasures' and of the 'One Health' concept into the WHO Pandemic Agreement. The latter has been proposed to mean the following: 'an integrated, unifying approach that aims to sustainably balance and optimize the health of people, animals, and ecosystems. It recognizes the health of humans, domestic and wild animals, plants, and the wider environment (including ecosystems) are closely linked and inter-dependent.'[82] Exactly this definition is an element of the Draft Pandemic Agreement (24 May 2024). Its draft article 5 on the 'One Health approach' reads as follows:

> The Parties shall promote a One Health approach for pandemic prevention, preparedness and response …, recognizing the interconnection between the health of people, animals and the environment, that is coherent, integrated, coordinated and collaborative among all relevant organizations, sectors and actors, as appropriate, in accordance with national and/or domestic law, and applicable international law, and taking into account national circumstances.[83]

Whether the promotion of the 'One Health' concept shall be obligatory or voluntary is still being negotiated at WHO level at the time of writing. In any event, the EU seems to be successful in supporting the further entrenchment of the doctrine of Global Health Security (GHS) into the WHO Pandemic Agreement. The GHS doctrine promotes a centralised (top-down), technocratic and biomedical approach to the prevention and response to health emergencies.

> [It] prioritizes the mitigation of biological risks in a biosecurity context. In this way, it combines two previously separate areas: public health protection and national/international security. As a result, biohazard mitigation and bioweapon warfare strategies are combined with those of public health protection. More specifically, the GHS integrates classic security and defence policy approaches and military

---

82 EU Textual Proposals Zero Draft Pandemic Agreement (28 March 2023) (n 76) 3.

83 Draft Pandemic Agreement (24 May 2024) (n 79), article 5.

approaches with the traditional medical field of prevention and containment of communicable diseases.[84]

The EU further requested that a provision, the place of which is yet to be determined, with regard to the declaration of a pandemic by the WHO Director-General is included in both instruments, the Pandemic Agreement and the revised IHR, either by identical provisions or by cross-reference.[85] Indeed, the EU's proposal was implemented via an amendment of article 12 IHR in May 2024. The title of this amended article is now: 'Determination of a public health emergency of international concern, including a pandemic emergency'. It demonstrates that not all public health emergencies of international concern (PHEICs) can necessarily also be classified as 'pandemic emergencies'.[86] It falls, however, under the new authority of the WHO Director-General to not only declare PHEICs but also a 'pandemic emergency' under the amended article 12 IHR (2024).

By proposing text for the new Pandemic Agreement regarding its objective, the general obligations of State Parties, plans and measures, and regarding the inclusion of a new Chapter II on 'Preventing, Detecting and Reporting Pandemic Situations', the EU undertook clear steps to significantly increase the obligations (and their effectiveness) in these areas.[87] By an EU-proposed article D.4, for example, WHO field missions for the purpose of verification and support are proposed which parties shall not unjustifiably refuse.[88] In case of rejection, short deadlines for providing an explanation and reaction are set in the EU proposal with the final consequence of involving the Conference of State Parties exercising its surveillance and monitoring powers.[89] Chapter II of the Draft Pandemic Agreement (24 May 2024) largely appears to follow the EU's proposals. Field missions are not formally mentioned, but could be introduced based on draft article 21.[90]

---

84 Amrei Müller, 'Die Pandemiegesetzgebung der WHO: Besorgniserregende Verhandlungen von internationaler Tragweite' (*Global Health Responsibility Agency*, October 2023) https://www.ghr.agency/?p=6760; on the GHS, see also the introduction to this volume.

85 EU Textual Proposals Zero Draft Pandemic Agreement (28 March 2023) (n 76), two versions for an article 3 (at 4 ff).

86 IHR (2024), article 12 (4bis).

87 EU Textual Proposals Zero Draft Pandemic Agreement (28 March 2023) (n 76), article 3 and additional articles, new Chapter II, articles A–D.

88 ibid, article D(4)(2): 'and shall strive to agree on the timing and terms of reference of the mission within 24 hours from receipt of the offer'.

89 ibid, articles D(4)(3) and (4).

90 Draft Pandemic Agreement (24 May 2024) (n 79).

The EU provided a detailed proposal for an article E on Access to and Sharing of Pathogen Samples and Data and a similarly elaborated article G on Benefit Sharing through Equitable Access to Countermeasures. These proposals include far-reaching obligations to ensure the availability of countermeasures, affordability of countermeasures, quality of countermeasures, stockpiling of countermeasures, and support for additional manufacturing facilities.[91] Article N of the EU's proposal supplements these obligations by the obligation to cooperate in the area of scientific research.[92] As can be seen from articles 11–14 of the Draft Pandemic Agreement (24 May 2024), many of these EU proposals remain part of the ongoing negotiations.[93]

The EU further proposed that the Zero Draft's article 12[94] on 'Strengthening and Sustaining a Skilled and Competent Health and Care Workforce' shall be complemented by obliging the parties to establish or designate multi-disciplinary emergency health teams at national and, where appropriate, regional levels, thereby providing mutual assistance.[95] Articles 7(3) and (4) of the Draft Pandemic Agreement (24 May 2024) have taken up this approach.[96] By proposing an additional article M(1), the EU wishes to effectively address mis- and disinformation by 'informing the public, communicating risk and providing evidence- and science-based information about pandemics and relevant countermeasures through effective channels, including social media, in cooperation with all stakeholders, including health professionals, local communities and civil society and the private sector'.[97] The EU proposes, in particular, to task the WHO-Secretariat 'at the request of the Conference of the Parties, to develop technical guidance, consult with experts, civil society organizations, the media and to monitor social media to identify relevant patterns of communication and need for information. It shall report to the Conference of the Parties on its activities.'[98] Article 18 of the Draft Pandemic Agreement (24 May 2024) on 'Communication and Public Awareness' has, however, not taken on these far-reaching EU proposals.[99]

---

[91] EU Textual Proposals Zero Draft Pandemic Agreement (28 March 2023) (n 76), articles G(2)–(6) respectively.

[92] ibid, article N.

[93] Draft Pandemic Agreement (24 May 2024) (n 79), articles 11–14.

[94] Zero Draft Pandemic Agreement (1 February 2023) (n 69).

[95] EU Textual Proposals Zero Draft Pandemic Agreement (28 March 2023) (n 76), addition to article 12(2) by article I.1.

[96] Draft Pandemic Agreement (24 May 2024) (n 79), articles 7(3) and (4).

[97] EU Textual Proposals Zero Draft Pandemic Agreement (28 March 2023) (n 76), article M.1(1(a)).

[98] ibid, article M.1(4).

[99] Draft Pandemic Agreement (24 May 2024) (n 79), article 18.

It hardly surprises that the EU furthermore sponsored a provision on supporting States in their implementation of the new Pandemic Agreement[100] and provided a proposal for setting up corresponding institutional arrangements. These arrangements would extend the sphere of action of the Conference of State Parties as the main institution for supervising implementation. They propose to streamline its competences and procedures, in particular the State reporting and advice system, and suggest the establishment of an 'Implementation and Compliance Committee' with the right to adopt recommendations to the Conference of State Parties, inter alia when reviewing compliance with the Pandemic Agreement. This includes adopting recommendations by three-fourths majority and a quorum of two-thirds of the members in the absence of consensus.[101] In this area, articles 21 and 22 of the Draft Pandemic Agreement (24 May 2024) deviate considerably from the proposals of the EU.[102] At least here the EU seems to fail. The current draft of article 24(2) of the Draft Pandemic Agreement (24 May 2024) reflects the reluctance of the negotiating parties to provide too much power to the WHO Secretariat and WHO Director-General. It states that:

> Nothing in the WHO Pandemic Agreement shall be interpreted as providing the WHO Secretariat, including the WHO Director-General, any authority to direct, order, alter or otherwise prescribe the national and/or domestic laws, as appropriate, or policies of any Party, or to mandate or otherwise impose any requirements that Parties take specific actions, such as ban or accept travellers, impose vaccination mandates or therapeutic or diagnostic measures or implement lockdowns.[103]

The proposals of the EU can be summarised on the one hand as an effort to globalise the EU's experience it has gained during the Covid-19 pandemic. On the other hand, it can be characterised as an effort to increase remarkably the scope of application and efficiency of EU law as developed during the Covid-19 pandemic to (alleged future) cross-border health threats in the broadest possible understanding by including these EU law concepts into an international pandemic treaty currently negotiated within the framework of the WHO. As far as the EU's proposals will be adopted in the continuing negotiations at WHO level, it will be HERA that will provide for and secure their implementation within the EU. The powers of HERA will increase considerably.

In this context, it should be kept in mind that the Zero Draft of the Pandemic Agreement in article 33(2) provided for the option of the EU to become a

---

100 EU Textual Proposals Zero Draft Pandemic Agreement (28 March 2023) (n 76), article O(1).

101 ibid, article P(4).

102 Draft Pandemic Agreement (24 May 2024) (n 79), articles 21 and 22.

103 ibid, article 24(2).

member of the WHO Pandemic Agreement.[104] If this happens without any of its Member States being a Party, the EU shall be bound by all the obligations under the Agreement. In the case where one or more of its Member States is a Party to the Agreement, the EU and its Member States shall decide on their respective responsibilities for the performance of their obligations under the Agreement. In such cases, the EU and the Member States shall not be entitled to exercise rights under the Agreement concurrently. Article 1(e) read together with articles 22, 33(1), and 34(2) of the Draft Pandemic Agreement (24 May 2024) fully upholds the approach taken in the Zero Draft and thereby incorporates the EU's proposal.[105]

In addition, the original proposal as to article 35 of the Pandemic Agreement (Zero Draft)[106] allowed for provisional application of the Agreement, in whole or in part, by the EU. This should have been possible by so notifying the Depositary, a procedure frequently followed in the treaty practice of the EU. According to the Draft Pandemic Agreement (24 May 2024), this possibility has not yet been adopted by the negotiating parties. However, it is indicated that the article will be revisited 'pending protocol discussions'.[107]

4.2 The Revision of the International Health Regulations

On 27 May 2022, by Decision of the 75th WHA, a Working Group had been established with the mandate to elaborate amendments to the IHR (2005).[108] The Working Group had its first meeting on 14–15 November 2022.[109] A final set of amendments to the IHR was adopted at the last hour of the 77th WHA on 1 June 2024.[110]

Proposals by States for amendment of the IHR could be submitted until 30 September 2022. In addition, two proposals were accepted after the deadline had passed. The then Czech EU Presidency, on behalf of the EU and its Member States and on its own behalf, submitted proposals relating to articles

[104] Zero Draft Pandemic Agreement (1 February 2023) (n 69), article 33(2).

[105] Draft Pandemic Agreement (24 May 2024) (n 79), articles 1(e), 22, 33(1) and 34(2).

[106] Zero Draft Pandemic Agreement (1 February 2023) (n 69), article 35.

[107] Draft Pandemic Agreement (24 May 2024) (n 79), article 35.

[108] WHA Decision 75(9) (27 May 2022) UN Doc WHA75(9).

[109] WGIHR, 'Report of the First Meeting of the Working Group on the Amendments to the International Health Regulations (2005)' (30 November 2022) UN Doc A/WGIHR/1/5.

[110] IHR (2024).

3, 6, 7, 11, 12, 15, 23, 35, 36, 43, 44, 48, and 49, added a new article 54bis, and proposed amendments to annex 1(4) and annex 6 to the IHR (2005).[111]

The EU proposed amendments to article 6 IHR (2005) and annex 1, section 4(b), which included a proposal for the extension of information that States must provide upon notification of an 'event' to the WHO. An 'event' means an outbreak of a disease, or an occurrence that creates the potential for a disease that presents or could present significant harm to humans. The additional information that the EU amendment envisaged to be provided included 'epidemiological and clinical data, as well as microbial and genomic data in case of an event caused by an infectious agent'.[112] This information shall be shared with all Parties of the IHR. By a new article 7(2), the EU proposed that this obligation should be further expanded to 'events' caused by an infectious agent and be complied with within a deadline yet to be specified. EU proposed amendments to article 11 IHR included a proposal for improvement of the WHO Event Information Site for National IHR Focal Points. This is a secured, web-based platform – the Event Information Site (EIS) – for communications with National Focal Points in order to fulfil their information sharing obligations, run by the WHO Secretariat.

The EU proposals to amend article 12 IHR are of particular importance. To the determination of the current PHEIC in the IHR (2005), they proposed to add the concept of a 'public health emergency of regional concern' and the concept of an 'intermediate public health emergency of international concern'.[113] Whilst EU proposals envisaged that the WHO Director-General determines the existence of these new health emergencies, their adoption would have also further enlarged the competencies of the EU cross-border health emergency system and the ensuing powers of HERA. These proposals were further supported by EU proposed amendments to article 44 IHR (2005), which would have required the WHO to strengthen 'regional planning, preparedness and response, in close cooperation with WHO Regional Offices and relevant international and regional organizations'.[114]

---

[111] EU Presidency, 'Submission of proposed amendments to the International Health Regulations (IHR) (2005), pursuant to decision WHA75(9) of the World Health Assembly, by the Czech Republic, the current Presidency of the Council of the European Union, as a State Party to the IHR and in coordination with the European Union, and on behalf of the Member States of the European Union' contained in WHO, 'Proposed Amendments to the International Health Regulations (2005) submitted in accordance with decision WHA75(9) (2022)' https://apps.who.int/gb/wgihr/pdf_files/wgihr1/WGIHR_Submissions_Original_Languages.pdf.

[112] ibid, article 6(2).

[113] ibid, article 12(6).

[114] ibid, article 44(2)(a).

The EU Explanatory Note to its proposed article 12 amendments did not disclose the above consequences but argued that the current IHR (2005) alert system is sometimes perceived as too restrictive. Therefore, the WHO Director-General should be given the possibility:

> to determine that an event constitutes a regional public health emergency of international concern or an intermediate public health emergency of international concern ('yellow light'). The introduction of the categories of regional as well as intermediate PHEICs aims to take into account that there can be a regional component to a 'yellow light' event, and that both the regional element as well as intensity need to be seen as interlinked.[115]

The EU proposal to amend article 15(2) IHR (2005) required that the Temporary Recommendations issued by the WHO Director-General and the Emergency Committees to address a PHEIC 'should be as evidence-based, concise and operational as possible, and refer to existing guidance and international technical standards, when appropriate'.[116]

With regard to health measures on arrival and departure at State borders regulated by article 23 IHR, the EU-proposed amendments attempted to globalise the EU's digital Passenger Locator Forms (PLFs) and link them to universal interoperable technological platforms. The EU-proposed amendments with regard to article 35 IHR (2005) followed a similar approach for health documents which, if in digital form, shall be universally interoperable and recognised. A proposed new paragraph 3 of article 36 IHR and respective proposed amendments to annex 6 added to certificates of vaccination or other prophylaxis the possibility to rely on other types of proof, in particular test and recovery certificates, and proposed to put the WHA in charge of developing technical specifications and recognition.[117]

The EU proposals with regard to amending article 43 IHR (2005) on additional health measures, that is, measures that go beyond those recommended by the WHO to address a PHEIC, can be understood as a reaction to such additional health measures imposed by the People's Republic of China and other States during the Covid-19 pandemic. The EU proposals aimed to bind such additional measures to substantial and procedural requirements. For example, the proposals demanded that such measures 'shall be based on regular risk assessments, provide a proportionate response to the specific public health risks', and 'be reviewed on a regular basis … . They should be compatible with measures taken by other Parties' and subject to consultations which, inter alia,

115 ibid, appendix 'explanatory notes', 2.

116 ibid, article 15(2).

117 ibid, article 36(3).

result in a report by the WHO Director-General to the WHA 'on the conduct and outcome of consultations, with particular regard to general challenges and problems revealed by them'.[118]

The EU proposal for a new article 54bis in the IHR suggested expanding the WHA's power to oversee the implementation of the IHR considerably, and to establish a Special Committee to assist the Assembly in fulfilling its monitoring powers. As a consequence, if they had been adopted, these amendments would have increased the effects on, and efficiency of, the IHR on national law of the Member States.

In November 2022, the WHO Secretariat had compiled all IHR (2005) amendments proposed by the Member States and regional organisations in one document, available to the public. The document showed the amendments article by article, but did not indicate the author(s) of each amendment.[119] In total, more than 300 proposals for amendment to 33 of the 66 articles of the IHR (2005), and to five of their nine annexes were submitted. In addition, six new articles and two new annexes had been proposed. Further, the WHO published a reference document with the technical recommendations of an IHR Review Committee on the proposed amendments, which had been prepared by the Secretariat for the third meeting of the WHO Working Group on the Amendments of the IHR (17–20 April 2023).[120] The Working Group originally intended to finish its work at its sixth and last meeting, scheduled for 7–8 December 2023.[121] By mid-December 2023, the Review Committee should have considered the package of amendments to the IHR prepared by the Working Group and forwarded it to the WHO Director-General before mid-January 2024. [122] In accordance with the four-month timeline set out in article 55(2) IHR (2005), the WHO Director-General should have distributed the final

118 ibid, article 43(7).

119 WHO, 'Article-by-Article Compilation of Proposed Amendments to the International Health Regulations (2005) submitted in accordance with decision WHA75(9) (2022) of November 2022' https://apps.who.int/gb/wgihr/pdf_files/wgihr1/WGIHR_Compilation-en.pdf.

120 WHO, 'Reference Document: Proposed Amendments and Technical Recommendations' (February 2023) https://apps.who.int/gb/wgihr/pdf_files/wgihr2/A_WGIHR2_Reference_document-en.pdf.

121 WGIHR, 'Report of the Second Meeting of the Working Group on Amendments to the International Health Regulations (2005)' (14 March 2023) UN Doc A/WGIHR/2/10, 2 https://apps.who.int/gb/wgihr/pdf_files/wgihr2/A_WGIHR2_10-en.pdf.

122 WGIHR, 'Report of the Review Committee Regarding Amendments to the International Health Regulations (2005)' (6 February 2023) UN Doc A/WGIHR/2/5, 97 https://apps.who.int/gb/wgihr/pdf_files/wgihr2/A_WGIHR2_5-en.pdf?sfvrsn=4b549603_12.

text of the amendments to all WHO Member States by January 2024 to permit States to carefully study the implications of all amendments for their domestic legal orders for four months before their planned adoption by the 77th WHA in May 2024. However, the Working Group and the WHO Director-General decided not to comply with these deadlines,[123] prolonged the negotiation process right through to the last day of the 77th WHA (1 June 2024), and, together with a number of States, pushed very hard for the adoption of the amendments at the very last hour of the WHA.[124]

Though the package of amendments adopted was more limited than expected, they include key elements of the original EU proposals, even though some were moved to other parts of the 2024 amended IHR. Thus, for example, the new paragraph A.2 of annex 1 to the IHR includes the obligation of States to develop, strengthen and maintain 'support [for] the local level in preventing, preparing for and responding to public health risks and events, including in relation to … (ii) on-site investigations; … (vi) risk communication, including addressing misinformation and disinformation …'.[125] At the national level, it added paragraph A.3(i) of annex 1, which requires the same with regard to risk communication, including addressing misinformation and disinformation.[126] Also, annex 2 on the 'Decision Instrument for the Assessment and Notification of Events that may Constitute a Public Health Emergency of International Concern'[127] and annex 3 on the 'Model Ship Sanitation Control Exemption Certificate/Ship Sanitation Control Certificate',[128] along with certificates required according to paragraphs 4 and 8 of annex 6 on 'Vaccination, Prophylaxis and Related Certificates',[129] clearly bear the EU's signature.

---

123 WGIHR, 'Report of the Fifth Meeting of the Working Group on Amendments to the International Health Regulations 2005' (25 October 2023) UN Doc WGIHR/5/3, para 5 https://apps.who.int/gb/wgihr/pdf_files/wgihr5/A_WGIHR5_3-en.pdf; and webcast of the 'Fifth Meeting of the Working Group on Amendments to the International Health Regulations (WGIHR)' (2 October 2023) with Steven Solomon (WHO Principal Legal Officer), via *YouTube* (7 October 2023) https://www.youtube.com/watch?v=1XvavE-p6VA.

124 'Bureau's Proposed Text' of 20 May 2024, appendix to the report of the WHO Director-General, 'Working Group on the Amendments of the International Health Regulations' (27 May 2024) UN Doc A77/9.

125 ibid, article A.2.

126 ibid, annex 1, article A.1(3).

127 ibid, annex 2.

128 ibid, annex 3.

129 ibid, annex 6, paras 6 and 8.

5. CROSS-BORDER HEALTH EMERGENCY FROM THE PERSPECTIVE OF THE TEU AND TFEU

On 21 October 2021, the European Parliament by resolution on EU Transparency in the Development, Purchase and Distribution of COVID-19 Vaccines (2021/2678(RSP))[130] expressed its 'deepest regret on the lack of transparency from the Commission, the Member States and pharmaceutical companies in the development, purchase and distribution of COVID-19 vaccines, especially in context of continuous breaches of contracts signed'[131] and called on the Commission to, inter alia:

> make a legislative proposal on future joint vaccine procurement with clear provisions on transparency and competence distribution among the actors of the EU institutional framework and the Member States and on future treatments against COVID-19 and orphan treatments within the framework of the pharmaceutical strategy for Europe; calls on the Commission to review the terms of price confidentiality agreements in order to address the current fragmentation of the European internal market.[132]

In addition, the European Parliament asked for further measures providing transparency on how and by whom medical countermeasures to address Covid-19 were dealt with, and how and by whom any future similar crises would be dealt with. In particular, the European Parliament criticised:

> the Commission's decision to refrain from using the ordinary legislative procedure through Article 168 TFEU in setting up the new European Health Emergency Preparedness and Response Authority (HERA), thereby failing to establish it as a fully-fledged independent agency that has a mandate to protect the public interest and is subject to the same rigorous scrutiny as other EU agencies; regrets the fact that the Commission's approach, which has led to Parliament being excluded from overseeing the work of HERA, can be regarded as yet another shortcoming that has undermined transparency and accountability for public spending and decision-making in the area of public health.[133]

By further resolutions, the European Parliament commented on accountability, including parliamentary monitoring of HERA, on HERA's mandate, and

---

130 European Parliament, Resolution of 21 October 2021 on EU Transparency in the Development, Purchase and Distribution of COVID-19 Vaccines (2021) 2678 (RSP).

131 ibid, number 2.

132 ibid, number 5.

133 ibid, number 11.

on the use of patent pools, open source research, and grants and subsidies.[134] It referred to stakeholders' comments on HERA, without, however, even to a minimum extent, reflecting on the criticism that arose in public of the EU's handling of the Covid-19 pandemic.[135] The European Parliament further described the overly broad role that HERA has started to play in the European Commission's and EU's handling of the conclusions drawn from the Covid-19 pandemic, and the impressive budgetary means and organisational tools assigned to it.[136] However, the European Parliament did not put into doubt that the TEU and the TFEU allow the EU's bodies to proceed as they do with HERA.

The method of how the EU Commission established HERA, the activities HERA engaged in until today, and, in particular, the options that the EU Commission is currently negotiating for its own and HERA's dominant future in EU health policies by means of the WHO Pandemic Agreement and the 2024 amendments to the IHR demonstrate that the EU tries to silently overcome the limits of its competence set by article 168(5) TFEU, without the EU having been able to use the Covid-19 pandemic to change the TEU and TFEU.[137]

As for the competence of the EU in health matters, the fundamental norm is indeed article 168(5) TFEU which reads as follows:

---

134 European Parliament, 'HERA, the EU's new Health Emergency Preparedness and Response Authority' (Briefing, February 2022) 3 ff https://www.europarl.europa.eu/RegData/etudes/BRIE/2022/698941/EPRS_BRI(2022)698941_EN.pdf.

135 Eg for the European Public Health Alliance: Rosa Castro 'HERA: Will the EU Lead Global Action Against Pandemics (1 October 2021) https://epha.org/hera-will-the-eu-lead-global-action-against-pandemics/, demanding that the EU (through HERA) will need to treat the medical tools resulting from public investments as global public goods. In addition, the European Parliament mentions the European Alliance for Responsible R&D and Affordable Medicines and the recommendations of Panel 3 'Climate Change and Environment/Health' of the Conference on the Future of Europe and, thus, no single voice critical at the EU as such. Eg also European Parliament, 'HERA, the EU's new Health Emergency Preparedness and Response Authority', 4 https://www.europarl.europa.eu/RegData/etudes/BRIE/2022/698941/EPRS_BRI(2022)698941_EN.pdf.

136 ibid, European Parliament, 4–10.

137 See for the consequences of the Covid-19 pandemic on EU treaty law and, in particular, the delimitation of competences between the EU and its Member States: Peter Becker et al, 'Die Pandemie und die EU: Integrationsimpuls mit ungewisser Wirkung' in Barbara Lippert, Stefan Mair, and Volker Perthes (eds), *Internationale Politik unter Pandemie-Bedingungen Tendenzen und Perspektiven für 2021* (SWP-Studie 26, 2020) 55, 57.

> The European Parliament and the Council, acting in accordance with the ordinary legislative procedure and after consulting the Economic and Social Committee and the Committee of the Regions, may also adopt incentive measures designed to protect and improve human health and in particular to combat the major cross-border health scourges, measures concerning monitoring, early warning of and combating serious cross-border threats to health, and measures which have as their direct objective the protection of public health regarding tobacco and the abuse of alcohol, excluding any harmonisation of the laws and regulations of the Member States.

Besides adopting 'incentive measures' at EU level, even when it comes to 'combating serious cross-border threats to health', no delegation of competences by the EU Member States has taken place. The aim of achieving a high level of health protection laid down in article 168(1) TFEU cannot overrule the limits set to the EU by the same article. Union action is restricted to complement national policies,[138] not to replace them. The EU Member States are led to cooperate with each other, with this cooperation to be supported by the EU.[139] Paragraph two of article 168(2) TFEU mentions 'Guidelines' as an example for a 'useful initiative to promote such coordination', but not Regulations, Decisions, or even Directives. The Council is expressly allowed to issue Recommendations for the purposes set out by article 168 TFEU.[140] Legislative measures, adopted in the procedure for ordinary legislation, that reach farther, are restricted by article 168(4) TFEU to:

> (a) … setting high standards of quality and safety of organs and substances of human origin, blood and blood derivatives; these measures shall not prevent any Member State from maintaining or introducing more stringent protective measures; (b) … in the veterinary and phytosanitary fields which have as their direct objective the protection of public health; (c) … setting high standards of quality and safety for medicinal products and devices for medical use.

Thus, to use the instrument of a Regulation based on article 168(5) TFEU must be considered overstepping the limits of competence by the EU bodies. This goes for the Regulation on Serious Cross-border Threats to Health and Repealing Decision No 1082/2013/EU[141] as well as for the Regulation establishing the ECDC.[142] Furthermore, the fact that the EU has chosen the instrument of a Regulation for reinforcing the EMA's role in crisis preparedness and management for medicinal products and medical devices may well be doubted based on article 168(4)(c) TFEU. The EMA has nothing to do with the EU

138 TFEU, article 168(1) para 2.
139 TFEU, article 168(2) para 1.
140 TFEU, article 168(5).
141 Regulation (EU) 2022/2371 (n 37).
142 Regulation (EU) 2022/2370 (n 9).

Common Foreign and Security Policy, with the latter justifying under narrow conditions that EU bodies become active under article 114 TFEU. Thus, the reference to article 114 in the context of the EMA, setting the EMA within 'approximation of laws in the internal market' can only be understood as a desperate effort to find any respective competence for the EU, which in fact is not given. Even if the protection of health is considered as a cross-section matter according to article 9 TFEU, which has to be considered whenever EU bodies become active, according to the jurisprudence of the Court of Justice of the European Union (CJEU), article 114 TFEU must not be used to circumvent the explicit exemption from approximation of laws under article 168(5) with the exceptions of article 168(4) TFEU. Concerning article 114 TFEU, the CJEU regularly examines whether a measure initiated by EU bodies 'actually contributes to eliminating obstacles to the free movement of goods and to the free movement to provide services, and to removing distortions of competition'.[143] Practice during the Covid-19 pandemic shows moreover that the EMA was an instrument of distortion of competition by providing an advantage to particular companies to supply countermeasures and keeping others away from the European market. Thus, the exception of article 165(4)(c) TFEU carries only what in the respective Regulation can be understood as 'setting high standards of quality and safety for medicinal products and devices for medical use'. Measures to fight pandemics like Covid-19 cannot, not even subsidiarily, be based on the internal market competence of article 114(1) TFEU.[144]

Legitimate doubts may be raised also about the current negotiations on a WHO Pandemic Agreement and the process that led to the 2024 adoption of the amendments to the IHR. In both cases, the EU has taken the lead – concerning the Pandemic Agreement through the European Commission, and in relation to the IHR amendment process through the EU Presidency. It must be doubted that this strong negotiation power of the EU is in line with article 168(3) TFEU, which provides that 'the Union and the Member States shall foster cooperation with … the competent international organisations in the sphere of public health', which points to the general coordination competence of article 2(5) TFEU.[145] In the reality of the negotiations at WHO level, the

---

[143] Case C-376/98 *Federal Republic of Germany v European Parliament and Council of the European Union* 2000 ECR I-08419, para 95.

[144] Christian Calliess, 'Die Gesundheitspolitik der EU in der Corona Krise (Covid-19-Pandemie) – Reformüberlegungen mit Blick auf die Konferenz zur Zukunft Europas', Berlin e-Working Papers on European Law No 128 (22 March 2021) 13 https://www.jura.fu-berlin.de/forschung/europarecht/bob/berliner_online_beitraege/Paper128-Calliess/BOB-128-Calliess-neu.pdf.

[145] TFEU, article 2(5), reads as follows: 'In certain areas and under the conditions laid down in the Treaties, the Union shall have competence to carry out

Member States, with the exception of the one State holding the Presidency of the EU, were and are not visible anymore. The EU has become active on behalf of its members within the WHO, and not in cooperation with them. From a cooperative approach one would expect that the EU Member States who are also members of the WHO elaborate and submit their own proposals that do not contradict each other, and are thus coordinated, but not that such proposals of individual States are replaced by one single proposal for all EU Member States made directly by the EU Presidency (concerning proposals to amend the IHR) or the European Commission (concerning draft articles for the new WHO Pandemic Agreement). This does not exclude that the EU is entitled to conclude the new WHO Pandemic Agreement side by side with the EU Member States once negotiations come to an end. Emphasis must be laid, however, on the negotiation process itself.

In view of the understanding of health as 'human health'[146] as opposed to 'animal health' in article 168(5) TFEU, the EU's reliance on the 'One Health' concept underlying its internal measures with regard to pandemic preparedness and prevention and the impact of this broad concept on the negotiations of a WHO Pandemic Agreement and the adopted 2024 amendments to the IHR must also be questioned. Relying on and promoting this concept may well overstep the limits of the EU's and, as a consequence, also HERA's competences.[147] To enlarge the understanding of 'threats to health' to also include environmental threats, thus, cannot be based on article 168(5) TFEU, but must be in line with article 191(1) TFEU, which is to be applied only in such a case.[148]

actions to support, coordinate or supplement the actions of the Member States, without thereby superseding their competence in these areas. Legally binding acts of the Union adopted on the basis of the provisions of the Treaties relating to these areas shall not entail harmonisation of Member States' laws or regulations.' And Christian Calliess, Matthias Ruffert, and Thorsten Kingreen, *EUV – AEUV mit Europäischer Grundrechtecharta. Kommentar* (6th edn, HC Beck (online) 2022), article 168 TFEU, margin number (mn) 18.

146 See for many others, eg Matthias Pechstein, Carsten Nowak, and Ulrich Häde (eds), *Frankfurter Kommentar EUV/GRC/AEUV* (1st edn, Mohr Siebeck (online) 2011), article 168 TFEU, mn 8.

147 See on HERA's link to the European Health Union: Commission, 'From the Commission to the European Parliament, the European Council, the Council, the European Economic and Social Committee and the Committee of the Regions Introducing HERA, the European Health Emergency Preparedness and Response Authority, the next step towards completing the European Health Union' COM (2021) 576 final, 3.

148 TFEU, article 191(1), reads as follows:

'1. Union policy on the environment shall contribute to the pursuit of the following objectives:

Article 191(1) TFEU entitles the EU, however, only to adopt an environmental policy measure which, inter alia, pursues the objective of protecting human health and not a human health measure meeting an environmental threat.[149]

As far as reference is made to article 35 ChEU,[150] the provision must be understood as not enlarging the competence of the EU and its institutions. It obliges them to pay due respect to this article when using their existing competences, among others those under article 168 TFEU.[151]

Since HERA has been established by the European Commission based on its own competences in the area of health, the lack of a legal fundament for the European Commission's competences in this area and the EU's respective activities also leads to HERA lacking a legal basis.

6. CONCLUDING REMARKS

With HERA, the EU has established and institutionalised a permanent and perpetual crisis mode in the European public health system. It expects new crises to come, not only naturally occurring pandemics but also man-made threats such as bioterrorism and threats falling under the scope of EURATOM. This chapter demonstrated that the EU, its Commission, and HERA are lacking a legal fundament in the Founding Treaties both for the activities they have set for themselves in the area of pandemic preparedness and prevention and by enlarging their activities and powers by negotiating the WHO Pandemic Agreement and the revision of the IHR. The EU and HERA turned out to be key drivers for the WHO Pandemic Agreement aiming to globalise the EU's own securitised Covid-19 measures and practices. This strategy has already proved largely successful in regard to the recent amendments to the IHR adopted in May 2024 on which the EU had considerable influence. It will not be

---

- preserving, protecting and improving the quality of the environment,
- protecting human health,
- prudent and rational utilisation of natural resources,
- promoting measures at international level to deal with regional or worldwide environmental problems, and in particular combating climate change.'

149 See the analysis of HERA's and the EU's underlying definitions in Section 3.

150 See Section 1.

151 See for many others, Hans Dieter Jarass, *Charta der Grundrechte der Europäischen Union: GRCh* (4th edn, HC Beck (online) 2021), article 35, mn 1 and 5.

easy for politicians and the public to stop the adoption of the WHO Pandemic Agreement in 2025. However, it is not too late to minimise the EU's impact on the final product in order to avoid that policies, measures, and instruments will be further globalised – policies, measures, and instruments that had disastrous effects in Europe during the Covid-19 pandemic and its aftermath.

6. Private law aspects of global pandemic preparedness, prevention, and response

Günter Reiner

1. INTRODUCTION

The administration of public health is a sovereign task. It essentially follows the rules of public law. Private law aspects of global pandemic preparedness, prevention, and response activities, and programmes and policies are therefore not evident at first glance. Of course, providing the general public with products and services in a market economy system is fundamentally a matter for private law entities that utilise private law contracts. In principle, this includes healthcare, even if this area has always been characterised by considerable State intervention in freedom of contract due to the overriding public interest in public health. This is so in particular in times of health emergencies, including a public health emergency of international concern (PHEIC) declared by the World Health Organization (WHO).

A second aspect – the global dimension of PHEICs and pandemic preparedness, prevention, and response activities and programmes – also has a strong connection to private law. It is true that the foundations of globalisation are based on agreements under public international law that are administered by international organisations governed by public international law. However, the de facto drivers of globalisation are frequently powerful private actors who enjoy the advantage over States that their activities are not limited by national borders in accordance with the principles of private international law. Private law actors act with private law instruments. The past has shown that cross-border emergencies not only promote the globalisation of law, but also the influence of international private law actors and instruments.

The aim of this chapter is to carve out and illustrate the enormous importance of the private law aspects, including the public-private hybridisation trend for public health emergency management and law, using the Covid-19-PHEIC and global responses to it as an example. This will highlight the dangers arising from the fact that acts of public administration performed under private law are subject to fewer obligations deriving from fundamental rights than acts performed under public law. This phenomenon has long been known in German administrative law and is discussed under the catchphrase '*Flucht in das Privatrecht*' ('escape into private law').[1]

First, the chapter examines the private actors that played a major role in the Covid-19-PHEIC (Section 2). Section 3 focuses on some private law instruments. Section 4 discusses the impact of WHO standards on private law. The last substantive part examines private law liability for damages in the global health emergency regime (Section 5), while Section 6 concludes. Despite the global dimension, national politics, law, and funding continue to play a major role. By way of example, this chapter focuses on the German and European perspectives.

2. PRIVATE LAW ACTORS

Together with States and international or supranational organisations, private law actors play a major role in global pandemic/PHEIC preparedness, prevention, and response law, policies, and institutions designed to address PHEICs. The investigative journalist and blogger Iain Davis has drawn up an informative diagram entitled 'The Global Public-Private Partnership (G3P)', in which he distinguishes between 'policy makers', 'policy distributors', 'policy enforcers', 'policy propagandists' and, last but not least, 'policy subjects' that enjoy or have to endure the consequences of policies. In addition to the public, he identifies private contributors among the 'policy makers', for example, the World Economic Forum and the Rockefeller Foundation. Among the 'policy distributors' he names, for instance, philanthropic foundations, global companies, non-governmental organisations (NGOs), and international expert bodies such as the Intergovernmental Panel on Climate Change (IPCC). Finally, among the 'policy propagandists' he lists prominent media corporations, fact-checking organisations, and social media platforms.[2] This is an insightful perspective that has inspired the following distinctions between various private actors involved in pandemic/PHEIC preparedness, prevention, and response activities and programmes: the actors of the health economy, the actors of civil

1 Christoph Gusy, 'Freiheit der Formenwahl und Rechtsbindung der Verwaltung' (1985) 7(11) JURA 578, 583.

2 'The Global Public-Private Partnership (G3P)' (*Iain Davis*, 2025) https://iaindavis.com/wp-content/uploads/2022/03/G3P-Chart.png. Unless otherwise stated all web links given in this chapter last accessed between 1 March and 4 April 2025.

society, the public-private partnerships, the actors of science, and the media and platforms.

2.1 Players in the Healthcare Industry

Naturally, companies that are able and willing to offer healthcare goods (eg vaccines) or services (eg medical treatments or laboratory analyses)[3] on a large scale on a global market across borders are direct actors in the area of pandemic/PHEIC prevention, preparedness, and response. One could even get the impression that the distribution of specific health products is now at the centre of the WHO's and the EU's efforts to address future health emergencies.[4]

Companies (and other private actors) also appear as indirect actors, for example by providing financial or moral support to other actors such as the WHO or civil society organisations (see Section 2.2) to ensure implementation of and compliance with WHO-recommended medical countermeasures to address a PHEIC. A prominent example during the Covid-19-PHEIC was the 'Go, get vaccinated!' ('*Dann geh doch impfen*') advertising campaign run by 150 German companies in support of the global vaccination campaign against Covid-19. In this campaign, the participating companies altered their well-known advertising slogans. The car manufacturer BMW, for example, temporarily changed its longstanding slogan 'Joy in Driving' ('*Freude am Fahren*') to 'Joy in Vaccination' ('*Freude am Impfen*').[5]

Private involvement also manifests itself in personnel moving between public and private actors involved in global pandemic/PHEIC prevention, preparedness, and response programmes and policy development. For example, Regina E Dugan from the US is a member of the Supervisory Board of

---

3 See eg the establishment of the 'EU reference laboratories' in accordance with article 15 of Regulation (EU) 2022/2371 on serious cross-border threats to health and repealing Decision No 1082/2013/EU [2022] OJ L314/26 (Regulation on serious cross-border threats to health).

4 See the new 'relevant health products' category added to the amended International Health Regulations (IHR) in 2024, which will play a major role from now on, discussed by Amrei Müller and Silvia Behrendt, 'The 2024 Amendments to the International Health Regulations: A Commentary (Part II: Selected Substantive Amendments)' (*Opinio Juris*, 20 September 2024) https://opiniojuris.org/2024/09/20/the-2024-amendments-to-the-international-health-regulations-a-commentary-part-ii-selected-substantive-amendments/.

5 'Dann geh doch zum Impfen! Marken ändern Slogans für Impfkampagne' (*Welt Online*, 7 December 2021) https://www.welt.de/wirtschaft/article235503422/Dann-geh-doch-zum-Impfen-150-Marken-aendern-Slogans-fuer-Impfkampagne.html.

the German Siemens AG, which is active in vaccine production, among other things, and cooperates with BioNTech,[6] since February 2023. She was the Director of the Defence Advanced Research Projects Agency (DARPA) (the research department of the US military) for several years before becoming CEO of Wellcome Leap, which is part of the British Wellcome Trust. Both DARPA and the Wellcome Trust/Leap have been involved heavily in research on messenger ribonucleic acid (mRNA) technology.

2.2 'Civil Society' Actors

Globally operating civil society actors in the form of NGOs also play a major role in pandemic/PHEIC preparedness and response programmes and policies. The Bill and Melinda Gates Foundation (BMGF), the Rockefeller Foundation, the Wellcome Trust and the Clinton Health Access Initiative, Inc. (CHAI) should be mentioned. These organisations are directly involved in global healthcare through their own activities and programmes, for example, in the distribution of medical products or through funding medical research.[7] They also exert indirect influence by funding other players, in particular the WHO,[8] but also domestic health authorities. For example, the BMGF has repeatedly made donations to the German Robert Koch Institute (RKI),[9] which is the national authority for the prevention of communicable diseases and for the

---

[6] 'Mehr Tempo bei der Entwicklung und Herstellung von Impfstoffen' (*Siemens*, 2021) https://www.siemens.com/de/de/unternehmen/stories/industrie/2021/pharma-impfstoff-digitalisierung.html; '*Siemens* und *BioNTech* bauen ihre Zusammenarbeit für eine weltweite Impfstoffproduktion aus' (*Siemens*, 23 June 2021) https://press.siemens.com/global/de/pressemitteilung/siemens-und-biontech-bauen-ihre-zusammenarbeit-fuer-eine-weltweite.

[7] Eg 'Health' (*The Rockefeller Foundation*, 2025) https://www.rockefellerfoundation.org/our-work/health/; 'About Us' (*Clinton Health Access Initiative*, 2025) https://www.clintonhealthaccess.org/about-us/; 'Who we Are' (*Wellcome*, 2025) https://wellcome.org/who-we-are; and 'Im Porträt: Gates Stiftung – Engagement für weltweite Gesundheit' (*Health Capital*, 7 October 2021) https://www.health-capital.de/news/artikel/im-portraet-gates-stiftung-engagement-fuer-weltweite-gesundheit/.

[8] The BMGF donated $591 million to the WHO and a further $700 million to other organisations (eg UNICEF) in 2020–21, which in turn donated to the WHO, see 'Factsheet WHO Finanzierung' (*Dialog Globale Gesundheit*, January 2024) https://globale-gesundheit.com/factsheet-who-3-finanzierung/.

[9] 'Bill Gates spendet fast halbe Million Dollar an das RKI' (*Deutsche Wirtschaftsnachrichten*, 10 January 2022) https://deutsche-wirtschafts-nachrichten.de/516814/Bill-Gates-spendet-fast-halbe-Million-Dollar-an-das-RKI.

early detection and prevention of the spread of infections in Germany.[10] The RKI reports to the German Federal Ministry of Health (BMG). Significantly, the agreement between the three political parties that formed the German coalition government between September 2021 and February 2025[11] mentions the term 'civil society' no fewer than 36 times.

The German Federal Government is explicitly in favour of cooperation with international foundations in the area of pandemic preparedness and response and in the health sector more generally (it has even declared that there is no alternative to such an approach). Accordingly, the largest private foundations in the field of global health, namely the BMGF, are funded directly or as part of 'cooperation projects' by the Federal Government, for example in the field of vaccine development and distribution.[12] In plain language: the German government supports the work of these foundations with billions in taxpayers' money. The WHO Draft Pandemic Agreement (24 May 2024) that is currently being negotiated implicitly favours promoting the involvement of 'civil society' in pandemic prevention, preparedness, and response activities as part of the whole-of-society approach (article 17).[13]

The informal influence of NGOs as 'advisors' to governments is also worth mentioning. Bill Gates himself, chair of the BMGF, made a personal appearance on German TV at the beginning of the Covid-19-PHEIC when

---

[10] Section 4I(1), German Infection Protection Act, *Gesetz zur Verhütung und Bekämpfung von Infektionskrankheiten beim Menschen – Infektionsschutzgesetz* (IfSG).

[11] 'Koalitionsvertrag 2021–2025 zwischen der Sozialdemokratischen Partei Deutschlands (SPD), BÜNDNIS 90/DIE GRÜNEN und den Freien Demokraten (FDP)' (*Frag Den Staat*, 2025) https://fragdenstaat.de/dokumente/142083-koalitionsvertrag-2021-2025/.

[12] See answer of the German Federal Government of 30 June 2023 to a 'Kleine Anfrage' by DIE LINKE parliamentary group, 'Stand der Zusammenarbeit zwischen der Bundesregierung und privaten Stiftungen', Bundestag-Drucksache 20/7512. This also includes the financing of PPPs like Gavi and the Coalition for Epidemic Preparedness Innovations (CEPI) by the federal government, which are dealt with separately in Section 2.3.

[13] WHA, 'Proposal for the WHO Pandemic Agreement', draft text of 24 May 2024, appendix to the report of the WHO Director-General, 'Outcome of the Intergovernmental Negotiating Body (INB) to Draft and Negotiate a WHO Convention, Agreement or Other International Instrument on Pandemic Prevention, Preparedness and Response' (27 May 2024) UN Doc A77/10 (Draft Pandemic Agreement (24 May 2024)). The corresponding draft article 16 of an earlier version of the draft Agreement explicitly mentioned 'civil society': INB, 'Zero Draft of the WHO CA+ for the Consideration of the Intergovernmental Negotiation Body at its Fourth Meeting' (1 February 2023) UN Doc A/INB/4/3.

he announced on the German evening news *Tagesthemen*, the daily flagship news programme of the first public television channel, that an effective vaccine should be developed that would immunise 7 billion people.[14] This is a statement that Chancellor Merkel later adopted as her own.[15]

2.3 Public Private Partnerships (PPPs)

There is also a growing tendency of State actors and international organisations such as the WHO and UNICEF to cooperate with NGOs including philanthropic foundations within the framework of public-private partnerships (PPPs) regulated by private law. This leads to a shift of public decision-making competences to non-State actors,[16] raising questions of accountability. An impressive example of such a PPP is the Coalition for Epidemic Preparedness Innovations (CEPI). This is a non-profit association established in Davos in 2017, founded by public, private, philanthropic, and civil society organisations under Norwegian law with the aim 'to accelerate the development of vaccines and other biologic countermeasures against epidemic and pandemic threats so they can be accessible to all people in need'.[17] Novavax, a manufacturer of a vaccine against Covid-19, announced in 2021 that CEPI's early support had helped the company 'to jump-start the development of a global supply network'.[18]

Another example is the aforementioned Vaccine Alliance Gavi, a foundation under Swiss private law which was established in 2000 with the aim of giving children in the world's poorest countries equal access to new and

---

14 'Tagesthemen' (*Tagesschau*, 12 April 2020) https://www.youtube.com/watch?v=083VjebhzgI.

15 Press conference from 19 February 2021, where Angela Merkel states that the pandemic will 'only be defeated when everyone in the world has been vaccinated'; see 'Pressekonferenz von Kanzlerin Merkel nach der G7-Videokonferenz' (*Bundesregierung*, 19 February 2021) https://www.bundesregierung.de/breg-de/service/archiv/archiv-mediathek/pressekonferenz-von-kanzlerin-merkel-nach-der-g7-videokonferenz-1860056.

16 Erika de Wet, 'Zur Zukunft der Völkerrechtswissenschaft in Deutschland' (2007) 67 ZaöRV 777, 795 ff, specifically with regard to the WHO, the author observes a 'relative decline of national governments as the main provider of services in the field of preventive medicine and health care' and an 'increasing role of corporations in determining global health governance'.

17 'Mission Statement' (*CEPI*, 2025) https://cepi.net/about-cepi.

18 '*Novavax* und *Gavi* schließen Vorabkaufvertrag über COVID-19-Impfstoff für COVAX-Facility' (*PR Newswire*, 7 May 2021) https://www.prnewswire.com/news-releases/novavax-und-gavi-schliessen-vorabkaufvertrag-uber-covid-19-impfstoff-fur-covax-facility-ab-875108139.html.

under-utilised vaccines. The WHO is one of the four permanent members of Gavi's Board of Directors, and co-chairs (alternately with UNICEF) the Gavi Executive Committee. During the Covid-19-PHEIC, Gavi managed the COVAX Facility (Covid-19 Vaccines Global Access), an 'initiative' that, in Gavi's words, aimed to 'bring together governments, global health organisations, manufacturers, scientists, private sector, civil society and philanthropy, with the aim of providing innovative and equitable access to COVID-19 diagnostics, treatments and vaccines'.[19]

2.4 Actors in Science

In the context of global health, 'science' can play a decisive role in legitimising the emergency measures. 'Follow the science' was one of the strongest arguments used by politicians to ensure compliance with medical and non-medical countermeasures to address the Covid-19-PHEIC. Pfizer even relied on the slogan 'Science will win' whilst promoting its vaccine against Covid-19.

Scientists working within the health administrations of States are at the forefront. They are integrated into the public administration and can face ethical dilemmas regarding their scientific integrity if, as has happened during the Covid-19-PHEIC, politicians express expectations demanding 'scientific' justifications for various health measures for the effectiveness of which there is, however, no, very little, or conflicting scientific evidence.[20] In a health emergency, a functioning independent scientific landscape that is immune to political influence, and whose representatives predominantly act in their own name (even if they belong to public universities) would be important as a corrective to public health institutions that are ultimately answerable to the executive. Like in other countries, the German government was, however, advised by a hand-picked 'Council of Experts on the Coronavirus' (*Corona-Expertenrat*) to justify its medical and non-medical countermeasures.[21] The WHO also relies on experts giving 'scientific advice' through its numerous expert advisory

---

19 'COVAX explained' (*Gavi*, 3 September 2020) https://www.gavi.org/vaccineswork/covax-explained.

20 Reinhard Werner, 'Corona-"Furchtappell": Politik drängte Expertenrat zu Änderung in Stellungnahme' (*Epoch Times Deutschland*, 31 August 2024) https://www.epochtimes.de/politik/deutschland/corona-furchtappell-politik-draengte-expertenrat-zu-aenderung-in-stellungnahme-a4849863.htm.

21 'Der ExpertInnenrat der Bundesregierung' (*Die Bundesregierung*, 3 May 2023) https://www.bundesregierung.de/breg-de/bundesregierung/bundeskanzleramt/corona-expertinnenrat-der-bundesregierung.

panels.[22] Advisory panels exist on various health topics[23] and expert members are selected by the WHO Director-General.

Finally, (private) publishers of high-ranked journals that approve 'scientific' studies are among the private scientific actors involved in pandemic preparedness and response programmes, thereby influencing the scientific discourse about pandemic response measures. It is worth remembering the highly influential but equally controversial publication by Corman and Drosten on the polymerase chain reaction (PCR) test at the beginning of the Covid-19-PHEIC,[24] the manuscript version of which was even published on the WHO's website.[25]

2.5 Media and Platforms

During the Covid-19-PHEIC, big media corporations, public broadcasting services and social media platforms played a decisive role in creating global acceptance for far-reaching public health measures. These actors also cooperated with State authorities and the WHO to pre-bunk, de-bunk, and censor discussions and questions raised by critical voices.[26]

One can speculate as to why so little criticism was voiced during the Covid-19-PHEIC, even by the private media outlets (and still is today). The fact is that these private outlets, such as the German weekly *Der Spiegel*, repeatedly received donations into the millions of Euros from one of the significant actors

---

22 'Expert Advisory Panels and Committees' (*WHO*, 2025) https://www.who.int/about/collaboration/expert-advisory-panels-and-committees accessed 4 April 2025.

23 *Deutscher Bundestag/Wissenschaftlicher Dienst*, 'Weltgesundheitsorganisation (WHO)' WD 2–3000–013/19 (14 March 2019) 7.

24 Victor Corman et al, 'Detection of 2019 Novel Coronavirus (2019-nCoV) by Real-time RT-PCR' (2020) 25 Eurosurveillance 2000045. The article was submitted on 21 January 2020, accepted on 22 January 2020 and published on 23 January 2020. Existing conflicts of interest were not declared. For a critical analysis, see Pieter Borger et al, 'External Peer Review of the RTPCR Test to Detect SARS-CoV-2 Reveals 10 Major Scientific Flaws at the Molecular and Methodological Level: Consequences for False Positive Results' (November 2020) https://www.researchgate.net/publication/346483715_External_peer_review_of_the_RTPCR_test_to_detect_SARS-CoV-2_reveals_10_major_scientific_flaws_at_the_molecular_and_methodological_level_consequences_for_false_positive_results.

25 'Diagnostic Detection of 2019-nCoV by Real-time RT-PCR' (*WHO*, 17 January 2020) https://www.who.int/docs/default-source/coronaviruse/protocol-v2-1.pdf?sfvrsn=%20a9ef618c_2.

26 See eg the WHO's 'infodemic management' programme discussed by McGrogan in Chapter 4 and by Müller and Behrendt in Chapter 3 in this volume.

in global pandemic preparedness and response, the BMGF.[27] Financial dependencies have also arisen for news outlets in relation to governments, which have published expensive adverts for vaccines against Covid-19 in private newspapers. In addition, journalists who supported the Covid-19 medical and non-medical countermeasures were frequently rewarded with honorary contracts and prizes.[28] However, there was apparently also direct influence from government representatives on the media. In an open letter dated 26 August 2024, Meta CEO Mark Zuckerberg complained that high-ranking members of the US Biden Administration had repeatedly exerted pressure on his employees to censor certain Covid-19 content for months in 2021.[29] The other global social media platforms have also censored critical voices on the global responses to the Covid-19-PHEIC, and continue to do so. *YouTube*, for example, cancelled in June 2023 the channel of the German association of critical medical professionals and scientists '*Mediziner und Wissenschaftler für Gesundheit, Freiheit und Demokratie, e.V.*'[30]

Legally, platforms justify their censorship with references to their terms and conditions under private law which users have agreed to by clicking on them.[31] However, general terms and conditions may not be used abusively, and it is recognised – at least in German private law – that fundamental rights, including the right to freedom of expression, must also be taken into account when assessing abusiveness,[32] even if the effect of fundamental rights protected in this way between private individuals is weaker than in the relationship between the individual and the State due to the entitlement to enjoy fundamental rights on both sides. Accordingly, it happens time and again that users

27 'Committed Grants: DER SPIEGEL GmbH & Co. KG' (*Gates Foundation*, 2025) https://www.gatesfoundation.org/about/committed-grants/2021/10/inv032089.

28 Jonas Aston, 'Das System Preisgelder' (*Apollo News*, 23 August 2023) https://apollo-news.net/das-system-preisgelder-regierungen-schanzten-lesch-mailab-und-kebekus-fuenfstellige-betraege-zu/.

29 Severin Tatarczyk, 'Dokumentiert: Das Schreiben von Mark Zuckerberg zu Content Moderation in sozialen Netzwerken' (*Das Blogmagazin*, 27 August 2024) https://www.severint.net/2024/08/27/dokumentiert-das-schreiben-von-mark-zuckerberg-zu-content-moderation-in-sozialen-netzwerken/.

30 'Woran merkt man, dass die Aufklärung Früchte trägt?' (*MWGFD*, 19 June 2023) https://www.mwgfd.org/2023/06/zensur-tube-hat-unseren-kanal-geloescht/.

31 See eg the judgment of the Federal Court of Justice (*Bundesgerichtshof*) of 29 July 2021, III ZR 179/20, BGHZ 230, 347, on the right of a social network (*Facebook*) to remove individual posts and block network access in the event of a breach of communication standards.

32 Lorenz Kähler, in *Beckscher Online-Großkommentar*, § 242 BGB, 160 (as of 1 June 2025).

successfully defend themselves against platforms when faced with the deletion of their posts or even accounts.[33] However, the experience also demonstrates the de facto effectiveness of instruments of private law for restricting open public discourse. This is not least due to the fact that most people whose posts are deleted do not have the time or money to go to court, often through several instances.

While social media platforms may have acted 'voluntarily' until recently, they are and will be increasingly pressed by legislators to suppress content that qualifies as 'disinformation'. Reference can be made here to EU Regulation 2022/2065 (the Digital Services Act (DSA)).[34] Since 25 August 2023, the DSA obliges the operators of 'very large online platforms and very large online search engines' to respect 'freedom of expression and information, including media freedom and pluralism'.[35] This sounds like a welcome development. However, in the name of the fight against 'disinformation', these very large online platforms and search engines are also responsible for 'any actual or foreseeable adverse effects' that the content disseminated may have on the 'protection of public health'. Severe sanctions can be imposed for violations.[36] Even more specific is EU Regulation 2022/2371 on serious cross-border threats to health, which also aims at 'fighting disinformation' in the area of health, among other things.[37]

Likewise, the WHO Draft Pandemic Agreement (24 May 2024) contains a draft provision that aims to ensure the dissemination of 'accurate' risk information about pandemics.[38] An earlier draft version of the agreement, the Bureau's Draft of 2 June 2023, was more explicit here, calling on the Contracting States to combat 'misinformation or disinformation' and build so-called 'infodemic management' capacities.[39] Similarly, the amendments to

---

33 Higher Regional Court (*Oberlandesgericht*) of Munich, judgment of 7 January 2020, 18 U 1491/19 Pre, *Facebook*.

34 Regulation (EU) 2022/2065 of the European Parliament and of the Council of 19 October 2022 on a Single Market for Digital Services and amending Directive 2000/31/EC (Digital Services Act) (2022) OJ L 277/1.

35 ibid, article 33.

36 ibid, article 52.

37 Regulation on serious cross-border threats to health (n 3), recital 34.

38 Draft Pandemic Agreement (24 May 2024) (n 13), article 18.

39 INB, 'Bureau's Text of the WHO Convention, Agreement or other International Instrument on Pandemic Prevention, Preparedness and Response (WHO CA+)' (2 June 2023) UN Doc A/INB/5/6, articles 1(b) and 18; see also the preamble of the Draft Pandemic Agreement (24 May 2024) (n 13): 'Recognizing the importance of building trust and ensuring the timely sharing of information to prevent misinformation, disinformation and stigmatisation.'

the International Health Regulations (IHR) adopted by the 77th World Health Assembly (WHA) in May 2024 oblige States to combat 'misinformation and disinformation' during a PHEIC.[40] The analysis now turns to the private law instruments prevalent in the area of pandemic/PHEIC prevention, preparedness, and response.

3. INSTRUMENTS OF PRIVATE LAW

3.1 Overview

The private law contract is the key legal instrument for the involvement of private actors in pandemic/PHEIC preparedness, prevention, and response activities, and to overcome the territorial limits of State (or supranational, eg the EU) sovereignty. Firstly, the organisation agreements under private law for the establishment of the aforementioned legal entities under private law (including PPPs) should be mentioned. Furthermore, there are cooperation and financing agreements. One example of the latter are the 'grant contracts' through which the EU provided funds for the supply of vaccines to low-income countries as part of the COVAX facility.[41] Another example is the 'Antiviral Vaccine RDI Finance Contract' concluded between the European Investment Bank and BioNTech SE dated 10 June 2020 for EUR 100 million for the development of a vaccine against Covid-19.[42]

Procurement contracts are undoubtedly of particular importance, as today's focus of the pandemic/PHEIC preparedness, prevention, and response agenda is on the worldwide distribution of health products. Back in 2011, the WHA created 'The Pandemic Influenza Preparedness Framework for the Sharing of Influenza Viruses and Access to Vaccines and other Benefits' ('PIP Framework' or 'Framework'). The PIP Framework is described as an 'innovative partnership among Member States, industry, civil society and other stakeholders' and aims to improve 'both the sharing of influenza viruses with pandemic

---

[40] WHA Res 77.17 (1 June 2024) UN Doc WHA77.17, annex 'Amendments to the International Health Regulations (2005)' (IHR (2024)), annex 1, section A(3)(i).

[41] The author succeeded in accessing the relevant contracts through a freedom of information request and made them available to the general public, see 'COVAX Facility' (*Frag den Staat*, 3 April 2023) https://fragdenstaat.de/anfrage/covax-facility/.

[42] The contract is available in redacted form on the website of the US Securities and Exchange Commission (SEC) under the company's mandatory disclosures: https://www.sec.gov/Archives/edgar/data/1776985/000119312520195916/d830259dex1046.htm.

potential (IVPP) and equitable access to the products necessary to respond to pandemic influenza – such as vaccines, antiviral medicines and diagnostic products'.[43] Within this framework, the WHO later concluded private-law contracts modelled on the Standard Material Transfer Agreement 2 (SMTA2) with manufacturers, research institutions (eg the German University of Marburg) and other institutions that receive biological material for doing research on influenza pandemic prevention. In these contracts, the manufacturers undertake to donate 10 per cent of their vaccine production to the WHO in the event of a pandemic and to provide the WHO with a reserve of a further 2.5 per cent of their vaccine production at 'affordable' prices. For its part, the WHO is providing manufacturers with high-quality 'biological material' that is important for the development and production of vaccines as part of the PIP Framework. The contracts were published by the WHO,[44] but unfortunately not in full. The 'term sheets', to which they refer, containing the main obligations of the manufacturers, including the provisions on 'Liability and Indemnity', remain undisclosed.[45]

During the Covid-19-PHEIC and on the initiative of the EU and France, among others, the WHO implemented the COVAX Facility, aiming at supplying low-income countries worldwide with Covid-19 vaccines. Within this framework (that also involved Gavi and CEPI), so-called 'Advance Purchase Commitments' were concluded with manufacturers for vaccine procurement contracts, even before market launch and approval (hence the use of the term 'advance'). Gavi acted as the purchaser of the vaccines against Covid-19 and coordinated the programme.[46]

The special and growing importance of advanced purchase agreements as part of the global pandemic/PHEIC preparedness, prevention and response

---

[43] WHO, 'Pandemic Influenza Preparedness Framework, Partnership Contribution High-Level Implementation, Plan III 2024–2030' (19 June 2024) 2 https://www.who.int/publications/i/item/9789240070141; and 'Pandemic Influenza Preparedness (PIP) Framework' (*WHO*, 2025) https://www.who.int/initiatives/pandemic-influenza-preparedness-framework.

[44] 'Category A: List of all Signed Agreements' (*WHO*, 2025) https://www.who.int/initiatives/pandemic-influenza-preparedness-framework/standard-material-transfer-agreement-2-(smta2)/list-of-signed-agreements-cat-a.

[45] The author looked at the contracts with *Seqirus UK Limited* (20 March 2017) and *Glaxo Group Limited* (29 June 2022) as examples.

[46] Since Gavi, as a private foundation, is not subject to freedom of information laws, these contracts are not public. Only the 'Template Commitment Agreements' between the individual States participating in COVAX procurement and Gavi and the 'Template Optional Purchase Arrangement' were published temporarily online at https://healthjsticeinitiative.org.za. They are still on file with the author in April 2025.

agenda is also evident outside of COVAX. Perhaps the most prominent of these agreements was the Advance Purchase Agreements (APA), which the EU Commission negotiated and concluded with eight Covid-19 vaccine manufacturers on behalf of the EU Member States, and which are analysed in more detail below (Section 3.2). The aforementioned EU Regulation 2022/2371 on serious cross-border threats to health[47] indicates that the joint procurement of vaccines within the EU will not remain an exception. The WHO's attempt to replicate the EU model of centralised European procurement structures via the new Agreement on Pandemic Preparedness and Response has so far been unsuccessful. The Draft WHO Pandemic Agreement (24 May 2024) only tentatively moves in this direction by setting up a global network to, among other things, enhance and facilitate work to remove barriers to equitable, timely, and affordable access to pandemic-related health products.[48] Unlike in the earlier Zero Draft of the Pandemic Agreement of February 2023, there is no longer any mention of the WHO 'managing' the supply through the network.[49]

Contracts under private law are fundamentally private and therefore confidential, unless the contracting parties decide otherwise. Certainly, States and some supranational organisations like the EU are fully committed to the principles of transparency and freedom of information. However, when it comes to citizens' requests for information, they are often satisfied to refer to the confidentiality clauses in their private-law contracts with private parties and to the relevant exceptions in favour of business secrets. It is therefore not surprising that some of the information about private law contracts relied on in this chapter had to be requested from the contracting State Parties via freedom of information requests, whilst other information only reached the public through unofficial channels. Some of the relevant contracts will probably never see the

---

47 Regulation on serious cross-border threats to health (n 3).

48 WHO Draft Pandemic Agreement (24 May 2024) (n 13), article 13; see also IHR (2024), article 13. According to the new article 13(8)(b) IHR (2024), the WHO Director-General shall 'make use of WHO-coordinated mechanisms, or facilitate, in consultation with States Parties, their establishment as needed, and coordinate, as appropriate, with other allocation and distribution mechanisms and networks that facilitate timely and equitable access to relevant health products based on public health needs'.

49 INB, 'Zero Draft of the WHO CA+ for the Consideration of the Intergovernmental Negotiation Body at its Fourth Meeting' (1 February 2023) UN Doc A/INB/4/3, article 6; and G20 High Level Independent Panel on Financing the Global Commons for Pandemic Preparedness and Response, 'A Global Deal for our Pandemic Age' (9 July 2021) https://g20.utoronto.ca/2021/G20-HLIP-Report.pdf, 15 (Roadmap): 'World Bank to support countries to participate in pooled global procurement mechanisms for entering into advance purchase contracts in the early phase of a pandemic', similarly, 57.

light of day. Is an improvement in sight? The WHO's Zero Draft Pandemic Agreement (1 February 2023) contained a clause stating that States should oblige manufacturers who receive public funding for the manufacturing of pandemic-related products to disclose the prices and terms of contract for the public procurement of pandemic products.[50] Unfortunately, this clause can no longer be found in the most recent draft of 24 May 2024 available at the time of writing, where the word 'disclose' does not even appear.[51]

3.2 Advance Purchase Agreements of the EU

To illustrate the use of procurement contracts in the area of pandemic/PHEIC preparedness, prevention, and response, the analysis now moves to taking a closer look at the Advance Purchase Agreements (APAs) which the EU Commission (Commission) concluded with eight different manufacturers of vaccines against Covid-19. EU Member States purchased a large proportion of their vaccine doses against Covid-19 through these agreements.[52] Regardless of the fact that the EU community of States saw itself competing with other countries in the race to supply their populations with vaccines against Covid-19 as early as possible, the EU approach could well become the blueprint for a global approach to purchasing health products deemed relevant to address a PHEIC/pandemic in the future.[53]

---

50 Zero Draft Pandemic Agreement (1 February 2023), (n 40), article 9.

51 WHO Draft Pandemic Agreement (24 May 2024) (n 13).

52 The EU Commission only published the Covid-19-APAs in the course of a freedom of information request from a fellow citizen; see https://ec.europa.eu/info/live-work-travel-eu/coronavirus-response/public-health/eu-vaccines-strategy_de#documents. The contracts were significantly redacted; even the page numbers were concealed. The author's following comments on the contracts are based on leaked versions that are on file with the author. An unredacted version of the 'Advance Purchase Agreement ("APA") for the development, production, priority-purchasing options and supply of a successful COVID-19 vaccine for EU Member States' with Pfizer/BioNTech SANTE/2020/C3/043–S1I2.838335, signed 20 November 2020 (Pfizer/BioNTech APA (2020)) is available at https://archive.org/details/contract_03/mode/2up. An unredacted version of the 'Advance Purchase Agreement ("APA") for the production, priority-purchasing options and supply of a successful COVID-19 vaccine for EU Member States' SANTE/2020/C3/054–SI2.838958, signed 4 December 2020 with Moderna (Moderna APA (2020)) is available at https://fragdenstaat.de/dokumente/9529-apa-moderna/.

53 G20 High Level Independent Panel (n 49) 15 (Key Proposals and Roadmap) 57 and 74.

3.2.1 Conclusion of contracts

When concluding the APAs, the Commission did not act in its own name, but on behalf of all Member States under private law. The power of representation (and the Commission's underlying mandate) results from an agreement between the Member States and the Commission of June 2020.[54] The majority of the Commission's APAs concluded with the various manufacturers of Covid-19 vaccines provided for a fixed total number of vaccine doses (eg 200 million Pfizer/BioNTech doses) as well as options for further vaccine doses at fixed prices within a certain period of time. In each case, the Commission promised to make a down payment, which would later be offset against the purchase price of the vaccines but would be lost for the EU if no (conditional) market authorisation of the vaccines under development was granted and the Commission therefore terminated the contract. The down payment was intended to support the development of the relevant health product (vaccine). Once the various vaccines had been authorised, the Member States placed their orders via forms attached to the APAs. The APA and orders formed a single contract.[55]

At the time the APAs were concluded, the vaccine products were not yet on the market and had not yet been authorised (even provisionally). As it was not yet clear which vaccine would be successful, the EU's aim was to secure sufficient quantities of all vaccines with the prospect of authorisation at a predictable (fixed) price as early as possible in view of the competition with countries outside the EU.[56] This was associated with the risk of ordering far too many doses at far too high a price. In its Special Report 19/2022 on 'EU procurement of COVID-19 vaccines', the European Court of Auditors described this

---

54 Agreement between the Commission and Member States on procuring COVID-19 vaccines on behalf of the Member States and related procedures, annexed to the Commission Decision of 18 June 2020 'approving the agreement with Member States on procuring Covid-19 vaccines on behalf of the Member States and related procedures' C(2020) 4192 final https://commission.europa.eu/system/files/2020-09/decision_approving_the_agreement_with_member_states_on_procuring_covid-19_vaccines_on_behalf_of_the_member_states_and_related_procedures.pdf.

55 Pfizer/BioNTech APA (2020) (n 52), annex I: Vaccine Order Form, article I(1): 'This Vaccine Order Form is submitted by [name of the Participating Member State] to Contractor in accordance with the terms of the APA, and forms an integral part of the APA.'

56 Similarly, Armin von Bogdandy and Pedro Villarreal, 'The Role of International Law in Vaccinating against COVID-19: Appraising the COVAX Initiative' (2021) 81(1) ZaöRV 89, 95 ff.

technique favourably as a 'novel risk-sharing approach' to ensure the availability of sufficient quantities of vaccines.[57]

Another point is worth noting concerning the vaccine manufacturers Pfizer/BioNTech and Moderna in particular. Only a few weeks passed between the conclusion of the contracts on 20 November and 4 December 2020 and the subsequent granting of a conditional market authorisation for these manufacturers' vaccines against Covid-19 by the Commission on 21 December 2020 and 6 January 2021 respectively. This indicates that the Commission and the manufacturers were possibly already in a position to assess the high chances of their products being authorised at the time of signing, especially because the US government had already concluded its advance purchasing contracts with Pfizer several months earlier. It does not appear that the aforementioned element of uncertainty had been significant here. The price per vaccine dose of EUR 17.50 for Pfizer/BioNTech and USD 22.50 for Moderna (according to leaked documents) seems high, and it is said to have been even higher for the repeat order that the President of the European Commission had placed with both manufacturers *by text message* on her own authority in 2021.[58] According to the EU Commission, it has 'secured' a total of 4.2 billion vaccine doses, ie 9.3 vaccine doses per EU citizen,[59] whereby the procurement contracts, as far as can be seen, did not include any obligation for manufacturers to adapt the product to (however foreseeable) mutations in the virus. A closer look at the contracts will be taken in the following sections.

3.2.2 The detailed content of the contracts

Contractual partners

First, the APAs were concluded by the Commission on behalf of all EU Member States. They are therefore multilateral (framework) agreements in which all EU Member States are involved. It is not easy to determine whether the Commission itself is also a party to the APAs and there are contradictory indications in the contracts. On the one hand, the Commission only signed the APA 'on behalf and in the name of the Participating Member States'.[60]

---

[57] European Court of Auditors, 'Special Report 19/2022, EU COVID-19 Vaccine Procurement: Sufficient Doses Secured after Initial Challenges, but Performance of the Process not Sufficiently Assessed', para 4 https://op.europa.eu/webpub/eca/special-reports/covid19-vaccines-19-2022/en/index.html.

[58] Shari Hinds, 'Milliarden-Deal per SMS?' *Welt am Sonntag* (Berlin, 9 June 2024) 19.

[59] 'Safe COVID-19 Vaccines for Europeans' (*European Commission*, 2023) https://commission.europa.eu/strategy-and-policy/coronavirus-response/safe-covid-19-vaccines-europeans_de.

[60] Eg the Pfizer/BioNTech APA (2020) (n 52) 28.

However, on the other hand, some parts of the agreement with Pfizer/BioNTech give the opposite impression. For example, clause II.22. reads: 'The relationship hereby established between the Contractor and the Commission is solely that of independent contractors.' Similarly, section II.6.2. indicates that '*Pfizer* and *BioNTech* are jointly and severally liable to the Commission or the Participating Member State for the implementation of the APA.' Under section I.8.1., the Commission even assumes an obligation: 'The Commission agrees to pay an upfront payment of €700 million … .'[61]

The question of whether the Member States are jointly and severally liable (ie each for the total price) for the total purchase obligations specified in the APA[62] or only as partial debtors in accordance with their own vaccine orders is neither expressly regulated in the APA nor is it regulated in the above-mentioned agreement between the Member States and the Commission of June 2020.[63] It therefore remains unclear. These questions must be determined according to the applicable law. In the case of the APAs concluded with Pfizer/BioNTech, Moderna, and AstraZeneca, the applicable law is Belgian law, as evidenced by the choice of law clauses in these agreements (accompanied by jurisdiction clauses in favour of Belgium). The interpretation of the will of the parties, taking into account the interests of all parties including those of the vaccine manufacturers, is likely to be decisive here. It is true that the Member States already informed the Commission of the quantities of doses they intended to purchase before the signing of the APAs. However, that does not mean that the internal quotas were known to the manufacturers when the agreements, which only stipulated total figures for purchase and payment, were concluded. Moreover, it is not to be expected that the manufacturers would have agreed to the Member States' quotas in the sense of partial debts, if they were known to them at the time of conclusion.

Relationship between the Member States

Second, the private law legal relationship between the Member States is another issue arising under the APAs. This concerns the question of internal compensation if an individual Member State is held liable by manufacturers in excess of its own quota in accordance with the above considerations. It is not obvious to base the internal allocation of liability for the total purchase price on the reported quotas. Rather, this could also be based on the size of the population of the respective Member State, for example. The annex to the agreement between Member States and the Commission of June 2020 contains the clause

61 ibid.

62 ibid, section I.6.2.

63 Agreement between the Commission and Member States on procuring COVID-19 vaccines (n 54).

suggesting that 'access to vaccine doses will be allocated to Participating Member States according to the population distribution key'.[64] Population size is therefore a criterion that was important to the contracting parties.

In 2023, it emerged that the Commission had ordered far too many vaccine doses for too short a period of time through its APA with Pfizer/BioNTech of May 2021. The question of the distribution of the purchase obligation became practically relevant. Under pressure from some Member States, the Commission entered renegotiations with Pfizer/BioNTech. This resulted in an agreement under which the Member States had to pay a non-purchase premium for some of the vaccine doses not yet purchased but were allowed to spread the remaining delivery over a longer period. In addition, the creation of an EU central warehouse for vaccines was stipulated. This made the answer to the question obsolete of how the total purchase obligation in relation to Pfizer/BioNTech would affect the Member States.[65] In a next third step, the discussion will turn to the owed properties of the vaccines against Covid-19.

Properties of the vaccines

The vaccine is named in the respective APAs, for example as 'BNT162b2' or 'a nucleoside-modified messenger RNA (modRNA)' vaccine. Necessary properties are not defined. In particular, the protection of the vaccinated person against severe cases of the Covid-19 disease or against transmission is not established. The contractual risk of the suitability of the purchased product is thus borne solely by the Member States (and of course, the citizens as taxpayers and vaccinated persons).

As expressly stated in the preamble to the APA concluded with Moderna in December 2020, the manufacturer makes no representation 'that the Product will be ultimately available or will produce the desired results, i.e. shows sufficient efficacy to prevent a COVID-19 infection, or be without unacceptable side effects'.[66] In contrast, the APA with Pfizer/BioNTech does not expressly exclude the warranty for the efficacy and safety of the product. In several places,[67] the obligation to supply and accept is even expressly subject to the provision that the company succeeds in 'develop[ing] a safe and effective vaccine according to the terms laid down in this APA'. However, no specific safety requirements are defined in the remainder of the agreement, which implies that the Commission and the Member States as purchasers are satisfied with

64 ibid, annex, section on 'Advanced Purchase Agreements and Conditions', 6.

65 'European Health Union: Commission Secures Agreement with *BioNTech-Pfizer* on the Delivery of COVID-19 Vaccines' (*Commission press release*, 26 May 2023) https://ec.europa.eu/commission/presscorner/detail/en/IP_23_2865.

66 Moderna APA (2020) (n 52), point K of the recitals.

67 Pfizer/BioNTech APA (2020) (n 52), sections I.3 and I.6.2.

the minimum requirements of the European Medicines Agency (EMA) conditional market authorisation procedure. Accordingly, the vaccine order form of the Pfizer/BioNTech APA contains the following clause: 'The Participating Member State further acknowledges that the long-term effects and efficacy of the Vaccine are not currently known and that there may be adverse effects of the Vaccine that are not currently known … .'[68]

At least, both Moderna and Pfizer/BioNTech promise that their vaccines fulfil the manufacturing specifications listed in the contract and that they are produced in accordance with 'current Good Manufacturing Practice' in line with the existing European legal requirements.[69] However, should this duty be violated, it is expressly stated that 'the Commission's and the participating Member States' sole and exclusive remedy will be for the Contractor to deliver replacement Vaccine'.[70] Moreover, recourse claims for damages suffered by Member States as a result of being sued by third parties, in particular by individuals suffering from adverse effects caused by the vaccines, are excluded. In addition, claims for damages by the Member States are limited to 50 per cent of the purchase prices paid and claims for damages by the Commission are limited to the amount of the advance payment made.

The present author is not in a position to judge whether these clauses are compliant with the applicable Belgian law. There are attorneys who doubt this in confidential legal opinions. However, when examining the appropriateness of the exclusion of liability for the effectiveness and safety of the vaccines, it could be necessary to take into account that the Commission, advised by the EMA, had the power to thoroughly assess the quality of the products as part of the EMA's conditional marketing authorisation procedure. The Commission could do so precisely *before* it set, with its authorisation decision, the condition for the Member States' obligation to accept the vaccine. Although the Commission is not identical to the Member States, it is and was on the side of the Member States when the contract was concluded. From the standpoint of individuals suffering from vaccine injuries, many of them serious,[71] the problem is not so much the limited warranty of manufacturers as the suspicion that

---

[68] ibid, section I.4.

[69] ibid, section II.8.2; and Moderna APA (2020) (n 52), section I.5.1.

[70] Pfizer/BioNTech APA (2020) (n 52), section II.8.2; and Moderna APA (2020), section I.5.7.

[71] Kristyna Faksova et al, 'COVID-19 Vaccines and Adverse Events of Special Interest: A Multinational Global Vaccine Data Network (GVDN) Cohort Study of 99 Million Vaccinated Individuals' (2024) 42 Vaccine 2200; Joseph Fraiman et al, 'Serious Adverse Events of Special Interest Following mRNA COVID-19 Vaccination in Randomized Trials in Adults' (2022) 40 Vaccine 5798; and James Gill et al, 'Autopsy Histopathologic Cardiac Findings in 2 Adolescents

the EMA did not investigate the safety and efficacy of the products thoroughly enough when rapidly granting them conditional market authorisations.[72]

Indemnification clauses

Fourth, and most interesting, are the indemnification clauses of the EU APAs. They are redacted in the copies of the agreements the Commission officially published following a freedom of information request. The Commission has justified the extensive redactions with the need to protect the commercial interests of the manufacturers[73] and with reference to the confidentiality clauses[74] in the agreements, which have also been redacted. When the unredacted APAs were leaked, the indemnification clauses in particular caused a considerable uproar in media critical of governments' and the EU's responses to Covid-19.[75] However, they should not have come as a surprise since similar clauses were already included in the aforementioned agreement of June

---

following the Second COVID-19 Vaccine Dose' (2022) 146 Archives of Pathology & Laboratory Medicine 925.

[72] See the detailed report by Sonia Elijah, 'What the Leaked EMA Emails & Docs Reveal: Major Concerns with Pfizer C-19 Vaccine Batch Integrity and the Race to Authorize, with Numerous Excerpts from the Emails' (*Childrens' Health Defense EU*, 12 September 2022) https://childrenshealthdefense.eu/eu-affairs/what-the-leaked-ema-emails-docs-reveal-major-concerns-with-pfizer-c-19-vaccine-batch-integrity-and-the-race-to-authorize/.

[73] But see EU General Court judgment of 17 July 2024, Case T-689/21 *Margrete Auken et al v EU Commission*, paras 151–71, which concern an action brought by citizens against a Commission decision rejecting their request for further disclosure of the Pfizer/BioNTech and AstraZeneca APAs. With regard to the refusal to disclose the indemnification clauses, the General Court stated that this was not justified by commercial interests because the principle of indemnification already resulted from the agreement of 18 June 2020 published on the Commission's website and because the indemnification clauses in the various APAs were roughly identical.

[74] Eg sections II.9.1 and 9.5 as well as section 9.9 in conjunction with section I.2 of the Pfizer/BioNTech APA (2020) (n 52). Section 9.5 expressly mentions the indemnification provision as the subject of confidentiality. Confidentiality must be maintained for up to 10 years after the end of the contract term.

[75] Eg Urs Gasche, 'Behörden täuschen Öffentlichkeit über Corona Haftungsklauseln' (*Infospreber*, 23 August 2021) https://www.infosperber.ch/gesundheit/public-health/behoerden-taeuschen-oeffentlichkeit-ueber-corona-haftungsklauseln/; and Hannes Strasser, '*Pfizer*-Verträge: Der größte Skandal der Medizingeschichte?' (*Journalistenwatch*, 29 October 2023) https://journalistenwatch.com/2023/10/29/pfizer-vertraege-der-groesste-skandal-der-medizingeschichte/.

2020 that was publicly available all along.[76] In this agreement, the Member States and the Commission promised each other that the Member States would bear 'any liability' associated with 'the deployment and use of the vaccines under their national vaccination strategies' and indemnify vaccine manufacturers for product liability 'under the terms and conditions of the relevant APA for liability related to the use and deployment of vaccines normally borne by such manufacturer'.[77] The indemnification clause in section I.12.1 of the Pfizer/BioNTech APA reads:

> … each Participating Member State shall indemnify and hold harmless the Contractor … and officers, directors, employees … (together, the 'Indemnified Persons') from and against any and all liabilities … arising from or relating to the use and deployment of the Vaccines in the jurisdiction of the Participating Member State in question.

The EU Member States are therefore obliged to reimburse Pfizer and BioNTech for the amount that these companies may have to pay to individuals suffering from adverse effects of Covid-19 vaccines. This even includes the costs for the services of the (top) law firms representing the manufacturers in proceedings brought against them by those injured by the vaccine. The obligation to indemnify is only excluded, to the extent that:

(i) the Losses were caused by the Wilful Misconduct … of such Indemnified Person; or
(ii) the Losses were caused by a material breach of Good Manufacturing Practice …, leading to a Quality Defect in the Vaccine … and resulting in a determination by the competent regulatory authority to recall or suspend the supply of the Vaccine, or in a withdrawal or Suspension of the Authorisation by the European Commission.[78]

The exclusion is therefore subject to very strict conditions that would not even be met by the serious differences in the quality of individual batches of the vaccines observed in a Danish study in 2023.[79]

---

[76] Agreement between the Commission and Member States on procuring COVID-19 vaccines (n 54).

[77] ibid, article 6.

[78] Pfizer/BioNTech APA (2020) (n 52), section I.12.1.

[79] Max Schmeling et al, 'Batch-dependent Safety of the BNT162b2 mRNA COVID-19 Vaccine' (2023) 53(8) European Journal of Clinical Investigation e13998. The German Paul Ehrlich Institute was critical of this study in a statement: 'Keine chargenbezogene Häufung von Verdachtsmeldungen zu Impfnebenwirkungen nach COVID-19-Impfungen mit *Comirnaty*' (18 August 2023) https://www.pei

The reason given for the generous indemnification obligation is that it is extremely difficult for manufacturers of pharmaceuticals in general, and even more so for manufacturers of vaccines relying on a novel modRNA-technology, to find liability insurance.[80] This may be true. However, given the high prices paid per vaccine dose by the EU Commission and its Member States – another piece of information that was redacted from the APAs officially released by the Commission – it is not apparent that the Member States have been granted a discount in the amount of a fictitious insurance premium. Furthermore, Pfizer's APA, for example, expressly provides that the indemnification obligation applies even if the manufacturer has taken out liability insurance.[81] The Moderna APA even obliges the manufacturer to 'take out an insurance policy or self-insurance against risks and damage or loss relating to the implementation of the APA' if required 'by the relevant applicable legislation' or by 'common practice in the pharmaceutical industry for a COVID-19 vaccine'.[82]

Whether the APAs' indemnification clauses comply with the applicable Belgian contract law is unclear. Again, there are confidential legal opinions of Belgian lawyers who consider these clauses problematic. They argue that with these clauses, manufacturers no longer have an incentive to supply effective and safe vaccines, and that the manufacturers' obligations to supply are therefore insubstantial. A comparison with the COVAX Facility is interesting in this context. The 'Terms and Conditions for Self-Financing Participants', ie countries that pay for their vaccines themselves, mentioned the possibility of vaccine suppliers requesting a liability exemption (however without prescribing this to the participating States) and expected that exemption to be excluded not only in the case of 'wilful misconduct' by the manufacturer/supplier but also in the case of 'gross negligence of the manufacturer' and in the case of a 'defect in the … vaccine due to non-compliance with, for example, terms of the marketing authorisation or current Good Manufacturing Practices'.[83]

.de/DE/newsroom/positionen/covid-19-impfstoffe/stellungnahme-keine-chargen-bezogene-haeufung-verdachtsfallmeldungen-covid-19-impfstoffe.html.

[80] Commission, 'Communication from the Commission to the European Parliament, the European Council, the Council and the European Investment Bank, EU Strategy for COVID-19 vaccines' COM (2020) 245 final, section 2.2: 'This proposed framework is therefore an insurance policy, which transfers some of the risk from industry to the public authorities in return for assuring Member States equitable and affordable access to a vaccine, should one become available.'

[81] Pfizer/BioNTech APA (2020) (n 52), section II.6.1.

[82] Moderna APA (2020) (n 52), section II.4.2.

[83] COVAX Facility, 'Terms and Conditions for Self-Financing Participants' (Gavi) https://www.gavi.org/sites/default/files/covid/covax/COVAX-Facility

The indemnification clause in the Pfizer/BioNTech APA quoted above would therefore not fulfil these requirements of the global vaccine distribution system run by COVAX. However, when evaluating that clause (under Belgian law), the special circumstance will again have to be taken into account that the Commission (associated with the Member States) had the quality control of the vaccines in its own hands via the EMA authorisation procedures at the time when the APAs were concluded.[84]

4. IMPACT OF WHO STANDARDS ON PRIVATE LAW

So far, the discussion has revealed how concrete coordinated vaccine procurement by the global pandemic/PHEIC preparedness, prevention, and response agenda at the level of the EU catered to the interests of big pharmaceutical corporations. Next, it is examined at a more abstract level how WHO standards find direct entry into European and national private law. The focus of the WHO standards, above all the IHR, is measures to be taken by States Parties under these Regulations. Accordingly, at the domestic level, the IHR predominantly influence and shape public health administrative law. Since this forms part of public law, it is not explored here further.

However, the IHR (in the 2005 version[85] as well as in the amended version of 1 June 2024[86]) formulate some requirements for private market participants that also influence their contractual relationship with customers. According to article 24 IHR on 'Conveyance Operators', the State Parties must, for example, oblige the operators of means of transport to, among other things:

(a) Comply with the health measures recommended by WHO and adopted by the State Party;
(b) Inform travellers of the health measures recommended by WHO and adopted by the State Party for use on board; and
(c) keep the means of transport for which they are responsible free at all times from sources of infection or contamination, including vectors and reservoirs.

German law implementing the IHR (2005), for example, passes on these requirements directly to market participants, posing an obligation on them to

_Terms_and_Conditions-Self-Financing-Participants.pdf.

[84] For the domestic regime corresponding to the exemption obligation, see Section 5.

[85] International Health Regulations (2005) (adopted 23 May 2005, entered into force 15 June 2007) 2509 UNTS 79 (IHR (2005)).

[86] IHR (2024).

provide relevant information.[87] These domestic law obligations are also likely to be of a public law nature and therefore primarily sanctionable by State authorities. However, it can be assumed that they also affect the content of contracts of carriage, with the result that a passenger can assert a contractual claim for damages against the carrier if he suffers damage as a result of the breach of duty.

As had become clear during the Covid-19-PHEIC, the WHO's recommendations for medical and non-medical emergency measures that it can issue under the IHR (2005) once the WHO Director-General has declared a PHEIC can have even greater, albeit indirect, significance for questions of whether and/or how private law contracts are concluded. This impact is indirect because it comes via restrictions adopted by governments and public health authorities on contact between persons, freedom of movement, or other activities following the WHO's recommendations.[88] Newly concluded contracts are invalid if they contradict these requirements,[89] and existing contracts may become unfulfillable or lose their economic sense, which, according to German law, justifies the defence of impossibility or of the disruption of the business basis.[90] For example, in Germany the law prohibited employees who could not provide proof of full vaccination against Covid-19 to work in certain areas. The law assumed 'full vaccination against Covid-19' if, among other things, one of the individual vaccinations was carried out with a vaccine that was 'recognised by the World Health Organization as part of the Emergency Use Listing'.[91] Certain activities, for example in the catering or sports sectors, were outright prohibited, or people who had not been vaccinated or not recovered from a Covid-19 infection were not permitted to carry them out. The legal basis for the German government's decrees authorising such restrictions was (and is) the

---

87 See sections 5 and 6 of the German Law on the implementation of the IHR (2005), *Gesetz zur Durchführung der Internationalen Gesundheitsvorschriften (2005), (IGV-Durchführungsgesetz – IGVDG).*

88 IfSG (n 10), section 28(a).

89 German Civil Code, *Bürgerliches Gesetzbuch – BGB*, section 134.

90 ibid, sections 275 or 313. In some cases, the agreements contain their own regulations in the event that WHO measures affect their implementation; see eg the 'Framework Contract for Supplies' (HERA/2023/NP/00 10) concluded by the Commission on behalf of 15 EU Member States with the British manufacturer *Seqirus* for the supply of avian influenza vaccine. Section I.15.4 states: 'Declaration of an influenza pandemic by the World Health Organization or another competent authority is considered as a Force Majeure event in the meaning of this FWC [framework contract]' https://fragdenstaat.de/anfrage/pre-pandemic-vaccines-agreement-zw-eu-kommission-und-csl-seqirus/.

91 IfSG (n 10), section 22(a)(1) no 1.

existence of an 'epidemic situation of national significance' to be determined by the German parliament, the *Bundestag*. According to the law, such a situation can be determined in particular because 'the World Health Organization has declared a public health emergency of international concern' (PHEIC).[92] On 25 March 2020, the *Bundestag* did not hesitate to make use of this provision once the WHO Director-General had declared the Covid-19-PHEIC.[93]

In addition, even non-binding WHO recommendations have a 'soft' impact on private law. Treated as what one may call 'congealed expert opinions', they can shape private law standards of care for companies and citizens in the context of contractual or tortious liability. Even the German Federal Constitutional Court (*Bundesverfassungsgericht*) relies on standards set by the WHO in its proceedings. An example is the case of a child who objected to the legal obligation to provide proof of a measles vaccination as a prerequisite for admission to a childcare facility. The Federal Constitutional Court rejected the constitutional complaint and referred (among other things) to a corresponding WHO recommendation to prove a positive risk-benefit assessment of the measles combination vaccination.[94]

Another recent example from Germany of the soft influence of the WHO's recommendations is a judgment of the Berlin Regional Court (Landgericht) of 2 July 2024, which has not been published so far. It concerns a LinkedIn user's lawsuit against the platform for the deletion of his profile after he had posted three contributions that were critical of the measures taken to address the Covid-19-PHEIC. One of the issues at stake was whether the linked posts constituted 'disinformation' within the meaning of the DSA insofar as they dealt with the adverse effects of vaccines against Covid-19. The Regional Court acknowledges that LinkedIn may 'refer to the findings of the World Health Organization' to assess whether a post contains misleading information that violates the provisions of its terms of use. Further, it states that the newspaper quote objected to by LinkedIn, according to which the safety of the Covid-19 vaccines has been insufficiently tested, contradicts 'the WHO's findings … that more serious or long-lasting side effects are extremely rare'.[95] The WHO standards apparently function here as expert opinion of the highest, unquestioned authority.

---

92 ibid, section 5(1).

93 *Deutscher Bundestag*, 'Stenografischer Bericht, 154. Sitzung' (25 March 2020) https://dserver.bundestag.de/btp/19/19154.pdf.

94 Bundesverfassungsgericht, decision of 21 July 2022, 1 BvR 469/20 et al, juris para 29.

95 Landgericht Berlin II, judgment of 2 July 2024, 27 O 270/22, 13 and 14.

5. PRIVATE LAW LIABILITY FOR DAMAGES IN THE GLOBAL HEALTH EMERGENCY REGIME

The final part of this chapter examines how the relevant actors involved in global pandemic/PHEIC preparedness, prevention, and response activities, and programmes and governance may be held accountable under private law for their decisions and the negative influence and effects these decisions have had (and may have in future) on individuals and companies. Medical and non-medical countermeasures adopted to address the Covid-19-PHEIC have caused numerous health problems, including adverse effects from vaccinations,[96] as well as material damages to people and companies.[97] Whether these effects can be classified as unavoidable collateral damage or far-reaching violations of fundamental rights and injustices will not be discussed here. Rather, the present chapter is concerned with the question of whether liability under private law is possible at all.

5.1 Liability of Interstate Actors?

First, the liability of intergovernmental players at the pinnacle of global health decision-making institutions – the WHO and EU – is discussed.

5.1.1 The WHO

It is difficult to imagine the WHO being liable towards individuals. The WHO Constitution of 1946 (WHOC)[98] read in conjunction with the Convention on the Privileges and Immunities of the Specialised Agencies (of the UN)[99] grants the WHO legal capacity. This implies, among other things, the ability to conclude contracts under private law and to acquire property as well as non-contractual rights and obligations. The organisation also expressly has the ability to initiate legal proceedings itself.[100] However, the organisation and its representatives are granted extensive immunity from 'any form

---

[96] Eg National Academies, 'Evidence Review of the Adverse Effects of COVID-19 Vaccination and Intramuscular Vaccine Administration' (2024) http://nap.nationalacademies.org/27746.

[97] Eg 'EU Monitor COVID-19: Interaktive Grafiken und Statistiken zu den Folgen der Pandemie in den EU Staaten' (*Destatis (Federal Statistical Office)*, 2020) https://www.destatis.de/Europa/DE/Thema/COVID-19/_inhalt.html.

[98] Constitution of the World Health Organization (adopted 22 July 1946, entered into force 7 April 1948) 14 UNTS 185 (WHOC).

[99] Convention on the Privileges and Immunities of the Specialised Agencies (adopted 21 November 1947, entered into force 2 December 1948) 33 UNTS 261.

[100] ibid, article II(3).

of legal process'.[101] Particularly in the context of the Emergency Use Listing Procedure, the WHO expressly rejects any responsibility for the unlicensed medical products it may recommend for use under this procedure to address a PHEIC and for its findings and recommendations on these products.[102] In view of the comprehensive immunity of the organisation under international treaties, the question of whether, and if so, under what conditions such a substantive exclusion of liability is to be denied under the applicable national private law of the place of damage is only of academic value.

The finding that it is not possible to hold the WHO accountable under private law is problematic. Individuals negatively affected by medical and non-medical countermeasures during a PHEIC will, however, rarely be in contact with the WHO and its staff directly, since most programmes in the area of pandemic/PHEIC preparedness, prevention, and response are carried out by PPPs that do not enjoy immunity (with the exception of Gavi, see Section 5.2).[103] The PPPs as executing actors may, however, claim that they have merely carried out the WHO's instructions in good faith. This argument could become particularly important if and insofar as the WHO standards claim to be legally binding.

5.1.2 The EU

The situation is different for the EU. According to article 340(2) TFEU,[104] the 'Union shall, in accordance with the general principles common to the laws of the Member States, make good any damage caused by its institutions or by its servants in the performance of their duties' and may be sued on this basis before the Court of Justice of the EU (CJEU).[105] The reference to the 'general principles of law' is understood to mean that 'the rule of law which has been infringed is intended to confer rights on individuals, that the infringement is sufficiently serious and that there is a direct causal link between the infringement and the damage caused to the injured parties'.[106]

---

101 ibid, article III(4).

102 WHO, 'Emergency Use Listing Procedure' (9 August 2022), annex 8, 65. On the Emergency Use Listing Procedure, also see Müller and Behrendt Chapter 3 in this volume.

103 Also critical of the transfer of decision-making competences to private entities from the point of view of human rights protection is Erika de Wet (n 16) 796, using the example of WIPO and WHO.

104 Consolidated version on the Treaty on the Functioning of the European Union (TFEU) [2012] OJ C326/47, article 340(2).

105 TFEU, article 268.

106 Eg C-352/98 P *Laboratoires pharmaceutiques Bergaderm SA*, guiding principle 2 and para 42; and Thomas Oppermann et al, *Europarecht* (9th edn, CH

Restrictions on public life in the context of health emergencies are normally based on legal measures. With regard to the accusation of legislative injustice, European case law ensures that the legislature retains a 'sufficient margin of discretion'.[107] The same can be assumed with regard to the administrative discretion of the EU Commission and the EMA[108] when deciding on the conditional market authorisation of medicinal products, in particular vaccines, whose safety and effectiveness have not been fully proven. Therefore, the EU institutions must have 'manifestly and significantly exceeded' the limits of their (legislative) discretion to be held liable.[109] It is difficult to imagine that this requirement would be assumed for EU measures that have been prepared, recommended, or, possibly in the future, even mandated by the WHO.

5.2 Liability of the PPPs

The PPPs relied on by the WHO and Member States in association with NGOs and philanthropic foundations are organised under private law. As persons under private law, they are subject to the liability provisions of the applicable private law (according to the principles of the relevant *lex fori*), in particular contract and tort law. As far as damage to health in the context of emergency measures is concerned, non-contractual liability for organisational negligence is likely to come into consideration. However, there are PPPs that have so much power that they are granted comprehensive immunity in the headquarters agreements they conclude with their host States. Gavi, which managed the COVAX Facility, is an example of this.[110]

Beck 2021), § 14, para 4, with further references.

107 *Laboratoires pharmaceutiques Bergaderm* (n 106), headnote 3.

108 According to article 71 of Regulation (EC) 726/2004 laying down Community procedures for the authorisation and supervision of medicinal products for human and veterinary use and establishing a European Medicines Agency (2004) OJ L 136/1, the EMA has its own legal personality. According to article 72(2) of the Regulation, the EMA itself is consequently subject to (contractual and) non-contractual liability. However, the EMA's own liability will hardly relieve the EU as decision-maker from its own external liability.

109 *Laboratoires pharmaceutiques Bergaderm SA* (n 106), para 43.

110 'Accord du 23 juin 2009 entre le Conseil fédéral suisse et GAVI Alliance (Global Alliance for Vaccines and Immunisation) en vue de déterminer le statut juridique de GAVI Alliance en Suisse', article 5 https://www.droit-bilingue.ch/fr-de/0.1/0.19/0.192.122.818.12-index.html.

5.3 Liability of the German State for Damages

The liability of the German State for damages due to the medical and non-medical countermeasures it adopted to address the Covid-19-PHEIC (and other PHEICs in the future) follows the general principles set out in German law. Accordingly, in addition to the violation of a legal norm that protects individuals, the State must also be at fault.[111] This presupposes the individual culpability of the unlawful behaviour in the person of an acting public servant. Therefore, State liability is likely to fail in the present context if the damage is based on the fact that the national authorities have implemented binding international requirements, even if these are later qualified as (fundamentally) unlawful by a national or international court (which is highly unlikely). But even non-binding recommendations, for example, those of the WHO Director-General under the IHR, should exempt national officials who follow them from allegations of negligence.

In addition to the claim for damages, the law on 'social compensation' according to Social Code XIV[112] grants citizens injured by acts of the State claims to a State pension (for medical treatment, sickness benefit and rehabilitation measures, basic pension payments and benefits for surviving dependants). This also applies to injuries caused by State-recommended or mandated vaccinations.[113] Unlike claims under private law, these do not require any unlawful or even culpable behaviour on the side of the State. Proof of causal damage is sufficient. However, the amounts granted are small, falling within the minimum subsistence level. In addition, the German authorities have been very reluctant to recognise vaccination injuries.[114] The existing legal facilitation of proof of causality has done nothing to change this.[115]

No-fault compensation by States for those injured by vaccines is also a concern of the WHO. As part of COVAX, a 'No-Fault Compensation Programme for Advance Market Commitment (AMC) Eligible Economies' was set up for

---

111 Basic Law, *Grundgesetz für die Bundesrepublik Deutschland* (GG), article 34; and *BGB* (n 89), section 839.

112 *Sozialgesetzbuch Vierzehntes Buch – Soziale Entschädigung (SGB XIV).*

113 ibid, section 24.

114 Jonas Koch and Tobias Schmidt, '467 anerkannte Corona-Impfschäden seit Beginn der Pandemie' *Neue Osnabrücker Zeitung* (Osnabrück, 22 January 2024). According to this article, only 467 cases of 11,827 applications for social compensation due to injuries caused by vaccinations against COVD-19 were recognised by January 2024.

115 See Günter Reiner, 'Haftung der Corona-Impfstoffhersteller für Impfschäden in Deutschland' (2024) 4 Deutsch-Georgische Zeitschrift für Rechtsvergleichung 21, 48 https://lawjournal.ge/wp-content/uploads/DGZR-4-2024-DE.pdf.

victims in 92 'low- and middle-income countries and economies'.[116] The programme, which is financed by 'a small levy on each dose distributed through COVAX to these countries and economies', sees itself as 'an important part of COVAX's commitment to vaccine equity' and is intended to minimise 'the number of instances in which these economies may be required to indemnify manufacturers, and ensures that affected eligible individuals have access to fair compensation'. It is also intended to reduce 'the risk of litigation for manufacturers'.[117]

As discussed in Section 3.2.2, the manufacturers are already in a privileged position since the States participating in the COVAX Facility are allowed to release them from their product liability responsibility. The no-fault compensation programme is reducing the residual risk that the States will not fulfil this obligation and permit the injured parties to take legal action against the manufacturers. It is not self-evident that this calculation works, because COVAX compensation will regularly be lower than damages under the applicable domestic law.[118] However, the risk of high litigation costs may well discourage the vaccine injured from taking the private law route. This brings the discussion to the last point, the liability of manufacturers in the area of pandemic/PHEIC prevention, preparedness, and response.

5.4 'Liability Risk Management' in Favour of Vaccine Manufacturers

The chance for people and companies who are harmed by the health products distributed during a PHEIC to claim damages from the manufacturers of these products is also limited. Indications of this can already be found at the WHO level. It then materialises at EU and national level.

5.4.1 The WHO level

As already mentioned, the COVAX programme provided for the participating countries the possibility to exempt the vaccine manufacturers from liability.

116 'COVAX No-Fault Compensation Program' (*WHO*, 2022) https://www.who.int/initiatives/act-accelerator/covax/no-fault-compensation.

117 'COVAX No-Fault Compensation Program: Explained' (*WHO*, 2022) https://www.who.int/initiatives/act-accelerator/covax/no-fault-compensation/covax-no-fault-compensation-program-explained.

118 In addition, the No-Fault Compensation Programme has not been very successful for vaccine-injured people. The number of claims made has been very low; see COVAX No-Fault Compensation Program for AMC Eligible Economies, 'Applications and Claims Data' (31 May 2025) https://covaxclaims.com/wp-content/uploads/2024/02/COVAX-Compensation-Program-Data.pdf.

Efforts are being made to generalise this model as part of the new WHO Pandemic Agreement. The latest draft of 24 May 2024 provides for 'the establishment and implementation of national, regional and/or global no-fault compensation mechanisms and other strategies for managing liability related to novel pandemic vaccines during pandemic emergencies'.[119] However, according to the colour code used in the draft, no consensus has yet been reached on this part. An earlier draft of the Pandemic Agreement from 2 June 2023 contained a separate article 10 on 'Liability risk management'.[120] This shows that this is less about care for individuals suffering from vaccine injuries and more about reducing risk of legal battles for vaccine manufacturers. In the drafts of the Pandemic Agreement of 30 October 2023 and 13 March 2024 respectively, the scheme was then referred to as 'Liability and Compensation Management'.[121] However, it seems that the idea for including a no-fault compensation scheme into the Pandemic Agreement is not yet off the table.

5.4.2 The EU level

It has been argued in Section 3.2.2 above that the most important aspect of liability risk management – the obligation of Member States to indemnify manufacturers against liability for vaccine damage – has been implemented within the EU framework of the APAs. However, a joint no-fault compensation programme of the Member States has not been included. The reason for this could be that most EU Member States already have national programmes in place. In addition, the EU lacks the legislative powers to set up such a scheme, and these powers could not be established with the necessary speed once the Covid-19-PHEIC had been declared. Another circumstance may have played an even greater role: in the event that manufacturers were ordered in court to pay damages to victims of vaccine injuries, the likelihood that EU Member States would actually honour their indemnification obligations to manufacturers was and is high. From the manufacturers' point of view, there was therefore less reason to try to prevent those injured by vaccines from suing the manufacturers for damages through the availability of a State compensation scheme. That aside, the EU also participated in the COVAX programme.

---

119 WHO Draft Pandemic Agreement (24 May 2024) (n 13), article 13bis.

120 Draft Pandemic Agreement (Bureau's Text (2 June 2023)) (n 39).

121 INB, 'Proposal for a Negotiating Text of the WHO Pandemic Agreement' (30 October 2023) UN Doc A/INB/7/3, article 15; and INB, 'Revised Draft of the Negotiating Text of the WHO Pandemic Agreement' (13 March 2024) UN Doc A/INB/9/3, article 15.

5.4.3 National German level

Finally, a look shall be taken at a provision of German national law that corresponds to the European emergency regime. It makes it even more difficult for those injured by vaccines to successfully take legal action against manufacturers and thus activate the indemnification obligation (see Section 3.2.2) than it already is. First, it is important to note that an ordinance issued, based on the German Medicines Act, by the Federal Government to address the Covid-19 crisis, the Medical Needs Supply Security Ordinance,[122] exempts vaccine manufacturers from certain labelling and information obligations as well as security measures (eg State batch testing) under the German Medicines Act. In addition, and consistently in this respect, this ordinance limits the general strict liability of manufacturers of vaccines against Covid-19 to intentional or grossly negligent misconduct, provided that the vaccines were placed on the market by the Federal Government and there is a possibility that the vaccine damage occurred as a consequence of the aforementioned exemptions.[123] Product liability due to pharmaceutical product defects, in particular design defects, remains conceivable, but is unlikely to come into play. As the current author has explained elsewhere, the German courts have so far refused to recognise a product defect giving rise to liability simply because the Commission, as the approval authority, has found the risks from the vaccines to be acceptable.[124]

For other health emergencies, another legal ordinance based on the German Medicinal Products Act, the Medicinal Products Act Civil Protection Exemption Ordinance[125] of 2003 in the version of 18 October 2022, contains a similar exemption from liability in favour of manufacturers of (as yet) unlicensed medicinal products or medicinal products with an expired use-by date that are placed on the market by the State authorities to counter an emergency or disaster situation. Such provisions show that legislators go far to ensure easy and (nearly) risk-free involvement of pharmaceutical manufacturers in pandemic/PHEIC preparedness, prevention, and response programmes and activities.

6. CONCLUSION

Private actors and instruments play a major, indeed crucial, role in the global health framework for pandemic/PHEIC preparedness, prevention, and response. Providing people with commercial healthcare products is at the

122 *Medizinischer Bedarf Versorgungssicherstellungsverordnung – MedBVSV*, section 3 I.
123 ibid, section 3.IV.
124 Reiner (n 115) 31 ff.
125 *AMG-Zivilschutzausnahmeverordnung – AMGZSAV*, section 7.

forefront of PHEICs and pandemic preparedness, prevention, and response activities and programmes. Multinational corporations, NGOs, and PPPs exercise economic power, but also, as the WEF and BMGF show, political power. Governments accept and even support this, probably not only out of respect for the private sector and freedom of contract in line with the principle of subsidiarity. Rather, the public-private hybridisation also grants them legal and – because of the public's reduced ability to monitor the endeavours of (often globally acting) private entities – factual room for manoeuvring and opportunities to shape policy, combined with less responsibility. Acting within the narrower framework based directly on fundamental rights would not allow for this flexibility and reduced responsibility.

A different type of private law aspect is the impact of global public health law on private law: for example, the IHR contain binding standards for health-related duties of certain market participants. These include, for instance airlines, which have an impact on the corresponding contracts with their clients via the national implementation laws. Non-binding WHO standards indirectly influence the interpretation of due diligence standards under private law as (alleged) institutionalised expert opinions of the highest authority.

The possibilities for people and companies to claim compensation for the damage caused by emergency measures during a PHEIC against the responsible actors, from the WHO to the manufacturers of health products, are very limited. The example of Covid-19 vaccines has shown that manufacturers are even privileged under the special emergency rules when compared to general rules applicable in normal times.

All in all, it is difficult to say whether the private sector, especially pharmaceutical companies, should be perceived as an extended arm of governments or rather the other way round. Overall, the growing influence of private law as pushed by governments is a threat to ensure accountability of State and non-State actors on different levels.

PART III

Securitisation and public-private hybridisation: the (European) domestic level

7. Governing during Covid-19: comparative insights on how health emergencies tested democracy

Marie-Luce Paris

1. INTRODUCTION

The World Health Organization's (WHO) declaration in March 2020 on the SARS-CoV-2 virus as a public health emergency of international concern (Covid-19-PHEIC) had far-reaching implications for governments. One of the striking features of the period was the use of, in some jurisdictions, war-like language in framing the disease. For various governments, the 'fight' against the virus was all about mobilising against the invisible enemy. For instance, on 16 March 2020, the French President announced that the nation was 'at war' with Covid-19:

> We are at war and faced with what is looming, this peak of the pandemic that is before us; I have decided, on the proposal of the Minister of the Armed Forces and the Chief of Staff of the Armed Forces, to launch *Opération Résilience*.[1]

This declaration served as Macron's strategy of legitimation to justify the strict countermeasures imposed in France, leading to significant disruptions in

[1] Emmanuel Macron 'Déclaration de M. Emmanuel Macron, président de la République, sur la mobilisation face à l'épidémie de Covid-19, en particulier le rôle des soignants, et sur le lancement de l'opération militaire Résilience en soutien à lutte contre la diffusion du coronavirus, Mulhouse, le 25 mars 2020' (*Mulhouse*, 25 March 2020) https://www.vie-publique.fr/discours/273982-emmanuel-macron-25-mars-2020-discours-de-mulhouse; and Ministère des Armées, 'Opération Résilience' (28 April 2021) https://archives.defense.gouv.fr/actualites/operations/operation-resilience.html. Unless otherwise stated all web links given in this chapter last accessed 27 October 2024. All errors in this chapter are my own.

the existing legal framework.[2] Although not every country embraced such an alarming narrative, an almost common feature was the centralised (top-down) approach to the health emergency response,[3] somehow itself encouraged by the securitised approach adopted by the WHO.[4] Almost overnight, governments around the world implemented an array of both medical and non-medical countermeasures, including widespread testing, contact tracing, curfews, large-scale quarantines (commonly referred to as 'lockdowns'), and more. Such actions resulted in severe restrictions on rights and freedoms, as well as disruptions to legislative bodies, judicial systems, and, sometimes, elections. Governments declared public health emergencies and, in some cases, enacted emergency health legislation without respecting normal procedures and without a formal vote, as seen in Ireland. Legal and political institutions struggled to adapt, creating a catalyst for democratic decline and weakening of the rule of law. Typically, this expansion of governmental power aligns with the broader securitisation trend found in the legal, policy, and institutional responses to the pandemic.[5]

This chapter offers comparative insights into the legal response to the Covid-19-PHEIC in the context of Ireland and France.[6] Despite the transnational

---

[2] Ruth Wodak, 'Légitimer la gestion de crise pendant la Covid-19' (2022) 28 OpenEditions Journal, paras 33–4 https://doi.org/10.4000/aad.5999 (accessed 29 May 2025). Pursuant to Wodak's analysis, Macron changed strategy a month later though, having significantly lost popularity due to the high mortality rate, overcrowded hospitals, and shortage of nurses and doctors. He now called on solidarity and equality.

[3] On the role of governments in the Covid-19 pandemic, see OECD, 'Building Resilience to the Covid-19 Pandemic: The Role of Centres of Government' OECD Policy Responses to Coronavirus (COVID-19) (OECD Publishing 2020) https://doi.org/10.1787/883d2961-en.

[4] Silvia Behrendt and Amrei Müller, 'Do We Need to Protect the Entire World Population from Health Threats through One Global Biomedical Surveillance and Response System?' (2021) 64(1) German Yearbook of International Law 41.

[5] For a similar response from governments beyond Europe, see the case of Zimbabwe, for instance, in Alison Mhazo and Charles Chiedza Maponga, 'Governing a Pandemic: Biopower and the COVID-19 Response in Zimbabwe' (2022) 7(12) BMJ Global Health e009667. For an explanation of the securitisation trend, see the introduction to this volume.

[6] For a description of the legal response in Ireland, see Eoin Carolan et al, 'Ireland: Legal Response to Covid-19' in Jeff King et al (eds), *The Oxford Compendium of National Legal Responses to Covid-19* (OUP online 2021); for the same in France, see Estelle Chambas and Thomas Perroud, 'France: Legal Response to Covid-19' in King et al (eds), ibid. For general works on legal responses, see Arnaud Lami (ed), *La pandémie de Covid-19: Les systèmes*

nature of the health crisis, the responses were primarily national, as intergovernmental efforts to coordinate the management of the Covid-19 pandemic were arguably failing.[7] The domestic level of analysis is therefore valuable. It also helps us understand what impact the new securitised approach, driven by the WHO, had at the domestic level, including as regards the protection of human rights and democratic procedures. As valuable is the comparative analysis to understand how, and to what degree, government responses disrupted the institutional framework and, more broadly, the functioning of democracy and the rule of law in jurisdictions with comparable democratic structures (both being unitary majoritarian systems).[8]

The second section presents the overall legal framework of the health emergency legislation and the extraordinary processes it entailed for the institutions. The third section delves into the disruption of decision-making processes, particularly in relation to democratic oversight and judicial review of violations of rights and freedoms. The chapter concludes with insights drawn from the experiences of Ireland and France, focusing on the robustness of their democratic systems, especially in the context of the WHO reform debate.

2. THE ENACTMENT OF HEALTH EMERGENCY LEGISLATION

To address the challenges posed by the Covid-19-PHEIC and implement countermeasures, many governments enacted emergency powers legislation.[9] In principle, this type of legislation is designed to manage crises effectively by granting to the executive branch both ordinary and exceptional powers to adopt

juridiques à l'épreuve de la crise sanitaire (Bruylant 2021); and Joelle Grogan and Alice Donald (eds), *Routledge Handbook on Law and the COVID-19 Pandemic* (Routledge 2022).

7 Renaud Gay and Kevin Guillas-Cavan, 'La gestion sanitaire de l'épidémie de Covid-19 par les États: Recettes communes et logiques nationales' (2020) 171(3) Chronique Internationale de l'IRES 3, 22.

8 For a comparative work that includes France but not Ireland, see Sabine Kuhlmann et al, 'Tracing Divergence in Crisis Governance: Responses to the COVID-19 Pandemic in France, Germany and Sweden Compared' (2021) 87(3) International Review of Administrative Sciences 556 .

9 There has been debate as to whether these measures were indeed 'necessary', given the low infection fatality rate of SARS-CoV-2; see Angelo Maria Pezzullo et al, 'Age-stratified Infection Fatality Rate of COVID-19 in the Non-elderly Population' (2023) 216(3) Environmental Research 114655; and Kevin Bardosh, 'How Did the COVID Pandemic Response Harm Society? A Global Evaluation and State of Knowledge Review (2020–21)' (14 May 2023) http://dx.doi.org/10.2139/ssrn.4447806.

ordinary law.[10] Such devolution or transfer of the legislative function from parliament to the government is a classical mechanism used in times of crisis. The First World War highlights a situation where the French government, for instance, operated through decrees under the concept of 'necessary illegality'. At the time, the French Parliament frequently turned to this practice, which was not explicitly allowed by the French Constitution, to grant the executive branch the authority to enact laws through decrees, resulting in a substantial expansion of the government's legislative powers.[11]

Emergency powers legislation typically shares certain characteristics. Evidently, such laws require popular legitimation since the executive takes extreme measures to protect the government.[12] This need for legitimation was expressed in various ways throughout the Covid-19 pandemic, particularly through narratives focused on securitisation, especially in France as mentioned above. Furthermore, emergency powers are fundamentally meant to be temporary. Once the emergency has passed, ordinary legal and political processes should resume.[13] This raises questions regarding the repeal of such laws but also regarding the precedent created by the implementation of such regimes of exception.[14] The examination of the emergency powers framework under Irish law and French law serves as a backdrop for analysing the public health emergency legislation that was implemented in both jurisdictions during the Covid-19 pandemic.

2.1 Background to Emergency Legislation

Although the legislation governing emergency powers is mainly derived from constitutional provisions, other legislative and institutional frameworks exist in both jurisdictions.

Article 28.3.3° of the Irish Constitution makes provision for emergency legislation under the specific context of 'war or armed rebellion'.[15] This clause

[10] John Ferejohn and Pasquale Pasquino, 'The Law of the Exception: A Typology of Emergency Powers' (2004) 2(2) International Journal of Constitutional Law 210, 216–17.

[11] Elina Lemaire, 'Le Parlement face à la crise du Covid-19 (2/2)' (*Jus Politicum* blog, 13 April 2020) https://blog.juspoliticum.com/2020/04/13/le-parlement-face-a-la-crise-du-covid-19-2-2-par-elina-lemaire/.

[12] Ferejohn and Pasquino (n 10) 220.

[13] ibid, 217.

[14] There is also the question of whether there was an emergency at all, a controversial question that can arguably be raised.

[15] Gerard Hogan et al, *Kelly: The Irish Constitution* (5th edn, Bloomsbury Professional 2018) 438 ff.

permits the *Oireachtas* (Irish Parliament) to enact laws deemed necessary 'for the purpose of securing the public safety and the preservation of the State' when a 'national emergency has been declared to exist by the two houses [of the *Oireachtas*]'. Such legislation specifically precludes the possibility of a court challenge.[16] The adoption of the Emergency Powers Act in 1939 was, in that vein, aimed at protecting Ireland's neutrality. It granted the government authority to issue orders that could, for instance, lead to the internment of individuals without trial and impose restrictions on freedom of expression and communication, all in an effort to mitigate threats to the State.[17] Alongside this constitutionally established framework, Ireland has implemented a comprehensive system for managing major emergencies. Adopting an 'all hazards' approach, this system aims 'to set out common arrangements and structures for front-line public-sector emergency management in Ireland'.[18] While the legal foundation for this system is somewhat ambiguous, it appears to depend on a range of governmental decisions.[19]

In contrast, France has established several regimes of exception. Article 16 of the Constitution grants the President of the Republic certain 'exceptional powers'.[20] This regime, which is the most severe – and somewhat atypical in a democratic context as it resembles a form of 'republican dictatorship'[21] – is activated only under circumstances where 'the institutions of the Republic, the independence of the Nation, the integrity of its territory or the fulfilment of its international obligations [are] under grave and immediate threat'. Moreover, these circumstances must lead to a disruption of 'the proper functioning of the constitutional public powers'. Meanwhile, article 36 addresses the state of siege, which applies during armed conflict, particularly 'in cases of imminent

16 Desmond Clarke, 'Emergency Legislation, Fundamental Rights and Article 28.3.3° of the Irish Constitution' (1977) 12 The Irish Jurist 217.

17 'The Emergency Powers Act, 1939: Far-Reaching Legislation to Ensure Public Safety' (1939) 5 The Irish Jurist 54.

18 Department of Housing, Local Government and Heritage, 'A Framework for Major Emergency Management' (24 September 2021) https://www.gov.ie/en/collection/ca182-a-framework-for-major-emergency-management/.

19 See eg the government decision to establish, at national level, a National Steering Group (NSG), replacing the Inter-Departmental Committee on Major Emergencies. Subsequently, the NSG formed a National Working Group to handle the responsibilities associated with the plan or programme, see 'A Framework for Major Emergency Management' (n 18).

20 Marie-Luce Paris, *Constitutional Law in France, International Encyclopaedia of Laws* (2nd edn, Wolters Kluwer 2024) 315–16, paras 596–9.

21 Under article 16 of the French Constitution, the President of the Republic can take any 'acts required by the circumstances', whether of a regulatory, legislative or judicial nature. These acts are not subject to judicial review.

danger arising from a foreign war or armed insurrection'. This provision effectively shifts police powers and the authority of civil authorities responsible for maintaining order to military forces, thereby instituting martial law.[22]

Lastly, the state of emergency proper is governed by law in France.[23] This regime of exception is linked to colonial policies. During the 1950s, amid insurrection in Algeria, the French Parliament enacted an ad hoc piece of legislation. The 1955 Law on the state of emergency significantly increased the powers of administrative authorities, enabling them to impose restrictions on individual freedoms, including movement, assembly, and press activities. The 1955 Law was invoked three times during the Algerian conflict – first in 1955 across the territories of French Algeria, then again in 1958 and 1961 within mainland France. It has since been utilised on several other occasions, either in part of the French territory (ie in 1984 and, recently, for a couple of weeks in May 2024, in relation to overseas troubles in New Caledonia; and in 2005 to quell riots in various French suburbs), or nationwide (ie in November 2015, following the Islamist terrorist attacks perpetrated in Paris and Saint Denis). This last state of emergency was prolonged on six separate occasions by the French Parliament. It eventually ended with the enactment of the 2017 Law aimed to enhance domestic security and combat terrorism.[24] However, throughout this period, significant amendments were made that intensified the limitations imposed on individual freedoms within the framework of this special regime. These amendments took a decidedly stricter approach, leading to a state of emergency from 2015 to 2017 that was far more severe than the measures implemented by colonial France in the wake of the Algerian war of independence.[25] In essence, this situation contributed to the 'normalisation' of the state of exception in France, transforming it into 'a new mode of governance in the field of national security that, rather than destined to be merely temporary or "exceptional", affirm[ed] its hold on the "normal" and permanent structure of

---

22 Paris (n 20) 317, para 600. Notwithstanding the state of siege, all the rights guaranteed by the Constitution continue to be exercised when their enjoyment is not suspended under the provisions of the Code of Defence.

23 Law No 55-385 of 3 April 1955 on the state of emergency (as amended in 2018); see also Paris (n 20) 317–8, paras 601–2. The state of emergency and the state of siege are mutually exclusive, meaning that the provisions relating to the state of emergency and those relating to the state of siege cannot be applied simultaneously in the same territory (article L 2131-1 of the Code of Defence).

24 Law No 2017-1510 of 30 October 2017 strengthening domestic security and the fight against terrorism.

25 Stéphanie Hennette-Vauchez, 'The State of Emergency in France: Days without End?' (2018) 14(4) European Constitutional Law Review 700, 704.

the legal order'.[26] This development holds considerable relevance for the below discussion surrounding the Covid-19 emergency and the securitisation framing of possible future health crises.

2.2 Covid-19 Health Emergency Legislation

In the context of the Covid-19-PHEIC, Ginsburg and Versteeg observed that legislative measures emerged as the predominant response to the crisis in many countries, though the difference was not significant.[27] Approximately 52 per cent of the countries included in their study – with France being one of them, but not Ireland – utilised legislation as a key component of their pandemic strategies. In many instances, this legislation was focused on infectious disease control or public health, but countries also invoked various other legal frameworks related to disasters and emergencies.[28] Both Ireland and France enacted emergency legislation to implement the countermeasures recommended by the WHO. Although these legislative measures were temporary in nature, it is noteworthy that Ireland did not formally declare a state of emergency, whereas France did. Regardless of the declaration of a state of emergency, both jurisdictions exhibited a strong dependence on governmental interventions, which was anticipated.

Ireland did not declare a formal state of emergency to respond to the Covid-19-PHEIC. Public health is indeed not a stated reason for invoking the emergency powers in article 28 of the Constitution (relating to the executive power). Yet, the actions taken by Ireland displayed characteristics typical of emergency measures, with a strong dependence on governmental intervention.[29] Specifically, the response relied on a set of primary pieces of legislation, two of which formed the core of Ireland's early actions.[30] Describing the Covid-19 pandemic as an 'emergency',[31] the *Oireachtas* swiftly enacted, in March 2020,

[26] ibid, 702–3.

[27] See Ginsburg and Versteeg's large-scale study in Tom Ginsburg and Mila Versteeg, 'The Bound Executive: Emergency Powers during the Pandemic' (2021) 19(5) International Journal of Constitutional Law 1498, 1515.

[28] ibid.

[29] Conor Casey et al, 'Ireland's Emergency Powers during the Covid-19 Pandemic' (COVID-19 Law and Human Rights Observatory for the Irish Human Rights and Equality Commission, 2021) 22.

[30] There were more than a dozen Acts adopted in this framework as well as amendments to the Health Act 1947, see Carolan et al (n 6), paras 18 and 24 ff.

[31] The use of the language of 'emergency' in primary legislation does not have any formal legal consequences in Irish law, see Carolan et al (n 6), para 17.

the Health Preservation Act[32] and the Emergency Measures Act,[33] at specially convened sittings of the Houses and without the need for a formal vote.[34] The preamble of the former referred to the 'manifest and grave risk to human life and public health posed by the spread of the disease known as Covid-19' and acknowledged the link between the urgent need to safeguard public health and the protection of constitutional rights. It emphasised the importance of implementing 'extraordinary measures and safeguards to prevent, minimise, limit or slow the risk of persons being infected', which was tied to the 'constitutional duty of the State to respect and, as far as practicable, by its laws to defend and vindicate the rights of citizens to life and to bodily integrity'. The latter granted extensive statutory powers to deal with the harsh economic and social effects of the Covid-19 pandemic, in addition to modifying the procedures for approving detention under the Mental Health Act 2001. This was supplemented by additional enforcement measures authorised through the Enforcement Powers Act[35] and the Health Amendment Act,[36] which were enacted in September and October of 2020, respectively. The Irish Human Rights and Equality Commission (IHREC) considered that while the powers granted under the Health Preservation Act were quite broad, the Act itself established adequate principles and policies to constitute a legitimate delegation of legislative authority.[37] On that legal basis, a number of measures were adopted, aimed at imposing considerable limitations on everyday life, encompassing a wide range of potential lockdown scenarios.[38]

---

[32] The Health (Preservation and Protection and other Emergency Measures in the Public Interest) Act 2020.

[33] The Emergency Measures in the Public Interest (Covid-19) Act 2020.

[34] Carolan et al (n 6), paras 18–19. Article 25.2.2° of the Irish Constitution allows the President of Ireland, under an expedited process, and acting on a request from the government as approved by the Seanad, to disapply the usual five-day waiting period required by the Constitution (between the moment the bill is presented to the President and the moment when s/he must sign it into law) and to sign the bill into law almost immediately. This is what happened in relation to the Covid-19-related Acts although it is not clear whether the TDs (members of parliament) skipped the formal vote or if a formal vote took place but with a reduced number of TDs actually sitting in person in the *Dáil* (lower house of the Irish Parliament). Ancillary enforcement measures were authorised in the Criminal Justice (Enforcement Powers Act) (Covid-19) Act 2020 (September 2020), and the Health (Amendment) Act 2020 (Health Amendment Act) (October 2020).

[35] The Criminal Justice (Enforcement Powers) (Covid-19) Act 2020.

[36] The Health (Amendment) Act 2020.

[37] Casey et al (n 29) 23.

[38] ibid, 32 ff; see eg how the Report presents the different stage-divided restrictions: Stage A – Total Lockdown: 8 April 2020 to 8 June 2020; Stage B – Easing

Unlike Ireland, France took the step of declaring a state of emergency, albeit not a constitutional one. Neither the exceptional powers under article 16 nor martial law under article 36 of the Constitution would have been appropriate for a pandemic.[39] The French government's initial response to the Covid-19 crisis aimed at adopting a 'flexible and progressive response' relying on existing legal frameworks to implement a first set of countermeasures. The Health Minister issued, under the provisions of the Public Health Code, a series of orders in early March 2020 aimed at gradually prohibiting gatherings, starting with limits of over 5,000 participants, then reducing to 1,000 and ultimately capping them at 100. Additionally, this response entailed shutting down nurseries, schools, universities, and a wide range of public venues. To further reinforce these actions, the Prime Minister invoked the judicially established 'doctrine of exceptional circumstances', which enabled the government to regulate individual movement and mandate a national lockdown at the start of the health crisis.[40]

However, to establish a strong legal foundation for the countermeasures to combat the Covid-19 pandemic, the French government promoted the enactment of a first law in March 2020 (March 2020 Law), which introduced a statutory 'state of health (or sanitary) emergency' (*état d'urgence sanitaire*).[41] A state of health emergency is defined as a health calamity which, by its nature and seriousness, endangers the health of the population. It is normally declared over all or part of the territory, like the state of emergency referred to in the 1955 Law, by the Council of Ministers through a decree. Nevertheless, exceptionally in this context, the March 2020 Law declared it directly on

Lockdown: 8 June 2020 to 29 June 2020; Stage C – Eased Lockdown: 29 June 2020 to 31 August 2020, although not in every county; Stage D – Modified Lockdown: 31 August 2020 to 7 October, although not in every county; Stage E – Tightened Lockdown: 7 October to 22 October, although Kildare, Laois, Offaly, Dublin, and Donegal were in this stage earlier; Stage F – Renewed Lockdown: 7 October 2020 to 30 November 2020.

39 Chambas and Perroud (n 6), para 7.

40 Although the doctrine was initially employed merely to address the interim period prior to the enactment of the main legislation, its use was not insignificant since it reveals that the executive can always override the absence of delegation of powers by the Parliament in exceptional cases, see Chambas and Perroud (n 6), para 27.

41 Law of Emergency No 2020-290 of 23 March 2020 to deal with the Covid-19 epidemic and Decree No 2020-293 of 23 March 2020 prescribing the general measures necessary to deal with the Covid-19 epidemic within the framework of the state of health emergency (both repealed by subsequent texts).

23 March 2020.[42] Similarly to the Irish case, the hasty mode of enactment of the main legislation and its broad scope were out of the ordinary. Because it was fast-tracked,[43] the March 2020 Law, adopted after four parliamentary sitting days, created an entirely new exceptional legal regime in less than a week, leaving no realistic prospect for the French Parliament to exercise its scrutiny and adopt resolutions expressing confidence or distrust about governmental actions.[44] From a political perspective, French opposition parties did not vehemently oppose the declaration of the state of health emergency, though some human rights and civil society organisations voiced their dissent.[45] Besides, while grounded in the model of the 'ordinary state of emergency' provided for by the above-mentioned 1955 Law, the March 2020 Law presented a broader scope.[46] It had the primary objectives of protecting the French people, bolstering the national economy, and temporarily adapting the rules of law to the upheavals caused by this crisis in economic, social, and administrative matters. It also aimed at organising the postponement of the second round of municipal elections – this last aspect being an important factor in the proper functioning of democratic rules.[47] Because it allegedly aimed at responding to one of the first missions of the State, that is to ensure public order and safeguard public health, the March 2020 Law was regarded as a public order law. It stipulated that a health emergency had to be 'proclaimed by ministerial decree in cases of a health crisis that pose[d] a threat to public health'. Such proclamation was promptly made for a duration of two months, lasting until May 2020 – noting that the two-month period was exceptional to the typical duration of this emergency regime, which is usually one month.[48] The recurring extensions of

---

42 Article L 3131-13 Code of Public Health. Whenever this legal regime is used, Parliament must be informed and can demand any complementary information to scrutinise it, see Chambas and Perroud (n 6), para 12.

43 Under articles 45 and 46 of the French Constitution; see Decision No 2020-799 DC of 26 March 2020 *Loi organique d'urgence pour faire face à l'épidémie de covid-19.*

44 Chambas and Perroud (n 6), para 26.

45 ibid, para 12.

46 It also inserted a whole new set of provisions in the Code of Public Health.

47 Ordinance No 2020-390 of 1 April 2020 relating to the postponement of the second round of the general renewal of municipal and community councillors, Paris councillors, and Lyon metropolitan councillors from 2020 and the establishment of public aid for 2021.

48 Decree No 2020-293 of 23 March 2020 prescribing the general measures necessary to deal with the Covid-19 epidemic within the framework of the state of health emergency. The two-month period was an exception to the typical duration of this emergency regime, which is usually one month.

this legislation, from the first time in May 2020 (May 2020 Law),[49] installed a long period of regime of exception with a complete return to the regular functioning of the State coming only much later. Interestingly, the May 2020 Law was regarded as compatible with the Constitution. However, the Constitutional Council prescribed several interpretative requirements, primarily related to the implementation of tracing measures and the safeguarding of personal data. Additionally, concerns were expressed regarding quarantine, house confinement and the possibility of judicial review of such confinement after a twelve-hour period.[50] This legislative framework granted the executive vast rule-making powers. The French government took a variety of regulatory measures, directly (via decrees or other types of measures) or through secondary legislation,[51] to address the health crisis encompassing a range of actions from restrictions on individual freedoms[52] to economic relief measures aimed at supporting a dormant economy during lockdown,[53] as well as purely medically related measures.[54]

Clearly, the Irish and French governments reacted determinedly to the health crisis, not only in initiating the exceptional legislation but also in acting on it. The unitary centralised system, of which France can be regarded as a prime example,[55] certainly aided this. However, the abundance of measures imposing lockdowns, masks, vaccines, or the vaccine pass provoked heated debates in both jurisdictions. Critics voiced concerns that these actions resembled the

---

[49] Law No 2020-546 of 11 May 2020 extending the state of health emergency and supplementing its provisions. For further detail, see Chambas and Perroud (n 6), para 13.

[50] Decision No 2020-800 DC of 11 May 2020 *Loi prorogeant l'état d'urgence sanitaire et complétant ses dispositions* ('Law extending the state of health emergency and supplementing its provisions').

[51] Under article 38 of the French Constitution, Parliament can temporarily enable the government to take measures by ordinances (ie to exercise regulatory power) in areas that normally pertain to the legislative power, see Paris (n 20) 66–7, paras 96–7; and Chambas and Perroud (n 6), para 15.

[52] These restrictions included measures that limited or entirely barred the movement of individuals and vehicles during designated times and locations as established by official decree; prohibiting residents from leaving their homes, except for essential travel related to family or health necessities; and mandates for quarantine, among other directives.

[53] These economic measures included temporary measures aimed at regulating the prices of specific goods, implemented to alleviate or rectify the imbalances noted within the market for those items.

[54] Medical measures aimed to provide patients with appropriate medications to eradicate the health disaster.

[55] Kuhlmann et al (n 8) 559–60.

onset of a 'health dictatorship', implying a gradual erosion of individual rights and freedoms, and, by extension, democratic principles.[56]

3. DECISION-MAKING DURING THE STATE OF HEALTH EMERGENCY

The Covid-19 pandemic presented a significant challenge for governmental decision-making. With uncertainty surrounding its origins, spread, prevention, and consequences, along with evolving scientific insights and recommendations changing daily, policy-makers were confronted with the difficult task of responding swiftly, yet appropriately, to the unfolding situation.[57] In both compared jurisdictions, the period led to an intense normative activity with the enactment of various countermeasures, accompanied by the establishment of ad hoc bodies tasked with overseeing their implementation. While these countermeasures were aimed at effectively addressing the risks and uncertainties associated with the Covid-19 pandemic, their impact on individual rights led to an equally intense judicial activity when the courts became actively engaged in assessing the legality and proportionality of these measures. This backdrop of heightened normative and litigious activity was interpreted as a manifestation of, first, the essential responsibility of the State – that of ensuring the

[56] For further detail as regards France, see Ruth Amossy, '"Health Dictatorship" and "Civil Disobedience": Political Extremists and French Debates on Democracy during Covid-19' (2023) 30(1) Javnost. The Public (Journal of the European Institute for Communication and Culture) 18 https://doi.org/10.1080/13183222.2023.2162287; Marie-Laure Basilien-Gainche, 'The French Management of COVID-19: Normalisation of Regimes of Exception and Degradation of the Rule of Law' in Joelle Grogan and Alice Donald (eds), *Routledge Handbook on Law and the COVID-19 Pandemic* (Routledge 2022) 434; and Le Club des Juristes, *Le droit face au coronavirus (Comment une pandémie inédite a mis à l'épreuve notre système juridique)* (LexisNexis 2021).

[57] There were also other opinions about the level of uncertainty of the health situation. See, for example, Norman Fenton and Martin Neil, *Fighting Goliath: Exposing the Flawed Science and Statistics behind the COVID-19 Event* (Sovereign Rights Publishing 2024). More generally, there was always critical questioning of the evidential basis (including scientific basis) for both the existence of a health emergency due to SARS-CoV-2 and the medical and non-medical countermeasures adopted to address the Covid-19-PHEIC, right from the beginning. See, for example, US House of Representatives Select Subcommittee on the Coronavirus Pandemic, Committee on Oversight and Accountability, 'After Action Review of the Covid-19 Pandemic: The Lessons Learned and a Path Forward' (*Wenstrup Report*, 4 December 2024) https://oversight.house.gov/wp-content/uploads/2024/12/12.04.2024-SSCP-FINAL-REPORT.pdf.

safety of its people; second, the role of the experts – that of providing clarity and insight despite prevailing uncertainties brought about by the crisis; and third, the duty of the judge – that of administering justice with independence and impartiality.[58] This environment prompted notable changes in the government's usual decision-making processes, reflecting the aforementioned trend of securitisation, particularly illustrated by the establishment of ad hoc bodies for crisis management and an increase in parliamentary oversight and judicial review of the countermeasures in place, aspects of which are examined in the following section.

3.1 Governing via ad hoc Bodies

Both Ireland and France established ad hoc bodies to support the government in making purportedly informed and effective decisions in response to the Covid-19 pandemic. While the Irish government set up the National Public Health Emergency Team (NPHET) for Covid-19, which served as an expert advisory body focused on Covid-19, the French government relied on a governmental body, the Health Defence Council, supplemented by two additional expert bodies. In both cases, concerns arose regarding not only the composition and role of these bodies, but also the oversight of their actions, a situation that typically reflects the tensions between the politicians and the experts. Politicians are usually compelled to make firm decisions and demonstrate resoluteness, whereas experts' advice often tends to be uncertain and contested, especially as understanding of the crisis evolves and initial evaluations shift.[59]

NPHET was formed in January 2020 as part of the Irish Department of Health. Chaired by the Chief Medical Officer, NPHET comprised representatives from various government bodies, including the Department of Health, along with individuals possessing 'relevant experience in health and/or other matters'.[60] The team was further assisted by the Expert Advisory Group and

[58] Florence Chaltiel, 'À propos de l'état d'urgence sanitaire, textes et contextes' (*Actu-Juridique.fr* blog, 9 September 2020, Les Petites Affiches, No 155a3) 16 https://www.actu-juridique.fr/constitutionnel/a-propos-de-letat-durgence-sanitaire-textes-et-contextes/. Some other, more critical, opinions were put forward from very early on during the pandemic.

[59] Kuhlmann et al (n 8) 570.

[60] In addition to members of the Department of Health, members were drawn from the Health Service Executive (HSE), the Health Protection Surveillance Centre (HPSC), the Health Information and Quality Authority (HIQA), and the Health Products Regulatory Authority (HPRA).

various NPHET subgroups.[61] Its general mandate was to 'oversee and provide national direction, guidance, support and expert advice on the development and implementation of a strategy to contain Covid-19 in Ireland'.[62] This was done by facilitating the sharing of information between the Department of Health and its agencies, as well as providing a forum for agreement on strategic approaches to public health emergencies.[63] NPHET's membership was regarded as broadly multi-disciplinary and multi-sectoral, which was arguably sufficient, in the eyes of the government that selected the members, to represent the diversity of scientific opinions, aligning with established WHO international standards. Additionally, the government position was that NPHET was not intended to function as a representative body.

The composition of NPHET was criticised on two fronts. Some questioned whether the group represented a wide enough range of medical and scientific viewpoints, while others expressed concern over the absence of expertise in human rights matters.[64] However, the main issue revolved around its purpose. NPHET was fundamentally an advisory body for the government. Functioning through a consensus-based approach, NPHET provided recommendations on the public health components of a coordinated governmental response to the pandemic, as informed by Ireland's National Action Plan in response to Covid-19. It had no juridical role in the making of laws or in the distribution of official public health guidance. Nevertheless, there were ongoing claims that the executive governance of NPHET had, in reality, accumulated more authority than its official position in the policy-making process would suggest, leading to a risk of 'an accountability trap'.[65] In other words, NPHET functioned as a de facto decision-maker on public health matters, overshadowing the government's role, despite being an unaccountable body.[66] This situation was exacerbated

---

61 Government of Ireland, Department of Health, 'National Public Health Emergency Team (NPHET) for COVID-19: Governance Structures' (2nd edn, 26 June 2020) https://www.gov.ie/en/publication/de1c30-national-public-health-emergency-team-nphet-for-covid-19-governance-/.

62 ibid, 4.

63 ibid, 6.

64 Casey et al (n 29) 55 ff.

65 ibid, 57; and Alan Eustace, Sarah Hamill, and Andrea Mulligan, 'Public Health Law during the COVID-19 Pandemic in Ireland', Public Policy Report (COVID-19 Legal Observatory, Trinity College School of Law 2021) 27 https://www.tcd.ie/law/2020.21/COVID-19%20Public%20Health%20Law%20Report.pdf.

66 Eustace et al (n 65) 27.

by a level of parliamentary oversight that, although still operational, remained relatively weak when it came to monitoring government actions.[67]

In France, the Health Defence Council (*Conseil de défense sanitaire*) was established in early 2020 as an emanation of the Defence and National Security Council (*Conseil de défense et de sécurité nationale*).[68] Its composition was at the highest level of the State, with the President of the Republic serving as its chair. Key ministers, including the Prime Minister, the Minister of Health, the Minister of Defence, as well as the Minister of Economy and the Minister of Employment, were also part of its membership. Other stakeholders drawn from major public institutions in the health sector were also invited to join. Two other bodies, established in March 2020, assisted the Health Defence Council, namely the Scientific Council for Covid-19 (*Conseil scientifique Covid-19*)[69] and the Analysis, Research and Expertise Committee (*Comité Analyse Recherche et Expertise* or *CARE*).[70] Both were governmental initiatives – the Scientific Council was established at the behest of the Minister for Health, while *CARE* was initiated by the government itself. Their primary role was to provide the government with independent expert opinions and recommendations to enhance its fight against the pandemic. The French government emphasised the unique and complementary functions of each body to mitigate any concerns regarding potential overlap in their responsibilities.[71] While the Scientific Council enlightened the government and public authorities on their strategic decisions regarding the management of the pandemic,[72] the primary focus of *CARE* was on foresight and anticipation. *CARE* aimed to promptly inform the government about the scientific, therapeutic, and technological advancements recommended by the scientific community in combating Covid-19. This included updates on the development and implementation of

---

67 Casey et al (n 29) 44–5.

68 Paris (n 20) 304, para 565.

69 See the rules of procedure and opinions of the Scientific Council issued between March 2020 and July 2022 at https://sante.gouv.fr/actualites/presse/dossiers-de-presse/article/conseil-scientifique-covid-19.

70 For the establishment of *CARE*, see 'Installation du comité analyse, recherche et expertise (CARE)' (*Ministère du travail, de la sante, des solidarites et des familles*, 24 March 2020) https://sante.gouv.fr/archives/archives-presse/archives-breves/article/installation-du-comite-analyse-recherche-et-expertise-care.

71 A couple of members were part of both bodies.

72 The Scientific Council comprised 13 experts from various scientific disciplines. It was tasked with addressing specific inquiries related to public health policies during the crisis, including the potential impacts of containment measures and strategies for virus testing and screening. Their recommendations were subsequently made available to the public.

testing and trial treatments, particularly highlighting experiments conducted internationally.[73]

Like the Irish NPHET, the French Health Defence Council faced criticism concerning both its makeup and role. The makeup of the Council allowed for great flexibility as its modular size membership could accommodate members from outside the government.[74] This proved advantageous when addressing the unpredictable challenges posed by the Covid-19 pandemic. However, this flexibility also raised concerns in terms of transparency and accountability. Additionally, these issues were exacerbated by ongoing criticism of the Council's role in managing public health responses. In normal times, the Defence and National Security Council serves as a pivotal high-level entity that outlines key strategies and establishes priorities related to 'military programming, deterrence, conduct of external operations, planning of responses to major crises, intelligence, economic and energy security, internal security programming contributing to national security and the fight against terrorism'.[75] Prior to the Covid-19 pandemic, the Council had already seen an increase in the frequency of its meetings[76] as 'defence' intervened in new matters to include issues like health and environmental concerns and possibly, in the future, food and digital matters, among others. Presidential practice of the last five years has tended to verify this potential extension of the Council's reach, since beyond the weekly frequency of its meetings, the subjects treated in the 'restricted' Council have considerably expanded. In the context of the Covid-19 pandemic, subjects dealt with within the Council ranged from the virus circulation map to the measures to lift the lockdown, including

[73] The *CARE* committee comprised 12 distinguished medical doctors and researchers, led by the esteemed virologist Professor Barré-Sinoussi, a Nobel Prize laureate recognised for her groundbreaking contributions to HIV research.

[74] Membership in the Defence and National Security Council is inherently discretionary, allowing for various configurations based on specific needs. The Council can convene in several formats: a plenary session that includes the President of the Republic, the Prime Minister, and the ministers responsible for implementing decisions – specifically the Ministers of Defence, Home Affairs, Economy and Budget, and Foreign Affairs. Additionally, a restricted formation comprises solely relevant ministers according to the day's agenda, along with the military chief of staff. Furthermore, there are specialised groups within the Council addressing particular areas, such as a Defence and National Security Council dedicated to national intelligence, another focused on nuclear weapons, and, as seen during the Covid-19 pandemic, a Council specifically for health-related matters.

[75] Article R 1122-1 Code of Defence.

[76] Originally meeting several times a year, the Council transitioned to weekly meetings after the 2016 terrorist attack in Nice, enhancing its ability to address the ongoing terrorist threat.

the launch of the so-called 'blue plan' for nursing homes, the reopening of a *Vendée* amusement park, schools, and beaches.[77] Nonetheless, this broader scope of the Council's activities is now being regarded as a potential threat to the effectiveness of parliamentary oversight of government action, leading to a weakening of the very nature of the Fifth Republic parliamentary regime.[78] Moreover, the ascendancy of the President of the Republic, who chairs the Council, has been described as 'an uninhibited hyper-presidentialism, even of a monarchical conception of power',[79] deviating significantly from democratic principles. It is not surprising that experts have referred to the Defence and National Security Council using terms like 'black cabinet', 'secret committee', or 'war room'.[80] As one academic expressed it:

> presidential practice has gradually erased the specialisation of [the Defence and National Security Council] resulting in its transformation into a restricted council of government, potentially competent in an ordinary way and, since 2015 [Islamist terrorist attacks], permanent. … The institutionalisation of the restricted Council in ordinary presidential decision-making body, … and the trivialisation of a war-related discourse which promotes the use of military means and organs, as well as encourage resort to exceptional measures, are useful tools in the hands of the President and the executive.[81]

In its formation for Covid-19, the Health Defence Council was empowered to make significant decisions regarding the pandemic. This power complemented the ongoing operation of traditional institutions, including the Council of Ministers, which typically serves as the primary body for government decision-making. However, in contrast to the Council of Ministers, whose proceedings are accessible to the public,[82] the Health Defence Council, like any other Defence Council formation, is covered by *secret défense*.[83] Such functioning was thus also seen as a risk to the constitutional balance between the executive and judicial branches since the secrecy surrounding the Council's meetings

---

77 Thibault Desmoulins, 'La formalisation du présidentialisme sous la Cinquième République: le Conseil de défense et de sécurité nationale' (*Jus Politicum* blog, January 2021) 221, 243–4 https://www.juspoliticum.com/articles/La-formalisation-du-presidentialisme-sous-la-Cinquieme-Republique-le-Conseil-de-defense-et-de-securite-nationale.

78 ibid, 250.

79 ibid, 221.

80 ibid.

81 ibid, 253.

82 For the proceedings of the French Council of Ministers, see 'Conseil des ministres' (*Gouvernement*, 2025) https://www.info.gouv.fr/conseil-des-ministres.

83 Article R 413-6 of the Code of Defence.

could impede judicial oversight of executive actions.[84] Therefore, in France the health crisis was predominantly managed by a political body (ie the Health Defence Council), flanked by two expert bodies (ie Scientific Council for Covid-19 and *CARE*) that operated without parliamentary or judicial scrutiny, leading to a significant lack of transparency. This situation has epitomised the securitisation trend through the two-fold phenomenon of an aggrandisement of executive authority and an institutionalisation of the Council as a standard mechanism for governmental decision-making in the context of a normalisation of the state of emergency amid a broadly defined framework of 'major crises' and 'threats'.[85]

3.2 Rights Limitations and Weak Oversight

In both jurisdictions, the legislature and the courts,[86] despite difficulty in convening normally,[87] played an important role in the context of the Covid-19 pandemic, given that the optimal course of action remained uncertain due to the unknown nature of the 'enemy'. As explained above, the Irish and French Parliaments promptly implemented emergency legislation to establish a legal framework to address the evolving crisis.[88] Meanwhile, the courts were tasked with reviewing the validity of various measures aimed at managing the emergency, particularly those that affected fundamental rights and liberties, including the right to privacy, freedom of movement, freedom of assembly, and the right to conduct business.

Nevertheless, it is important to provide additional context to these observations, as both democratic oversight and judicial scrutiny were not entirely effective in the unprecedented environment brought about by the Covid-19 pandemic.

---

[84] Desmoulins (n 77) 253.

[85] ibid, 241–5.

[86] See also the role of other official bodies such as the Irish Human Rights and Equality Commission (IHREC), and the French National Consultative Commission on Human Rights (*Commission Nationale Consultative des Droits de l'Homme, CNCDH*) via their reporting (eg reports of the IHREC) and opinions (eg CNCDH, *Etat d'urgence sanitaire et Etat de droit*, 28 April 2020).

[87] For the disruption of ordinary business in Ireland, see Carolan et al (n 6), paras 63 ff (legislature) and paras 80 ff (courts). For the same in France, see Chambas and Perroud (n 6), paras 28 ff (legislature) and paras 31 ff (courts).

[88] For general observations, see Ginsburg and Versteeg (n 27).

3.2.1 Democratic control

The precipitation of events brought about by the Covid-19 pandemic significantly altered the regular law-making process (as we have seen primarily concerning the health emergency legislation). The time constraints imposed by the urgency of the crisis hindered the ability to deploy expertise to properly evaluate legislation. In the Irish case, the absence of (or probable absence of) regulatory impact analysis, which typically assesses the potential effects of proposed regulations on 'the rights of the citizen/human rights', was highlighted by the IHREC.[89] Overall, the delegation of legislative power to the Minister of Health resulted in 'a black hole' in addressing human rights and equality issues within the *Oireachtas* whose brief was too wide to realistically be able to devote significant attention to all relevant measures.[90] The IHREC Report on the emergency powers during the Covid-19 pandemic explained:

> Members of the Oireachtas could not meaningfully raise such concerns [ie, human rights and equality concerns] because it was unclear precisely what restrictions would be introduced. The sunset provisions and procedures allowing the Oireachtas to annul measures have had little, if any, purchase. The interaction between NPHET and the Government in approving the policy direction and preparing legislation may allow for some consideration of human rights and equality concerns. However, this is largely done by those with neither expertise, nor insight into the needs of disadvantaged groups, nor democratic accountability. Such consideration, if it occurs, is not available for public scrutiny. This is a significant defect in Ireland's COVID-19 response, breaching international law norms relating to the rule of law.[91]

Similarly, in the French case, the unprecedented amount of derived legislation produced in a short period of time posed challenges. For instance, between 25 March and 8 April 2020, the French government enacted a remarkable total of 41 ordinances under the enabling 2020 March Emergency Law.[92] The issue was further complicated by concerns regarding the quality of these measures. One example was the Decree outlining the 'general measures necessary to cope with the epidemic within the framework of the state health emergency', which remarkably underwent 38 amendments in the space of six

---

89 Casey et al (n 29) 54–5.

90 On one occasion, a deputy attempted to overturn a series of Covid-19 regulations but was unsuccessful. Though the proposer of the motion focused primarily on economic grounds, several deputies who opposed the regulations highlighted concerns regarding civil liberties, specifically regarding punitive measures, see Casey et al (n 29) 50.

91 ibid, 62.

92 See article 11 of the March 2020 Law which allowed the government to take, by ordinance, the temporary economic and social measures that the emergency (allegedly) required to tackle the Covid-19 pandemic.

months (between its enactment in October 2020 and April 2021), averaging a change every four days. This was certainly problematic in terms of foreseeability of the law. The situation became even more perplexing with the amending Decree of 19 March 2021, which was equally ambiguous. Its first provision, intended to replace, eliminate, and alter various elements of the previous Decree, was extremely lengthy, spanning over 1,000 words! It was not just the way the measures were adopted or modified, that was questionable, but also their legal meaning and status as legal norms.[93] The regulatory definition of masks, which became mandatory for public use, was a case in point.[94] Four categories of authorised masks were defined, including those reserved for non-health uses. All these masks had to meet four characteristics, one of which was itself divided into three sub-characteristics(!).[95] Additional examples that illustrate the quite confusing normative production were the so-called 'health (sanitary) protocols' and the infamous 'self-certifications' that permitted individuals to leave their homes and travel during lockdowns. The issue with the health protocols, particularly those governing public life,[96] was that, although they set out precise standards of behaviour by adding additional obligations (eg compulsory wearing of masks), they did not have the form nor the appearance of regulatory texts. These were unsigned documents that were merely distributed to authorities and the public.[97] Under French administrative law,

---

[93] In addition, of course, to the problem of the legality of such norms as regards the potential violations of fundamental freedoms that could arise. See below, on judicial review, text accompanying (nn 123–32).

[94] Apart from the political controversy that emerged when it became clear that there were not enough masks and that it was revealed that the French government had previously destroyed its stocks, see Fabrice Lhomme and Gérard Davet, '2017–2020: comment la France a continué à détruire son stock de masques après le début de l'épidémie', *Le Monde* (Paris, 7 May 2020); and Clément Schouler and Laurent Mucchielli, 'Covid, état d'urgence et libertés publiques: Les libertés qui fondent la démocratie sont-elles solubles dans la lutte contre une épidémie?' (2022) 449(4) Futuribles 73, 74–5.

[95] See point III of annex I of the 2020 Decree. These characteristics were of a complexity that cannot but escape common sense; they required 'an efficiency in filtering particles of three micrometres emitted towards the outside greater than 90%, breathability that allows them to be worn for a period of four hours and air permeability greater than 96 litres per square meter per second, for a depression of 100 pascals sic.'

[96] Schouler and Mucchielli (n 94) 75; see, for example, the health protocol for the 2020–21 school year entitled 'Guide relatif au fonctionnement des écoles et établissements scolaires dans le contexte Covid', which established an obligation for students to wear a category 1 mask, albeit not provided for in the 2020 Decree.

[97] Schouler and Mucchielli (n 94) 75.

an administrative authority may only issue a regulatory text if it possesses the legal authority to do so. This authority must be exercised by a civil servant, an elected official, or a member of a regularly appointed constitutional body, whose personal accountability or the validity of their delegated authority can be subject to judicial review. Consequently, such regulatory texts cannot be issued anonymously. As for the self-certifications, although not based on any regulatory text, they were unexpectedly mandated, at the end of March 2021, by a simple announcement on the website of the Ministry of the Interior.[98] Yet, in a 2022 decision, the Council of State, the highest administrative court, validated the practice of these 'unidentified normative objects'.[99] The Council of State notably justified the obligation to carry, for any travel, a self-certificate by arguing that this obligation did not constitute 'a disproportionate measure, despite the seriousness of the infringement … caused to the freedom of movement'. Furthermore, the Council of State asserted that this obligation did not violate 'the principles of legality of offences and penalties', nor did it undermine the principle of 'the necessity of penalties'.[100]

Hence, the importance of greater political and judicial scrutiny of pandemic measures. In Ireland, where the oversight by the *Oireachtas* of the law-making process fell short in several respects, recommendations were made by a special committee of the *Oireachtas* to address them. These all pointed towards the need for better ex post oversight of all legislation and regulations made pursuant to the pandemic by the sectoral committees,[101] or specifically of the regulations made by the Minister of Health through the establishment of a Joint *Oireachtas* Committee on Equality, Human Rights and Diversity, as suggested by the IHREC.[102] The same situation prevailed in the French case where parliamentary oversight was described, by an apt but obvious metaphor, as being 'on life support'.[103] As a general measure, the Code of Public Health

98 ibid; the self-certifications were to be produced by any individual who had a compelling reason (eg accompanying their children to school, going to the doctor, attending a police or court summons) to leave their home and travel around.

99 ibid.

100 Council of State, 10e et 9e chambres réunies, 22 December 2020, No 439 956, ECLI:FR: CECHR:2020:439956.20201222, paras 5–6.

101 Houses of the *Oireachtas*, 'Special Committee on COVID-19 Response: Final Report' (6 October 2020) para 172, cited in Casey et al (n 29) 50. Sectoral committees or departmental joint committees are typically established to consider matters of expenditure, administration and policy connected with each of the Departments of State and associated public bodies.

102 Casey et al (n 29) 50.

103 Jean-Philippe Derosier and Gilles Toulemonde, 'Le Parlement français et la pandémie: un Parlement sous assistance respiratoire', Etude, Fondation Robert

was amended at the start of the pandemic to introduce a specific requirement regarding the information that should be made available to the National Assembly and the Senate:

> The National Assembly and the Senate are informed without delay of the measures taken by the government under the state of health emergency. [They] may request any additional information as part of the scrutiny and evaluation of these measures.[104]

Due to the significant disruption in the functioning of the French Parliament, the assemblies swiftly chose to oversee the management and consequences of the Covid-19 crisis through other means than parliamentary questions. In this exercise, the Senate took a more pro-active approach by opting to leverage its various standing committees and establish monitoring missions and to carry out essential hearings. This detailed examination through committees proved to be somewhat more effective than the scrutiny conducted in the National Assembly,[105] particularly given that the Senate was in opposition to the government. Additionally, the Senate opted to establish a committee of inquiry responsible for assessing France's preparedness in response to the Covid-19 pandemic. This committee was also tasked with looking into how political and administrative leaders managed the health crisis and the decisions made by France in comparison to those of other European countries.[106] Despite this, the scrutiny operated by the French Parliament certainly failed in exercising, particularly within the National Assembly, thorough hearings and inquiries,

---

Schuman (2020) 7 https://old.robert-schuman.eu//fr/doc/ouvrages/FRS_Parlement_francais_Covid-19.pdf; and Jean-Baptiste Jacob, 'À propos d'un inédit familier: le contrôle parlementaire de l'état d'urgence sanitaire' (*Actu-Juridique.fr* blog, 28 April 2020, Les Petites Affiches, No 153g9) 6 https://www.actu-juridique.fr/constitutionnel/a-propos-dun-inedit-familier-le-controle-parlementaire-de-letat-durgence-sanitaire/.

104 Article L 3131-13, para 2 of the Code of Public Health.

105 The National Assembly, through its Conference of Presidents, decided to establish an information mission on the impact, management, and consequences in all its dimensions of the Covid-19 pandemic. However, favouring a general and cross-cutting mission, where the various parliamentary groups and committees were represented, it did not prove to be sufficiently efficient, see Derosier and Toulemonde (n 103) 9.

106 Senate Commission of Inquiry, 'Rapport fait au nom de la commission d'enquête pour l'évaluation des politiques publiques face aux grandes pandémies à la lumière de la crise sanitaire de la covid-19 et de sa gestion' (8 December 2020), No 199, Vol 1 https://www.senat.fr/rap/r20-199-1/r20-199-11.pdf and Vol 2 (hearings) https://www.senat.fr/rap/r20-199-2/r20-199-21.pdf.

the objective being to avoid putting the government and the majority in difficulty. This was made worse by the fact that the adapted rules for the exercise of the scrutiny rested on relatively weak legal foundations.[107]

The relative apathy of Parliament in both jurisdictions was further exacerbated by the shortcomings of judicial review exercised by the courts.

3.2.2 Judicial review

The state of health emergency was not meant to impede the administration of justice. In both legal systems, the courts continued to operate without interruption, albeit with mitigating measures. Judicial review of laws and regulations proved essential given the numerous claims brought to challenge these, particularly concerning the necessity of proportionality in relation to public health objectives.[108] Nonetheless, the weakness of the review carried out by courts must be acknowledged.

In Ireland, a 'highly mediated case',[109] started during the complete lockdown period (from 27 March to 5 May 2020), saw the Supreme Court upholding a decision of lower courts to dismiss a challenge regarding the constitutionality of laws introduced in response to the Covid-19 pandemic.[110] The applicants had considered that the two main Acts – the Health (Preservation and Protection and other Emergency Measures in the Public Interest) Act 2020 and Emergency Measures in the Public Interest (Covid-19) Act 2020 – were unconstitutional. They sought leave to seek judicial review claiming it was in the public interest. Before the High Court, the applicants made forceful statements because they saw, in the 'draconian, regressive and unnecessary' measures that the government acted upon, some kind of 'fraudulent science' leading to the arrival of a 'police State' which could be paralleled with Nazi Germany. While the applicants certainly had standing (since the restrictive measures in question were meant to affect every person residing in the State, including

---

[107] Derosier and Toulemonde (n 103) 10.

[108] More Covid-19 related cases will arrive at European level too, before the European Court of Human Rights in particular, about the conciliation of public order (including health) with the protection of fundamental rights; see European Court of Human Rights Press Unit, 'Factsheet – COVID-19 Health Crisis' (October 2024) https://www.echr.coe.int/documents/d/echr/fs_covid_eng.

[109] Carolan et al (n 6), para 291.

[110] *Gemma O'Doherty & John Waters v The Minister for Health & Ors* [2022] IESC 32. The applicants had invoked article 40 of the Irish Constitution, the personal rights of the citizens (they also mentioned unenumerated rights), the right to the inviolability of the dwelling, the right to assemble peaceably, as well as the right to family life under article 41 and the right to practice religion under article 44.2.

the applicants), they failed to make an arguable case properly backed up by relevant facts.[111]

In one of the most recent cases about the health crisis, the High Court ruled that the emergency measures, particularly those which imposed criminal sanctions for certain gatherings and leaving home without reasonable excuse, were constitutional.[112] The High Court ruled that:

> It was clearly the intention of both houses of the Oireachtas that this legislation should be put in place, for the proper and indeed constitutionally appropriate step of vindicating lives, as the preamble of the Act clearly states. It cannot be overemphasized that the reason why these remarkable and unprecedented steps were being taken, was to save lives. … This step was not done on some party-political whim, or some attempted power grab, carried out by an unconscionable dictatorship. It was done to defend and vindicate the rights of citizens of the State to life and to bodily integrity, pursuant to the Constitution.[113]

Besides, the High Court recalled the 'extraordinarily difficult position' the Irish government was placed in due to the political circumstances at the time, which coincided with a general election (January 2020) and the process of forming a new government. Still, the Court emphasised 'how effective[ly] [the] democratic system operated' since the Houses of the *Oireachtas* could sit again normally after the dissolution.[114] Nevertheless, these legal arguments – and in particular the unwillingness of courts to engage with scientific evidence not 'approved' by NPHET and the WHO – may appear specious when viewed from a more critical perspective, as has been observed in certain circles.[115]

The same trend of validation of the exceptional measures decided by the government can be observed in the French case, whether under constitutional review or (administrative) judicial review processes.[116] First of all, judicial oversight regarding the declaration of the state of health emergency itself was

---

111 *Gemma O'Doherty & John Waters v The Minister for Health & Ors* [2020] IEHC 209 [55]; see also Marie-Luce Paris, 'Legal Actions against the State: Comparative Perspectives with Reference to Ireland and France' (*British Association of Comparative Law* blog, 6 July 2020) https://british-association-comparative-law.org/2020/07/06/legal-actions-against-the-state-comparative-perspectives-with-reference-to-ireland-and-france/ (accessed 26 April 2025).

112 *Nial Ring & Ors v The Minister for Health & Ors* [2024] IEHC 323.

113 ibid, [47].

114 ibid, [39–41].

115 Fenton and Neil (n 57).

116 Schouler and Mucchielli (n 94) 84. For an overview of how the health crisis impacted the administration of justice in France, see Hélène Pauliat and Séverine Nadaud (eds), *La crise de la Covid-19: Comment maintenir l'action publique*? (LexisNexis 2020).

minimal.[117] The constitutionality of the state of health emergency was only established as regards the May 2020 Law which extended the emergency.[118] Yet, the Constitutional Council largely endorsed the health emergency legislation, often diverging from its established precedents. The Council ruled that 'the Constitution [did] not exclude the possibility for the legislature to provide for [a state of health emergency]' and that it was up to the legislature 'to ensure the reconciliation between the objective of constitutional value of protecting health and respect for the rights and freedoms recognised to all those residing in the territory of the Republic'.[119] In that particular context, the Council concluded that the legislature achieved an appropriate balance between safeguarding public health and maintaining individual freedoms.[120] Besides, the Council did not hesitate, at the very start of the health crisis, to renounce one of its prerogatives – which is nevertheless essential in a period of suspension and restriction of freedoms – that of reviewing ex post the constitutionality of laws.[121] This level of self-restraint enabled the Council to refrain from examining the question of whether the home confinement of over 67 million individuals for 55 straight days represented a deprivation of liberty that warranted judicial oversight by the ordinary courts in application of article 66 of the Constitution, or if it was merely a restriction of liberty. The general stance of the Council was, unsurprisingly, severely criticised by lawyers and experts.[122]

As for the Council of State, it experienced a significant surge in its activities, handling numerous cases during the initial year of the Covid-19 pandemic.[123] In that context, the Council issued important rulings in interim relief and injunction proceedings, particularly regarding limitations on freedom of movement.[124] Emblematic cases included challenges against the use

---

117 See Decision No 2020-799 DC (n 43).

118 The President of the Republic referred the May 2020 Law to the Constitutional Council, which is a rare occurrence in the practice of the Fifth Republic.

119 Decision No 2020-800 DC of 11 May 2020 *Loi prorogeant l'état d'urgence sanitaire et complétant ses dispositions*, para 17.

120 ibid, para 23.

121 Decision No 2020-799 DC (n 43). The Constitutional Council censored part of the legislation though, such as the automatic extensions of pre-trial detentions that could be made without the guarantee of judicial review by ordinary courts in a reasonable timeframe, see Decision No 2020-878/879 QPC of 29 January 2021 *M Ion Andronie R. et autre [Prolongation de plein droit des détentions provisoires dans un contexte d'urgence sanitaire]*, paras 10–11.

122 Schouler and Mucchielli (n 94) 84–5.

123 Charlène Collet, 'Covid-19 et liberté d'aller et venir' (2021) 47(2) Civitas Europa 231, 232.

124 These cases were judged under the specific remedy of *référé-liberté*, a fast-track proceeding in the form of a petition based on a serious and illegal violation

of drones,[125] government restrictions affecting French citizens living abroad wishing to return to France,[126] the right of nursing home residents to leave their facilities,[127] and even restrictions on cycling.[128] Concerning the latter case, one can only note the oddity of the situation where the Council of State requested the government to clarify publicly why the prohibition on using bicycles was to be addressed in the midst of one of the most critical emergencies in recent history.[129] The review carried out by the supreme administrative court was meant to play a crucial role in safeguarding public freedoms, notably by ensuring that the restricting countermeasures were 'necessary, adequate and proportionate'. This series of cases certainly allowed the Council of State to remind the executive of certain essential principles.

Yet, the Council of State dismissed nearly all applications in interim relief and injunction proceedings, thus demonstrating a questionable leniency towards the executive branch, some critics even describing the administrative case law of this period as 'an extension of executive propaganda via judicial means'.[130] While the objective of protecting public health was perfectly legitimate, it raised a broader question: Were the restrictive measures implemented by authorities truly effective in achieving this goal, and were they proportionate to the desired outcome? Besides, whose health are we really discussing? According to the WHO's Constitution, health is defined as 'a state of complete

---

of individual freedoms. This remedy was extended in the context of the state of health emergency by article L. 3131-18 of the Public Health Code. For orders made during the first months of the health emergency, see 'Dernières décisions (référés) en lien avec l'épidémie de Covid-19' (*Conseil d'Etat*, 2025) https://www.conseil-etat.fr/actualites/dernieres-decisions-referes-en-lien-avec-l-epidemie-de-covid-19.

125 CE, ord., 18 May 2020, *Association la Quadrature du net,* and *Ligue des droits de l'homme*, Applications No 440442 and 440445, ECLI:FR: CEORD:2020:440442.20200518.

126 CE, ord., 12 March 2021, *Briand and Union française de l'étranger*, Applications No 449743, ECLI:FR: CEORD:2021:449743.20210312.

127 CE, ord., 3 March 2021, *Demay*, Application No 449759, ECLI:FR: CEORD:2021:449759.20210303.

128 CE, ord., 30 April 2020, *Fédération française des usages de la bicyclette*, Application No 440179, ECLI:FR: CEORD:2020:440179.20200430; see also CE, ord., 30 April 2020, *Ligue des droits de l'homme & Ors*, Application No 440250, ECLI:FR: CEORD:2020:440250.20200430, about the limitations pertaining to the process for seeking asylum.

129 The order of the Council of State was limited to addressing this request for clarification, as it lacked the necessary authority to address the plaintiffs' allegations regarding the infractions they had committed.

130 Cited in Schouler and Mucchielli (n 94) 84.

physical, mental and social well-being and not merely the absence of disease or infirmity'.[131] Considering this comprehensive perspective on health, can we conclude that the imposed limitations, especially those pertaining to freedom of movement, which extended to confining nursing home residents to their rooms, were likely to ensure their physical, mental, and social well-being?[132]

4. CONCLUSION

As the disease quickly faded from the public consciousness when life got back to (almost) normal over the course of 2022, the WHO eventually declared, on 5 May 2023, that Covid-19 no longer represented a PHEIC, although it stopped short of stating that the pandemic was over. Ireland and France had already disbanded their Covid-19 emergency regimes, although both governments continued to issue guidance to help prevent the spread of the virus. In March 2022, Covid legislation was ended in Ireland[133] while, in France, the Law enacted on 30 July 2022 officially terminated the state of health emergency.[134]

It is widely perceived to be the case that the national response to the Covid-19 pandemic, by conferring wide powers on the government, altered the legal order and, particularly in France, disrupted the constitutional equilibrium, resulting in a more powerful executive branch.[135] Parliaments found themselves forced to reconcile two apparently contradictory intentions: on the one hand, to recognise that the fight against the Covid-19 pandemic required a promptness of decision and execution that did not allow for accommodation of the traditional modalities of parliamentary debate and control; and on the other hand, to succeed in imposing, in the gap then opened between State power and the ordinary legal order, a scrutiny of government action.[136] In that context, the pandemic response has certainly sparked a broader discussion about the role of government power during times of crisis, one of the oldest topics in constitutional and political theory. Such discussion has been regarded

---

131 Constitution of the World Health Organization (adopted 22 July 1946, entered into force 7 April 1948) 14 UNTS 185 (WHOC), preamble.

132 Collet (n 123) 239.

133 The Health (Preservation and Protection and Other Emergency Measures in the Public Interest) Act 2020 ended at the end of March 2022.

134 Law No 2022-1089 of 30 July 2022 ending the exceptional regimes created to fight the Covid-19 pandemic.

135 Chambas and Perroud (n 6), para 6.

136 Guillaume Le Floch (ed), *Covid-19, approches de droit public et de science politique* (Berger-Levrault 2021).

as substantial by some[137] or remarkably submissive by others.[138] To say it truly, the health emergency crisis has provided a unique opportunity to examine how our representative democracies operate when confronted with the experience of their vulnerability.

The persistent concern about emergency powers is that their use can lead to executive aggrandisement and an erosion of civil liberties and democracy. While the strict governmental countermeasures certainly challenged the existing legal and political frameworks in the two compared jurisdictions, they did not entail the disappearance of the rule of law and testified to the robustness of the democratic systems, where creative ways were found to ensure the normal functioning of the institutions and a heightened vigilance with regard to the reconciliation between the rule of law and the health emergency was at the least maintained.

However, the exceptional Covid-19 regimes have created a concerning precedent. From now on, it will indeed appear as legitimate to reinstate a regime of exception, and limit rights and freedoms and perhaps provide an opportunity to accelerate the establishment of a system of generalised surveillance of the population, should any situation considered to be of a similar intensity to that caused by the 2020 pandemic occur.[139] Will the people accept this situation? Will they be able to count on their Parliament to exercise proper scrutiny in the face of the executive branch, given that they largely censored themselves the first time around? More generally, would it not be important to question whether the next health crisis attains a critical level of intensity? Accountability issues are also likely to further arise since more de facto power is vested in technocratic public health advisors, away from the political executive democratically accountable to Parliament and the electorate. This is very much the case in France, for instance, where the evocation of an Ecological Defence Council to deal with climate change and the environment, or of an Energy Defence Council to deal with the energy crisis, sounds like a highly questionable way to tackle key political issues 'democratically'. In Ireland, it remains to be seen how the announced new health agency on infectious diseases, pandemic preparedness, and other emerging public health threats,

---

137 Ginsburg and Versteeg (n 27) 1499.

138 Eg Toby Green and Thomas Fazi, *The COVID Consensus. The Global Assault on Democracy and the Poor – A Critique from the Left* (Hurst 2023); Laura Dodsworth, *A State of Fear. How the UK Government Weaponised Fear during the Covid-19 Pandemic* (Pinter & Martin 2021); and Eric Windholz, 'Governing during a Pandemic: From Parliamentary Sovereignty to Autocratic Technocracy' (2020) 8(2) Theory and Practice of Legislation 93.

139 Schouler and Mucchielli (n 94) 83.

on the recommendations from the Public Health Reform Expert Advisory Group,[140] will act and be accountable, if established.

In sum, if the domestic response to the Covid-19 pandemic has been robust enough, governments need to carefully monitor how they envisage the reconciliation between (the next) health emergencies and the rule of law. This is important to keep their margin of action and appreciation in check, especially in light of the recent enhancements to the powers of the WHO via the 2024 amendments to the IHR and the potential adoption of a new Pandemic Agreement on the global stage.

140 Department of Health, 'Report of the Public Health Reform Expert Advisory Group' (2023) https://www.drugsandalcohol.ie/41979/1/Public_Health_Reform_Expert_Advisory_Group.pdf (accessed 26 April 2025).

8. 'Lockdowns', rights violations, remedies, and the new global health security order: lessons to be learnt from the German experience?

Kai Ambos

1. INTRODUCTION

This chapter examines the German policies in response to Covid-19 and tries to draw some lessons from this experience for the World Health Organization's (WHO) efforts to reform the international legal framework on pandemic preparedness and response. First, it takes issue with the unexpected career of the lockdown concept, often used interchangeably to capture the meaning of *Ausgangsbeschränkung* (exit restriction) and *Ausgangssperre* (exit prohibition) (Section 2). Then, a chronological overview and a preliminary assessment of the German Covid-19 countermeasures is offered (Section 3). Section 4 analyses exit restrictions in more detail, given that they can be considered as paradigmatic interferences with a series of fundamental rights and that the ensuing rights restrictions can rarely be considered proportionate. Finally, it is discussed whether the German experience can offer any lessons for the envisaged new Global Health Security (Law) Order driving the WHO reform efforts (Section 5).

2. THE COVID-19 'PANDEMIC' AND THE UNEXPECTED CAREER OF THE 'LOCKDOWN' CONCEPT

The term 'lockdown' received the questionable award of the 'Anglicism of the Year' in 2020 in Germany.[1] It was, in fact, an invention or creation by the

[1] '2020' (*Anglizismus des Jahres*, 2020) www.anglizismusdesjahres.de/anglizismen-des-jahres/anglizismen-des-jahres-adj-2020/. Unless otherwise

media at the beginning of the Covid-19 outbreak, declared 'pandemic'[2] by the WHO on 11 March 2020,[3] employing – to be noted in passing – a new and broader concept of 'pandemic'.[4]

---

stated all web links given in this chapter last accessed between 4 January and 16 May 2025.

[2] Etymologically, the term pandemic comes from the Greek 'Pandēmía' meaning '(affecting) the whole nation'. It can be defined as 'an outbreak of a disease that occurs over a wide geographic area (such as multiple countries or continents) and typically affects a significant proportion of the population' ('Pandemic', *Merriam Webster*, January 2025) www.merriam-webster.com/dictionary/pandemic.

[3] WHO, 'Director-General's Opening Remarks at the Media Briefing on COVID-19' (*WHO*, 11 March 2020) www.who.int/director-general/speeches/detail/who-director-general-s-opening-remarks-at-the-media-briefing-on-covid-19---11-march-2020.

[4] The current WHO definition (1999, revised 2005 and 2009) distinguishes between six phases (cf WHO, 'Pandemic Influenza Preparedness and Response. A WHO Guidance Document' (3 March 2009) 10 ff https://www.who.int/publications/i/item/9789241547680. This constitutes a 'description' rather than a 'definition' of a 'pandemic' (see Peter Doshi, 'The Elusive Definition of Pandemic Influenza' (2011) 89(7) Bulletin of the World Health Organization 532, 533). Phases 1–3 refer to 'preparedness', phases 4–6 react to 'community level outbreaks'. In the context of the H1N1 influenza outbreak in 2009, the definitions on the WHO's website have been changed from 'disease severity' with 'enormous numbers of deaths and illness' to 'wider global dissemination' and lack of immunity (cf Doshi, ibid, 533–4 with figure 1). The Council of Europe criticised this change, inter alia suspecting 'possible influence of the pharmaceutical industry' (see Parliamentary Assembly of the Council of Europe, 'The Handling of the H1N1 Pandemic: More Transparency Needed' (23 March 2010) AS/SOC (2010)12), paras 17–21 https://assembly.coe.int/CommitteeDocs/2010/20100329_MemorandumPandemie_E.pdf). While the 'Pandemic Influenza Preparedness Framework' adopted by the World Health Assembly (WHA) in 2009 did not define 'pandemic', it defined an 'influenza virus with human pandemic potential' as 'any wild-type influenza virus that has been found to infect humans and that has a haemagglutinin antigen that is distinct from those in seasonal influenza viruses so as to indicate that the virus has potential to be associated with pandemic spread within human populations with reference to the International Health Regulations (2005) for defining characteristics' (see WHO, 'Pandemic Influenza Preparedness Framework for the Sharing of Influenza Viruses and Access to Vaccines and other Benefits' (2011) 9 https://apps.who.int/gb/pip/pdf_files/pandemic-influenza-preparedness-en.pdf). In February 2020, a WHO spokesperson announced that '[F]or the sake of clarification', the six phases and the category of 'pandemic' will no longer be used, but Covid-19 continues to be an 'international emergency' (see Stephanie Nebehay, 'WHO Says It No Longer Uses "Pandemic" Category, but Virus Still Emergency' (*Reuters*, 24 February 2020) www.reuters.com/article/uk-china-health-who

Generally, 'lockdown' refers to the closure of institutions, the sealing off of areas up to entire countries, and the standstill of public life for weeks and months.[5] Thus, 'lockdown' is used, for example, to describe 'an emergency measure or condition in which people are temporarily prevented from entering or leaving a restricted area or building (such as a school) during a threat of danger' or – more broadly – 'a temporary condition imposed by governmental authorities … in which most people are required to refrain from or limit activities outside the home involving public contact …'.[6] In more simple terms, 'lockdown' refers to the condition resulting from various restrictive measures by which public life (and probably as a consequence private life) is severely restricted.[7] The term is also used – more specifically with regard to imprisonment – to capture 'the confinement of prisoners to their cells for all or most of the day as a temporary security measure'.[8] At any rate, an (internationally) accepted definition does not exist.[9]

The broader understanding referring to the prohibition or limitation of (even private) contacts is especially relevant in our context where the term is used

-idUKKCN20I0PD). The WHO nonetheless still referred to the 2009 definition in its 2022 Covid-19 strategy (see WHO, 'Strategic Preparedness, Readiness and Response Plan to End the Global COVID-19 Emergency in 2022' (30 March 2022) 22 www.who.int/publications/i/item/WHO-WHE-SPP-2022.1). The Director-General classified Covid-19 on 11 March 2020 as a 'pandemic', albeit cautioning against a careless misuse of the term (see WHO, 'Director-General's Opening Remarks' (n 3)).

5 Oliver Bendel, 'Lockdown' (*Gabeler Wirtschaftslexikon*, 8 March 2022) https://wirtschaftslexikon.gabler.de/definition/lockdown-122433/version-385414.

6 cf 'Lockdown' (*Cambridge Dictionary*, January 2025) https://dictionary.cambridge.org/dictionary/english/lockdown (where the first meaning is not even mentioned).

7 'Lockdown' (*Digitales Wörterbuch der Deutschen Sprache*, January 2025) www.dwds.de/wb/Lockdown. Stressing the impact on public life also *Sachverständigenausschuss* (Expert Committee), 'Evaluation der Rechtsgrundlagen und Maßnahmen der Pandemiepolitik' (*Bundesministerium für Gesundheit*, 30 June 2022) 66 https://www.bundesgesundheitsministerium.de/fileadmin/Dateien/3_Downloads/S/Sachverstaendigenausschuss/220630_Evaluationsbericht_IFSG_NEU.pdf). This Expert Committee was established by the Federal Government in autumn 2021. For more information see www.bundesgesundheitsministerium.de/service/begriffe-von-a-z/s/sachverstaendigenausschuss-infektionsschutzgesetz.html.

8 'Lockdown' (*Merriam Webster*, January 2025) www.merriam-webster.com/dictionary/lockdown; 'Lockdown' (*Dictionary.com*, January 2025) www.dictionary.com/browse/lockdown.

9 See *Sachverständigenausschuss* (n 7) 66.

rather loosely or imprecisely. Take, for example, the statement by Maria Van Kerkhove, Technical Lead of the WHO's Health Emergencies Programme, according to whom lockdowns are 'a set of measures countries have taken that include individual- and community-level restrictions of movement. They can include full- or partial closures of different types of facilities, such as schools or workplaces.'[10] On this understanding, movement restrictions and closures are mixed up. Similarly, on the WHO's website one reads of '[l]arge scale physical distancing measures and movement restrictions, often referred to as lockdowns'.[11] This again is confusing, blurring the line between social distancing and movement restrictions. The author notes in passing that the WHO has sent contradictory messages as to the usefulness of lockdowns.[12] In a similar vein, the term was used in Germany for a whole series of measures under the *Infektionsschutzgesetz* (Infection Protection Act, IfSG)[13] to which we will return below.

Notwithstanding the definitional issues, it is clear that 'movement restrictions' fall short of a 'lockdown' as defined above. The distinction between the former and the latter is well captured by the German terms *Ausgangsbeschränkung* and *Ausgangssperre*, that is, a mere restriction of the freedom of movement (literally: 'exit restriction')[14] or (social) contact (eg prohibit sport in groups) as opposed to an effective prohibition to leave one's home ('locking' someone

---

10 Linda Lacina, 'WHO Officials Warn against "Magical Thinking" Regarding Lockdowns – COVID-19 Briefing' (*World Economic Forum*, 14 May 2020) www.weforum.org/agenda/2020/05/13-may-who-briefing-magical-thinking-lockdowns/.

11 WHO, 'Coronavirus Disease (COVID-19): Herd Immunity, Lockdowns and COVID-19' (31 December 2020) www.who.int/news-room/questions-and-answers/item/herd-immunity-lockdowns-and-covid-19.

12 Eg 'WHO Advice on Lockdowns – In the News' (*Science Media Centre New Zealand*, 13 October 2020) www.sciencemediacentre.co.nz/2020/10/13/who-advice-on-lockdowns-in-the-news/.

13 Klaus Weber, 'Lockdown', in Klaus Weber (ed), *Rechtswörterbuch* (33rd edn, CH Beck online 2024) with various examples of measures.

14 Note that the translation service of the Federal Constitutional Court translates a mere '*Ausgangsbeschränkung*' as 'curfew'; but this rather corresponds, as explained in the main text, to a '*Ausgangssperre*'. Thus, in this chapter the term 'curfew' will only be used for a lockdown ('*Ausgangssperre*') while 'exit restriction' means a mere '*Ausgangsbeschränkung*'.

'down', 'up').[15] Other languages also reflect the distinction.[16] This distinction is taken up in the German discussion by those authors who argue that the legislator used on purpose the more lenient *Ausgangsbeschränkung* in order to make clear that a stricter *Ausgangssperre* was never envisaged.[17] Yet, further restrictions, for example, school and business closures come close to an *Ausgangssperre* although they have been decreed as separate measures.

Interestingly, though, it was not until 18 November 2020 with the third Population Protection Act (*Bevölkerungsschutzgesetz*) that § 28a IfSG was introduced using the term *Ausgangsbeschränkung* in § 1 number 3.[18] § 28a(2) number 2 then provided for a restriction on leaving the home allowing it only for certain purposes or at certain times. This has been considered the legal basis for *Ausgangssperren*.[19]

It is clear from the above that a mere contact prohibition/restriction is to be distinguished from a lockdown in factual and legal terms. A contact prohibition tries to avoid physical contacts between persons (as a kind of enhanced social distancing), whereas *Ausgangsbeschränkungen*, albeit possibly entailing the same consequence (no social contact), are legally speaking preventive prohibitions subject to permission.[20]

---

15 cf also *Verwaltungsgerichtshof* (VGH) Higher Administrative Court München, Order of 14 December 2020, 20 NE 20.2907, margin number (mn) 28; Jens Gerhardt, '§ 28a Besondere Schutzmaßnahmen zur Verhinderung der Verbreitung der Coronavirus-Krankheit-2019 (COVID-19)' in Jens Gerhardt (ed), *Infektionsschutzgesetz* (6th edn, CH Beck 2022) 468, 488 ff, mn 25; and Jörn Kämmerer and Leif Jischkowski, 'Grundrechtsschutz in der Pandemie' (2020) 19 GesundheitsRecht 341, 345–6.

16 In Spanish the '*toque de queda*' is different to a simple 'confinement' just as in French the '*couvre-feu*' does not amount to a 'confinement'.

17 Gerhardt (n 15) 488 ff, mn 25; also Andrea Kießling, '§ 28a Besondere Schutzmaßnahmen zur Verhinderung der Verbreitung der Coronavirus-Krankheit-2019 (COVID-19)' in Andrea Kießling (ed), *Infektionsschutzgesetz* (3rd edn, CH Beck 2022) 435, 456, mn 40 ('*Ausgangssperre*' as a special form of '*Ausgangsbeschränkung*').

18 *Bundesgesetzblatt* (BGBl) Federal Law Gazette I 2020, 2397.

19 cf Andrea Kießling, '§ 28b Bundesweit einheitliche Schutzmaßnahmen zur Verhinderung der Verbreitung der Coronavirus-Krankheit-2019 (COVID-19) bei besonderem Infektionsgeschehen, Verordnungsermächtigung' in Andrea Kießling (ed), *Infektionsschutzgesetz* (2nd edn, CH Beck 2021) mn 31; and Kießling (n 17), § 28a, mn 110 ff.

20 Kießling (n 17) 456, mn 38.

Absolute lockdowns/curfews are generally considered to be 'always disproportionate'.[21] They are also problematic with regard to article 104(2) sentence 1 of the *Grundgesetz* (German Constitution, hereinafter GG) which requires a judicial decision in the case of deprivation of liberty.[22]

3. THE GERMAN COUNTERMEASURES AGAINST COVID-19: A CHRONOLOGICAL OVERVIEW AND PRELIMINARY ASSESSMENT

In Germany, there have been two general 'lockdown' phases with differences in detail.

3.1 'Lockdown I'

The first lockdown was decreed on 16 March 2020 legalising certain countermeasures on the level of the German States (*Bundesländer* or *Länder*).[23] On 22 March 2020, the Federal and *Länder* governments agreed to enact area-wide exit and contact restrictions through executive decrees, including several travel and contact restrictions as well as the closure of many shops and institutions (such as day-care centres, schools, educational institutions, and venues).[24]

21 ibid, 458 mn 44; Gerhardt (n 15) 488 ff, mn 25; Christian Johann and Moritz Gabriel, '§ 28 Schutzmaßnahmen' in Christian Eckart and Michael Winkelmüller (eds), *BeckOK Infektionsschutzrecht* (23rd edn, CH Beck online 2023), mn 35.

22 Kießling (n 17) 458, mn 44; Johann and Gabriel (n 21), § 28, mn 35; see also *Bundesverwaltungsgericht (BVerwG)* Federal Administrative Court, Judgment of 22 November 2022, 3 CN 2.21, mn 26 ff.

23 Thorsten Kingreen, 'Grundlagen des deutschen Infektionsschutzrechts' in Stefan Huster and Thorsten Kingreen (eds), *Handbuch Infektionsschutzrecht* (2nd edn, CH Beck 2022) 3, 21, mn 26; and *Sachverständigenausschuss* (n 7) 65.

24 'Besprechung der Bundeskanzlerin mit den Regierungschefinnen und Regierungschefs der Länder am 12. März 2020', Decision of 12 March 2020 by the Federal Chancellor and the heads of government of the *Länder* www.bundesregierung.de/breg-de/themen/coronavirus/beschluss-zu-corona-1730292; on this basis, all *Länder* decided to close the schools by way of executive decrees on 13 March 2020 (see 'Wo bleiben Schulen zu – und wie lange?' (*tagesschau*, 14 March 2020) www.tagesschau.de/inland/corona-schulschliessungen-103.html). On 22 March 2020, the guidelines of 12 March were extended; cf 'Erweiterung der beschlossenen Leitlinien zur Beschränkung sozialer Kontakte, Besprechung der Bundeskanzlerin mit den Regierungschefinnen und Regierungschefs der Länder vom 22.03.2020', Decision of 22 March 2020 by the Federal Chancellor and the heads of government of the *Länder* www.bundesregierung.de/breg-de/themen/coronavirus/besprechung-der-bundeskanzlerin-mit-den-regierungschefinnen-und-regierungschefs

On 27 March, the (first) Population Protection Act[25] was adopted – after an exceptionally fast procedure in the legislature, the *Bundestag* and *Bundesrat*. Originally, the draft provided that the Federal Government as a collective entity would have to decide whether there was an 'epidemic situation of national scope'. The *Bundestag* did not accept this 'surprising self-empowerment'[26] by the Federal Ministry of Health, accompanied by its disempowerment, and retained this right for itself.[27] Given the considerable factual uncertainties at the time, there was practically no intervention by the specialist (administrative) courts, and § 28(1) IfSG was recognised almost without exception as a temporarily suitable basis for authorising restrictive measures[28] – despite the fact that it was never intended for a pandemic.[29]

-der-laender-vom-22-03-2020-1733248; and *Sachverständigenausschuss* (n 7) 62. As an example of the *Länder* legal ordinances cf Brandenburg, 'Verordnung über Maßnahmen zur Eindämmung des neuartigen Coronavirus SARS-CoV-2 und COVID-19 in Brandenburg (SARS-CoV-2-Eindämmungsverordnung – SARS-CoV-2-EindV) (*Brandenburg State Government*, 17 March 2020) www.landesrecht.brandenburg.de/dislservice/disl/dokumente/8581/dokument/14161; Hesse, 'Dritte Verordnung zur Bekämpfung des CoronaVirus' (*State Government of Hesse*, 14 March 2020) https://starweb.hessen.de/cache/GVBL/2020/00008.pdf#page=13; Mecklenburg-Vorpommern, 'Verordnung der Landesregierung über Maßnahmen zur Bekämpfung der Ausbreitung des neuartigen Coronavirus SARS-CoV-2 in Mecklenburg-Vorpommern (SARS-CoV-2-Bekämpfungsverordnung – SARS-CoV-2-BekämpfV)' (*Mecklenburg-Vorpommern State Government*, 17 March 2020) www.regierung-mv.de/static/Regierungsportal/Ministerium%20für%20Wirtschaft%2c%20Arbeit%20und%20Gesundheit/Dateien/Downloads/GVOBl%20Nr%206%20vom%2018.%20März%202020%20-%20Corona.pdf.

[25] BGBl I 2020, 587.

[26] Christoph Möllers, 'Parlamentarische Selbstentmächtigung im Zeichen des Virus' (*Verfassungsblog*, 26 March 2020) https://verfassungsblog.de/parlamentarische-selbstentmaechtigung-im-zeichen-des-virus/.

[27] This was generally welcomed; cf Klaus F Gärditz and Maryam Kamil Abdulsalam, 'Rechtsverordnungen als Instrument der Epidemie-Bekämpfung' (2020) 3 Zeitschrift für das Gesamte Sicherheitsrecht 108, 113; Anna-Lena Hollo, '§ 5 Epidemische Lage von nationaler Tragweite' in Andrea Kießling (ed), *Infektionsschutzgesetz* (3rd edn, CH Beck 2022) 46, 55 ff, mn 3; Möllers (n 26); and Katrin Gierhake, 'Ist das Recht suspendiert worden?' (2022–2023) 6–7 Zeitschrift für Rechtsphilosophie Neue Folge 132, 148.

[28] Eg *VGH* München, Order of 30 March 2020, 20 NE 20.623, mn 34; *Oberverwaltungsgericht* (OVG) Higher Administrative Court Münster, Order of 6 April 2020, 13 B 398/20.NE, mn 28 ff.

[29] cf Kingreen (n 23) 22, mn 28.

On 15 April 2020 the Federal and *Länder* governments decided to extend the exit and contact restrictions until 3 May.[30] However, at the same time they allowed a gradual opening of schools from 4 May onwards.[31] Then Federal Chancellor, Angela Merkel, criticised that cautious and well-considered relaxations led to 'opening discussion orgies'.[32] On 30 April[33] and 6 May[34] more relaxation followed in certain areas. The specialist courts started to take on a more important role in this phase, especially in the area of trade and commerce.[35]

In view of the (allegedly) increasingly rapid rise in the number of infections, restrictions were imposed on 14 October 2020 for regions with more than 50 new infections in seven days.[36] A 'lockdown light'[37] was decided on 28 October which came into force on 2 November.[38] Yet, this time, in contrast to 'Lockdown I', schools and retail outlets remained open. Given that the

---

30 'Telefonschaltkonferenz der Bundeskanzlerin mit den Regierungschefinnen und Regierungschefs der Länder am 15. April 2020', Decision of 15 April 2020 of the Federal Chancellor and the heads of government of the *Länder* www.bundesregierung.de/resource/blob/973812/1744226/bcf47533c99dc84216eded8772e803d4/2020-04-15-beschluss-bund-laender-data.pdf.

31 ibid, 5.

32 'Bundeskanzlerin kritisiert "Öffnungsdiskussionsorgien"' (*Zeit Online*, 20 April 2020) www.zeit.de/politik/deutschland/2020-04/angela-merkel-lockerungen-corona-beschraenkungen-kritik-oeffnungsdiskussion.

33 'Telefonschaltkonferenz der Bundeskanzlerin mit den Regierungschefinnen und Regierungschefs der Länder am 30. April 2020', Decision of 30 April 2020 of the Federal Chancellor and the heads of the governments of the *Länder* www.bundesregierung.de/resource/blob/973812/1749804/353e4b4c77a4d9a724347ccb688d3558/2020-04-30-beschluss-bund-laender-data.pdf.

34 'Telefonschaltkonferenz der Bundeskanzlerin mit den Regierungschefinnen und Regierungschefs der Länder am 6. Mai 2020', Decision of 6 May 2020 of the Federal Chancellor and the heads of government of the *Länder* https://vdvo.de/fileadmin/user_upload/Coronavirus/Bund_Laender_Beschluss_06-05-2020.pdf.

35 cf Kingreen (n 23) 24, mn 32 and 44, mn 78 with references.

36 'Konferenz der Bundeskanzlerin mit den Regierungschefinnen und Regierungschefs der Länder am 14. Oktober 2020', Decision of 14 October 2020 of the Federal Chancellor and the heads of the governments of the *Länder* www.bundesregierung.de/resource/blob/974430/1798920/907336cb30061987d8d14340778a662e/2020-10-14-beschluss-mpk-data.pdf?download=1.

37 This term is in fact a paradox for it is only possible to talk of a 'lockdown light' if 'lockdown' is understood strictly as explained at the beginning of this chapter.

38 'Videokonferenz der Bundeskanzlerin mit den Regierungschefinnen und Regierungschefs der Länder am 28. Oktober 2020', Decision of 28 October 2020 of the Federal Chancellor and the heads of the governments of the *Länder* www

incidence figure required for contact tracing was not reached,[39] these measures, first limited until 30 November, were then extended on 25 November until 20 December – also accompanied by some tightening of contact restrictions.[40]

3.2 'Lockdown II'

As not even the tightening of the contact restrictions brought down or at least stopped the rising number of infections,[41] 'Lockdown II' was decreed on 13 December 2020. Some *Länder* introduced additional measures such as night-time curfews (9 pm to 5 am)[42] and bans on leaving a 15 kilometres zone around one's place of residence without justification.[43] The second lockdown lasted far longer than the first one: originally envisaged to last until 10 January 2021, a phased plan with opening options was only agreed on 3 March.[44] Notwithstanding all these measures, the infection rates increased again beginning in March 2021. On 22 March, Chancellor Merkel and the Minister-Presidents of the *Länder* agreed to enforce the so-called 'emergency

---

.bundesregierung.de/resource/blob/975232/1805024/5353edede6c0125ebe5b5166504dfd79/2020-10-28-mpk-beschluss-corona-data.pdf.

39 The figure was set at 50 new infections per day in a given region; cf Kingreen (n 23) 24 ff, mn 34.

40 'Videokonferenz der Bundeskanzlerin mit den Regierungschefinnen und Regierungschefs der Länder am 25. November 2020', Decision of 25 November 2020 of the Federal Chancellor and the heads of the government of the *Länder* https://www.bundesregierung.de/resource/blob/976074/1820174/ccce6d20309c4339bd80b5ab66c2f7f5/2020-11-25-mpk-beschluss-data.pdf?download=1.

41 For the daily new infection rates see '7-Tage-Inzidenz der Coronainfektionen (COVID-19) in Deutschland seit Juni 2020' (*Statistica*, 10 July 2023) https://de.statista.com/statistik/daten/studie/1192085/umfrage/coronainfektionen-covid-19-in-den-letzten-sieben-tagen-in-deutschland/. An additional problem consisted in the new variants of the Coronavirus, which were far more infectious, albeit less harmful, than the original one.

42 See eg § 3 of the 11th Bavarian infection control measures ordinance of 15 December 2020, BayMBl. 2020 Nr 737 www.verkuendung-bayern.de/files/baymbl/2020/737/baymbl-2020-737.pdf.

43 See eg § 25(1) first sentence of the amended Bavarian Ordinance, BayMBl. 2021 Nr 5 https://www.verkuendung-bayern.de/files/baymbl/2021/5/baymbl-2021-5.pdf.

44 'Videokonferenz der Bundeskanzlerin mit den Regierungschefinnen und Regierungschefs der Länder am 3 März 2021', Decision of 3 March 2021 of the Federal Chancellor and the heads of the governments of the *Länder* www.bundesregierung.de/resource/blob/974430/1872054/66dba48b5b63d8817615d11edaaed849/2021-03-03-mpk-data.pdf?download=1.

brake' in a stricter way.[45] An 'Easter rest', coming very close to a complete lockdown,[46] was first decreed but then lifted again only 24 hours later, in the face of massive protest.

On 23 March 2021, the fourth Population Protection Act came into force.[47] It included a new § 28b IfSG, a self-executing law from which protective measures (including night-time curfews) should follow automatically when the incidence rate reached 100 (the so-called 'Federal Pandemic Emergency Brake').

When by mid-April 2021 the number of infections began to decrease, the *Länder* decided to end protective measures gradually. Despite another surge in November 2021 with more than 50,000 positive tests a day[48] for the first time on 11 November, the 'epidemic situation of a national scope' ended on 25 November.[49] However, there was a certain normative confusion, for instance concerning the new § 28a(8) IfSG excluding exit restrictions[50] and the new § 28(9) IfSG maintaining the measures in force until 19 March 2022 (including exit restrictions).[51]

The new Omicron variant of the SARS-CoV-2 virus led to higher infection numbers at the end of 2021, but fewer people went to hospital. Against

---

45 'Videokonferenz der Bundeskanzlerin mit den Regierungschefinnen und Regierungschefs der Länder am 22 März 2021', Decision of 22 March 2021 of the Federal Chancellor and the heads of governments of the *Länder* https://www.bundesregierung.de/resource/blob/974430/1879672/aebe890b8eb7a6c1656bbf90c7acb0a9/2021-03-22-mpk-data.pdf.

46 Maundy Thursday and Holy Saturday 2021 should have been defined as additional one-off days of rest and combined with far-reaching (public) contact restrictions as well as a ban on gathering from 1 to 5 April. Only food retail in the narrow sense should be open on Saturday; see 'Decision of 22 March 2021' (n 45) (as of 24 March). Yet, once again, it would rather have amounted to a restriction of *public* life instead of a complete lockdown since the focus was on *public* contact restrictions.

47 BGBl I 2021, 802.

48 It can be noted that the number of 'positive tests' did not equal the number of people infected. An increase in 'infections' was also due to the fact that more tests were carried out because testing became mandatory for persons who were not vaccinated against Covid-19 disease. For a discussion and critique of the testing strategies driving 'infection rates' see Norman Fenton and Martin Neil, *Fighting Goliath. Exposing the Flawed Science and Statistics behind the COVID-19 Event* (Sovereign Rights Publishing 2024) chapter 3 (29–44) and chapter 21 (293–310).

49 See article 20(b) of the reformed IfSG of 22 November 2021, BGBl 2021, 4906.

50 BGBl I 2021, 4906.

51 First, it was to last only until 15 December 2021. Later it was extended; see BGBl I 2021, 5162, and 5167.

this background, combined with a decrease in the number of infections from mid-February 2022, the Federal Government and the *Länder* governments decided, on 16 February 2022, to relax the measures until 20 March 2022.[52] Although 24 March 2022 was the day with the highest number of new infections (positive tests) in Germany (more than 318,000 in total),[53] normality in daily life slowly came back by April 2022 with a 'basic protection' (eg wearing masks on public transport) still in force. In another decisive move, the *Bundestag* rejected a draft law to introduce compulsory vaccination from the age of 60 on 7 April. In the summer of 2022, there were (allegedly) significantly more intensive care treatments in hospitals due to a 'summer wave';[54] also, there were two more peaks in the registration of new infections (positive tests) on 19 July and 11 October 2022.[55]

On 8 September 2022, further amendments to the IfSG were accepted by the *Bundestag* preparing for a possible new wave of infections in the autumn.[56] The obligation to wear masks was maintained while curfews and exit restrictions were no longer considered necessary.[57] In December 2022, Federal Health Minister Karl Lauterbach and his colleagues at *Länder* level could not agree whether masks should continue to be compulsory in closed places/locations. This led to different measures in different *Länder*.[58]

On 26 December 2022, the Charité virologist Christian Drosten, who can be described as the 'godfather' in the German Covid-19 saga as he significantly influenced the policies of the German Government, voiced the momentous

---

52 'Videokonferenz der Bundeskanzlerin mit den Regierungschefinnen und Regierungschefs der Länder am 16. Februar 2022', Decision of 16 February 2022 of the Federal Chancellor and the heads of the governments of the *Länder* www.bundesregierung.de/resource/blob/974430/2005140/6d5d1ba7b997e2231f545f798f677382/2022-02-16-mpk-beschluss-data.pdf?download=1.

53 'Täglich gemeldete Neuinfektionen und Todesfälle mit dem Coronavirus (COVID-19) in Deutschland seit Januar 2020' (*Statistica*, 18 April 2023) https://de.statista.com/statistik/daten/studie/1100739/umfrage/entwicklung-der-taeglichen-fallzahl-des-coronavirus-in-deutschland/.

54 'Sorgen wegen Corona-Personalausfällen an vielen Kliniken' *Süddeutsche Zeitung* (Munich, 13 July 2022).

55 Statistica (n 53).

56 'Neufassung des Infektionsschutzgesetzes beschlossen' (*Deutscher Bundestag*, 2022) www.bundestag.de/dokumente/textarchiv/2022/kw36-de-infektionsschutzgesetz-903658.

57 BGBl I 2022, 1454.

58 'Landesgesundheitsminister ohne Einigung zu weiteren Corona-Lockerungen' (*Zeit Online*, 5 December 2022) www.zeit.de/politik/deutschland/2022-12/corona-massnahmen-gesundheitsminister-bundeslaender-maskenpflicht-keine-einigung.

opinion that the pandemic was over.[59] This was the beginning of the end of the Covid-19 restrictions. On 4 April 2023, the Council of Experts (*Expertenrat*), not to be confused with the (already-mentioned) Expert Committee (*Sachverständigenausschuss*),[60] ceased its work because the pandemic had, allegedly, 'returned to normal'.[61] On 5 April 2023, the Federal Health Minister Lauterbach pronounced that the pandemic had been 'successfully overcome'.[62] Finally, on 7 April 2023, the Infection Protection Act expired.

3.3 Summary and Preliminary Assessment

In sum, the following measures were adopted to address the appearance of SARS-CoV-2 in Germany:[63]

- exit restrictions and contact restrictions in the strict sense;
- closure of or restrictions on the operation of trades, businesses, cultural, recreational, and sporting facilities;

---

59 'Christian Drosten zur Corona-Lage in Deutschland: Nach meiner Einschätzung ist die Pandemie vorbei' *Der Tagesspiegel* (Berlin, 26 December 2022).

60 While the *Council of Experts*, which had its constituent meeting on 14 December 2021, was an advisory body for the Federal Government (see German Federal Government, 'Bewältigung der Pandemie: Der ExpertInnenrat der Bundesregierung' (4 May 2023) www.bundesregierung.de/breg-de/bundesregierung/bundeskanzleramt/corona-expertinnenrat-der-bundesregierung), the *Expert Committee* (n 7), with half of its members appointed by the Federal Government and the *Bundestag* respectively, was supposed to evaluate the consequences of the provided measures as requested by § 5(9) IfSG. Originally, it was envisaged that this evaluation was to be carried out only by the German National Academy of Sciences Leopoldina (see *Deutscher Bundestag*, 'Gesetzentwurf der Fraktionen der CDU/CSU und SPD, Entwurf eines Gesetzes zur Fortgeltung der die epidemische Lage von nationaler Tragweite betreffenden Regelungen' (9 February 2021) BT-Drs 19/26545).

61 According to government spokesman Steffen Hebestreit, '"Pandemie-Lage normalisiert" Corona-Expertenrat der Bundesregierung stellt Arbeit ein' (*Tagesspiegel*, 31 March 2023) https://www.tagesspiegel.de/gesundheit/pandemie-lage-normalisiert-corona-expertenrat-der-bundesregierung-stellt-arbeit-ein-9595178.html.

62 The press conference is available at: Phoenix (via *YouTube*), 'Arzneimittel-Engpässe: Pressekonferenz mit Gesundheitsminister Prof. Karl Lauterbach' (*YouTube*, 5 April 2023) www.youtube.com/watch?v=mltCLdsUMXQ.

63 See the list in *Sachverständigenausschuss* (n 7) 67.

- closure of or restrictions on the operation of schools, day-care centres, and universities;
- prohibitions or restrictions on events, meetings, and other gatherings;
- restrictions on travel, including prohibitions, on accommodation; and
- wearing of masks.

The measures taken by the Federal Government as well as by the *Länder* in March 2020 – during the 'first lockdown' – have been qualified as the beginning of 'the most unusual withdrawal from everyday life that Germany has ever experienced'[64] and as the 'most massive collective encroachment on fundamental rights in the history of the Federal Republic',[65] characterised by the 'overly hasty' adoption of unsystematic legislation that is difficult to reconcile with the fundamental *Rechtsstaatsprinzip* (rule of law principle).[66] Arguably, this amounted to a kind of state of exception[67] (not explicitly provided for in the Constitution),[68] albeit not in a Schmittian sense[69] and not amounting to

[64] Kingreen (n 23) 21, mn 26; critical also Dietrich Murswiek, 'Die zwei Schutzgüter des Rechts auf Leben: Über Abwägungsfehler bei der Anwendung des Rechts auf Leben am Beispiel der Corona-Politik' in Peter Hilpold and Christoph Perathoner (eds), *Völkerrecht – Europarecht – Deutsches Recht. Festschrift für Professor Gilbert Gornig, Band II* (Nomos 2023) 475, 484.

[65] Möllers (n 26); Murswiek (n 64) 483: 'Restrictions on freedom on a scale never before seen in a state under the rule of law in peacetime'.

[66] cf Jens Gerhardt, '§ 5 Epidemische Lage von nationaler Tragweite' in Jens Gerhardt (ed), *Infektionsschutzgesetz* (6th edn, CH Beck 2022) 36, 47–51, mn 2–3.

[67] cf Robert van Ooyen and Hendrik Wassermann, 'Zur Einführung: Freiheit, Demokratie und Grundgesetz im Pandemie-Notstand' (2021) 7 Recht und Politik 7; and Oliver Lepsius, 'Grundrechtsschutz in der Corona-Pandemie' (2021) 7 Recht und Politik 40, 46 ff speaks of a 'parallel legal order'.

[68] The GG does not explicitly speak of a '*Staatsnotstand*' (state of exception) but provides for (six) different emergency-like situations; cf articles 35, 80a, 91, and 115a ff GG.

[69] cf Carl Schmitt, *Politische Theologie* (10th edn, Duncker & Humblot 2015) 18. Yet, the Schmittian full suspension of the law in a state of exception did not take place; cf Stephan Rixen, 'Grenzenloser Infektionsschutz in der Corona-Krise?' (2021) 7 Recht und Politik 67, 67 (especially fn 3); also Sarah Ripucci and Amy Slipowitz, 'Democracy under Lockdown' (*Freedom House*, 2020), graph on page 2 https://freedomhouse.org/sites/default/files/2020-10/COVID-19_Special_Report_Final_.pdf, finding that 'the condition of democracy and human rights has grown worse in 80 countries' in 2020. Germany was, however, not among these 80 countries. For a more nuanced analysis Gierhake (n 27) 132 ff, 150–1, and 164 (while not seeing a formal state of exception, identifying a harmful impact on the law's substance given the government's failure to acknowledge the

the end of democracy.[70] To be sure, in this phase the courts mostly upheld the executive Covid-19 countermeasures; yet, this was due to the considerable factual uncertainties resulting in the courts accepting the general authorisation.[71] These uncertainties at the beginning arguably also explain why the mainstream view considers that the first lockdown has been proportionate. According to the Expert Committee:

> An intervention that proves appropriate at one point in time may prove unjustified at another. Thus, it appears as largely uncontroversial to consider the first lockdown at the beginning of the Corona pandemic in the spring of 2020 as appropriate. Knowledge about the disease and its consequences as well as about the effectiveness of the possible protective measures was low and the presumed potential harm extremely high. It therefore had a *certain plausibility* to put health protection first in this phase.[72]

In contrast, the 'second lockdown' has been far more controversial. This is also due to the fact that new measures were introduced. Perhaps the most controversial ones were the night-time curfews[73] and the prohibition against leaving a 15 kilometres zone around one's place of residence without justification.[74]

State's essential role as a guarantor of freedom). For an altogether different critique, see Luis Greco, 'Ausnahmezustand, Beamter, Bürger. Vorüberlegungen im Sinne eines alternativen Modells zur Begründung von Rechtspflichten (anlässlich der Pandemieeindämmungsmaßnahmen)' (2022–2023) 6–7 Zeitschrift für Rechtsphilosophie Neue Folge 89, arguing that a state of exception was not even necessary since the limitations to individual rights could well take place within the ordinary system of rights protection.

70 While indeed any state of emergency is a test for any democracy, the involvement of different experts with different views, assessments, and recommendations advocates against an alleged 'expertocracy' undermining democracy. A non-consensual or controversial expert opinion leaves sufficient discretion for the democratically elected and thus legitimate legislator. In addition, the experts' special role ends with the end of the pandemic; cf Christoph Gusy, 'Grundrechte unter Quarantäne?' (2021) 7 Recht und Politik 64, 66.

71 cf *OVG* Münster (n 28) 423, which states (in mn 41) that a special authorisation for measures was not necessary in view of 'such an extraordinary and unprecedented event in the history of the Federal Republic of Germany'.

72 *Sachverständigenausschuss* (n 7) 22–3 (emphasis added).

73 See text accompanying n 41 above.

74 Bavarian Ordinance (n 43). As these measures did not directly curtail the possibility to leave the home, their *legal classification was disputed*: either they were subsumed under § 28a(1) first sentence number 3 IfSG on the basis of a broad understanding of the concept of exit restriction, or they were seen as travel restrictions according to § 28a(1) first sentence number 11, or the classification was left

While the former measure was mostly qualified as disproportionate by the special courts,[75] the case law on the second measure was ambiguous.[76] The announced (but not implemented) 'Easter rest' of March 2021, a period considered 'epidemiologically and politically extraordinarily difficult',[77] would hardly have survived judicial review.[78] Politically it resulted in a public '*mea culpa*' by Federal Chancellor Angela Merkel,[79] who at the same time threatened that the Federal Government would take the reins if the *Länder* did not take adequate action.[80]

In sum, it is fair to say that judicial review by the (lower) administrative courts increased and became more effective over the course of the pandemic,

---

open. The 15 km radius differs from the exit restriction in that it is *not linked to leaving the home* and thus is not primarily aimed at restricting the freedom of the person protected by article 2(2) second sentence GG, nor is it a comparable intensive restriction; cf Gerhardt (n 15) 489, mn 25a and Kießling (n 17) 456, mn 40.

75 *VGH* Mannheim, Order of 5 February 2021, 1 S 321/21, mn 30 ff; *OVG* Lüneburg, Order of 6 April 2021, 13 ME 166/21, mn 18 ff; for a critical analysis, Andreas Haratsch, 'Zur Verhältnismäßigkeit nächtlicher Ausgangssperren – Eine Lüneburger Spezialität' (2021) 74 Die Öffentliche Verwaltung 538; *OVG* Greifswald, Order of 23 April 2021, 1 KM 221/21, mn 32 ff; in contrast, upholding this measure *VGH* München (n 15) mn 20 ff; for a critical analysis, Andrea Kießling, 'Anmerkung zu VGH München, Beschluss vom 14.12.2020 – 20 NE 20.2907' (2021) 74 Neue Juristische Wochenschrift 182, 182–3.

76 See eg *VGH* München, Order of 26 January 2021, 20 NE 21.162, mn 13 ff (considering the measure unlawful; concurring Markus Ogorek, 'Bewegungsbeschränkungen für Bewohner von Corona-Hotspots' (2021) 74 Neue Juristische Wochenschrift 824, 826–7); contrary, *OVG* Berlin-Brandenburg, Order of 14 January 2021, OVG 11 S 3/21, mn 14 ff (not obviously unlawful).

77 Kingreen (n 23) 27, mn 40.

78 ibid; see also Jens Kersten and Stephan Rixen, *Der Verfassungsstaat in der Corona-Krise* (3rd edn, CH Beck 2022) 35, referring to 'political and legal confusion around the "Easter rest"'.

79 cf 'Gründonnerstag und Karsamstag werden keine Ruhetage' (*Bund-Länder-Beschluss*, 24 March 2021) www.bundesregierung.de/breg-de/suche/budeskanzlerin-ostern-ruhetage-1881286.

80 Merkel during an interview in the political talk show *Anne Will* on 28 March 2021; see Das Erste (via *YouTube*) 'Anne Will 28.03.2021 mit Bundeskanzlerin Angela Merkel' (*YouTube*, 29 March 2021) https://youtu.be/rwE9l0dfOIs?si=E_jPmrjhjllXwpT0. The German tabloid *Bild* ran the headline 'Merkel Threatens Mega-Lockdown!'; see Johannes Bockenheimer and Benedikt Weimer, 'Merkel droht mit Mega-Lockdown!' (*Bild*, 29 March 2021) www.bild.de/bild-plus/politik/inland/politik-inland/angela-merkel-in-tv-interview-kanzlerin-droht-mit-mega-lockdown-75894594.bild.html.

especially during the second lockdown.[81] The Federal Administrative Court (*Bundesverwaltungsgericht, BVerwG*), in a clear and straightforward decision, considered the Bavarian Covid decree of 27 March 2020 imposing[82] inter alia, exit restrictions during daytime, to be partly unconstitutional.[83] In contrast, the case law of the Federal Constitutional Court (*Bundesverfassungsgericht, BVerfG*)[84] remained overly restrained, even after the end of the pandemic, and this has generated widespread criticism. We will return to this below.

81 cf Kingreen (n 23) 24, mn 32, referring to a 'more active role' of the courts; Thorsten Kingreen, 'Jenseits der Pandemie' (*Verfassungsblog*, 7 March 2023) https://verfassungsblog.de/jenseits-der-pandemie/; and Frank Schorkopf, 'Grundrechtsbeschränkungen in der Pandemie: Freiheit – ein Schönwetterkonzept?' *Der Spiegel* (Hamburg, 28 February 2023) www.spiegel.de/politik/deutschland/corona-und-grundrechtsbeschraenkungen-freiheit-ein-schoenwetterkonzept-a-04dd068c-4615-4a3c-bf3d-7bcd18939285.

82 Bayrisches Ministerialblatt (BayMBl) 2020 No 158 of 27 March 2020. The Court ruled on the version amended as of 31 March 2020, BayMBl 2020 No 162.

83 *BVerwG* (n 22), arguing that, already in the context of necessity, restrictions on contact in public and private spaces could have been considered as a more lenient measure (mn 16). It also stated that spending time outdoors without meeting people living in another household was in itself insignificant from the perspective of the aim to prevent the spread of an infectious disease (mn 33). Yet, the *BVerfG* accepted the general clause of the infection protection law as a sufficient constitutional basis to close catering establishments by means of an executive order (mn 34). On this, see also *BVerwG*, Judgment of 16 April 2023 – BVerwG 3 CN 4.22 and 3 CN 5.22, 16 May 2023, mn 26. For a discussion, Ladislav Vyhnánek et al, 'The Dynamics of Proportionality: Constitutional Courts and the Review of COVID-19 Regulations' (2024) 25 German Law Journal 386, 403.

84 cf *Bundesverfassungsgericht (BVerfG)* Federal Constitutional Court, Order of 19 November 2021, 1 BvR 781/21 et al (*Federal pandemic emergency brake I*, regarding contact and exit restrictions), available in English at www.bundesverfassungsgericht.de/SharedDocs/Entscheidungen/EN/2021/11/rs20211119_1bvr078121en.html and Order of 19 November 2021, 1 BvR 971/21 (*Federal pandemic emergency brake II*, regarding school closures) www.bundesverfassungsgericht.de/SharedDocs/Entscheidungen/EN/2021/11/rs20211119_1bvr097121en.html).

4. EXIT RESTRICTIONS (*AUSGANGSBESCHRÄNKUNGEN*) AS EXEMPLARY INTERFERENCES WITH HUMAN RIGHTS

4.1 Conceptual Clarification

As already mentioned above, besides contact prohibitions, exit restrictions were the most common and controversial measures adopted. The term broadly refers to any leaving of one's home subject to certain conditions or otherwise restricted, for example, by temporal limitations.[85] More broadly, the restriction may be understood to go beyond one's home and encompass the leaving of any place where one is temporarily accommodated or stays. It goes too far, however, to include other restrictions on freedom of movement, for example, the above-mentioned 15 kilometre rule, since the term 'exit' implies a connection to a place to be left.

As indicated above, exit restrictions are also to be distinguished from exit *prohibitions*, ie a curfew or any measure amounting to a lockdown *stricto sensu* (*Ausgangssperre*). Given the lack of a legal authorisation as of March 2020, these even more restrictive measures have been considered unlawful.[86] In addition, a strict curfew is equivalent to segregation (*Absonderung*) and thus only permissible under infection control law in accordance with § 30 IfSG;[87] yet, it is generally considered disproportionate under any circumstance.[88] At any rate, most of the measures taken in Germany did not amount to a lockdown *stricto sensu* since there always has been a series of exceptions – for

85 Kießling (n 17) 456, mn 40.

86 Anika Klafki, 'Corona-Pandemie: Ausgangssperre bald auch in Deutschland?' (*JuWissBlog*, 18 March 2020) www.juwiss.de/27-2020/; Andrea Kießling, 'Ausgangssperren wegen Corona nun auch in Deutschland (?)' (*JuWissBlog*, 19 March 2020) www.juwiss.de/29-2020/; Andrea Edenharter, 'Freiheitsrechte ade?' (*Verfassungsblog*, 19 March 2020) https://verfassungsblog.de/freiheitsrechte-ade/; see also Thorsten Kingreen, 'Whatever it Takes?' (*Verfassungsblog*, 20 March 2020) https://verfassungsblog.de/whatever-it-takes/.

87 Gerhardt (n 15) 488 ff, mn 25; Andrea Kießling, '§ 28 Schutzmaßnahmen', in Andrea Kießling (ed), *Infektionsschutzgesetz* (3rd edn, CH Beck 2022) 413, 427, mn 53; Johann and Gabriel (n 21), § 28, mn 35; Josef Lindner, '§ 18 Öffentliches Recht' in Hubert Schmidt (ed), *COVID-19, Rechtsfragen zur Corona-Krise* (3rd edn, CH Beck 2021) 665, 691, mn 75; André Sangs, 'Das dritte Gesetz zum Schutz der Bevölkerung bei einer epidemischen Lage von nationaler Tragweite und Gesetzgebung während der Pandemie' (2020) 39 Neue Zeitschrift für Verwaltungsrecht 1780, 1785 in fn 58.

88 Kießling (n 17) 458, mn 44.

instance, refuelling vehicles, withdrawing money, dropping off parcels at the post office[89] – relaxing the respective restriction.[90] Thus, the term 'lockdown' was normally used in a more symbolic sense to express the alleged seriousness of the situation or even create a certain sensation of fear.[91]

4.2 Possible Rights Interferences

As to exit restrictions proper, there are, apart from the question of the correct legal basis (an act of parliament[92] which at least provides for sufficiently precise guidance with a view to executive decrees),[93] a series of rights interferences that result from them.

---

89 The first '*Ausgangssperre*' was issued in the region of Tirschenreuth, east of Bavaria; see Edenharter (n 86); Kießling (n 86); for more examples from different *Länder* see Sebastian Kluckert, *Das neue Infektionsschutzrecht* (2nd edn, Nomos 2021) § 3, mn 18.

90 Kießling (n 86); Hannah Ruschemeier and Sascha Peters, 'Allein im öffentlichen Raum' (*Verfassungsblog*, 22 March 2020) https://verfassungsblog.de/allein-im-oeffentlichen-raum/; Kämmerer and Jischkowski (n 15) 341 and 345.

91 cf Kießling (n 19), § 28b, mn 31; see also *VGH* München (n 15), mn 28, noting the term being 'used in the political sphere … not decisive for the legal qualification'.

92 Regarding this requirement ('*Parlamentsvorbehalt*') in the context of the Covid-19 pandemic, cf Hans-Jürgen Papier, 'Corona-Krise als Herausforderung für den Rechtsstaat' (2021) 38 Deutschland & Europa 6, 7. According to the 'Wesentlichkeitstheorie' – developed by the Federal Constitutional Court – the legislator itself must make all essential decisions as far as fundamental rights are concerned; cf BVerfGE 40, 237 (249); 49, 89 (126); 83, 130 (142, 151 f); 95, 267 (307).

93 In particular, exit restrictions cannot be issued, as done in Bavaria by a so-called '*Allgemeinverfügung*', ie a general executive decree – an administrative act (*Verwaltungsakt*) addressed to a *group of persons determined or determinable according to general characteristics* (§ 35 second sentence *Verwaltungsverfahrensgesetz* Administrative Procedure Act) – since a concrete, definable factual situation required by this form of an executive measure is lacking (cf *Verwaltungsgericht (VG)* Lower Administrative Court München, Order of 24 March 2020, M 26 S 20.1255, mn 23; Thorsten Siegel, 'Verwaltungsrecht im Krisenmodus' (2020) 39 Neue Zeitschrift für Verwaltungsrecht 577, 579; Anika Klafki, 'Verwaltungsrechtliche Anwendungsfälle im Kontext der COVID-19-Pandemie' (2020) Juristische Schulung 511, 512; Kingreen (n 23) 21 ff, mn 27; but see also *VG* Saarlouis, Order of 30 March 2020, 6 L 340/20, mn 6; and *VG* Dresden, Order of 30 March 2020, 6 L 212/20, mn 20 (relevant factual situation results from the 'Corona-pandemic')).

Article 2(2), second sentence, read in conjunction with article 104(1) GG protects the freedom of movement, which first and foremost relates to the right to *leave* a certain place.[94] If this is prohibited under a threat of public force/coercion,[95] as in the case of an exit restriction, the right to freedom of movement is interfered with.[96] More restrictive measures like a curfew or quarantine affect, a fortiori, the ambit of protection or scope of this right.[97] The third sentence of article 2(2) GG allows for a restriction – by means of infra-legal provisions or administrative acts[98] – *pursuant to* a law (*'auf Grund eines Gesetzes'*) but the Federal Constitutional Court found that the issuing of restrictive measures *by* (*'durch'*) law was as such not unconstitutional.[99] This position has been widely rejected.[100]

---

[94] cf Hans Jarass, 'Art. 2 [Handlungsfreiheit, Persönlichkeitsrecht, Leben und körperliche Unversehrtheit, Freiheit der Person]' in Hans Jarass, Bodo Pieroth and Martin Kment (eds), *Grundgesetz* (18th edn, CH Beck 2024) 62, mn 130; and Manuel Brunner, 'Das Grundrecht auf Freiheit der Person (Art. 2 II 2, 104 GG)' (2020) 42 Juristische Ausbildung 1328, 1330–1.

[95] *BVerfG* (n 84), mn 242; Kingreen (n 23), c41 ff, mn 73; Tristan Wißgott, 'Keine "self-executing" Ausgangssperre' (*Verfassungsblog*, 24 April 2021) https://verfassungsblog.de/keine-self-executing-ausgangssperre/. This was seen differently by *OVG* Münster, Order of 13 July 2020, 13 B 968/20.NE, mn 46 ff; *Verfassungsgerichtshof (VerfGH)* Bayern Constitutional Court Bavaria, Decision of 23 November 2020, Vf. 59-VII-20, mn 74 and *VerfGH* Bayern, Order of 17 December 2020, Vf. 110-VII-20, mn 32 requiring direct coercion; for a discussion, see Thorsten Kingreen and Ralf Poscher, *Grundrechte, Staatsrecht II* (40th edn, CF Müller 2024), mn 596.

[96] *BVerfG* (n 84), mn 242 ff (on night-time curfew); *VG* München (n 93), mn 31–2; *VGH* München, Order of 30 March 2020, 20 NE 20.623, mn 72; cf in detail on this Wißgott (n 95).

[97] As to quarantine measures, § 30 IfSG did not provide for the requirement of judicial control. This has been considered unconstitutional; cf Kingreen (n 23) 42 mn 74 with further reference and in detail Daniel Stach, 'Die häusliche Quarantäne nach Ein- oder Rückreise aus dem Ausland' (2021) 74 Neue Juristische Wochenschrift 10.

[98] For the distinction, cf eg Hans Jarass, 'Vorbemberkung vor Art. 1: Allgemeine Grundrechtslehren' in Hans Jarass, Bodo Pieroth and Martin Kment (eds), *Grundgesetz* (18th edn, CH Beck 2024) 15, mn 42.

[99] *BVerfG* (n 84), mn 267 ff, especially mn 268.

[100] Against an interference 'by' law (already before the *BVerfG* decision) Udo di Fabio, 'Art. 2 Abs. 2 Satz 2: Freiheit der Person' in Günter Dürig, Roman Herzog, and Rupert Scholz (eds), *Grundgesetz Kommentar* (supplement 55, CH Beck 2009) 83, mn 42 (further references in fn 7); and Wißgott (n 95); subsequently Tristan Wißgott, 'Doch eine "self-executing" Ausgangssperre' (*Verfassungsblog*, 2 December 2021) https://verfassungsblog.de/doch-eine-self-executing

While the Court acknowledges the above-mentioned differentiation,[101] it backs its more flexible interpretation allowing for a direct interference based on the wording ('pursuant to law') with the same wording in the first sentence of article 10(2) GG.[102] With the drafting history being 'unproductive',[103] the Court seems to argue with a view to the desired result[104] in order to give the legislator a free hand to interfere with fundamental rights directly by law. Thus, in the words of the Court:

-ausgangssperre/; John Thurn, 'Grenzenlose Vorverlagerung' (*Verfassungsblog*, 3 December 2021) https://verfassungsblog.de/grenzenlose-vorverlagerung/, but accepting this result in terms of an appropriate legal examination; Kingreen (n 23), c41 ff mn 73; Oliver Lepsius, 'Zerstörerisches Potential für den Verfassungsstaat' (*Legal Tribune Online*, 3 December 2021) www.lto.de/recht/hintergruende/h/bverfg-1bvr78121-1bvr97121-corona-bundes-notbremse-massnahmen-kontakt-ausgang-schule-kinder-grundrechte-kommentar-verfassung-rechtstaat/; Ralf Poscher, 'Das Infektionsschutzrecht als Gefahrenabwehrrecht' in Stefan Huster and Thorsten Kingreen (eds), *Handbuch Infektionsschutzrecht* (2nd edn, CH Beck 2022) 155, 208, mn 140 ('*Petitio Principii*'); see also the critical statements on the legislative process by Christoph Möllers, 'Stellungnahme zum Entwurf eines Vierten Gesetzes zum Schutz der Bevölkerung bei einer epidemischen Lage von nationaler Tragweite' Bundestag-Drucksache 19/28444 (15 April 2021) www.bundestag.de/resource/blob/834614/9ace24a12b228c12a677f4b05aec4865/19_14_0323-2-_Prof-Dr-Moellers_-viertes-BevSchG-data.pdf; and Andrea Kießling 'Stellungnahme als geladene Einzelsachverständige für die öffentliche Anhörung im Gesundheitsausschuss des Deutschen Bundestages am 16.4.2021' *Bundestag* (16 April 2021) www.bundestag.de/resource/blob/834718/f9d7dff3462d982b089359365a45624a/19_14_0323-6-_ESV-Dr-Andrea-Kiessling_-viertes-BevSchG-data.pdf; sceptic also Heiko Sauer, 'Gediegene Gegenerzählung' (*Verfassungsblog*, 1 December 2021) https://verfassungsblog.de/gediegene-gegenerzahlung/; but in favour Jarass (n 94), Art. 2, mn 138; and Jarass (n 98), Vorbemerkung vor Art 1, mn 42.

101 *BVerfG* (n 84), mn 268.

102 ibid, mn 269. In doing so, the *BVerfG* refers to an earlier decision (BVerfGE 125, 260 (313)), which only states that the interference directly by law is not excluded by article 10(2) first sentence. The reference to an earlier decision (BVerfGE 85, 386 [396 ff]) does not deal with the problem either; cf Wißgott (n 100). The Court does not mention the similar provisions of articles 6(3), 13 (7), and 16 (1) second sentence; see also Thurn (n 100).

103 The Court refers to the considerations of the Drafting Committee of the Parliamentary Council which indeed are rather ambiguous and can be interpreted in both ways; cf *BVerfG* (n 84), mn 270.

104 cf Wißgott (n 100); Thurn (n 100).

> There is nothing to suggest that the purpose of Art. 2(2) second sentence and Art. 104(1) GG is to establish an absolute or unlimited right vis-à-vis the legislator. … Where the freedom of physical movement is directly interfered with by a law, this does not entail any loss of legal protection that would be incompatible with the protective purpose of the limitation clauses.[105]

However, most scholars consider precisely the lack of an effective (judicial) remedy as the main problem of a *direct* restriction by law. For in such a situation there is no infra-legal measure/act against which a citizen could lodge a complaint before the administrative courts;[106] one could only file a constitutional complaint directly against the respective law, which is a much more complex and normally slower procedure. More generally, the Court was criticised for having failed to take into account the wide range of controversial positions expressed in the public and academic debate.[107]

At the same time, these measures interfere with the more specific protection of the freedom of movement in the sense of *Freizügigkeit* ('permissiveness') by article 11(1) GG. While the Federal Constitutional Court refrained from examining this right,[108] the Munich Administrative Court stressed that indirect and de facto 'impacts' also amount to an interference with this right in terms of their objective and effect. Exit restrictions prohibit not only a longer visit to friends or family or a holiday stay but also a change of residence that is not absolutely necessary. Hence, they have a significant influence on the formation of the free will of persons and ultimately the exercise of this will. The ensuing interference with the right to free movement may be 'considerable' depending on the circumstances of the respective case, going beyond a mere reflex and an unintended side effect.[109] In addition, exit restrictions have the same effect as

---

105 *BVerfG* (n 84), mn 272.

106 Möllers (n 100) 3 ff; Kießling (n 100) 6 ff; Kießling (n 17), § 28b, mn 8; Wißgott (n 95); see, however, in favour Sauer (n 100).

107 See Kyrill-Alexander Schwarz, 'In dubio pro imperio?' (2022) 41 Neue Zeitschrift für Verwaltungsrecht Beilage 3, 5; and Thurn (n 100).

108 *BVerfG* (n 84), mn 92, holding that the complainants' submissions did not meet the requirements to sufficiently substantiate their arguments.

109 *VGH* München (n 91), mn 29; see also Thorsten Kingreen, 'Das Studium des Verfassungsrechts in der Pandemie' (2020) 42 Juristische Ausbildung 1019, 1022; and Kingreen (n 23) 41, mn 72, seeing a substantial impact if the right of residence is restricted to the vicinity of one's own home, as especially in the case of night-time exit restrictions, which, even if only temporary, have the de facto effect of a full exit restriction.

residence orders aiming to prevent harm or danger,[110] which have always been considered to constitute an interference with article 11(1) GG.[111]

The broader right of free development of the personality (article 2(1) GG), understood as a general freedom of action and a general right of personality (entailing the right to meet other people beyond family as constitutive for the development of personality),[112] is interfered with by contact restrictions of all kind,[113] especially if these are enforced by fines.[114] The Federal Constitutional Court states that '[s]imply being able to meet other people is of foundational importance for personality development'.[115] This is even more the case with exit restrictions.[116] The general right of personality in its manifestation as self-determination of the individual about his/her identity is also affected by the obligation to wear a mask in public.[117]

The marriage and family rights protected by article 6(1) GG are concerned in that exit restrictions – in the form of enforceable requirements for private gatherings in both public and private spaces (§ 28b(1) first sentence number 1 IfSG) – limit the right to meet with one's relatives or spouse in a freely chosen manner and frequency and to maintain family relations.[118]

Given the significant impact on the retail sector, catering, and other service sectors, there may also exist an interference with the occupational freedom protected by article 12 GG and the right to property protected by article 14 GG.[119] Yet, the Court does not even mention these rights.

---

110 These orders are one of several special police powers to be exercised for preventative purposes. The police can order a person to leave or not to enter a certain place for a certain period of time; cf Thorsten Kingreen and Ralf Poscher, *Polizei- und Ordnungsrecht* (12th edn, CF Müller 2022), § 11, mn 1 and § 15, mn 1.

111 Kingreen (n 23), c41, mn 72; and regarding these orders, cf Kingreen and Poscher (n 110), § 15, mn 4 with references.

112 *BVerfG* (n 84), mn 111–13.

113 ibid, mn 110. This is an interference with the right to the free development of one's personality.

114 cf § 73(1a), number 11 b IfSG; this constitutes an interference with the general freedom of action, *BVerfG* (n 84), mn 252; on the violation of threat by a fine, see *BVerfG*, Judgment of 26 February 2020, 2 BvR 2347/15 et al, mn 333.

115 *BVerfG* (n 84), mn 113.

116 ibid, mn 251.

117 Kingreen (n 23), c40 ff, mn 70.

118 *BVerfG* (n 84), mn 251.

119 cf Volker Boehme-Neßler, 'Anmerkung' (2022) 41 Neue Zeitschrift für Verwaltungsrecht Beilage 34.

4.3 Balancing/Proportionality Test

As we have seen with regard to article 2(2) GG, the fact that a certain measure/act interferes with a fundamental right does not automatically entail the violation of the respective right. Rather, the interference may be justified if it pursues a legitimate purpose, is suitable and necessary to achieve it, and finally proportionate in the narrower sense, that is, reasonable/appropriate.[120]

If one takes a closer look, already the *legitimate purpose/aim* of exit restrictions can be questioned. On the one hand, these measures – as the others – allegedly aimed at maintaining the functioning of the healthcare system.[121] This is not only a somewhat vague purpose but it also rests on uncertain and unpredictable assumptions.[122] On the other hand, the protection of life and health has been advanced as a legitimate purpose/aim.[123] Yet, as to the former (article 2(2) first sentence GG) one must distinguish between the *protection of life proper* (that is, against killing) and the (preceding) *freedom* (or: being free) *from risks to life*.[124] While the former protection is absolute and tolerates, in principle, no balancing pursuant to the proportionality principle, the latter is relative and subject to such a balancing. Covid-19 countermeasures whose aim was to limit the spread of the virus cannot be said to protect life proper but only to reduce the risk to life as a consequence of getting infected.[125] Thus, the (liberty) rights restricted by these measures must not be balanced against the right to life but against the preceding freedom from risks to life, ie freedom is to be balanced against freedom (not life).[126]

Such measures may at best contribute to risk reduction and at worst they have no effect at all since the persons targeted do not carry the virus and thus cannot infect others and/or the virus is spread/transmitted otherwise. At any

120 cf *BVerfG* (n 84), mn 166.

121 cf § 28a(3) first sentence IfSG; and *BVerfG* (n 84), mn 176.

122 Critical regarding the vagueness also Kießling (n 17) 448 ff, mn 20.

123 See, again, § 28a(3) first sentence; and on this, Kießling (n 17) 448, mn 18.

124 The Constitutional Court speaks vaguely of 'threats to the enjoyment of fundamental rights' ('*Grundrechtsgefährdungen*'), which, under certain conditions, may have to be put on an equal footing with rights violations proper ('*Grundrechtsverletzungen*') and thus are equally protected by the respective fundamental right, here the right to life (including risks to life) pursuant to article 2(2) first sentence GG; cf *BVerfG*, Order of 19 June 1979, 2 BvR 1060/78, BVerfGE 51, 324, 346 ff; Order of 3 October 1979, 1 BvR 614/79, BVerfGE 52, 214, 220; and Order of 16 December 1983, 2 BvR 1160/83 et al, BVerfGE 66, 39, 57 ff. For a critical analysis, see Murswiek (n 64) 475 ff, 478 who speaks more precisely of the protection of life and the freedom from risks to life.

125 Murswiek (n 64) 485.

126 ibid, 486.

rate, such measures, for example exit restrictions, are indiscriminate and thus lack differentiation, for they affect all persons equally, including those that do not carry the virus and thus do not pose a potential danger to the life of others with regard to a possible transmission, and the alleged possible subsequent death.[127] In addition, the risk to life sought to be avoided is distributed unequally, ie a possible Covid-19 infection entails very different consequences depending on a series of (partly interrelated) factors and only rarely turns out to be the sole cause (if any) of a subsequent death. In fact, the dilemma of these measures is that they are general and unspecific while the risks to the lives of given persons are highly individualised, depending on a series of (individual) factors (age, previous diseases, general health, lifestyle, etc) which escape generalisation.[128]

From a rights perspective, a State intervention aiming at reducing risks to life by curtailing or restricting other rights and general liberties can only be justified if the respective risk passes a certain threshold of severity going beyond the general life risk,[129] ie if it turns from a general, unspecific, unclear risk into a concrete danger for the rights (here life) of a certain group of persons sought to be protected.[130] If this is the case, the balancing of rights exercise, consisting of the above-mentioned balancing of freedom (from liberty interferences) against freedom (from risks to life caused by a virus) amounts to a comparison of risks to life with the liberty interferences that are more tangible. Here the State must, first of all, demonstrate beyond any reasonable doubt that the measures are suitable (*geeignet*) and necessary (*erforderlich*) with a view to effective risk reduction. As to the proportionality *stricto sensu* (reasonable/appropriate measures), it must be considered that the citizens themselves could take measures of self-protection (ultimately total self-isolation) instead

---

127 In terms of German police law, people infected by the virus would allegedly qualify as '*Störer*' ('spoiler', representing a danger/threat to others) while those not infected, for that matter, as '*Nichtstörer*' ('non spoiler'). Only the former can, in principle, be lawfully subjected to (police/administrative) countermeasures while the latter can only be targeted exceptionally, pursuant to principles of necessity; cf Murswiek (n 64) 484, 487–8.

128 cf also Frauke Rostalski, 'Masernimpfpflicht: Zur Notwendigkeit einer Debatte über die Grenzen des (bislang) erlaubten Risikos' (*Verfassungsblog*, 29 August 2022) https://verfassungsblog.de/masernimpfpflicht/, referring to a 'permanent "Triage"' in the health system because of different lifestyles.

129 cf Murswiek (n 64) 477.

130 ibid, 475: '... duty on the state to protect individuals from dangers to their lives, but not to minimize risks to life below the *danger threshold*.' On the concept of danger – leading in the ordinary course of events to a harm with probability – in this (public order) context see ibid, 479–80; and Kingreen and Poscher (n 110), § 8.

of delegating this decision to State authorities of questionable legitimacy and thus renouncing their autonomy.[131]

4.4 Conclusion

Exit restrictions can rarely be proportionate in the context of a virus like SARS-CoV-2 that is transmitted only by human physical contact.[132] They are either not suitable for achieving the alleged (legitimate) aim, namely the successful control of the spread of the virus, or they are not necessary because less invasive contact restrictions are available, being a more lenient and even more appropriate measure.[133] On a more general level, the discussion of the right to life and the preceding right to freedom from risks to life shows that a key question is to precisely identify which right is actually and effectively protected by certain Covid-19 countermeasures, including by exit restrictions. Only if this is correctly done, notwithstanding all the empirical uncertainties, can a proper balancing of the rights (and corresponding State duties) affected be carried out.

And what to make of the performance of the Constitutional Court with regard to Covid-19 countermeasures? It has not played its role well. In general terms, the distance to politics, and in particular the executive power, has become strangely small. 'President of the Constitutional Court defends Corona

---

131 Murswiek (n 64) 487; Stephan Rixen, 'Abschied von der Verhältnismäßigkeit?' (*Verfassungsblog*, 25 May 2022) https://verfassungsblog.de/abschied-von-der-verhaltnismasigkeit/, speaks of a 'health prevention State'; and Rostalski (n 128).

132 Kießling (n 17) 457, mn 43; different, however, *BVerfG* (n 84), mn 274–303.

133 *VerfGH* Saarland, Order of 28 April 2020, Lv 7/20, mn 35, 37; *VGH* München, Order of 4 October 2021, 20 N 20.767, mn 77, 85; confirmed by *BVerwG* (n 22), mn 14 ff; Kießling (n 17) 457, mn 43; Kießling (n 86); Ruschemeier and Peters (n 90); Christian Katzenmeier, 'Grundrechte in Zeiten von Corona' (2020) 38 Medizinrecht 461, 465; and Felix Schmitt, 'Die Verfassungswidrigkeit der landesweiten Ausgangsverbote' (2020) 73 Neue Juristische Wochenschrift 1626 stressing that it was only six of the 16 *Länder* (Bavaria, Berlin, Brandenburg, Saarland, Saxony, und Saxony-Anhalt) that used exit restrictions at that time. However, for the different view see Annette Guckelberger, 'Kontaktverbote anlässlich Corona' (2020) 39 NVwZ-Extra 1, 11; *VGH* München (n 28), mn 60, noting that unambiguous determination is not possible due to numerous uncertainties; and very uncritical regarding exit restrictions ('*Ausgangssperren*' in terms of exit restrictions with certain reasons for leaving one's home) is Eike Ziekow, 'Die Verfassungsmäßigkeit von sogenannten "Ausgangssperren" nach dem Bundesinfektionsschutzgesetz' (2020) 135 Deutsches Verwaltungsblatt 732.

policy'[134] – is a headline that reads as if this president were a politician, and not a judge. A judge rather speaks through judgments. Then, judges of the Constitutional Court and Chancellor Merkel meet for dinner.[135] All this creates, to say the least, mixed public perceptions and it also raises doubts with regard to the Court's case law, especially in an area as controversial as Covid-19 policy. At any rate, there are various aspects which deserve criticism.[136]

First, contact restrictions and curfews – but also exit restrictions – are not just controversial restrictions on individual freedom. Rather, they also have the potential to threaten democracy. A functioning democratic discourse requires that citizens can meet at any time. The Court failed to recognise this and the 'collateral damage' it created (which is still not fully understood and recognised).[137]

Second, the Constitutional Court only examined contact and exit restrictions (federal pandemic emergency brake I) and school closures (federal pandemic emergency brake II) but did not take into account other rights, including children's right to education that the measures interfered with. It thus disregarded the special dangers which result from simultaneous additional interference with fundamental rights.[138]

Third, the Court largely uncritically adopted the narrative of mainstream politics as well as the assessment of the invited experts and public health institutions, which are not fully independent but subject to the instructions of the

---

134 cf eg the headline of RedaktionsNetzwerk Deutschland, 'Präsident des Verfassungsgerichts verteidigt deutsche Corona-Politik' (*RND*, 2 April 2021) www.rnd.de/politik/prasident-des-verfassungsgerichts-verteidigt-deutsche-corona-politik-32AAPZT5ILUBIS5QZ565CGIG54.html (accessed 4 January 2024).

135 cf eg, Jost Müller-Neuhof, 'Vorwürfe gegen Richterinnen und Richter' *Der Tagesspiegel* (Berlin, 12 July 2021).

136 See for considerable scholarly criticism, Boehme-Neßler (n 119) 35; Kingreen (n 81); Schwarz (n 107) 3; Schorkopf (n 81); and concerning the time before 'Federal pandemic emergency brake I and II' already Oliver Lepsius, 'Anmerkung' (2021) 67 Juristenzeitung 955, 959; Lepsius (n 100); Rixen (n 131); and Rostalski (n 128).

137 cf Boehme-Neßler (n 119) 34–5.

138 ibid.

executive and its invited experts.[139] As to the latter, it has been rightly criticised that the invited experts did not fully reflect the respective scholarly disputes.[140]

In sum, the Court very much limits its constitutional scrutiny and only roughly examines whether the measures were justifiable and reasonable (*Vertretbarkeitskontrolle*).[141] It did not examine whether the exit restrictions *were* proportionate, but whether the legislature was *entitled to consider* them proportionate. It accords the legislator – in line with the deferential approach also common in other jurisdictions[142] – a margin of appreciation with regard to the examination of appropriateness (proportionality *stricto sensu*)[143] and

---

139 The highly influential Robert Koch Institute (RKI) (on its influence Anna-Lena Hollo, '§ 4 Aufgaben des Robert-Koch-Instituts', in Andrea Kießling (ed), *Infektionsschutzgesetz* (3rd edn, CH Beck 2022) 35, 40, mn 6) is a higher federal authority that reports to the Federal Ministry of Health (*Bundesgrundheitsministerium* (BMG)), see § 2 *Gesetz über Nachfolgeeinrichtungen des Bundesgesundheitsamtes* (BGA-NachfG) https://www.gesetze-im-internet.de/bga-nachfg/BJNR141610994.html. The BMG exercises some supervision over the RKI (cf § 3(1) *Gemeinsame Geschäftsordnung der Bundesministerien* (GGO) https://www.verwaltungsvorschriften-im-internet.de/bsvwvbund_21072009_O11313012.htm). Hence, the activities of the RKI are not covered by the freedom of science within the meaning of article 5(3) GG; see https://www.rki.de/SharedDocs/FAQ/COVID-19/FAQ-Liste-Krisenstab.html. This seems to be confirmed by the so-called RKI files, available at 'RKI-Files – Ungeschwärzt' (*RKI-transparenzbericht*, 2024) https://rki-transparenzbericht.de, noting: 'Eine derartige Einflussnahme seitens des BMG in RKI-Dokumenten ist ungewöhnlich' ('unusual for the BMG to exert such influence on RKI documents') (RKI-Files (2021) 982); 'Eine Herabstufung vorher würde möglicherweise als Deeskalationssignal interpretiert, daher politisch nicht gewünscht' ('downgrade not politically desirable') (RKI-Files (2022) 148); 'Reduzierung des Risikos von sehr hoch auf hoch wurde vom BMG abgelehnt' ('Reduction of the risk from very high to high was rejected by the BMG) (RKI-Files (2022) 210). In sum, there is certainly a tension between the RKI as a 'scientific authority' and political decision-makers; see Nadine Bader, Tina Handel, and Birthe Soennichsen, 'Wie unabhängig ist das RKI?' (*tagesschau.de* 9 August 2024) https://www.tagesschau.de/inland/innenpolitik/corona-aufarbeitung-rki-100.html.

140 cf Schwarz (n 107) 6; Boehme-Neßler (n 119) 35; and Rixen (n 131).

141 cf Boehme-Neßler (n 119) 35; Rixen (n 131); and Rostalski (n 128).

142 Vyhnánek et al (n 83), therefore calling for a 'semi-procedural review' that focuses on the 'procedural rationality' of the respective measures evaluating the policy formation process and the underlying empirical evidence.

143 *BVerfG* (n 84), mn 217, holding that 'when assessing whether a measure is appropriate, too, the legislator in principle has a margin of appreciation'; Order of 19 November 2021 – 1 BvR 971/21, NJW 2022, 167, mn 135; see also more recently, Order of 27 April 2022 – 1 BvR 2649/21, mn 204.

thus goes beyond previous practice where this could only be taken into account with regard to the question of whether the respective measure was suitable and necessary.[144] Of course, the Constitutional Court is not a 'trial court' and thus cannot substitute a factual assessment by the first instance administrative courts or even undertake such a factual assessment. Yet, more guidance could have been expected. After all, this Court is tasked with the protection of individual rights and considers itself as the 'guardian of the constitution'.[145] If the Court wants to live up to this self-attribution it has to enhance constitutional scrutiny and stress its distance from daily politics and current politicians. It remains to be seen whether the Court will take its task more seriously in future pandemics.

5. PERSPECTIVES: LESSONS LEARNT FOR THE NEW GLOBAL HEALTH SECURITY (LAW) ORDER?

At the time of writing, the revised International Health Regulations (IHR as amended 2024) have been adopted[146] but the envisaged WHO Agreement on Pandemic Prevention, Preparedness and Response had not yet been finally adopted. However, WHO Member States have – after three years of negotiations[147] – agreed on a preliminary text of a Pandemic Agreement on 16 April

144 cf Rixen (n 131).

145 cf eg, *BVerfG*, Order of 10 June 1975, 2 BvR 1018/74, BVerfGE 40, 88 (93).

146 WHA Res 77.17 (1 June 2024) UN Doc WHA77.17, annex 'Amendments to the International Health Regulations (2005)'; for a first assessment see Caroline Foster, 'Compliance and Accountability Mechanisms in the 2024 Revisions to the WHO International Health Regulations (2005)' (*EJIL: Talk!*, 21 June 2024) https://www.ejiltalk.org/compliance-and-accountability-mechanisms-in-the-2024-revisions-to-the-who-international-health-regulations-2005/ ('patchwork', 'insufficient').

147 The 77th World Health Assembly (WHA) decided to continue negotiations until the 78th WHA in May 2025, see WHA, Decision 77(20) (1 June 2024) UN Doc WHA77(20). Generally, on the reform and the historical development and legal framework see Pedro Villarreal, 'The Law of the WHO and COVID-19 Pandemic Reformism' (2021) 64 German Yearbook of International Law 11, 11 ff and 34 ff; more critical, Silvia Behrendt and Amrei Müller, 'Do We Need to Protect the Entire World Population from Health Threats through One Global Biomedical Surveillance and Response System?' (2021) 64 German Yearbook of International Law 41, 41 ff and 45 ff (critical of the influence of the Global Health Security doctrine entailing far-reaching interferences with human rights and stressing the EU's and G7's promotion of the reform). On the relationship between the two instruments, Nasiya Daminova and Shisong Jiang, 'The First Working Draft of the WHO's "Pandemic Treaty": Attempting to Cover Normative Gaps

2025.[148] The final text aims to build on the existing global health architecture. It attempts in various ways to ensure the 'coherence and complementarity between the process of developing the new instrument and the ongoing work … with regard to implementing and strengthening the IHR (2005)',[149] which was already recognised as necessary in 2021.[150]

Whether any lessons can be drawn from a domestic experience like the German one depends on several factors, above all whether the reform leads to a further strengthening and centralisation of the global health system and what role States – as opposed to the powerful private actors – will play in this system. It is also not yet clear what the envisaged WHO reform will mean for human rights. In fact, it is not even clear what rights we are talking about: the right to global health, ie human rights of equal access to adequate medical care and supplies/vaccines (which is often advocated by States from the global south) for every human being;[151] or the human rights restricted by a WHO system of global health governance (liberty, free movement, assembly, health,

---

Indicated by the COVID-19 Pandemic?' (*EJIL:Talk!*, 13 October 2022) www.ejiltalk.org/the-first-working-draft-of-the-whos-pandemic-treaty-attempting-to-cover-normative-gaps-indicated-by-the-covid-19-pandemic/.

[148] An unofficial (unedited) version of the draft Pandemic Agreement of 16 April 2025 is available at https://www.keionline.org/wp-content/uploads/Proposal_for_WHO_Pandemic_Agreement_E-Onscreen-16-April-2025-at-01_57-CEST.docx.pdf accessed 6 May 2025; see also WHO, 'WHO Member States Conclude Negotiations and Make Significant Progress on Draft Pandemic Agreement' (16 April 2025) https://www.who.int/news/item/16-04-2025-who-member-states-conclude-negotiations-and-make-significant-progress-on-draft-pandemic-agreement. For a first analysis, see Richard Clements, 'The WHO Pandemic Agreement: Equity for Developing States or Business as Usual?' (*EJIL:Talk!*, 8 May 2025) https://www.ejiltalk.org/the-who-pandemic-agreement-equity-for-developing-states-or-business-as-usual/. For an earlier (official) version of the Pandemic Agreement of 24 May 2024, see WHA, 'Proposal for the WHO Pandemic Agreement', draft text of 24 May 2024, appendix to the report of the WHO Director-General, 'Outcome of the Intergovernmental Negotiating Body (INB) to Draft and Negotiate a WHO Convention, Agreement or Other International Instrument on Pandemic Prevention, Preparedness and Response' (27 May 2024) UN Doc A77/10.

[149] WHA, Decision 2(5) (1 December 2021) UN Doc SSA2(5), para 4.

[150] Clements (n 148).

[151] In this vein see UN Committee on the Elimination of Racial Discrimination (CERD), 'Statement 2 (2022), Statement on the Lack of Equitable and Non-discriminatory Access to COVID-19 Vaccines' (25 April 2022), adopted at CERD's 106th session 11–29 April 2022; and IHR as amended 2024 (WHA77.17) (n 146), article 3(1); and Abbie-Rose Hampton et al, '"Equity" in the Pandemic Treaty: The False Hope of "Access and Benefit-Sharing"' (2023) 72 International & Comparative Law Quarterly 909.

bodily integrity, education, etc) which may issue regulations with immediate effect at the domestic level (usually advocated by liberal-minded people from more developed countries with more or less functional health systems).

As to the right to global health, the consideration of different resources and circumstances in the individual States can be identified as a 'clear theme throughout the text' of the draft Pandemic Agreement.[152] The Parties shall be guided by '[f]ull respect for the dignity, human rights and fundamental freedoms of all persons' (article 3(2)). Accordingly, Winnie Byanyima, Executive Director of UNAIDS, spoke of 'an agreement with human rights at its heart' which 'can lay the foundations for a more effective and equitable response to future health crises' and ensure a 'fairer, safer, and more resilient' global health system.[153] However, the final text fails to meet further (equity) demands of the developing countries.[154] Despite the almost anachronistic multilateral approach, the final text also reflects the current focus on the nation State, when it recognises right at the beginning 'that states bear the primary responsibility for the health and well-being of their peoples' (preamble para 1). Thus, it is probably fair to say that we talk about both levels – rights protection *versus* rights interference – and thus the question of the concrete balancing (right to access to 'pandemic products'[155] or the protection against risks to health *versus* restrictions of numerous other rights) arises. Here the German constitutional debate – or similar debates in other jurisdictions[156] – may help to find an adequate mechanism of judicial review.

---

[152] Clements (n 148); the WHO Pandemic Agreement (n 148) aims to prevent, prepare for, and respond to pandemics 'guided by equity' (article 2(1)). In the context of prevention and surveillance, 'national capacities and national and regional circumstances' should also be taken into account (article 4(1)); see also article 6(1): 'Each Party, *within the means and resources at its disposal*, shall take appropriate measures to develop, strengthen and maintain a resilient health system' (emphasis added).

[153] 'UNAIDS reacts to WHO Member States reaching Pandemic Agreement consensus' (*UNAIDS Press Release*, 16 April 2025) https://www.unaids.org/en/resources/presscentre/pressreleaseandstatementarchive/2025/april/20250416_PR_pandemic_agreement.

[154] Clements (n 148).

[155] See the 2024 amendments to articles 15(2) and 16(1) IHR (WHA77.17) (n 146); and Amrei Müller and Silvia Behrendt, 'The 2024 Amendments to the International Health Regulations: A Commentary (Part II: Selected Substantive Amendments)' (*Opinio Juris*, 20 September 2024) http://opiniojuris.org/2024/09/20/the-2024-amendments-to-the-international-health-regulations-a-commentary-part-ii-selected-substantive-amendments/.

[156] cf Vyhnánek et al (n 83).

A few further open questions may be identified. First, the comparison of the global health system with a domestic one is complicated by the involvement of private actors in the former with the ensuing marginalisation of the WHO and, more importantly, lack of transparency, conflicts of interest, and the risk of capture.[157] This leads to a situation where the main actors are no longer public ones. That is, there no longer is a public international organisation primarily controlled and directed by its Member States like the WHO, but public-private partnerships (PPPs) dominated by the private actors. This may be different in domestic health systems, at least those of the rich global north, where the State is the main actor; although one must not underestimate the influence of the pharmaceutical industry in these systems too.[158]

Secondly, the domination of a public actor (WHO) by private actors forces us to rethink the public/private law dichotomy and ultimately to overcome it in order to be able to control and hold the new/dominant private actors accountable. In other words, legal responsibility may have to be shifted to these private actors by way of a broader concept of (international) public authority/power that also extends to such hybrid public-private powers like PPPs.[159] To be sure, the argument rests on the premise that the public/private dichotomy has largely disappeared in the international health system given the influence of the private sector and the dominance of PPPs. Against this background, a legal responsibility of private actors must be established.

---

[157] cf Anne Peters, 'International Law between COVID-19 and the Next Pandemic' (2022) 18 MPIL Research Paper Series 6.

[158] See eg Rebecca Strong, 'The Anatomy of Big Pharma's Political Reach' (*Brownstone Institute*, 8 April 2022) https://brownstone.org/articles/the-anatomy-of-big-pharmas-political-reach/ concerning EMA; see Leïla Miñano et al, 'Investigation: Big Pharma Influence Hangs over Europe's Medicines Regulator' (*EU Observer*, 17 June 2024) https://euobserver.com/Health%20&%20Society/ar6d0b9023; 'Wie die Pharmaindustrie Europas Arzneimittelbehörde EMA beeinflusst' (*Der Standard*, 21 June 2024) https://www.derstandard.at/story/3000000225143/wie-die-pharmaindustrie-europas-arzneimittelbehoerde-ema-beeinflusst.

[159] cf Jelena von Achenbach, 'Die globale Verteilung von COVID-19-Impfstoffen durch die Public Private Partnership COVAX in öffentlich-rechtlicher Perspektive' (2022) 60 Archiv des Völkerrechts 23, 43; concurring Andreas Fischer Lescano, 'Verteilungsfragen im Weltgesundheitssystem' in Anne Peters, Stephan Hobe, and Eva-Maria Kieninger (eds), *Koloniale Kontinuitäten im internationalen Recht* (CF Müller 2024) 179; and positively evaluating COVAX, Armin von Bogdandy and Pedro Villarreal, 'The Role of International Law in Vaccinating against COVID-19: Appraising the COVAX Initiative' (2021) 81 Zeitschrift für ausländisches öffentliches Recht und Völkerrecht 89, 116.

Third, and linked to the previous point, if we assume that the real problem of the global health governance system is indeed the dominant involvement of private actors and its public-private hybridisation through PPPs, the question arises how this dominance/influence of private actors can be challenged, or generally how the privatisation can be pushed back and reduced. And how can the principles of accountability and transparency – which arguably also informed the amendment process of the IHR and keep informing the ongoing negotiations of the WHO Pandemic Agreement[160] – be implemented with regard to these private actors? Don't we need a 're-publicised' WHO for this, that is, isn't it necessary to strengthen the public powers of the WHO, but not so much vis-à-vis States but vis-à-vis these private actors? Isn't the Pandemic Agreement, as a classic international law instrument, in principle the right instrument to do this? And, more generally, isn't it high time then to push for more international health law and judicialisation[161] and to emancipate it from its 'underdog' role with regard to hegemonic regimes like world trade and investment protection law?[162]

ACKNOWLEDGEMENT

I acknowledge the indispensable research assistance of Jonathan Stelter. Due to space constraints, we have omitted all original quotes and either translated or summarised them.

---

160 See article 3(5) Pandemic Agreement (April 2025) (n 148). But also see the more critical view regarding the IHR amendments by Müller and Behrendt (n 155).

161 On the 'uneven judicialisation' in this regard, see Benedict Kingsbury, 'International Courts: Uneven Judicialisation in Global Order' in James Crawford and Martti Koskenniemi (eds), *The Cambridge Companion to International Law* (CUP 2012) 203, 203 ff.

162 Peters (n 157) 9.

9. Top-down versus bottom-up. WHO PHEIC declarations and the protection of human rights in Switzerland: a libertarian analysis

David Dürr

1. EMERGENCY MEASURES VERSUS INDIVIDUAL HUMAN RIGHTS

As outlined in other chapters of this volume, a salient feature of international health strategies in the area of pandemic preparedness, prevention, and response is their strong trend towards securitisation. This means that health policy is combined with strategies deployed in matters of military defence or in other emergency scenarios.[1] This has an impact on the structure of the legal instruments used. Their focus is usually more on effectiveness and not so much on legitimacy; enforcement becomes more important than legal foundation, and individual liberties are less important than 'winning the war' against a pathogen. This, in turn, recalls the old and even more fundamental dichotomy of legal positivism versus natural law: official emergency measures (typically 'imposed' by governmental authorities) are rather attributable to the former, human rights (having their 'natural' source within each individual) to the latter.[2]

---

1 Military units were deployed in Switzerland shortly after the first measures to address Covid-19 were adopted in February 2020. This was the first military mobilisation since the Second World War; see decision by Swiss parliament about military assistance in the fight against the Covid-19 pandemic of 5 May 2020 (BBl *Bundesblatt* 2020, 4669).

2 Beside many others; cf a 'classic' and a 'libertarian' on this dichotomy: Hans Kelsen, *Reine Rechtslehre* (2nd edn, Österreichische Staatsdruckerei 1960) 196 ff with Murray Rothbard, *The Ethics of Liberty* (New York University Press 2002) 17 ff.

It is therefore no coincidence that approaches to implement countermeasures against pandemic 'aggression' have gradually become structured in a centralised top-down fashion, as opposed to bottom-up, where responses are determined through local democratic processes and institutions. When such a top-down approach is taken, 'winning the war' or overcoming the health emergency frequently gains priority over the respect for human rights, 'public health interests' are easily given preference over individual interests, national responses are preferred over local, and international interests and responses over regional (eg European) or national responses and interests. This was not always the case. All pre-Covid-19 domestic pandemic response plans[3] followed a much more decentralised approach. However, all these plans were disregarded in response to SARS-CoV-2.

1.1 An Idealised Picture of Switzerland

This tension between security-oriented top-down strategies and liberty-oriented bottom-up approaches was strongly accentuated in the responses to Covid-19 in many countries of the Western world, predominantly in Europe, the United States, and Canada where there are strong traditions of liberal constitutions. The same is true for Switzerland with its Federal Constitution going back to earlier versions of the 19th century, developed in mutual influence with the late US Constitution of 1887.[4] Besides this, in Switzerland there is a particularly strong tradition of direct democracy with the people having the right to call for referenda, ie to put parliamentary legislation to public vote. This right was introduced on the federal level in 1874 and has since been used frequently. The same is true on the level of the cantons.[5] These relatively frequent votes have created an image of Switzerland as a country with a particularly

---

[3] The case of SARS 2003 was handled in Switzerland in a much more decentralised way. The only measure implemented by the Federal Government was the Federal Government authorising the Federal Health Agency to implement entry bans for visitors out of areas affected by infectious disease outbreaks. This was used for a few Asian exhibitors at a watch fair in Basel-City (see https://www.admin.ch/cp/d/3e8aa265_2@pressel.admin.ch.html (accessed 7 May 2025)). The adoption of any other measures was left in the competence of the Cantons (see, ordinance 818.101.22 of 1 April 2003, AS *Amtliche Sammlung* 2003 785).

[4] Andreas Kley, 'Der Einfluss der Articles of Confederation der U.S. Constitution auf die schweizerische Bundesverfassung 1848' (2024) I Zeitschrift für schweizerisches Recht 59.

[5] Each Canton in Switzerland has its own constitution which – according to the Federal Constitution – must grant a democratic system; see article 51 of the Swiss Federal Constitution.

democratic, people-based political system, where the State and its agencies are servants of the people, and thus human rights prevail over public emergency strategies.

The implementation of countermeasures against Covid-19 in Switzerland has shown that this idealised image does not correspond to reality. For many people in Switzerland, the strong top-down interventions by the State have led to disappointment, if not an outright shock,[6] probably more so than in countries with a traditionally more centralised structure of government such as France, Spain, or even China.

It is not within the scope of this chapter to more broadly compare the current Swiss political system with other political systems. Whilst relying on examples from Switzerland, this chapter instead aims to present some fundamental thoughts about top-down and bottom-up approaches to respond to emergency situations like pandemics, and to reflect on the question as to whether bottom-up approaches that give strict priority to the protection of individual human rights are nevertheless able to address supra-individual problems like pandemics.

1.2 An Alternative Approach

Due to being organised in the form of States, all countries are today probably characterised by a vertical top-down structure with the government as holder of a prerogative position above any other actors.[7] Even where liberal constitutions prominently support human rights, such as in Switzerland, their implementation depends on a wide discretion of the government that has the power to grant, to limit or – in times of an 'emergency that threatens the life of the nation'[8] – even derogate from them. Limitations or derogations cannot be instituted arbitrarily but in accordance with the flexible principles of legality and proportionality.[9] Once restrictions to, or derogations from, human rights are

---

[6] An association called 'Friends of the Constitution' founded in July 2020 within a few weeks grew to more than 25,000 members, a number that very few associations in Switzerland ever reach. Since then, it has been divided into several sub-entities, one of which retained the original name (https://verfassungsfreunde.ch/en/ (accessed 7 May 2025)).

[7] In Switzerland, such an emergency competence of the Federal Government is based on articles 184(3) and 185(3) of the Federal Constitution; however, there are some uncertainties as to the interpretation of their wording.

[8] Such as according to article 4(1) of the International Covenant on Civil and Political Rights (adopted 16 December 1966, entered into force 23 March 1976) 999 UNTS 171 (ICCPR).

[9] Swiss Federal Constitution, article 36(3).

contested by individual human rights-holders, it is the State's judicial authorities that have the power to decide about their validity. The partiality inherent in this set-up is mitigated by the State creating separate bodies to make such decisions, known as the separation of powers.[10] This does not, however, change the prerogative position of the State.

The analysis in this chapter contrasts this with an alternative approach, in which the prerogative position is based exclusively on each individual member of society, creating an essentially decentralised structure of societal organisation that is nevertheless able to support solutions that address collective dangers such as the international spread of disease. The approach presented here is based on two theories going back to the 19th and early 20th centuries. They originate from two politically quite different directions but lead to closely comparable, if not identical, conclusions.

The first approach is one of natural science developed in the 19th century following the Darwinian change of paradigm and leading to social and particularly to socialist theories, namely by anarchists like Mikhail Bakunin,[11] Peter Kropotkin,[12] and later Gustav Landauer.[13] These theories were never implemented via real-world political systems,[14] but found their continuation in the second half of the 20th century in scientific fields that oscillate between social and natural science such as sociobiology.[15]

This anarchist approach is relevant for our analysis insofar as it looks at human behaviour as a natural phenomenon that does not depend on external powers giving directions – such as God, king, or State – but that follows innate natural laws of behaviour, just like other natural laws such as the law of gravity. What those early socialist scientists as well as the apolitical sociobiologists notice is that these natural laws of behaviour do not just lead to the proverbial

---

[10] cf also below Sections 4.2 and 5.2.

[11] Mikhail Bakunin, *God and the State* (1871, imprimerie jurassienne 1882); *Statism and Anarchy* (1873); and *Man, Society, and Freedom* (1871).

[12] Peter Kropotkin, *Mutual Aid. A Factor of Evolution* (1902).

[13] Gustav Landauer, 'Durch Absonderung zur Gemeinschaft' in Rolf Kauffeldt and Michael Matzigkeit (eds), *Gustav Landauer: Zeit und Geist* (Boer 1997, essay originally published in 1901) 80.

[14] What led to a socialist 'reality' was the opposite to what Bakunin and Kropotkin envisaged, namely Marxism; cf Mikhail Bakunin, *Marxism, Freedom, and the State* (1872), chs III and V.

[15] Franz Wuketits, *Soziobiologie, die Macht der Gene und die Evolution sozialen Verhaltens* (Springer Spectrum 1997); David Dürr, 'The Ethics of Physics' in Jörg Guido Hülsmann and Stephen Kinsella (eds), *A Life in Liberty* (Papinian Press 2024) 255; Edward Wilson, *Sociobiology: The New Synthesis, 25th Anniversary Edition* (Harvard University Press 2000); and Edward Wilson, *Genesis: The Deep Origin of Societies* (Allan Lane 2019).

jungle of 'eat and be eaten', but also, and even strongly so, to altruistic and responsible behaviour within situations of collective concern.[16]

The second approach is an economic one going back to the same epoch, ie to the late 19th century, when the 'Austrian School of Economics' thoroughly analysed the regularities of human behaviour in individual as well as societal contexts. Prominent names of that school include Carl Menger and Ludwig von Mises,[17] as well as the later and better-known Friedrich von Hayek.[18] Those economists were critical of statist interventions in economic relations but did not go as far as the socialist anarchists of that time in their urge to overcome the State. Later scholars, however, did precisely this, among them Murray Rothbard[19] and Hans-Hermann Hoppe.[20]

These theories are relevant for the analysis in this chapter insofar as one of their central elements is the premise that everyone shall have ownership of his or her body. It is out of this starting point that normative criteria for societal relationships are derived. Therefore, individual human rights lie at the very centre of these theories.[21] But unlike typical constitutional theories, these human rights are not granted top-down by some official authority but originate bottom-up out of their own intrinsic reality. And regardless of its individualist starting point, this approach opens the possibility for individuals to build a wide range of relationships by voluntary cooperation, including on levels beyond mere individual spheres.[22]

---

[16] Kropotkin (n 12), referring to Darwinian research, ch I; and Charles Darwin, *The Descent of Man, and Selection in Relation to Sex* (John Murray 1871) ch IV.

[17] Carl Menger, *Untersuchungen über die Methode der Sozialwissenschaften und der politischen Ökonomie insbesondere* (Dunker & Humblot 1883); Ludwig von Mises, *Human Action: A Treatise on Economics* (Yale University Press 1949, 2010); also Guido Hülsmann, *Mises: The Last Knight of Liberalism* (Ludwig von Mises Institute 2007).

[18] Friedrich August von Hayek, *The Constitution of Liberty* (University of Chicago Press 1960); in addition to political appeals like Friedrich August von Hayek, *The Road to Serfdom* (University of Chicago Press 1944).

[19] Murray Rothbard, *For a New Liberty, The Libertarian Manifesto* (Ludwig von Mises Institute 1978) 55 ff; and *The Ethics of Liberty* (n 2) 201 ff.

[20] Hans-Hermann Hoppe, *Economy, Society, and History* (Ludwig von Mises Institute 2021) lectures 6 and 7; and Hans-Hermann Hoppe, *A Theory of Socialism and Capitalism* (Ludwig von Mises Institute 2010) ch 8.

[21] Rothbard (n 2) 113 ff; and Hoppe, *A Theory* (n 20) 158 ff.

[22] Jörg Guido Hülsmann, *Die Wirtschaft und das Unentgeltliche: Kostenlose Güter zwischen Kapitalismus und Staat* (Landt Verlag 2023).

These two approaches can today be categorised as 'libertarian'.[23] They will guide the analysis in what follows and explore alternatives to statist interventions to address global pandemics such as those driven by the World Health Organization (WHO) and by States in response to SARS-CoV-2. On the one hand, the alternatives proposed here are based on trust in the factual reality of natural behavioural laws, especially in collective matters. On the other hand, they are grounded in taking human rights seriously, especially the right to bodily integrity and to control one's own body.

It goes without saying that this alternative approach is not perfect. Like the statist approach, it is a regime of *this* world with all its shortcomings. But some specific shortcomings painfully experienced during the Covid-19 pandemic – namely State dominance not only severely interfering with the enjoyment of human rights but also having jurisdiction over legal challenges of such interferences – might be avoided or mitigated by an alternative libertarian approach presented here.

2. THE HIERARCHY OF POWER

2.1 Higher and Lower Levels

The subject to explore in this chapter consists of a complex network of societal organisation with smaller and bigger communities, local, or more far-ranging institutions, all of which have varying degrees of influence on and over each other. According to libertarian theories, such structures function exclusively on the basis of power and not (democratic) legitimacy.[24]

This is what manifested itself in the WHO-led, multi-level response to the Covid-19 public health emergency of international concern (PHEIC) and is depicted in Figure 9.1. It started with the WHO declaring the Covid-19-PHEIC on 30 January 2020, and the adoption of subsequent WHO recommendations on medical and non-medical countermeasures to States on how to address this PHEIC. Though not formally binding in law, in practice, State compliance with WHO recommendations appeared high with the effect that most national

---

23 The notion of 'Libertarianism' came up in the 19th century from leftist anarchists. Today, it is primarily used in order to differentiate 'Libertarianism' from 'Liberalism'. In politics, 'liberals' are associated rather with collective positions, while 'libertarians' are associated with individualist positions, such as presented in this chapter.

24 Rothbard (n 2) 161 ff; Bakunin, *Statism* (n 11), chs III and IV; and Gustav Landauer, '*Die vereinigten Republiken Deutschlands und ihre Verfassung*' (1918) 3 Das Flugblatt, later reprinted in *Zeit und Geist: Kulturkritische Schriften 1890–1919* (Klaus Boer 1997) 294.

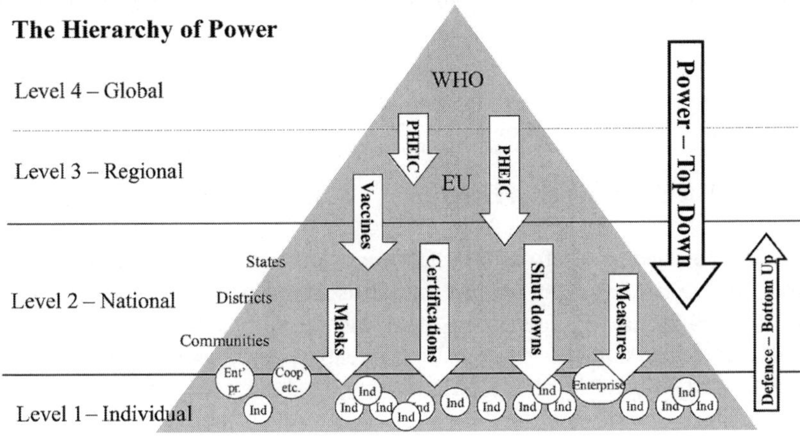

Figure 9.1 *The hierarchy of power*

governments no longer felt free to decide on their own how to respond to the Covid-19-PHEIC. On the national level, the top-down approach was reflected in the reliance on emergency law or emergency-law-like provisions providing for extraordinary powers to executive institutions, mostly suspending parliamentary control and heavily restricting human rights.[25]

When it comes to the implementation of these measures, including their physical impact on individuals, Level 1 depicted at the bottom of Figure 9.1 tends to be given a merely passive or complying role as an addressee of what is recommended, urged or enforced from above. The only non-passive function attributed to Level 1 is one that is usually referred to as the role of the democratic 'sovereign', ie to have elected parliamentary representatives that in turn empower the government to implement the measures recommended by the higher levels, including the WHO.

In Switzerland with its direct democracy, this chain of democratic legitimacy seems to be more than just theory. Either people themselves have approved the respective statute in a referendum, or they have voluntarily decided not to call for a referendum. But in practice, less than 1 per cent of all statutes at the federal level are put to public vote and the cause for this is not that

[25] In Switzerland, parliamentary functions were closed on 15 March 2020 by a spontaneous decision of the two chambers and resumed not before 4 May 2020, while the Federal Government issued more than 20 ordinances containing severe restrictions of human rights.

people agree with those statutes but that the hurdles for a referendum are very high.[26] Therefore, in reality, the 'direct democracy' of Switzerland does not function in a way substantially different from the 'indirect democracies' in other Western countries where people are just passive addressees of measures implemented from the top down.

2.2 The Sovereignty of Defence

There is, however, one active (or rather re-active) role the bottom Level 1 might take. This role is to defend against the intrusions from higher levels (depicted in Figure 9.1 by the 'defence-arrow' pointing bottom-up). Such reactions might violate domestic statutes or international treaties, and therefore result in reactions from the higher level in the form of physical enforcement or as penalties such as fines.[27] But from the viewpoint of natural science in human societal behaviour proposed by the libertarian thinkers introduced above, these bottom-up reactions are 'justified' in a specific sense, ie as natural phenomena: they 'must' happen, not at someone's order and not following abstract principles but because they correspond to *natural regularities* of human behaviour.[28]

In other words, such reactions to aggression, intrusion, or encroachment are something like the basic engine of how human behaviour develops. They induce specific kinds of social behaviour between individuals and groups.[29] If they prove useful, they will remain or even be optimised further by new reactions. If they fail, they will disappear. Theories of behavioural evolution stipulate that it is ultimately the physical law of *actio = reactio* which underlies the evolution not only of cells, plants, and more complex organs but also of behaviour of species within their social contexts.[30]

---

[26] According to article 141 of the Federal Constitution, 50,000 signatures must be collected and legalised within 100 days. This is much more difficult than the constitutional initiative which requires 100,000 signatures within 18 months (Federal Constitution, article 138).

[27] Not by the WHO but by national authorities, eg Swiss Epidemics Act (n 70) and (n 71) below, articles 82–4.

[28] Namely according to the sociobiological approach; cf Wuketits (n 15), ch 7; and David Dürr, 'The Inescapability of Law' (2019) 23 Journal of Libertarian Studies 161.

[29] Such as families, tribes, voluntary cooperatives, etc; cf Wuketits (n 15), ch 7; and Kropotkin (n 12).

[30] Discussing this subject is beyond the scope of this chapter, ie to what extent positive laws are laws in the same way as physical laws, such as the law of gravity. Reference is made, eg, to von Mises (n 17) 2: 'One must study the laws of human action and social cooperation as the physicist studies the law of nature.'

All this applies to *Homo sapiens* as well.[31] This means that humans too cannot but react defensively to certain transgressions imposed on them. This is what the Roman paroemia '*neminem laedere*' ('do harm to no one') expresses, '*neminem*' meaning 'no one' in the singular. The fact that humans have a 'built-in' regularity to resist individually to aggression corresponds to identifying them as holders of individual human rights.

3. THE HIERARCHY OF LEGITIMACY

Legal history shows that contracts as a legal institution have emerged much later than torts. Earliest cultures of law have dealt with simple conflicts. Contracts have emerged later, as ritualised solutions to such conflicts. Sale and purchase of a piece of land developed out of an agreement between an owner of the land and a trespasser whereby the latter delivers an amount of money against the owner giving up resistance.[32]

In other words, the bindingness of contracts is not primarily based on voluntary consent to be bound, but on the fact that lack of consent means having the right to resist – except one voluntarily waives the right: '*volenti non fit iniuria*'.[33] The bindingness of consent lies in the individual's promise not to resist. And thus, the 'legitimacy' to exceptionally overrule somebody's right to resist lies in the latter's waiver of such right. For the different levels at stake here – individual, national, regional, and global – this means the following.

3.1 The Level of the Individual (Level 1)

The positions involved at Level 1 as depicted in Figure 9.1 are individual positions.[34] The essence here is that individuals or voluntarily formed groups of individuals want to be left alone. They do not want to bother anybody, and they do not want to be bothered by others. This essentially negative position, according to the libertarian theorists, is the core of human rights.[35] All that human rights demand from others is not to do something, namely, not to

---

31 Wuketits (n 15) 138 ff; and Darwin (n 16), ch 12.

32 Max Kaser, *Das Römische Privatrecht* (HC Beck 1971), § 10 *in iure cessio.*

33 'The one who consents does not suffer injustice'.

34 See also the discussion in Section 2.1.

35 Of course, other newer theories tend to extend human rights to positive contents, ie to claims against the State to engage in 'positive' actions; concerning Switzerland see, eg, the much debated judgment of the European Court of Human Rights (ECtHR) granting claimants a 'human right' to more protection by the State against being harmed by climate change (*Verein Klimaseniorinnen Schweiz and ors v Switzerland* App no 53600/20 (ECtHR, 9 April 2024)).

encroach on, or intrude into, a person's decision on how to lead his or her own life. 'Don't tread on me' is an often-used phrase by libertarians.[36]

This essentially negative feature of human rights, and particularly of the right to liberty, is therefore not derived from any external source. The binding force of these rights is not a normative argument applied to facts, but a fact itself: the fact of the natural phenomenon that people react if they are confronted with aggression. Here we meet the approach of natural science mentioned in connection with anarchist theories of the 19th century: Once it is proven by the experiment of legal history[37] that humans inevitably resist aggression, there is no need for any authority to legally command such behaviour, just as there is no need for legally enforcing the law of gravity. These natural forces are there because they are there. This is not a circular argument but a proven fact.

3.2 The National Level (Level 2)

At the second level, the structure is currently collective. State legislation, political programmes, and governmental activities like public health strategies articulate positions not of individuals but of collective groups or networks. This is usually attributed to Rousseau's '*volonté générale*' ('general will') and '*volonté de tous*' ('will of all'), or to narratives of 'the people' as a collective body.[38]

But unlike on Level 1, the typical structure of such collective articulations in relation to their addressees is not negative or defensive but positive and often pro-active. What it typically demands from individuals is not to negatively 'leave the national body alone'[39] but to positively require individuals to provide services or to pay taxes for the collective – in alignment with the second part of John F Kennedy's famous sentence '... ask what you can do for

[36] In accordance with the 'classical' liberal right, such as advocated by John Locke in the *Second Treatise on Government* (1690), chs V and VIII on the defence of property and the beginning of political societies.

[37] cf in the 19th century, among others, Savigny's historical school of law, or Ehrlich's sociology of law; see Friedrich Carl von Savigny, *Vom Beruf unserer Zeit für Gesetzgebung und Rechtswissenschaft* (2nd edn, JEB Mohr 1828); and Eugen Ehrlich, *Grundlegung der Soziologie des Rechts* (4th edn, Duncker & Humblot 1989 (originally published 1913)).

[38] Jean-Jacques Rousseau, *Du contrat social* (Rey 1762), ch III.

[39] Except, eg, in matters of national defence; cf Hans Hoppe (ed), *The Myth of National Defence* (Ludwig von Mises Institute 2003).

your country'.[40] This statement contradicts the libertarian approach presented here, leading to the question of where such collective claims, expressed in law adopted by collective entities binding individuals equally, derive their justification from.

The most prominent argument to justify the binding nature of law adopted by collective entities on individuals is 'democracy'.[41] Accordingly, the people on Level 1 or their representatives are said to mandate the government on Level 2 to make law that is binding on all members of society on an equal basis, and to implement this law in the public interest. Restrictions to human rights determined by such legislation, including taxation, military service, and mandatory health measures are said to be justified (among other reasons) by reference to their democratic origin. In other words, the individuals on Level 1 are said to have democratically consented to the restrictions of their rights.

As has been argued above, from a libertarian perspective, this consent argument can only be accepted for a limited part of the people, ie for those who individually expressed their consent to being bound by the law that specifically implements the measures adopted at Level 2 or who elected representatives that then decided on those laws. But in any event, the fact that a majority only – directly or indirectly – consents cannot justify attributing their consent to those who *do not* consent. This is even more so in cases where only a minority consents.[42] Nevertheless, for those who *do* consent – be it many or a few – consent is a consistent justification.

3.3 The Regional Level (Level 3)

On the third level, the same democratic arguments are regularly invoked to legitimise treaties and policies adopted by regional collective institutions. Here too, the source for justifying the legally binding nature of regional multilateral treaties is argued to lie on the next lower Level 2. This is the typical structure of regional treaties. They are contracts between Level 2 entities, usually between States as autonomous subjects of international law.[43] The binding quality of regional treaties of public international law for Level 2 entities thus derives from these very entities' consent. Unlike norms on Level 2 that are never based

---

[40] John F Kennedy, *Inaugural Address* (delivered in Washington DC, 20 January 1961).

[41] Tracing back to Thomas Hobbes, *Leviathan* (Crooke 1651), chs 14, 17, and 18 on a covenant with the sovereign.

[42] See also Section 2.1.

[43] Individuals are, however, not typically parties to international treaties; see Urs Saxer, *Die internationale Steuerung der Selbstbestimmung und der Staatsentstehung* (Springer 2010) 238 ff.

on the consent of all individual actors on Level 1,[44] treaties on Level 3 are usually based on the consent of *all* States that ratify a treaty. It is in principle not possible to bind a State to an international treaty without its consent, even if a majority of other States decide to be bound by the respective treaty.[45]

There are, however, shortcomings at the interface with Level 1: Level 2 legitimacy to make and adopt international law through collective regional institutions at Level 3 derives its justification from the lower Level 1. Thus, Level 3 depends on Level 2, which in turn depends on Level 1. And since the competence of a State's government to enter into treaties with other States will have impacts on the individuals on Level 1, according to the approach presented here, such treaties can only be binding for those individuals who have individually consented to that delegation of competence.

3.4 The International or Global Level (Level 4)

On Level 4 consisting of international organisations, first and foremost the UN and its specialised agencies like the WHO, the same argumentative dependence applies as in the relation between Levels 2 and 3, that is, the legitimate powers of Level 4 to adopt legally binding treaties and regulations depend on a lower level, typically Level 2 of States, which in turn depends on Level 1.[46] Therefore, Level 4 ultimately depends on Level 1 as well.

This in turn means that, according to libertarian theories, the legally binding nature of a multilateral treaty like the International Health Regulations (IHR),[47] adopted at the level of the WHO, can only find its justification by and for those individuals at Level 1 that do consent (or have consented) either to such treaties limiting their human rights or to the respective delegation of competence.

---

44 As discussed in Section 3.2.

45 A prominent exception to this principle of international law is the foundation of the Swiss Confederation in 1848. This foundation was not accepted by all Cantons but only by a majority of the liberal Cantons against a minority of the Catholic Cantons.

46 Unless it is about mandatory international law that is valid without being formally approved in a treaty, such as the prohibition of crimes against humanity, genocide, slavery, and human trafficking; see Theodor Meron, *Human Rights and Humanitarian Norms as Customary Law* (Clarendon Press 1989).

47 International Health Regulations (IHR) (2005) (adopted 23 May 2005, entered into force 15 June 2007) 2509 UNTS 79 (IHR 2005). Amendments to the IHR were adopted on 1 June 2024 by the 77th World Health Assembly (WHA): WHA Res 77.17 (1 June 2024) UN Doc WHA77.17, annex 'Amendments to the International Health Regulations (2005)' (IHR 2024).

3.5 Putting the Pyramid Upside Down

In summary, what has been argued here based on libertarian theories is that all 'higher' levels (Levels 2, 3, and 4) ultimately depend on Level 1 and derive their ultimate legitimacy to adopt legally binding multilateral treaties, national statutes, or any kind of enforceable regulations from Level 1, and in particular from the consent given by each and every individual to be bound or to be represented. Expressed in a figurative sense: Level 1, which was presented so far at the bottom of the 'Hierarchy of Power', will rank at the top in what could be called the 'Hierarchy of Legitimacy'. The pyramid with its broad base consisting of all individual members of (global) society and with delegated organisations like the WHO at the top should be shaped upside down as illustrated by Figure 9.2.

Here, the arrows pointing from top down do not depict orders, commands, or enforcement measures imposed on subordinates. They rather constitute delegations, elections, or requests that may or may not be assumed by their addressees on Levels 2, 3, or 4. It is on the basis of individual voluntary consent that those on top Level 1 allow the lower levels to implement limitations of individual rights, such as organising countermeasures against pandemic risks. Voluntary delegations of this kind may be motivated by deeming bigger organisations more efficient in solving a certain problem than all individuals taking their own decisions and measures. The 'power' delegated this

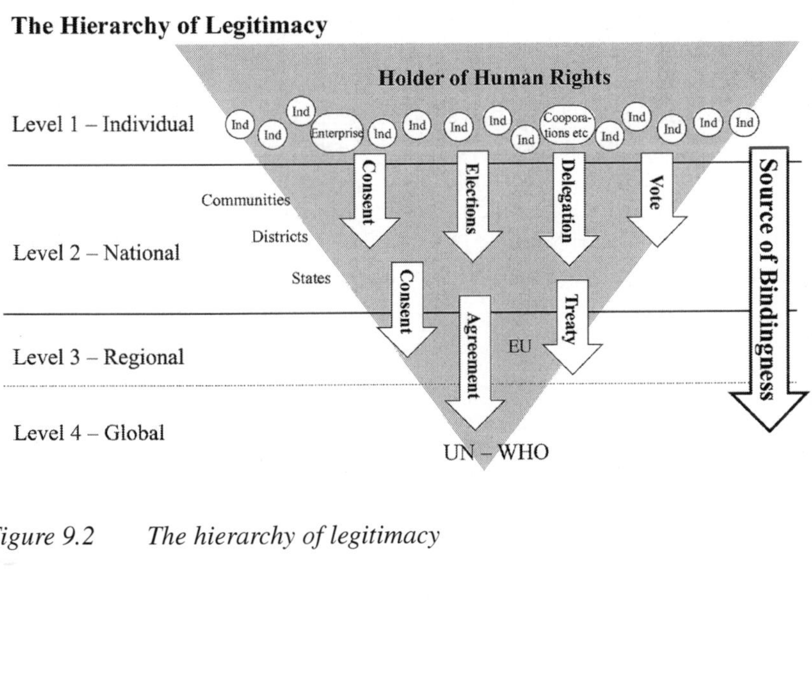

Figure 9.2 *The hierarchy of legitimacy*

way is essentially different from State power with its shortcomings mentioned above.[48] It rather corresponds to a power of attorney that is given individually and can typically be withdrawn any time by any individual's will.

On a practical level, it will never be possible to obtain voluntary consent by all members of a society or even the global population to delegate powers of attorney to either one or more than one organisation that will subsequently agree on measures similar to those that are regularly recommended by the WHO to address (alleged) global health emergencies. Nevertheless, as shall be argued in the following, the theoretical considerations inspired by libertarian thinkers that have been presented so far can assist in developing consistent approaches to reconcile the protection of human rights with the implementation of collectivised countermeasures to address a global health emergency recommended by the WHO.

4. RECONCILING INDIVIDUAL CONSENT WITH PANDEMIC COUNTERMEASURES: THE LIBERTARIAN APPROACH

For libertarians, the most consistent way to legitimately implement medical countermeasures like those recommended by the WHO is to ensure that consent is given by each individual addressee, be it directly or via voluntary delegations to suitable organisations. To the extent this is achieved, there is no conflict with the human right to liberty or to any other human rights involved. This is, of course, the best-case solution, discussed further in Section 4.1.

There is also a second-best case scenario for those who do not consent. This scenario involves submitting the claims of those who resist against certain health measures imposed by the State, including upon recommendations of the WHO or regional organisations like the EU, to a non-State mechanism of impartial arbitration. This scenario is discussed in Section 4.2.

In Section 4.3, the analysis moves to discussing the worst-case scenario from the perspective of libertarian theories, where individuals are subjected to health measures without their consent and without being given access to impartial non-State arbitration. The Covid-19 responses adopted by the Swiss government, the EU, and the WHO arguably fall into this category.

48 See Section 2.1.

4.1 The Libertarian Best-Case Scenario: Individual Consent to Comply with Countermeasures and the Human Right to Liberty

As soon as individuals agree to comply with countermeasures adopted at Levels 2, 3, and 4 to allegedly address the spread of a disease, restraining their otherwise free options of behaviour by implementing business lockdowns, vaccinations, protective masks, etc, such restrictions are justified in the eyes of libertarian theorists. For the principle of '*consenti non fit iniuria*' is respected.[49]

Hence, for those individuals giving consent to comply with the measures mandated by national, regional, or even global organisations such as the Swiss Confederation, the EU, or the WHO, endeavouring to protect people against diseases like Covid-19 by masks or vaccinations or other means, no problems arise. Moreover, from the perspective of libertarian scholars, nothing is wrong with these States and international organisations intensively recommending the application of these measures – as long as such advertisement does not become intrusive or even aggressive.[50] If by (non-aggressive) recommendations people become convinced of these measures and therefore voluntarily decide to adhere to them, true consent is achieved.

This is not different from the market when companies recommend their products or services and quite often do it by intensive marketing campaigns. If they go too far and try to 'force' people by incomplete, misleading, or even incorrect information, by exaggerating imminent dangers or by intrusive communication to apply their products like vaccines etc, their activities turn into an encroachment of individuals' freedom to consent and the potential 'customers' turn into victims. '*Consenti non fit iniuria*' cannot apply here because there is no true consent. This aspect is well known in traditional private law as 'lack of will' or 'defective will', with the consequence that such a contract is not binding.[51] The same is reflected in the concept of 'free and informed consent' to medical treatment.[52] According to the libertarian theory presented here, this concept applies not only to medical treatment (which, eg, would exclude

[49] Dürr (n 28) 161 and 163.

[50] Rothbard (n 2) 45 ff.

[51] In Roman Law cf Kaser (n 32), § 58 ff; and in Swiss Law, Code of Obligation, article 21 ff.

[52] Applicable also to private actors; cf Swiss Federal Office of Public Health, 'Traitements et soins: consentement libre et éclairé' ('Free consent to treatment or care after comprehensive briefing') (*OFSP [Federal Office of Public Health]*, 28 August 2024) https://www.bag.admin.ch/bag/en/home/medizin-und-forschung/patientenrechte/rechte-arzt-spital/2-freie-einwilligung-nach-aufklaerung.html (accessed 22 December 2024).

compulsory vaccination),[53] but to any other restrictions to human rights due to health measures, such as the right to freedom of movement, to freedom of assembly, private life, and to earn a living. This is so regardless of whether the organisation legislating for or recommending these restrictions is a private company, a State's government, or the WHO.

Libertarian theorists do not argue that States or other official 'political authority' shall be ignored. Rather, they recognise that they can be influential entities, sometimes even reputable actors, and that this might in turn have an influence on people's behaviour – but never more than this. The benchmark, when confronted with any State intervention, is: 'How would you react if any other organisation acted in the same way as the State?',[54] be it a commercial enterprise or a non-profit entity like a church or a charity foundation.[55] If any such organisation would present a strategy against a pandemic, strongly recommending wearing masks, vaccinations, locking down workplaces and schools, and proposing a scheme of taxation to finance all these measures, it might experience different responses – and the very same should be the case if this organisation is 'the State' or an international inter-State organisation.

Many people might follow the recommendations because they think 'States' or intergovernmental organisations embody their collective will and accept that 'States' or international organisations do their best for the good of everyone. This corresponds to the attitude of those who, during the Covid-19-PHEIC, followed what was ordered. In Figure 9.3, these people are depicted on Level 1 at the bottom of the Hierarchy of Power (left side of Figure 9.3).

On the other hand, there are individuals who question some or all medical or non-medical countermeasures or who want to learn more before accepting, or who just refuse to comply with them. In such cases, the 'State' or other organisations approaching them have no option but to convince the people of the effectiveness, proportionality, or reasonableness of the health measures and to subsequently acquire them as 'clients'. As far as the people of this group can be convinced to voluntarily adhere to health measures, they are on Level 1 at the top of the Hierarchy of Legitimacy (right side of Figure 9.3).

Figure 9.3 illustrates a combination of the Hierarchy of Power on the left and the Hierarchy of Legitimacy on the right. The left side depicts the WHO and/or governments urging or even forcing people top down to adhere to health measures. The right side shows people deciding on their own, with some of them

---

53 Even though this was not always respected during the Covid-19-PHEIC; see eg Austria (statute BGBl I Nr 4/2022 of 4. 4. 2022) envisaging mandatory vaccinations against Covid-19. However, this law was never enforced.

54 Michael Huemer, *The Problem of Political Authority* (Palgrave Macmillan 2013) 183 ff.

55 Rothbard (n 2) 161 ff and 183 ff; and Huemer (n 54) 3 ff and 145 ff.

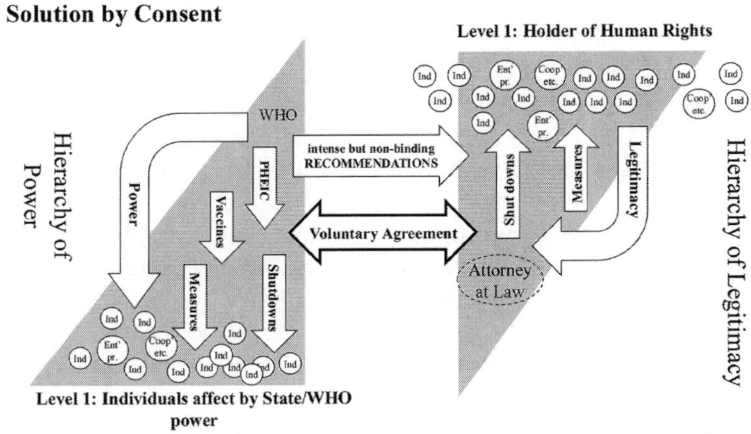

Figure 9.3 *Solution by consent*

complying voluntarily with the recommended measures, and others deciding not to do so or to choose alternative solutions. It is also possible that individuals on the right side voluntarily organise themselves and mandate other professional actors to coordinate and represent them in negotiations with 'the State' or with other organisations representing different groups of people. In any event, in the Hierarchy of Legitimacy, these representatives, agents, or attorneys are *below* the individuals who mandate them, that is, they have no power *over* them.

One may wonder about the individuals on the right side of Figure 9.3 – individuals who do not voluntarily consent to adhere to certain public health measures or who prefer other measures to those propagated by 'States' or intergovernmental organisations. To force them to adhere by law or by using physical force is not an option according to the libertarian approach. This would violate their human right to liberty. But one can also ask why individuals should be forced at all. Are there convincing arguments for this?

4.2 The Libertarian Second-Best-Case Scenario: Solving Conflicts of Rights with the Help of the Human Right to a Fair Trial

Yes, there are arguments, especially in the context of pandemics: wearing masks or administering vaccinations could prevent other people from being infected, becoming sick, or even dying. Such arguments contain two elements, both of which are often used as criteria to limit human rights: 'public interest' and the protection of human rights of third parties.[56] According to libertarians, 'public interest' is too vague a criterion to justify limitations of individual human rights.[57] Human rights of third parties are, however, highly relevant and can justify the limitation of human rights.

Thus, libertarians would not exclude that organisations like the WHO or States honestly try to represent and reconcile conflicting human rights of many people such as the human right to health or life. However, once more[58] the proposals of 'States' and 'intergovernmental organisations' are not inherently more (democratically or scientifically) legitimate than those of any other private organisations proposing to act in the interest of other people. In the view of libertarians, even if an organisation is able to show that their 'clients' have given power of attorney to them, they have no authority to do more than to *represent* their client. Giving power of attorney does not encompass the authority to *decide* conflicts with opposing claims including conflicts between the human rights of different people. Libertarians do not find any reason why this should not apply to organisations referred to as 'States' or 'intergovernmental organisations' like the WHO. They should act only like *attorneys for their clients* in court *but not as judges* on the bench of that court. Therefore, libertarians argue that organisations like the WHO or States claiming to *represent* the majority of the people on a territory do not have the power to *decide* on a conflict with the remaining minority.[59]

The task of deciding conflicts of human rights, libertarians suggest, shall not be taken on by the direct representative organisations of human rights holders that were given powers of attorney but by an independent body. Precisely this is the object of a prominent human right: the human right to fair trial. This human right is contained in all classical liberal constitutions as well as in international treaties like the European Convention on Human Rights[60] and the International Covenant on Civil and Political Rights (ICCPR).[61]

The human right to a fair trial means the right 'to a fair and public hearing by an independent and impartial tribunal established by law'.[62] This implies a human right not only to a public hearing of the parties' claims but also a right

---

56 Such as according to the Swiss Federal Constitution, article 36(2).

57 Rothbard (n 2) 113 ff and 145 ff, insists on human rights being property rights that cannot be disposed of except by contractual consent of their holders; and Hayek (n 18) 205 ff.

58 See also the discussion in Section 4.1.

59 Hoppe, *Economy* (n 20) 101 ff; and Huemer (n 54) 59 ff.

60 European Convention on Human Rights (adopted 4 November 1950, entered into force 3 September 1953) 213 UNTS 221 (ECHR), article 6.

61 ICCPR, article 14.

62 cf ECHR, article 6.

to obtain a final decision on how conflicting human rights shall be balanced. That is, which party's human right(s) prevail over the human right(s) of the other, and to what extent. Independence and impartiality forbid the tribunal to prefer one party to the other or to give more weight to one party's human right(s) than to the rights of the others. It must consider only how much the interests of the parties protected by their human rights mutually collide, ie to what extent they are incompatible.[63] This qualifies the human right to a fair trial not merely as a formal rule of court procedure[64] but as a material rule protecting human rights from being limited more than human rights of the counterpart they might collide with. The formula this leads to is the 'Golden Rule' of equal reciprocity: 'Do not do unto others as you would not have them do unto you.'[65] The Kantian categorical imperative can also be recalled in this context. It can be seen as a philosophical expression of the natural law of *actio equals reaction* introduced above.[66]

If this independent and impartial mode is applied when reaching a decision, none of the parties should be better or worse off than the other. Their human rights might be restricted but no more than the conflicting human rights of the other party.[67]

Figure 9.4 illustrates this. It resembles Figure 9.3, which depicted individuals' adherence to public health measures by consent. Figure 9.4 also combines the 'Hierarchy of Power' on the left with the 'Hierarchy of Legitimacy' on the right. But instead of linking the gap between the two groups by convincing and eventually obtaining consent to the same measures, here the gap is bridged by the work of an independent and impartial tribunal. Depending on the complexity at stake, such a tribunal would not consist of only a few judges like a conventional court bench. It should rather be a professional organisation that 'morphologically' resembles a scientific research institute primarily examining the facts including mutual impacts of the colliding standpoints and ultimately rendering an answer to the questions at stake.[68]

63 Dürr (n 15) 266 ff; and David Dürr, *Diskursives Recht, zur theoretischen Grundlegung rechtlicher Einflussnahme auf überindividuelle Konflikte* (Schulthess 1994) 138 ff.

64 Such as '*audiatur et altera pars*'.

65 Sermon on the Mount, Luke 6/13; Matthew 7/12; and Darwin (n 16), ch 4 summary.

66 See Section 2.2.

67 Dürr (n 15) 266 ff; and Dürr, *Diskursives Recht* (n 63) 136 ff.

68 More on this cf Dürr, *Diskursives Recht* (n 63) 206 ff.

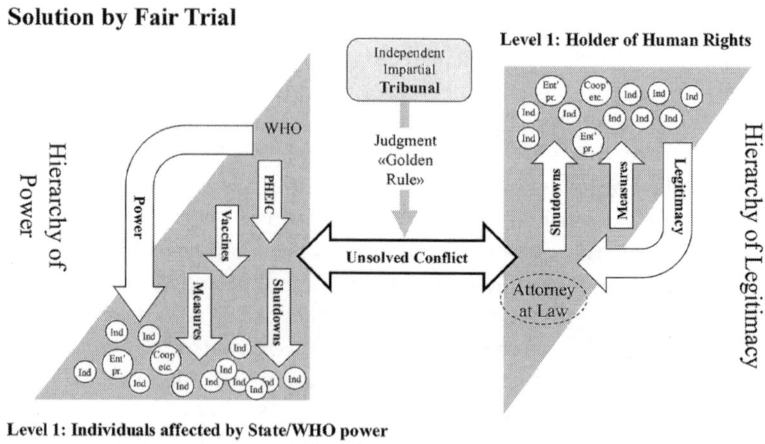

Figure 9.4 *Solution by fair trial*

4.3 The Libertarian Worst Case: Relying on Executive Enforcement Powers

While conflicts between health measures recommended by States or the WHO and the enjoyment of human rights can be legitimately solved by either consent (best case) or through an arbitration process respecting the material human right to a fair trial (second best case), any other restrictions to human rights remain illegitimate according to libertarian theory.

5. APPLICATION TO SWITZERLAND?

When applying the above libertarian considerations to Switzerland, one will notice that the political structure of this country, embedded inter alia in the intergovernmental structure of the WHO, is far from what has been referred to as the 'Hierarchy of Legitimacy' above. Two examples suffice to illustrate this within the frame of this short analysis.

5.1 Bindingness at What Level?

When the WHO's IHR Covid-19 Emergency Committee met on 30 January 2020, followed by the formal declaration of a PHEIC,[69] the federal statute *Epidemiengesetz* (Epidemics Act) of 28 September 2012 was activated in Switzerland.[70] Article 6[71] reads as follows:

> 1 There is a 'special situation' if:
> a. the ordinary law enforcement agencies are unable to control the outbreak and the spread of contagious diseases, and one of the following hazards is present:
> 1. an increased risk of infection and spread,
> 2. a particular risk to public health,
> 3. severe impacts on the economy or other spheres of life; an increased risk of infection and spread, a particular risk to public health, severe impacts on the economy or other spheres of life;
>
> b. *the World Health Organization (WHO) has determined that there is a public health emergency of international concern and, as a result, there is a risk to public health in Switzerland.*
>
> 2 After consulting the Cantons, the Federal Government may order the following measures:
> a. measures on individuals;
> b. measures on the population;
> c. obligation of physicians and other healthcare professionals to help fight contagious diseases;

---

[69] WHO Covid-19 Emergency Committee, 'Statement on the fourth meeting of the International Health Regulations (2005) Emergency Committee regarding the outbreak of coronavirus disease (COVID-19)' (1 August 2020) https://www.who.int/news-room/detail/01-08-2020-statement-on-the-fourth-meeting-of-the-international-health-regulations-(2005)-emergency-committee-regarding-the-outbreak-of-coronavirus-disease-(covid-19) (accessed 22 December 2024): 'The Director-General declared that the outbreak of COVID-19 continues to constitute a PHEIC. He accepted the advice of the Committee to WHO and issued the Committee's advice to State Parties as Temporary Recommendations under the IHR (2005).'

[70] *Epidemiengesetz* (2012), Official Publication Platform of Federal Law, SR 818.101. This statute is under review at the time of writing in December 2024. The review is, however, limited to formal matters. On the Swiss national level, the situation will thus remain the same in the future; cf Swiss Federal Office for Public Health 'Teilrevision Epidemiengesetz' ('Partial revision of the Epidemics Act') *(OFSP*, 22 December 2024) https://www.bag.admin.ch/bag/de/home/strategie-und-politik/politische-auftraege-und-aktionsplaene/revision-epidemiengesetz.html (accessed 22 December 2024).

[71] Translation by the author, emphasis added.

d. declaring compulsory vaccinations for vulnerable population groups, for those who are particularly exposed and for persons who carry out certain activities.

Under normal circumstances, measures listed in section 2 of this article are within the competence of the Cantons. Matters of public health are thus normally regulated on a level that is closer to individuals than the Federation.[72] Under normal circumstances, consultations with, and participation of, the Cantons must be ensured before any centralised measures in the area of public health can be implemented.

This can lead to differences between the Cantons and the Federal Government if the latter invokes facts described in section 1(a) of article 6, the existence of which is difficult to prove. Hence, it will be much easier for the Federal Government to refer to a PHEIC declaration by the WHO under section 1(b). This is precisely what happened on 28 February 2020, when the Swiss Federal Government issued an urgent decree referring to article 6(1)(b) of the Epidemics Act.[73] The Federal Government declared a 'special situation' in Switzerland and ordered the implementation of its first measures allegedly aimed at limiting the spread of Covid-19. It imposed a ban on events and gatherings with more than 1,000 participants like football games, carnival parades, Saturday night gatherings on the streets, etc. This was the start of a whole series of more and more severe measures taken in the weeks, months, and years that followed.

Hence, even though the implementation of countermeasures against Covid-19 in Switzerland was formally initiated by the Swiss government, the legal basis was the PHEIC declaration by the WHO. And since the reference to a PHEIC declaration by the WHO is part of a *binding* Swiss statute, the PHEIC declaration became legally enforceable. Interestingly, the references made by the Swiss government to the WHO Covid-19 Emergency Committee's declaration of the Covic-19-PHEIC did *not* examine the scientific foundation of this declaration. It contented itself with citing subparagraph (b) of article 6(1) of the Swiss Epidemics Act that refers to the PHEIC declaration by the WHO.[74]

---

72 This means that normally, the responsible administrations are smaller, and they are entities that, in the libertarian understanding, 'compete' with 25 other Cantons. Therefore, regulating health matters at this lower level is generally more 'client-oriented' than regulation by a monopolised Confederation.

73 AS 2020-0619, 573 ff, referring to WHO 'COVID-19 IHR Emergency Committee' and its statements at https://www.who.int/groups/covid-19-ihr-emergency-committee (accessed 22 December 2024).

74 ibid.

In line with the libertarian theories discussed above, for individuals who did agree with this implied delegation of decision-making powers to the WHO, permitting the WHO de facto to activate the relevant articles in the Epidemics Act amounting to limitations of the human rights of Swiss people, such limitations are presumably acceptable. This is, however, not the case for individuals who were not willing to accept these restrictions of their human rights. For these individuals, according to libertarian principles, the only consistent solution could have been the submission of their case to an impartial tribunal. During the Covid-19-PHEIC, some individuals tried to take this route and took their case to court, including the Federal Supreme Court of Switzerland.

5.2 Impartial Tribunal?

Impartiality, however, was far from being practised.[75] According to the libertarian viewpoints presented above, impartiality implies that the court does not judge on the viewpoints of the parties on the diverging interpretations and applications of human rights but only determines the extent to which they collide, and how much they are incompatible.[76]

Applied to conflicts between citizens defending themselves against Covid-19 countermeasures that limit their human rights and the 'State' claiming to protect the human rights of individuals who agree to comply with these measures, impartiality means weighing the incompatible standpoints of:

- On the one hand, the State may argue that certain measures such as mandatory mask requirements or school closures are effective in preventing the spread of Covid-19, based on facts, and therefore protecting the rights to health and life.
- On the other hand, individuals may claim that adhering to these measures unduly interferes, for example, with the enjoyment of their rights to physical integrity and health, and their children's right to education.

While the latter's viewpoints are given, the State's standpoint may be reasonably questioned and must be carefully examined. But one of the State's important arguments during the Covid-19-PHEIC was the large number of positive

---

75 Even though the hurdle for a breach of impartiality of courts in Switzerland, as in most western countries, is very low since following the rule that even mere appearance of partiality leads to the exclusion of the respective judge; see Swiss Federal Supreme Court, 2C_455/2020, 5.2.1 and 5.2.2; cf also *Aviso Zeta AG v Austria* App no 5734/14 (ECtHR, 21 June 2018).

76 As discussed in Section 4.2.

PCR test[77] results, which allegedly proved high levels of infection rates. When plaintiffs demanded release from quarantine measures that were ordered based on such tests, they argued that PCR tests from a medical and epidemiological point of view are not meaningful. The Swiss Federal Supreme Court, in a leading judgment, agreed with this by holding that 'it is not disputed, and incidentally it is common knowledge, that a positive PCR-test does not amount to a diagnosis of a disease and is not very meaningful on its own'.[78] Nevertheless, the Court dismissed the claims on rather weak grounds. It found that:

> In the case of newly emerging infectious diseases, there is typically a high degree of uncertainty about the causes, consequences and suitable control measures … . The measures to be taken cannot therefore be legally determined in advance with certainty but must be taken on the basis of the current, usually incomplete state of knowledge …, which requires a certain leeway on the part of the responsible authorities … .[79]

This reasoning shows a strong tendency of the Court to support the State's standpoint as being a priori justified, helpful for society, politically desirable, and generally positively connoted. There might be good reasons for that, even if the unreliability of PCR tests is recognised. These reasons can be that human rights – for example the rights to health and life – of many other citizens might be protected by these measures. These reasons must, however, be specified and sufficient evidence be provided by the government invoking them. If this is not possible, an impartial court must declare such measures inadmissible.[80]

6. CONCLUSION

To conclude, a return to the question asked at the beginning of this chapter is required: How to find a consistent approach to address the imminent conflict between globally structured WHO interventions on the one hand, and the protection of human rights of individuals on the other? From the perspective of libertarian theories that this chapter relied on, the following summary of approaches proposed throughout the discussion above is offered to address these conflicts.

---

[77] PCR (polymerase chain reaction) tests are a laboratory technique with a very high sensitivity for viruses, even before an infection or illness occurs.

[78] Swiss Federal Supreme Court, 2C_228/2021, 5.2.; and 2C_941/2021, 3.3.4.

[79] ibid, 2C_228/2021, cons. 4.7; 2C_941/2020, cons. 3.2.6; and BGE 132 II 449 E. 5.4; 131 II 670 E. 2.3 (unofficial translation by the author).

[80] See among other decisions of the Swiss Federal Supreme Court, 2E_3/2022, cons. 3.3; and 2F_4/2022, cons. E. 3.3.

First, any debate forthcoming in connection with public health measures implemented by States or indirectly by the WHO must be compatible with individual human rights. Human rights have priority over other subjects such as pandemic preparedness, prevention or response, or any other public interests. The only limitation to human rights might be justified by protecting the human rights of others.

Second, approaches that support individuals in giving their voluntary (free and informed) consent to public health measures as much as possible should be adopted. This should be achieved by providing well-founded, evidence-based, and convincing, but neither aggressive nor intrusive, recommendations. This permits States to uphold the right to liberty during infectious disease outbreaks.

Third, in order to support the principle of free and informed consent, libertarian theorists suggest building institutional structures on different societal levels with smaller or larger territorial impact. Their positions and competences should be defined according to the 'Hierarchy of Legitimacy' where the individuals and their human rights are positioned on the top level, while all other institutional structures are dependent on this top level. This may advocate for a transformation of sovereign States like the Swiss Confederation, other public institutions, and intergovernmental organisations like the WHO, and reshaping these institutions into structures that resemble commercial enterprises, *pro bono* foundations, insurance cooperatives, and the like.

Fourth, remaining conflicts between such organisations and/or between individuals and their human rights arising in the context of the implementation of medical and non-medical countermeasures against an infectious disease outbreak should be resolved through arbitration by independent tribunals, deciding based on facts presented by both parties. That is, such conflicts are not resolved by political structures where majorities overrule minorities but by smaller or larger independent and impartial organisations such as private courts or mediators. This would in turn secure the protection of the human right to a fair trial.

Tensions and conflicts emerging from pandemics or other severe events will not be fully extinguished by approaches drafted here. However, taking on some of the libertarian viewpoints suggested may result in a more balanced approach than the one taken by the WHO and many States during the Covid-19-PHEIC.

Concluding remarks: emergency regimes for global health law

Amrei Müller and Silvia Behrendt

The chapters in this volume set out to trace the securitisation and public-private hybridisation of public health emergency of international concern (PHEIC)/ pandemic preparedness and response law, policy, and institutions at the international (World Health Organization, WHO), the regional European (EU), and the domestic levels. They also examined some of the numerous effects on various areas of law, health policies, and public institutions.

1. CONSOLIDATION

The analyses in many chapters reveal that both the securitisation and the blurring between the public and the private spheres has been reiterated and consolidated over time, in particular by the global WHO-led responses to the Covid-19-PHEIC. They are reflected in pandemic/PHEIC preparedness, prevention, and response law and policies, and institutions – both at the domestic, the regional (EU), and the international WHO level.

As highlighted by David Bell,[1] both trends re-emerged at the level of the WHO in the early 1990s, re-connecting to utilitarian, technocratic, and top-down patterns in global health policy from colonial times, and moving towards commodity-based strategies to secure public health. The Global Health Security (GHS) doctrine came to revive and dominate the WHO's pandemic preparedness, prevention, and response programmes with the adoption of the respective resolution in 2001 by the World Health Assembly (WHA);[2] and by re-modelling the International Health Regulation of 1969 (IHR (1969)) in a thorough revision process of 1995–2005 in line with the tenets of the GHS,

1 Chapter 1 by Bell in this volume.

2 WHA Res 54.4 (21 May 2001) UN Doc WHA54.4; see also earlier, WHA Res 48.13 (12 May 1995) UN Doc WHA48.13.

cumulating in the adoption of the IHR (2005).[3] The WHO's focus on supporting the building of health systems, training of health workers in sanitation, and the provision of better nutrition through local initiatives of the 1950s into the 1980s was successively replaced once more by more centralised and prescriptive measures aimed at population health and behavioural control, favouring more uniform responses and a focus on health products and commodities, pushed by the growing influence of private funders on the WHO. More and more of the WHO's work and programmes were conducted through public-private partnerships (PPPs) since the early 2000s, and the WHO – and in particular the WHA – lost control over most of its budget, 80 per cent of which is today earmarked for priorities set by private and major State funders.[4]

The declaration of the Covid-19-PHEIC saw a further increase in the number of PPPs created to implement WHO-recommended medical and non-medical countermeasures and to prevent and prepare for new pandemics/PHEICs in the future.[5] They were established under the lead of the WHO Secretariat, reducing the influence of the WHA and the Executive Board further over WHO policies, law, and institutional set-ups.[6] Moreover, new expert committees gained more influence. This technicised and centralised the WHO's global health policies and guidelines further; and opened additional (revolving) doors for individuals with ties to private institutions and philanthropic foundations, and for their enjoying of privileges and immunities, traditionally limited to public persons and institutions.[7]

The Covid-19-PHEIC galvanised programmes and medical and non-medical countermeasures driven by the main priorities of the GHS doctrine. First to mention is the declaration of the Covid-19-PHEIC by the WHO,[8] triggering parallel declarations under EU law[9] and domestic law[10] despite the non-bindingness under international law of such a PHEIC declaration. Neither at the international (WHO), nor the regional (EU), nor the domestic level was

---

[3] Chapter 2 by Ramakrishnan and Namboodiri; and the introduction to this volume.

[4] Chapter 1 by Bell in this volume.

[5] Chapter 2 by Ramakrishnan and Namboodiri; and Chapter 6 by Reiner in this volume.

[6] Chapter 2 by Ramakrishnan and Namboodiri in this volume.

[7] Chapter 6 by Reiner in this volume; and Chapter 3 by Müller and Behrendt, especially on expert committees involved in the WHO's EUL procedure.

[8] Chapter 4 by McGrogan; and Chapter 3 by Müller and Behrendt in this volume.

[9] Chapter 5 by Geistlinger in this volume.

[10] Chapter 7 by Paris (concerning France); Chapter 6 by Reiner (concerning Germany); and Chapter 9 by Dürr (concerning Switzerland) in this volume.

the fundamental question raised by the respective authorities over the three and a half years that the Covid-19-PHEIC lasted as to whether the appearance of SARS-CoV-2 and the Covid-19 illness with its low infection fatality rate (IFR)[11] indeed constituted such a PHEIC and/or 'health emergencies' under the respective domestic legislation, justifying the implementation of far-reaching medical and non-medical countermeasures.

Second, the rapid development, emergency authorisation/listing, and subsequent administration of investigational vaccines against Covid-19 promoted by the WHO, especially through its Emergency Use Listing (EUL) procedure and large-scale advertisement campaigns reflect and follow the GHS doctrine.[12] The EUL procedure permits the WHO to de facto emergency licence medicinal products like vaccines as global medical countermeasures.

Third and similarly, the WHO's infodemic management programmes – assessing and controlling what type of health information, and in what volume, should be communicated globally and what information should be suppressed as medical or other 'mis- or disinformation' – came to full fruition during the Covid-19-PHEIC,[13] including through cooperation between the WHO and big technological companies and media outlets.[14] This corresponds to the GHS's demand for effective 'risk communication' during PHEICs, no matter whether these PHEICs are due to naturally occurring infectious disease outbreaks or outbreaks ascribed to biowarfare or laboratory accidents.[15]

Chapters observe that the securitised approaches, as well as additional influence of private corporations and philanthropic foundations, have become further entrenched also in the international legal framework on PHEIC/pandemic prevention, preparedness, and response via the 2024 amendments to the IHR[16] and the new Pandemic Agreement.[17] For example, the 'exception-

---

[11] Angelo Pezzullo et al, 'Age-stratified Infection Fatality Rate of COVID-19 in the Non-elderly Population' (2022) 114655 Environmental Research 216, concluding that the median IFR was 0.0003% at 0–19 years, 0.002% at 20–29 years, 0.011% at 30–39 years, 0.035% at 40–49 years, 0.123% at 50–59 years and 0.506% at 60–69 years.

[12] Chapter 3 by Müller and Behrendt in this volume.

[13] Chapter 4 by McGrogan in this volume.

[14] Chapter 3 by Müller and Behrendt in this volume.

[15] Introduction to the volume.

[16] WHA Res 77.17 (1 June 2024) UN Doc WHA77.17, annex 'Amendments to the International Health Regulations (2005)'.

[17] WHA, 'Proposal for the WHO Pandemic Agreement', draft text of 24 May 2024, appendix to the report of the WHO Director-General, 'Outcome of the Intergovernmental Negotiating Body (INB) to Draft and Negotiate a WHO Convention, Agreement or Other International Instrument on Pandemic Prevention, Preparedness and Response' (27 May 2024) UN Doc A77/10.

ally broad executive function'[18] of the WHO Director-General to declare a PHEIC and new 'pandemic emergencies'; and to make temporary and standing recommendations on how to address them, including by recommending the use of 'relevant health products', are expanded by the 2024 IHR amendments. Authors praised the latter – together with other 2024 amended articles of the IHR that will give additional powers to the WHO in the area of promoting and expediting the production and allocation of 'relevant health products' – as a win for 'equity', which will ensure more equitable distribution of medical countermeasures in future PHEICs benefiting in particular low-income countries.[19] However, these amendments will also boost the global distribution and administration of emergency licensed medicinal products in future PHEICs and further entrench a global top-down, unitary response framework regardless of local contexts, and thus further promote this GHS-preferred countermeasure without having answered open questions as to its effectiveness and compatibility with human rights law and medical law.[20] At the same time, the amendments entrench the product-focused approach to pandemic/PHEIC prevention and response – a commodified approach which aligns with the interest of WHO's PPPs, the pharmaceutical industry, and philanthropic foundations.[21] The 2024 amended IHR also increases surveillance activities and reporting obligations in line with the GHS doctrine.[22]

Many of these securitised and commodified approaches to pandemic/PHEIC preparedness and response and their strengthening via the 2024 IHR amendments are due to the work of the EU, and, in particular, its Commission and its Directorate-General on Health Emergency Preparedness and Response (HERA) established in 2021.[23] These approaches have been adopted *in toto* at EU level, developed further, institutionalised, and benefited from the allocation of considerable EU funds, despite a missing legal basis in the EU treaties.[24] HERA has been active in the area of surveillance, intelligence gathering, and health threat assessment, advancing research and clinical trials on pathogens with pandemic potential and the development of medical countermeasures, their distribution, and stockpiling – creating a constant state of 'health emergency' alert also at the level of the EU.[25] When it comes to the involvement

18 Chapter 4 by McGrogan in this volume.
19 Chapter 2 by Ramakrishnan and Namboodiri in this volume.
20 Chapter 3 by Müller and Behrendt; and Chapter 1 by Bell in this volume.
21 Chapter 1 by Bell in this volume.
22 Chapter 4 by McGrogan; and Chapter 2 by Ramakrishnan and Namboodiri in this volume.
23 Chapter 5 by Geistlinger in this volume.
24 ibid.
25 ibid.

of private corporations at EU level, investments have been pushed by HERA Invest to develop innovative countermeasures, in particular vaccines for infectious diseases with pandemic potential; and an EU FAB that created a network of vaccine manufacturing sites with an 'ever-warm' capacity to produce 500–700 million vaccines per year, investing EUR 160 million annually.[26]

Among other reasons, because of the 2024 amended provisions of the IHR, domestic PHEIC/pandemic preparedness, prevention, and response law, policies, and institutions are also securitised further. The WHO's centralised and uniform approach to public health threats is implemented through IHR National Focal Points and – as required by the 2024 amendments to article 4 IHR – all States are to establish *additional* national IHR authorities responsible for further coordinating the implementation of the IHR at the domestic level.[27] In addition, new core capacities – for example, in relation to combating mis- and disinformation during PHEICs – are to be built at domestic levels in line with the 2024 amendments to the IHR.[28]

Securitisation trends at the domestic level are also reflected in the high level of compliance with WHO recommendations for medical and non-medical countermeasures against the Covid-19-PHEIC by States despite the fact that these recommendations are not legally binding on States.[29] In numerous countries, a PHEIC declaration by the WHO activates domestic legal provisions on 'health emergencies' authorising governments in turn to adopt various countermeasures domestically.[30] Many of these health emergency measures were decreed by executive authorities with minimal or no parliamentary oversight;[31] and included typical securitised countermeasures like lockdowns[32] and mass vaccination campaigns with investigational products.[33]

Another feature reflecting the securitised approach at the domestic level was the setting up of ad hoc bodies for crisis management – dominated by

---

[26] ibid. EU FAB is an EU mechanism created to ensure that manufacturing capacities for vaccines are operational and can be activated quickly in case of a public health emergency.

[27] Chapter 4 by McGrogan in this volume.

[28] ibid; and Chapter 2 by Ramakrishnan and Namboodiri in this volume.

[29] Chapter 9 by Dürr in this volume.

[30] ibid, concerning Switzerland; and Chapter 6 by Reiner (concerning Germany) in this volume.

[31] Chapter 7 by Paris (concerning France and Ireland); and Chapter 8 by Ambos in this volume.

[32] Chapter 8 by Ambos; Chapter 7 by Paris; and Chapter 1 by Bell in this volume.

[33] Chapter 6 by Reiner in this volume.

the executive and selected experts to provide scientific advice.[34] Most prominently demonstrating the militarised/defence approach to addressing infectious disease outbreaks is the French 'Health Defence Council' – an executive body that redefined health as a matter of national defence policy and operating under military secrecy – that devised and decreed many of the French Covid-19 countermeasures backed up by 'expert advice'.[35]

The blurring of the public and the private can be observed at the domestic level too. Chapters, for example, highlighted that public health authorities – like the German Robert Koch Institute – receive funding from private corporations and philanthropic foundations, whilst, at the same time, funding is provided by governments for projects carried out by these foundations and/or the PPPs they form part of with the WHO and governments.[36] Domestic media reporting on health issues, and Covid-19 matters in particular, was and is also funded by both philanthropic foundations and governments.[37] And, as examined in detail by Reiner in this volume,[38] the privatisation of profits from the mass vaccination campaigns against Covid-19 and the 'publicisation' of their costs – including through providing public funds for such countermeasure development; reducing requirements for manufacturers to prove safety and effectiveness of countermeasures in emergency authorisation or EUL processes; and by States indemnifying manufacturers for product liability – creates numerous conflicts of interests undermining the important (democratic) control functions of public institutions over private corporations.

2. EFFECTS

The (legal) effects of the securitisation of pandemic/PHEIC preparedness, prevention, and response law, policies, and institutions, as well as the continued blurring of the public-private distinction are manifold.

First, various chapters highlighted the interferences with, and often violations, of States' human rights duties and the WHO's responsibilities for human rights resulting from securitised medical and non-medical countermeasures recommended and implemented in countries around the world. Lockdown policies, including school closures, had adverse effects on children in particular. They lost years of education, were subjected to abuse more frequently, became

34 Chapter 7 by Paris, concerning Ireland and France; and Chapter 8 by Ambos in this volume, concerning the German 'Council of Experts' (*Expertenrat*) that gave scientific advice to the executive on its Covid-19-PHEIC responses.

35 Chapter 7 by Paris in this volume.

36 Chapter 6 by Reiner in this volume.

37 ibid.

38 ibid.

more food insecure (together with their families), and were and continue to be affected by increasing levels of poverty.[39] Burdens of infectious diseases that had traditionally been priorities for the WHO, like malaria and tuberculosis, increased, with Covid-19 responses absorbing vast portions of health budgets at domestic and WHO levels.[40]

The WHO's EUL procedure, its global recommendation and advertising of EUL vaccines to address the Covid-19-PHEIC as 'safe and effective' and its involvement in stifling scientific, medical, and other critique of such policies by classifying it as 'mis- or disinformation' via its infodemic management programme are not compatible with the WHO's responsibilities for various human rights, and the WHO's duties under the IHR (2005) and (2024).[41] These procedures and policies cannot be considered valid limitations of the WHO's responsibilities for the human right to health, and in particular for the right to secure access to safe and efficacious medicinal products of good quality, access to reliable health information, and the right not to be subjected to medical and scientific experimentation or medical treatment without free and informed consent.[42] And they can lead to States violating their corresponding human rights duties at the domestic level. Many of the WHO's recommendations were taken on by State authorities without these authorities – including domestic courts – carrying out thorough assessments as to whether their implementation was in line with States' obligations under international and European human rights law as well as with domestic constitutional law.[43]

This highlights a second effect of the securitised approach to infectious disease management: increased centralisation and uniformisation, and the taking over by executive authorities at the domestic level at the expense of legislative and judicial control.[44] And, at the levels of the EU and the WHO, an expansion of competencies of the EU executive organ – the Commission (and its HERA);[45] or that of the WHO Director-General and the WHO Secretariat, among others through the 2024 amendments of the IHR and the negotiation of the new Pandemic Agreement.[46]

---

39 Chapter 1 by Bell in this volume.

40 ibid.

41 Chapter 3 by Müller and Behrendt; and Chapter 4 by McGrogan in this volume (concerning the infodemic management programme).

42 Chapter 3 by Müller and Behrendt in this volume.

43 ibid.

44 Chapter 7 by Paris; Chapter 8 by Ambos; and Chapter 9 by Dürr in this volume.

45 Chapter 5 by Geistlinger in this volume.

46 Chapter 4 by McGrogan in this volume.

Chapters covering securitisation processes at the domestic level point to the loss of parliamentary control over securitised executive health policies and law. The French executive 'Health Defence Council' operated without parliamentary control or judicial review; and in Ireland, a scientific 'expert body' set up by the executive engaged in de facto executive decision-making with no or very little parliamentary oversight.[47] In Switzerland, emergency laws provided extraordinary powers for executive institutions, mostly suspending parliamentary control; and permitting the Federal Government to disregard the strong competences of the Cantons in the area of health protection and their rights to be consulted.[48] In Germany, decisions on responses to the Covid-19-PHEIC were made primarily by the Federal Chancellor and the heads of government of the *Länder* in regular telephone conferences.[49]

Domestic courts were little involved in reviewing executive medical or non-medical countermeasures in all the countries studied in this volume, often displaying high levels of self-restraint.[50] This was despite the unprecedented interferences with human rights that these measures constituted, including even with non-derogable rights like the right not to be subjected to medical or scientific experimentation or medical treatment without free and informed consent. In Ireland, almost all executive measures against Covid-19, including criminal sanctions, were upheld by the courts, arguing that any claims to unconstitutionality were not backed by facts or were clearly justified by the aim to (diffusely) 'protect lives'.[51] Minimal judicial oversight was exercised in France by the Constitutional Council, endorsing much of the emergency legislation, often in divergence from earlier established precedents.[52] Swiss courts appear to have been predisposed to confirm executive health measures too, relying in particular on State health authorities' and the WHO's scientific expertise.[53] As in Ireland, in Germany, courts failed to even identify both which human rights – the right to life or rather, the right to freedom from risks to life that have reached a sufficient threshold of severity beyond general life risks – were to be protected by the Covid-19-PHEIC countermeasures, and the numerous other human rights these countermeasures interfered with, often severely. This led the courts to conduct incomplete balancing exercises of different conflicting rights with the State generally failing to demonstrate beyond

47 Chapter 7 by Paris in this volume.

48 Chapter 9 by Dürr in this volume.

49 Chapter 8 by Ambos in this volume.

50 Chapter 7 by Paris; Chapter 8 by Ambos; and Chapter 9 by Dürr in this volume.

51 Chapter 7 by Paris in this volume.

52 ibid.

53 Chapter 9 by Dürr in this volume.

reasonable doubt that Covid-19 countermeasures, for example exist restrictions, are indeed suitable (*geeignet*) and necessary (*erforderlich*) with a view to effectively reducing risks to life by a virus, and are proportionate *stricto sensu*.[54] Overall, it thus appears that domestic courts were reluctant to engage in thorough lawfulness, suitability, necessity, and proportionality analyses of far-reaching limitations of human (and constitutional) rights due to medical and non-medical countermeasures; and relatedly, scientific expertise provided by the WHO, the European Medicines Agency (EMA), and State health or medical authorities were (and are) not normally scrutinised or questioned.

At the level of the EU, parallel developments can be detected with the activities of HERA, including significant budgetary allocations to it, not overseen by the European Parliament. This is so because HERA was not established as a fully fledged independent EU Agency but as a Commission Directorate and thus an executive body.[55] There has been no judicial review of HERA's activities. HERA's performance has only been reviewed by *OpenEvidence* in consortium with *PricewaterhouseCoopers*[56] which then, among others, informed a report of the European Commission on HERA's operations to the European Parliament and the Council in March 2025.[57] The establishment of HERA constitutes, in addition, an acquisition of additional competences in the field of health by the EU and its Commission that are not covered by the EU Founding Treaties. These EU competences may become permanent through the prominent role that the EU has taken on in negotiating both the 2024 amendments to the IHR and the new Pandemic Agreement, and by the perspective of the EU becoming a signatory to the latter in the near future.[58]

At the level of the WHO, centralisation of decision-making powers in the hands of the WHO Director-General and the WHO Secretariat became clear

---

54 Chapter 8 by Ambos in this volume, critical of the German Constitutional Court's approach in particular.

55 Chapter 5 by Geistlinger in this volume.

56 European Commission, 'Study Supporting the Review of the Health Preparedness and Emergency Response Authority (HERA) with Regard to its Operations, Structure, and Governance', written by OpenEvidence in consortium with PricewaterhouseCoopers EU Services EESV between October 2023 and April 2024 https://op.europa.eu/en/publication-detail/-/publication/c8ab8a41-09f8-11f0-b1a3-01aa75ed71a1/language-en (accessed 17 May 2025). This is another aspect evidencing the progressing public-private hybridisation trend.

57 European Commission, 'Report from the Commission to the European Parliament and the Council. Review of the Implementation of the Operations of the Health Emergency Preparedness and Response Authority (HERA)' COM (2025) 147 final.

58 Chapter 5 by Geistlinger in this volume.

during the Covid-19-PHEIC, strengthened further via the 2024 IHR amendments and the new Pandemic Agreement.[59] Moreover, as the WHO's EUL procedure illustrates, small expert committees enjoy considerable influence to recommend unlicensed medical products for potential global use, with the overall procedure being under the full control of the WHO Director-General and the WHO Secretariat.[60] More and more PPPs are established by the WHO Secretariat to 'support' States in implementing pandemic prevention and response measures.[61]

This shows that third, the securitisation, but also the successive public-private hybridisation of pandemic/PHEIC prevention, preparedness, and response law, policies, and institutions, leads to accountability deficits at the domestic, regional (EU), and in particular, the international level of the WHO, with accountability understood broadly.

Political and democratic accountability are undermined by decreasing involvement of domestic parliaments, the European Parliament, and the WHA.

Accountability through critical analysis and reporting of the media and ensuing transparency is undermined by the blurring of public and private rights and obligations, with the WHO closely cooperating with big technology companies and media outlets to make available to the general public only 'correct' information about a PHEIC and its underlying disease; and by fighting 'mis- and disinformation'. Government, philanthropic foundations, or corporate funding for global and national media outlets reinforces this pattern further;[62] as do the privatised or increasingly conditioned public funding structures of scientific and medical research. Expert committees, which do not, or only in a limited way, publish the reasoning and evidential basis for their decisions and recommendations, and which do not usually offer fora for public debate and scrutiny, undermine transparency and accountability as well.[63] This is worsened by the extension of immunities and privileges to members of, for example, WHO expert committees, as well as to PPPs carrying out many of WHO's programmes in the area of PHEIC/pandemic prevention, preparedness, and response, exempting them from any judicial procedures.[64] Moreover, when WHO and governments rely on private law contracts, like Advance Purchase

---

59 Chapter 4 by McGrogan; Chapter 2 by Ramakrishnan and Namboodiri; and Chapter 1 by Bell in this volume.

60 Chapter 3 by Müller and Behrendt in this volume.

61 Chapter 2 by Ramakrishnan and Namboodiri in this volume.

62 Chapter 6 by Reiner in this volume.

63 Chapter 7 by Paris; Chapter 8 by Ambos, concerning expert bodies at the domestic level; and Chapter 3 by Müller and Behrendt in this volume, concerning the WHO's expert bodies.

64 Chapter 3 by Müller and Behrendt in this volume.

Agreements (APAs), to deliver medical countermeasures, obligations to protect commercial secrets will further prevent public scrutiny and transparency, and limit free access to information by the general public.[65]

Judicial accountability for medical and non-medical countermeasures and their effects on individuals and institutions is also weakened both by the securitisation and the public-private hybridisation trends. As indicated, the logic of emergency and urgency led to minimal judicial scrutiny of executive emergency laws and policies at the domestic level during the Covid-19-PHEIC by most courts.[66] At the same time, States' assigning private entities to implement countermeasures – for example, by requiring and empowering social media platforms to pre-bunk, debunk, and remove alleged mis- or disinformation posted by users – impedes access to remedies for affected individuals as platforms will justify their activities with reference to terms and conditions under private law accepted by users. Activating judicial remedies is time-consuming and expensive for individuals.[67] Holding the WHO, its PPPs, or WHO experts liable under private law for damages caused by medical and non-medical countermeasures is regularly excluded due to immunities granted[68] – once more an example that shows how the gradual taking on of public privileges like immunities by private entities undermines accountability. EU organs and agencies like EMA will rely on their 'administrative discretion' to justify the development and implementation of countermeasures; and private corporations like vaccine manufacturers will regularly be indemnified or benefit from no-fault compensation schemes.[69] States, on their part, can be reluctant to accept claims for social damages,[70] for example for vaccine injuries caused by medical countermeasures, as this implies a recognition that State (or EU) medical regulators – potentially themselves relying on the WHO's EUL procedure – may not have shown due vigilance and rigour in the process of authorising medical products and recommending, advertising (or even mandating) them for mass administration. Indemnifying manufacturers will also increase States' costs to pay damages and legal fees for manufacturers.

All in all, this leads to diminished responsibility of both public and private persons and institutions acting at the domestic, regional, and international levels for their pandemic/PHEIC policies promoted and empowered by the skewed international legal framework on pandemic/PHEIC prevention, preparedness,

65 Chapter 6 by Reiner in this volume.

66 Chapter 7 by Paris; Chapter 8 by Ambos; and Chapter 9 by Dürr in this volume.

67 Chapter 6 by Reiner in this volume.

68 ibid; and Chapter 3 by Müller and Behrendt in this volume.

69 Chapter 6 by Reiner in this volume.

70 ibid.

and response like the 2024 amended IHR and the new Pandemic Agreement (2025). This is to the detriment of affected individuals and the enjoyment of their human rights, transparency and public scrutiny, the political self-determination of peoples through the functioning of democratic systems with checks and balances in place, and ultimately, to the detriment of the rule of law itself.

3. TIME TO REVERT SECURITISATION AND RE-AFFIRM THE DISTINCTION BETWEEN THE PUBLIC AND THE PRIVATE

Where from here? The 2024 amendments to the IHR and the new Pandemic Agreement, as well as numerous WHO programmes and initiatives by WHO's PPPs promote further securitisation and the blurring of the public-private distinction in PHEIC/pandemic prevention, preparedness, and response law and subsequently in policies and institutions at international, regional, and domestic levels. However, as asked by McGrogan in this volume:[71] is it not time to pause and raise the question as to whether moving down this route leads us towards achieving the stated goal of fundamentally improving global public health protection? That is, global public health that ideally benefits all individuals on this planet?

In light of the analyses conducted in many of the chapters in this volume, the argument can be made that the time has come to first revert the securitisation and current move towards ever greater centralisation, uniformity, and population control in global public health law, policies, and institutions in general, and in particular in the area of infectious disease management. And second, to re-establish the distinction between the public and the private in public health.

The alternative to the securitised approach would consist of a return to more holistic and decentralised approaches to pandemic/PHEIC preparedness, prevention, and response that were still prevalent in numerous domestic pandemic response plans, and in guidelines issued by the WHO before the appearance of SARS-CoV-2. As recently as 2019, the WHO itself argued against securitised responses to infectious disease outbreaks.[72] Based on numerous scientific studies available in 2018–19,[73] it excluded far-reaching school and business

[71] Chapter 4 by McGrogan in this volume.

[72] WHO, 'Non-pharmaceutical Public Health Measures for Mitigating the Risk and Impact of Epidemic and Pandemic Influenza' (19 September 2019) https://iris.who.int/bitstream/handle/10665/329438/9789241516839-eng.pdf (accessed 8 May 2025).

[73] Eg Thomas Ingelsby et al, 'Disease Mitigation Measures in the Management of Pandemic Influenza' (2006) 4(4) Bioterrorism and Biosecurity 366.

closures (lockdowns), mask-wearing, and contact-tracing.[74] Instead, it recommended focused protection, care, and treatment for the elderly and people with weak immune systems on a voluntary basis, and simple measures like washing hands frequently and staying home when sick for younger people.[75]

Thus, such an alternative approach could move away from classifying infectious disease outbreaks primarily as (global) health emergencies requiring strict, centralised top-down countermeasures for control, and from seeing (sick) individuals (and animals) primarily as 'biological risks' to be managed and controlled by a central authority. Rather, it could re-recognise human beings as holders of the human right to health and other human rights who can decide as sovereign individuals which medical treatments they wish to undergo with free and informed consent, and who can critically absorb and participate in open, public scientific, and medical debates about any medical or non-medical measures that may reasonably be taken to address an infectious disease outbreak in local context, and in decisions on what portion of a community's public health budget should be allocated to it. People would ideally do so as equal rights-holders within a political community ('democratic society'[76]) that secures everyone's human right to health through the building of democratically controlled public health systems accessible to everyone. In line with the positive and negative elements of the human right to health and corresponding State duties, such systems would provide at least primary health services of good quality[77] to everyone along with adequate water, sanitation and nutrition;[78] and, successively, additional services addressing most prevalent health problems in local context. At the 'negative' end, health systems would always respect and safeguard the bodily and mental integrity of

---

74 WHO, 'Non-pharmaceutical Public Health Measures' (n 72).

75 ibid.

76 Eg references to 'democratic societies' in the International Covenant on Economic, Social and Cultural Rights (adopted 16 December 1966, entered into force 3 January 1976) 993 UNTS 3 (ICESCR), articles 4 and 8(1)(a) and (c); in the International Covenant on Civil and Political Rights (adopted 16 December 1966, entered into force 23 March 1976) 999 UNTS 171 (ICCPR), articles 14(1), 21, and 22(2); and in the European Convention on Human Rights (adopted 4 November 1950, entered into force 3 September 1953) 213 UNTS 221 (ECHR), articles 8(2)–11(2).

77 CESCR, 'General Comment No 3: The Nature of State Parties' Obligations' (14 December 1990) UN Doc E/1991/23, para 10; 'General Comment No 14: The Right to Health' (11 August 2000) UN Doc E/C.12/2000/4, paras 43(a), (d)–(f) and 44; and UN International Conference on Primary Health Care, 'Declaration of Alma-Ata' (1978), para VII(3) https://cdn.who.int/media/docs/default-source/documents/almaata-declaration-en.pdf (accessed 8 May 2025).

78 CESCR, 'General Comment No 14' (n 77), paras 4, 11, and 43(b) and (c).

individuals, including by upholding the rights not to be subjected to medical experiments or to medical treatment without free and informed consent.[79] This would appear to be in line with general public health principles too.[80]

Ensuring 'participation of the population in all health-related decision-making at the community, national, and international levels',[81] including in relation to health responses to infectious disease outbreaks, would be crucial in this context of devising an approach alternative to the securitised approach too. This participation could be realised via decentralised and democratised domestic public health systems and democratic political institutions – legislative, executive/administrative, judicial – at the domestic level; and be supported by collective deliberation and decision-making at the level of the WHO by (equal) States in its central organ – the WHA – with (democratic) States (ideally) representing their people at the WHA.

Such re-focusing could also re-establish a clear distinction between the public and the private in the area of public health and pandemic/PHEIC prevention, preparedness, and response. It would re-establish the primacy of the public over the private in law and institutions, re-assert democratic control via public law and institutions, uphold human rights protection and open-ended scientific enquiries, and ensure accountability of both public and private persons and institutions involved in public health at domestic and international levels. It could assist in turning back the disproportionate and unaccountable influence on global health law, policies, and institutions of powerful private entities; and prevent States and the WHO from evading their public responsibilities and duties by performing public rights and obligations under private law or conferring such public rights and obligations to private persons or institutions.

---

79 ibid, para 8; and Chapter 3 by Müller and Behrendt in this volume.

80 Chapter 1 by Bell in this volume.

81 CESCR, 'General Comment No 14' (n 77), para 11; and 'Declaration of Alma-Ata' (n 77), para VI and VII.5.

Index